Dressing à la Turque

Costume Society of America
Book Series

Editor
Jennifer Mower

Editorial Board
Linda Baumgarten
Jean L. Druesedow
Rebecca Jumper-Matheson
Darnell-Jamal Lisby
Jean L. Parsons
Sarah J. Rogers
Arti Sandhu
Casey Stannard

The Costume Society of America book series includes works on all subjects related to the history and future of fashion, dress, costume, appearance and adornment, including historical research, current issues, curatorial topics, contemporary design and construction practices, and conservation techniques. These books range from scholarly to more general interest and vary widely in format as well, from primarily textual to heavily illustrated. The series embraces a variety of specialties, including anthropology and cross-cultural studies, contemporary fashion issues, textiles, museums and exhibits, research methods, performance, and craft or fashion design.

Dressing à la Turque

Ottoman Influence on French Fashion, 1670–1800

KENDRA VAN CLEAVE

The Kent State University Press Kent, Ohio

© 2023 by The Kent State University Press, Kent, Ohio 44242
All rights reserved
ISBN 978-1-60635-459-9
Published in the United States of America

Portions of this book were previously published as:

Van Cleave, Kendra. "The Lévite Dress: Untangling the Cultural Influences of Eighteenth-Century French Fashion." *The Social Fabric: Deep Local to Pan Global; Proceedings of the Textile Society of America 16th Biennial Symposium,* January 1, 2018. https://digitalcommons.unl.edu/tsaconf/1119.

Van Cleave, Kendra. "Contextualizing Wertmüller's 1785 Portrait of Marie-Antoinette through Dress." *Costume* 54, no. 1 (2020): 56–80.

Van Cleave, Kendra. "'The Desire to Banish Any Constraint in Clothing': Turquerie and Enlightenment Thought in the French Fashion Press, 1768–1790." *French Historical Studies* 43, no. 2 (April 1, 2020): 197–221.

No part of this book may be used or reproduced, in any manner whatsoever, without written permission from the Publisher, except in the case of short quotations in critical reviews or articles.

Cataloging information for this title is available at the Library of Congress.

27 26 25 24 23   5 4 3 2

CONTENTS

Acknowledgments   vii

Introduction   1

1 Clothing Perspectives, East and West   11

2 Western and Eastern Approaches to Dress   33

3 Defining Ottoman Influence, 1760–90   53

4 Fashion and National Identity   111

5 *Turquerie,* Enlightenment Thought, and the French Fashion Press   139

6 Marie-Antoinette *à la Turque*   155

Conclusion   169

Appendix 1: Other Ottoman-Influenced Styles, 1775–92   181

Appendix 2: Extant Ottoman-Inspired Garments   187

Notes   197

Bibliography   223

Index   243

ACKNOWLEDGMENTS

Special thanks go to my research/writing group for their support and encouragement, particularly Brenna Barks, Trystan L. Bass, J. Leia Lima Baum, Dr. Carolyn Dowdell, and Lisa VandenBerghe for their feedback on drafts, and Sabrina Mark for proofreading patterns.

Mela Hoyt-Heydon's support was instrumental to receiving research funding.

Several colleagues shared their research about certain extant garments with me for which I am deeply grateful, including Dr. Serena Dyer, Dr. Carolyn Dowdell, and Lisa VandenBerghe.

Particular thanks go to Brooke Welborn, whose research intersected with my own and who joined me in writing a journal article that became the first output for our ideas.

Many museums, libraries, and archives provided research assistance and critical sources, including the Archives départementales des Yvelines, Archives nationales—site Paris, Bibliothèque du Musée des Arts décoratifs, Bibliothèque nationale de France—sites François Mitterrand and Richelieu, Bunka Gakuen University Library, and Victoria & Albert Museum. The interlibrary loan staff of the J. Paul Leonard Library, San Francisco State University, helped me obtain numerous sources. I am particularly thankful to the museum professionals who assisted me with their collections, including Neal Hurst at Colonial Williamsburg; Dr. Johannes Pietsch of the Bayerisches Nationalmuseum; David E. Ned Lazaro at Historic Deerfield Museum; Shelley Tobin at Killerton (National Trust); Anne de Thoisy-Dallem and Marie Olivier at the Musée de la Toile de Jouy; Karine Rodriguez at the Musée d'Histoire de Marseille; Chiara Squarcina and Luigi Zanini at the Museo di Palazzo Mocenigo; Dr. Marianne Larsson at the Nordiska Museet; and Pascale Gorguet-Ballesteros and Sylvie Brun at the Palais Galliera, musée de la Mode de la Ville de Paris.

I was honored to receive funding to support this research from several sources, including research travel grants from the Costume Society of America, Design History Society, San Francisco State University, and Society of Antiquaries London. San Francisco State University provided a sabbatical leave. The Costume Society of America granted funds for image licensing.

Several chapters were revised from published journal articles and symposium proceedings, and I am grateful to the editors of the journals *Costume* and *French Historical Studies,* as well as the Textile Society of American Symposium Proceedings, for permission to republish.

I would like to thank illustrator Michael Fleming for his illustrations and graphics (the map, charts, and technical drawings).

My family supported me emotionally and logistically over the many years I spent researching and writing this book, especially Michael and Laraine. I couldn't have done it without you.

INTRODUCTION

French dominance in the fashion world is rarely questioned, particularly in the early modern period. From the seventeenth century, cutting-edge clothing designs originated at the court of Louis XIV (1638–1715), then filtered out across Europe. However, those French styles did not exist in a national vacuum. When the *Magasin des modes* (Magazine of fashion) proclaimed that Frenchwomen's particular genius was taking the fashions of other countries, improving and embellishing them, then exporting them back to their native lands, it was observing the exoticism that had underscored French fashion for the past hundred years or more. While French style did indeed set the bar across Europe, what is too frequently obscured is the extent to which it was based in small or large part on dress from the Middle East, North Africa, and Asia—principally the Ottoman Empire.

From the late seventeenth century, French culture became increasingly obsessed with all things "oriental," as objects and ideas that were associated with the East came to represent luxury, comfort, and a worldly sense of style. Advances in communication and transportation meant that Middle Eastern, North African, and Asian things—material goods like textiles and coffee, but also concepts like stories, fashions, and home decor—became wildly popular across France. These Eastern things were embraced across class and geography: as imports grew and locally made copies abounded, they became part of the daily lives of not just the elites but also the bourgeois and working classes, including those living in the provinces. By the eighteenth century, Eastern commodities, designs, and references were fundamental to everyday

No one can deny that our French Ladies make the Ladies of almost all other Kingdoms adopt their fashions; however, we must agree that these [fashions] are almost always exchanges. Have they [French women] not borrowed, in less than two years, Polish, English, Turkish, Chinese [dress]? Today they borrow the Spanish [dress]. It is true that they improve these styles; & even, strictly speaking, they do not borrow anything but the names, & they give things [in return]. When they copy, they correct, they embellish. When they imitate, they create. Of a too inventive imagination, too helpful to slavishly follow their models, they seize it, they shape it. They become, in a word, the *masters* of their authors. This talent shines in today's Spanish hats & *bonnets,* as it shone in *robes à la Polonoise,* in English hats, in Turkish bonnets, & in the *poufs à la Chinoise.*
—Magasin des modes

life in France, where they were adapted and given new cultural associations, then exported to other Western European countries.

This obsession was focused on the Ottoman Empire, due in large part to its geographic proximity and comparatively open trading and diplomatic policies. Regions like India, China, Japan, and the Americas fascinated the French, but Ottoman culture was most accessible and thus became the model for all things exotic. Furthermore, although goods from farther east could move by sea, many still arrived overland through the Ottoman Empire and in so doing acquired Turkish connotations. Over time, what were called "oriental" references were integrated into French culture through architecture, decorative arts, fashion, food, literature, painting, and theater. In dress, beginning with the seventeenth-century trend for lounging clothing worn at home, which transformed into dress suitable for public wear (what we might today call "street wear"), fashionable female dress was based in part on Turkish approaches to garment cut and design (Ottoman clothing affected men's dress as well, but this is harder to document in this period).[1] French women began wearing Westernized versions of Middle Eastern caftans for both informal and formal wear, upending at least two centuries of an approach to dress founded on structured garments and complex pattern shapes.

This is not to say French women abandoned all Western dress precepts in the early modern period. As Eastern-inspired dressing gowns were turned into fashionable garments, their cuts and fits were refined and Westernized (and they received new, specialized names, some pointing to their foreign origins, others demonstrating just how profoundly they were considered French). Furthermore, despite their relaxed impression—what was called *négligé* or *deshabillé,* meaning comfortable, informal dress—any ensemble worn outside the home was done so over boned stays and, for most of the period, hoops or pads, creating an artificial understructure that reshaped the body's contours and created the controlled body deemed essential to Western ideas of female self-presentation. Moreover, numerous themes and artistic movements influenced dress in this era, including Rococo, chinoiserie, *paysannerie,* Anglomania, the troubadour style, and neoclassicism, as well as political events and themes such as ambassadorial visits, internal French politics, and the American and French revolutions.[2] French dress was a cross-cultural mélange, and the desire was to embrace and mix rather than separate and demarcate. Nonetheless, when it came to women's fashion, Ottoman influences were the strongest motif from about 1670 through 1780, and these continued to be significant in subsequent decades.

Thus, from the late seventeenth century through the mid-1780s, most garments worn by middling and upper-class French women were either based on, or incorporated significant influences from, the dress of the Ottoman Empire or areas under its cultural influence. Scholars have documented this phenomenon through the mid-eighteenth century, but the impact that Ottoman dress continued to have on French women's fashion in later decades has thus far been comparatively less explored. Certainly, research demonstrates the massive popularity of faux-Turkish costumes in portraiture and masquerade, as well as clothing worn by Western travelers to the Ottoman Empire. However, from the 1760s through the mid-1780s, Turkish dress continued to be the dominant influence in French fashion, which has thus far been underestimated. This is partly due to this period's proliferation of styles, which has complicated historians' ability to untangle their specifics. Nonetheless, in an era when French fashion was obsessed with (inter)national signage, popular modes at the end of the century continued to incorporate Ottoman elements, an understanding of which is necessary to fully comprehend French culture. As Barbara Lasic declares, "French fashions in the early modern period cannot be understood outside of the global commercial networks of exchanges between Europe and the rest of the world."[3]

In this book, I argue that Turkish dress had decided impacts on French women's fashion, far beyond "costume," in the eighteenth century's last decades, and this trend was an important precursor to the English and neoclassical trends. This fascination with the Ottoman Empire manifested in what scholars call "*turquerie*," Turkish-focused Orientalism, as information about the Empire's dress was disseminated through ambassadorial visits, travel writings, art, masquerades, and theater, reaching large numbers of French people across class and geography. The Turkish-inspired fashions that resulted in the late eighteenth century have been underestimated in terms of their popularity and cultural impact. These originated in the late seventeenth-century enthusiasm for Eastern dressing gowns, which were introduced for private lounging wear but quickly became fashionable everyday dress and formed the basis for the leading modes of the early and mid-eighteenth century. Fashion publications, artworks, extant garments, and published and personal writings prove that Ottoman-inspired fashions, particularly the *robes à la polonaise* (Polish-style dress), *circassienne* (Circassian), *turque* (Turkish), and *lévite* (Levite), were immensely popular in the 1760s through the 1780s, differed substantially from other styles, and demonstrate real connections to Ottoman dress. Style mixing and naming practices reveal the fluidity of national and cultural identity, and a talent for adapting and blending these was considered fundamental to the French national character. These Turkish-inspired styles had a relationship with Enlightenment fashion ideas that in some ways mimicked, and in others diverged from, rhetoric around English and neoclassical themes; all three should be understood as an interrelated continuum. Finally, Queen Marie-Antoinette's wardrobe further demonstrates the complicated cultural ideas associated with these fashions, which were connected to long-criticized ideas about luxury and female sexuality. As the century ended, English, patriotic, and neoclassical themes predominated in French fashion. Nonetheless, styles with Turkish names and aesthetics continued to proliferate. The impact of Ottoman clothing on French women's dress in the late eighteenth century is greater and farther reaching than most scholars have concluded, demonstrating that this fundamental aspect of daily life served as a site of important dialogue about, and with, Eastern perspectives.

FASHION AND IDENTITY

In this work, *fashion* and *dress* refer to the clothes, accessories, and other elements of self-presentation and self-decoration such as hairstyles or cosmetics worn by individuals, as well as the changing style cycle communally adopted, adapted, and abandoned. As Daniel Roche explains, "Fashion exists at the intersection of the fact of dressing, which an individual can launch and generalise within the clothing system where it becomes common property, and the fact of clothing generalised in a manner of dressing and reproduced on the collective scale."[4] *Costume* refers to the garments and other elements of self-presentation/self-decoration used to resemble someone or something else, particularly for art, masquerade, theater, or entertainment. Scholars are proving both are an excellent lens through which to study societies and cultures. First, fashion is critical to an individual's self-presentation and social definition: whether consciously or subconsciously, individuals and groups use dress to construct, communicate, and negotiate social and cultural identity. Second, dress is a global trade commodity, and a prime example of how "things" facilitate cross-cultural interchange and adaptation, a process that began long before the modern era.

The garments we wear—their materials, cut, construction, decoration, and wearing modes—allow the sending and receiving of nonverbal messages creating, to varying degrees, instantaneous understandings of ourselves and others as individuals and members of groups.[5] At a glance, dress communicates basic identity categories, whether those are age, class, gender, ethnicity, cultural or national background, occupation, and more.[6] These ideas are well encapsulated by Terence Turner's term *social skin,* which he uses to indicate how "the surface of the body seems everywhere to be treated, not only as the boundary of the individual as a biological and psychological entity but as the frontier of the social self as well ... Dress and bodily adornment constitute one such cultural medium, perhaps the one most specialised in the shaping and communication of personal and social identity."[7] Joanne Eicher and Mary Ellen Roach-Higgins define the term *dress* not only as "an assemblage of body modifications and/or supplements displayed by a person" but also stress that this is "in communicating with other human beings."[8]

Dress not only *reflects* identity, but also facilitates conscious and subconscious *choices* about self-presentation and self-fashioning. Dress constructs collective identity; according to Patrizia Calefato, it creates "social imagery," allowing a community to coalesce "through a series of small, yet significant bonds."[9] Diana Crane maintains it is "one of the most visible markers of social status and gender. . . . Clothing is an indication of how people in different eras have perceived their positions in social structures and negotiated status boundaries."[10] Individuals can choose among different garments and styles to both identify with and separate from larger communities, using what Adam Geczy terms clothing's "lived, performative intent . . . in asserting personality and identity."[11]

Geczy argues that as the concept of "fashion" as a changing cycle arose in seventeenth-century France, it became fundamentally linked with perception and role-play—the understanding and conscious manipulation of identities—within that culture, and this idea holds true in the subsequent century.[12] Of course, strong social and cultural forces shape the range of identity statements available as well as their reception.[13] Susan B. Kaiser explains fashion is a "social process of negotiation and navigation" that "involves becoming collectively with others."[14] These important functions are often disregarded given fashion's associations with surface, which can be interpreted as insubstantial or unimportant. Dani Cavallaro and Alexandra Warwick argue dress is a "*deep surface,* a system of signs that fundamentally relies on superficial modes of signification for the purposes of expressing the underlying beliefs of a given culture and the character of the subjects fostered therein."[15] In addition, the long-standing gendering of fashion as feminine means it has frequently been disregarded as unworthy of deeper reflection due to the devaluing of women's lives and interests.[16]

Dress is illuminating in cross-cultural studies because for centuries, textiles and garments have traveled between regions, countries, and continents, both as individual consumer goods and as ideas and information. Geczy contends that "the signs of nation, identity and novelty . . . are nowhere more evident" than in fashion and dress.[17] Historically, clothing may have been usually built locally, but textiles, dyes, and other materials were often imported from around the world.[18] Furthermore, stories, images, garments, and other representations of dress have long served as ambassadors between cultures and nations. As fashion goods travel, they bring not only their material self and commercial value but also exotic associations.[19] Alexander Bevilacqua and Helen Pfeifer argue, "Goods, practices and ideas were inextricably linked."[20] These are adopted, adapted, and recontextualized as they travel, speaking equally about the cultures into which they are incorporated as those from which they originated and creating a negotiable space.

Fashion's cross-cultural references are complex. Fred Davis cautions that signifiers may be similar across a given culture, but their meaning can differ depending on the audience, arguing dress allows for "registering the culturally anchored ambivalences that resonate within and among identities."[21] Several scholarly methodologies are employed in this book to parse these ambivalences. Consumption studies focuses on how the act of consuming goods, ideas, stories, allusions, and aesthetics is key to identity formation.[22] In "thing theory," a strand of material culture studies, scholars argue that artifacts can be understood only through the world view of the cultures that encountered (made, used, traded, discussed, imagined) them, and multiple readings of these meanings are valid.[23] In dress history, the analysis of extant garments is increasingly deemed important.[24]

Edward Said's seminal book, *Orientalism,* lays the groundwork for understanding how the Western world created a fictional "Orient" as Europe's fundamental "Other." Said articulates how the idea of an imagined Orient intensified a sense of self for the West "by dramatizing the distance and difference between what is close to it and what is far away."[25] Looking specifically at the eighteenth century, scholars are building on, countering, and adding nuance to Said's arguments, demonstrating how foreign "things" played consequential roles in identity formation. For example, Julia Landweber establishes that French people used Ottoman masquerade costumes to experiment with personal and national identities without political or psychological risk, so much so that Turkish goods and ideas "became an important tool in shaping individual identities in France and perhaps even in crafting a general vision of the French national character."[26] Meanwhile, Nebahat Avcıoğlu's study of architecture in this period demonstrates how Ottoman references helped to define and mark "Otherness."[27]

Geczy identifies three core processes by which Orientalism enters fashion: "assimilation, improvement, adoption and influence," which generally occurs unconsciously; "masquerade, repatriation or reidentification," where wearing the Other's costume affords "temporary release from social restrictions," and "inflection, inspiration, tokenism and galvanization," whereby Orientalism becomes a political tool for separating from the norm.[28] All three processes were at work in late eighteenth-century French fashion: conscious masquerade (Turkish costume worn for a masquerade, portrait, or on stage) combined with tokenism (adopting a style or element and calling it Turkish) led to conscious and unconscious assimilation and influence.[29] Fashion thus provides a lens through which to study this period's fascination with the Ottoman Empire specifically, and exoticism more generally, revealing strong themes of preoccupation with and ambivalence about national and cultural identity, and demonstrating when and how cultural appropriation and amalgamation became central to eighteenth-century French culture.

GEOGRAPHIC TERMINOLOGY

Geographic nomenclature is perhaps problematic in any cross-cultural study. On the one hand, countries such as France and the Ottoman Empire had their political boundaries and can be appropriately named as such. Similarly, land masses such as Anatolia—the peninsula extending into the Black and Mediterranean seas, located within the modern country of Turkey—as well as the Asian continent are relatively clearly defined, although the boundary between Asia and Europe is debatable. However, geographic terms like *East* or *Middle East* introduce an inherently Eurocentric perspective. *East* implies it is not the central reference point, thus creating an Orientalist distinction between Us (Europe) and Other.[30] Certainly *Orient* and *Oriental* are passé for modern scholarship but replacing them with *Middle East* or *Near East* still implies Europe's centrality.[31] Furthermore, these terms are ambiguous about *which* countries and regions are included. *Asia* and its subdivisions could be more appropriate, but these do not correspond to the entire Ottoman Empire, much of which existed on the continents of Europe and Africa.

On the other hand, this book considers how French people understood the Ottomans specifically and, more broadly, areas commonly referred to today as the *Middle East*, *North Africa*, and *Eastern Europe*, as well as *Asia*. Furthermore, countries and regions including most of the Ottoman Empire, as well as Hungary, Poland, Russia, China, India, and Japan, *were* indeed located east of France, and, to an eighteenth-century French perspective, were culturally similar in significant ways. Thus, while acknowledging the inherent Eurocentric bias of these words, I will use the terms *East*, *Middle East*, and *Eastern Europe* to name geographic areas in groupings that align with the eighteenth-century French world view and are understandable for modern readers. *East* refers to a loose and shifting definition of countries and regions to France's east that were considered non-European, including the Ottoman Empire, Hungary, Poland, Russia, and the entire Asian continent. *Middle East* denotes the

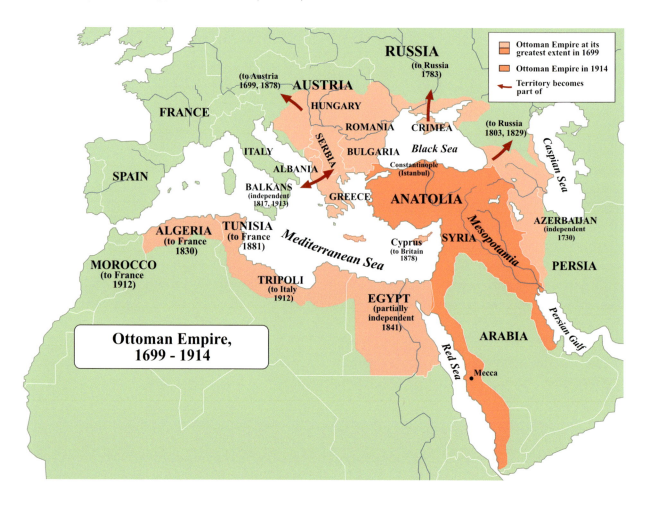

Fig. 1. The Ottoman Empire was primarily to the east of France, and included territories in Europe, the eastern Mediterranean, and North Africa. (Illustration by Michael Fleming.)

Ottoman Empire as well as Persia; this omits specifying North Africa for brevity's sake. Finally, *Eastern Europe* refers to Hungary, Poland, western Russia, and the Balkans area of southeastern Europe (see list below). I hope that by investigating cross-cultural interchanges, historical understandings of geography can be better understood in all their complexity.

It is also important to note eighteenth-century French perspectives on geography and national origin within the Ottoman Empire specifically. The political entity that was the Ottoman Empire in this era included not just modern Turkey but also all or parts of the following modern-day countries (Fig. 1):

Eastern Mediterranean:
- Jordan
- Lebanon
- Iraq
- Israel
- Palestine
- Saudi Arabia
- Syria
- Yemen

Northern Africa:
- Algeria
- Egypt
- Libya
- Tunisia

Southeastern Europe:
- Albania
- Bosnia and Herzegovina
- Bulgaria
- Cyprus
- Greece
- Moldova
- Montenegro
- Romania
- Russia and Ukraine (specifically the Crimean region)
- Serbia

However, eighteenth-century French people frequently included independent countries and regions that were under some degree of Ottoman influence in their ideas of the Empire, particularly Hungary, Poland, and western Russia. Furthermore, the terms *Ottoman* and *Turkey* or *Turkish* were used interchangeably, while a *Turk* was any Ottoman or Muslim living within or without the Empire.[32] Thus, any usage of *Ottoman* or *Turkish* in this book should be understood to be a flexible definition. Finally, the eastern Mediterranean region was often called *Levant*, a term dating back to sixteenth-century France that derives from the French word for *rising,* as in lying in the direction of the rising sun.[33]

FASHION IN FRENCH CULTURE

From the late seventeenth through the mid-twentieth centuries, France was the acknowledged fashion leader of Western Europe.[34] During the reign of Louis XIV (1643–1715), French society centered on the court of Versailles and the urban center of Paris. Jean-Baptiste Colbert, the king's finance minister, encouraged luxury manufacturing and purchasing, while Louis played an important role as style-setter.[35] In an era of conspicuous consumption, as Aileen Ribeiro writes, a "sense of the subtleties and nuances of existence [were] expressed in the right choice of dress."[36] Luxury goods, including fashion, were markers of elite status and critical to expressing taste and wealth.[37]

However, the exponential growth of consumption in this period meant that by the early eighteenth century, a substantial bourgeois class had ready money and thus access to consumer goods.[38] Furthermore, after Louis XIV's death in 1715, sumptuary law relaxation encouraged access to fashionable dress for rapidly growing numbers of people across social classes, while technology and transportation advances were making these goods more affordable.[39] Over the course of the eighteenth century, production and consumption grew astronomically, meaning exponentially more people from an ever-widening class spectrum could purchase an increasing number of products with significantly more choice.[40]

These shifts affected dress: rising numbers of middle- and working-class people participated in a growing fashion system, expanding not only the number of items purchased but also the amount of consideration for personal preference in clothing selection.[41] The size and value of wardrobes grew exponentially among the bourgeois and working classes, and even in rural communities, consumers sought innovation.[42] Kimberly Chrisman-Campbell argues that between more effective means of spreading fashion information, a flourishing market in secondhand clothes, and advances in manufacturing and trade that lowered clothing's cost, "Fashion was available to all and desired by all."[43]

Significantly, fashion—goods as well as information about new and changing styles—was a topic of growing social interest. For one thing, the style leaders were changing. In the seventeenth century, fashion had been the elite's realm, and those outside who could participate did so mostly through imitation. However, in the eighteenth century, a new fashion culture focused on Paris developed in which *marchandes de modes* (female merchants who were primarily responsible for designing, trimming, and accessorizing ensembles), actresses, courtesans, and those who had the funds to be au courant joined the royalty and aristocracy in defining what was fashionable.[44]

Another important development in this era was the gendering of fashion production and consumption. Parisian seamstresses gained independent guild status in 1675 with the right to make most of women's and children's wardrobes; previously, dressmaking had been the province of male tailors, at least officially.[45] Clare Haru Crowston demonstrates how increasing numbers of women were employed in the dress trades at cheap rates, while women's fashion consumption grew; both trends meant dress became increasingly feminized in a way that overshadowed class distinctions.[46] Meanwhile, Jennifer Jones argues that as fashion became a female occupation and therefore a female concern, it was trivialized in a way that obscured its meanings.[47]

In this period, French people were increasingly conscious that dress contributed to the construction of social identities.[48] Enlightenment philosophes debated and deconstructed connections between appearance and identity, arguing over which garments and styles were most physically and morally beneficial and would therefore contribute to an ideal society. By the 1770s, these concepts had achieved widespread popularity across French society, leading to a growing desire for naturalism and egalitarianism in appearance that had real effects on fashion.[49] Meanwhile, the rate of fashion change—new styles introduced, old styles abandoned—exponentially increased in the century's last decades, something both obvious to contemporaries and a matter of concern.[50] Chrisman-Campbell argues this quickening pace was caused by innovations resulting from the relaxation of the guild system; manufacturing, transportation, and communication advances; and, most importantly for this study, the development of fashion magazines.[51]

THE FRENCH FASHION PRESS

French print culture expanded dramatically in the eighteenth century.[52] Before the mid-1770s, people tended to learn about fashion trends from shops, traveling merchants, tailors and seamstresses, and social acquaintances.[53] Annual almanacs illustrated with fashion plates reached a large audience, but quickly went out of date.[54] Numerous short-lived attempts at fashion periodicals dated back to the seventeenth century and included *Le Courrier français* (The French courier, 1649), *Le Muse historique* (The historical muse, 1658–59), and *Le Cabinet des nouvellistes* (The office of novelists, 1728). The leader in these efforts was the *Mercure de France* (Mercury of France, 1672–1791), which through 1731 published intermittent articles on Parisian elite dress, as well as entirely fashion-focused, semiannual issues called *Extraordinaire*.[55] Almost three decades later, the short-lived *Feuille nécessaire* (Necessary sheet, 1759) and *L'Avant-coureur* (The forerunner, 1760–69) revived these attempts.

However, it was not until the late 1770s that the fashion press really established itself (due, in large part, to tax reforms) enough to have a major impact on French society.[56] The *Courrier de la mode ou le Journal du goût, Ouvrage périodique, contenant le détail de toutes les nouveautés du mois* (Courier of fashion or the journal of taste, periodical work, containing the details of all the novelties of the month, 1768–70) was the first magazine to focus solely on fashion, but it lasted only two years. The *Monument du costume*, a series of twelve fashion prints accompanied by short narratives, was an important source of fashion information when it was published in 1776, with another series published in 1783.[57] However, it was more focused on social mores than the newest trends. With the publication of the *Gallerie des modes et costumes français, dessinés d'après nature, Gravés par les plus Célèbres Artistes en ce genre, et colorés avec le plus grand soin par Madame Le Beau* (Gallery of French fashions and costumes, drawn from nature, engraved by the most famous artists of this genre, and colored with the greatest care by Madame Le Beau), regular fashion updates reached a small but influential audience.[58] The *Gallerie* was not technically a magazine but rather a series of fashion plates accompanied by detailed descriptions released irregularly but frequently as *cahiers* (notebooks) from 1778 until 1787.[59] Finally, beginning with the semimonthly *Cabinet des modes, ou les Modes nouvelles, décrites d'une manière claire & précise, & représentées par des planches en taille-douce, enluminées* (Office of fashion, or new fashions, described in a clear & precise manner, & represented by intaglio plates, illuminated, 1785–86), fashion magazines as we would understand them today—fashion plates with detailed descriptions, as well as texts reporting what was in style and out—began publication.[60] The *Cabinet* was followed by the *Magasin des modes nouvelles, françaises et anglaises, décrites d'une manière claire & précise, & représentées par des planches en taille-douce, enluminées* (Shop of new fashions, French and English, described in a clear & precise manner, & represented by intaglio plates, illuminated, 1787–89), then the *Journal de la mode et du goût, ou Amusemens du salon et de la toilette* (Journal of fashion and taste, or amusements of the salon and the dressing process, 1790–93).[61] The Revolution interrupted fashion publishing for several years, but the industry resumed with the *Journal des dames et des modes* (Journal of women and fashion, 1797–1839), *Tableau général du goût, des modes et costumes de Paris, par une société d'artistes et gens de lettres* (General table of taste, fashions and costumes of Paris, by a society of artists and men of letters, 1797–99), and *L'Arlequin, ou Tableau des modes et des goûts* (The harlequin, or table of fashions and tastes, 1798–99).[62]

The fashion press had several important effects on French culture. For one, it promoted the idea that styles were continuously changing, inventing new details, terminology, and other reasons for women to update their wardrobes.[63] As fashion was considered to be an important record of contemporary tastes, editors attempted to capture what was actually being worn in Paris and spread that information to readers in the provinces and other countries.[64] In fact, Caroline Rimbault's study found that bourgeois and provincial women were more likely to subscribe to these kind of exclusively female publications than Parisian noblewomen, who tended to join their spouses in subscribing to costly journals of interest to both.[65] Annemarie Kleinert estimates that sixty thousand copies of the prospectus for the *Cabinet des modes* were distributed across Europe, and about a thousand people subscribed annually.[66] Furthermore, the *Gallerie* and its successors devoted most of their coverage to women's dress, further gendering fashion as female.[67] Finally, fashion became something that *could* be encapsulated and communicated through the print medium, and a garment or style's name was as important as its appearance, something particularly evident in the late eighteenth-century vogue for fashion naming, whether it be varieties of dresses or jackets, hats or hairstyles, as well as small elements such as the bow worn on a gown or a particular sleeve cuff—something of specific import in this era when considering Ottoman influence on French fashion.[68]

Multiple creators drew, wrote, edited, and published these periodicals.[69] Parisian printmakers Jacques Esnault and Michel Rapilly edited the *Gallerie*, while at least five artists drew its plates: Claude-Louis Desrais, Pierre-Thomas Leclerc, J.-B. Martin, de Saint-Aubin, and Watteau fils.[70] Meanwhile, Jean-Antoine Le Brun ("Lebrun-Tossa," 1760–1837) was responsible for both the *Cabinet des modes* and the *Journal de la mode et du goût*.[71] A hatmaker's son, Le Brun studied for the priesthood and worked as a teacher before entering publishing. He was young and inexperienced when beginning the *Cabinet*, relying on printer, bookseller, and journalist François Buisson's assistance.[72] Thus, these creators were not necessarily fashion experts, multiple hands were involved, and creators contradicted one another and themselves.

Fashion magazines are not the only source for the history of dress in this period, but combined with published and personal writings, artworks, and surviving garments, they demonstrate the tangible impacts of Ottoman ideas and aesthetics on French women's dress from the late seventeenth through the end of the eighteenth century.

Clothing Perspectives, East and West

In the late seventeenth century, changing global politics culminated in the renewal of the Franco-Ottoman alliance, leading to a global trade explosion as French merchants received increased access to the highly valued commodities that came from or through the Ottoman Empire. Ottoman imports came wrapped in ideas and stories, which fed a rapacious French appetite for the exotic. In particular, dress served as a focal point for French interest in what scholars call *turquerie,* or Turkish-focused Orientalism. With increasing access to information about the Ottomans, costumes worn for art, masquerade, and the theater made frequent use of Turkish themes and brought information about Ottoman dress, real and imagined, to a broad swathe of French society. This omnipresence translated into widespread popularity for Turkish-inspired dress styles, as women's garments named and styled after the Ottoman Empire led French fashion from the late seventeenth through the mid-eighteenth centuries.

Madame de Broglie sent me to the *Comediennes* [Comédie française theater], to find a sultana's costume she wanted for her portrait. I visited [actresses Mademoiselle] Gaussian and [Mademoiselle] Grandval, and it was the second who gave me what I was looking for, which I immediately took to [painter Jean-Marc] Nattier.

—Comte de Tessin, 1742, quoted in Haydn Williams, *Turquerie: An Eighteenth-Century European Fantasy*

TURQUERIE AND FRENCH DRESS

Dress, including both fashion and costume, was a key site in which French fascination with *turquerie* materialized. The eighteenth-century French consumed Ottoman dress in several ways, some direct

11

and relatively authentic, others less so. Ambassadors and their envoys provided conspicuous examples of Turkish style, while French military regiments originating in Eastern Europe were widely admired for their flamboyant uniforms based on national dress. Travelers' accounts and costume albums documented and publicized the clothing worn in the Empire and surrounding regions. The French posed for and viewed Ottoman-themed paintings, drawings, and prints; created, wore, and observed Eastern masquerade costumes; and attended or participated in theatrical productions with Turkish settings and costumes. These sources combined to make Ottoman dress ubiquitous across France.

Said demonstrates how Western Europeans created the idea of the "Orient" as Europe's fundamental "Other," as a means of "dominating, restructuring, and having authority over the Orient."[1] According to his argument, this imagined East connected many disparate communities into one semihomogeneous idea, which was generally portrayed in a negative light (childlike, irrational, depraved, and different) compared to Europe (rational, virtuous, mature, and normal).[2] Later scholars have complicated this view, arguing that opinions of the East were frequently contradictory, encompassed accurate and fictional information, and ranged from positive to negative depending on the era.[3] Concerning the eighteenth century, historians debate to what extent *turquerie* served as a dominating force of West over East or whether it is better understood as cross-cultural exploration and questioning. Srinivas Aravamudan argues eighteenth-century Orientalism focused on understanding "civilizational differences both relativistically and universally," while Avcıoğlu cautions that the era's relatively balanced power structures meant *turquerie* was an experiment with "alternative aesthetic, cultural, and political role models."[4]

The Ottoman Empire formed in 1516–17 when Sultan Selim I (1470–1520) united Anatolia, the Balkans, and the Mamluk Empire of Syria and Egypt. It held power over virtually the entire eastern Mediterranean and added considerable amounts of territory in the sixteenth and seventeenth centuries. The Empire loomed large in the European political structure because it was Europe's primary non-Christian aggressor and was geographically closer than other "exotic" powers.[5] Its image began to change with the 1536 alliance between Suleiman I (1494–1566) and French King François I (1494–1547), which inaugurated official diplomatic and economic relationships with the West. The Empire took on an increasingly important role in the French experience and imagination after the failed Ottoman siege of Vienna (1683), as its military threat diminished and regular trade and diplomatic missions were established with Western Europe.[6] Growing numbers of Westerners visited the Ottoman Empire, and their resulting artworks and travel writings, as well as commercial goods, stories, and references, took on growing significance in the daily life of France. Although many non-Western cultures fascinated the French, information about the Ottomans was the most available of these, while impressions of other parts of Asia were comparatively vague and generalized based on assumptions about the Turks.[7]

Commercial routes into the Middle East and Asia expanded substantially in the early modern period, as did French demand for goods from these regions.[8] Western traders established direct sea routes with Asia, but significant trade continued to pass through Ottoman ports, meaning items from regions further east brought with them Turkish associations.[9] This interest in all things Turkish was integrated into eighteenth-century French culture via art, architecture, domestic goods, food, interior and exterior decor, gardens, entertainment, and fashion.[10] *Turquerie* permeated across the class spectrum, as the middling classes joined the elites in displaying wealth and status through access to exotic commodities.[11] Moreover, Western Europeans did not simply interact with Turkish goods, but also with concepts about what the Ottomans represented.[12]

TURQUERIE

In modern scholarship, the term *turquerie* is used to refer to Western fascination with genuinely Turkish goods and their copies, as well as any item, action, image, or allusion referring to the Ottoman Empire.[13] In the seventeenth and eighteenth centuries, the term referred to a "manner of being cruel & barbarous, as do the Turks."[14] Its modern definition originates with Charles Augustin Sainte-Beuve, who in 1831 used *turquerie* to mean literary or artistic works inspired by a fantasy of Turkey.[15] Among the eighteenth-century French, the term *oriental* was used to reference anything Eastern, including the Ottoman Empire.[16] However, that term is too broad for this study, so I will join the many scholars who use the term *turquerie* as a useful shorthand for Ottoman-focused Orientalism. It is important to clarify that concepts of, and fascination with, *turquerie*—particularly in the arena of dress—in the contemporary mindset also included the Ottoman-influenced cultures of Eastern Europe, specifically the Balkans, Hungary, Poland, and Russia.[17] Although today cultural links between Turkey and these regions may not immediately spring to mind, strong connections existed in the eighteenth century.[18] Much of the Balkans were then under Ottoman control, and independent countries like the Kingdom of Hungary (under Hapsburg rule), Poland (more specifically, the Polish-Lithuanian Commonwealth, which in 1772 was split between the Russian Empire, the Kingdom of Prussia, and Hapsburg Austria), and Russia's western regions had been under Ottoman rule in preceding centuries; thus clothing styles in Turkey and Eastern Europe had long intermingled.[19]

Fig. 2. Louis XV holds an audience for Ottoman ambassador Mehmed Said Efendi. Chiquet (ed.), *L'Audiance Magnifique dônée par le Roy Louis XV à Mehemet Effendi, Ambassadeur du Grand Seigneur le 21 Mars 1721* (The magnificent audience given by the king Louis XV to Mehemet Effendi, ambassador to the Great Lord the 21 March 1721), ca. 1721. (Print, etching, 31.3 cm × 20.2 cm, Paris, Musée Carnavalet.)

THE INFLUENCE OF AMBASSADORIAL VISITS

Ambassadorial visits provided some of the first introductions of Turkish dress to French society. While the Ottomans did not set up a permanent embassy in France until 1796, they sent delegations in 1669, 1720–21 (Fig. 2), and 1741–42; these were national spectacles, stimulating interest in *turquerie* in general and Turkish dress in particular.[20] Other non-Western ambassadors indirectly encouraged the phenomenon, like the 1684 Siamese visit that precipitated a fad for fashion "*à la Siamoise*," as well as the 1788 delegation from Mysore (modern India) that sparked dresses "*à la Tipoo-Saïb*" in reference to that kingdom's ruler.[21]

OTTOMAN DRESS IN TRAVEL WRITINGS

Published travel writings were another important means of disseminating information about the Ottomans and their dress. In particular, the letters of Englishwoman Lady Mary Wortley Montagu (1689–1772), which were edited and published in 1763, reached a broad audience across Western Europe.[22] Lady Montagu's husband was ambassador to the Ottoman Empire as well as a representative of the English Levant Company, and the couple lived in Constantinople for two years beginning in 1716. She was among the first Westerners to gain access to aristocratic female-only spaces like harems and bathhouses; she spoke Arabic, allowing her to communicate with Turkish women directly; and she often wore Ottoman clothing, both in Constantinople and upon her return home.[23] Scholars who analyze Montagu's writings argue she viewed dressing as an "Other" as a means of putting on, taking off, and reinforcing ethnic and

Fig. 3. A Turkish caftan allegedly belonging to Lady Mary Wortley Montagu. *Robe,* Turkey, ca. 1720. (Brocade, blended silk and cotton with silver-gilt design woven in, Victoria & Albert Museum, London, T.225-1958. Given by W. D. Clarke Esq. Author photograph. Courtesy of Victoria and Albert Museum, London.)

gender identity.[24] Lady Montagu brought Ottoman textiles back home with her, which may have included items of dress.[25] One fascinating example is the woman's caftan at the Victoria & Albert Museum, which, according to family tradition, belonged to Montagu (Fig. 3).[26]

Another notable traveler was Marie Thérèse Rodet Geoffrin (1699–1777), a Parisian *salonnière* whose gatherings included several Enlightenment luminaries.[27] She corresponded with Russian Empress Catherine the Great and Polish King Stanislaw August, visiting the latter in Warsaw in 1766. The letters she wrote home were a sensation in Paris, and according to the influential Friedrich Melchior, Baron von Grimm, read by nearly every French intellectual, although unfortunately most were never collected and published.[28] She may have described dress in these, or even returned with some examples.[29] Certainly, she later owned several Russian caftans, gifts from Catherine the Great, and if the circa 1760 portrait presumed to be her is authentic, she had access to a Turkish-, Polish-, or Russian-style caftan.[30]

OTTOMAN DRESS IN ART

Artistic representations of Ottoman dress were central to disseminating and popularizing Turkish fashion themes. Beginning in the sixteenth century, costume albums combined illustrations with descriptive texts and represented Western Europeans' desire to categorize nations and peoples via their dress and character, which were supposedly linked. European-produced albums contributed to the idea that cultures could be reduced to visual characteristics, as well as the "Othering" of foreign cultures.[31] Ottomans were ever present in these albums, and some included the peoples of Eastern Europe. These were widely circulated in France and beyond, serving as a direct source for artists and costume designers when depicting Ottoman clothing.[32] Whether or not these albums included local artists' contributions, the dress they illustrated was generally adapted for the European market for which they were intended.[33]

No costume album was more influential than the *Recueil de cent estampes representant différentes nations du Levant* (Collection of one hundred prints representing different nations of the Levant, 1712–15, Figs. 4, 5, 133, 138), which was widely disseminated throughout Western Europe and whose figures frequently served as the basis for successive artists' work.[34] Franco-Flemish painter Jean-Baptiste Van Mour (1671–1737) moved to Constantinople in 1699 as part of French ambassador Charles de Ferriol's entourage, remaining there until his death. His workshop of

European and Ottoman artists created multiple paintings for the Western market, many of which today are in the Rijksmuseum (Figs. 19, 20, 47, 51).³⁵ De Ferriol commissioned a series of one hundred engravings based on Van Mour's paintings, which was published in 1712–13, with second and third editions in 1714 and 1715.³⁶ Each plate in the *Recueil* represents one or more figures, inscribed as a particular "type" rather than an individual: positions like the sultan, grand vizier, and chief eunuch; jobs like scholar, patriarch, merchant, or coffee server; and numerous nationalities, ethnicities, and religions, including Armenians, Jews, Greeks, Serbians, and Persians. The *Recueil* was significant in its attempt to accurately portray Turkish dress, including that of women, although Van Mour could not have had personal access to Ottoman ladies.³⁷

The vogue for painting Europeans in Ottoman costume dates to the sixteenth-century trade between Venice and the Empire. By the mid-eighteenth century, it had become fashionable for French people to be painted in "Turkish" costume.³⁸ Artists and sitters, many of whom had never traveled, created what were usually fantasy costumes; signs that a subject was wearing Turkish dress include loose caftans, fur trimmings,

(*Left*) Fig. 4. An "Aga," an honorific Ottoman title for several kinds of civilians and officers. Gérard Jean Baptiste Scotin I after Jean Baptiste Vanmour, *Aga, ou Gentilhomme Turc,* plate 39 from *Recueil de cent estampes représentent differentes nations du Levant* (Collection of one hundred prints representing the different nations of the Levant), 1714–15. (Etching and engraving, 14 1/16 × 9 3/16 in., the Metropolitan Museum of Art, New York. Bequest of Mrs. Charles Wrightsman, 2019.)

(*Right*) Fig. 5. A Turkish girl is served coffee by an attendant. Jean-Baptiste Haussard after Jean Baptiste Vanmour, "Fille Turque, prenant le Caffé sur le Sopha," plate 48 from *Recueil de cent estampes représentent differentes nations du Levant* (Collection of one hundred prints representing the different nations of the Levant), 1714–15. (Etching and engraving, 14 1/16 × 9 3/16 in., the Metropolitan Museum of Art, New York. Bequest of Mrs. Charles Wrightsman, 2019.)

CLOTHING PERSPECTIVES, EAST AND WEST   17

sashes, striped fabrics, asymmetrically placed caps, veils, braided hair, and standing jewel or feather arrangements called *aigrettes* (egret feathers).[39] Being painted in this mode expressed worldliness, wealth, and taste on the part of both artist and sitter, and can be understood as acts of exoticism and luxury consumption.[40] By the 1760s, the growing influence of neoclassicism meant these costumes were condensed into what were considered "ancient" draperies, but their basis was still in pseudo-Turkish dress.[41]

One of *turquerie*'s most important artists was Jean-Étienne Liotard (1702–89), who accompanied an English lord on his grand tour and remained behind in Constantinople, living there from 1738 until 1742; he also traveled through Greece and Malta. While in the East, Liotard wore Ottoman dress (with a long beard), continuing to do so when he returned to Europe as self-promotion.[42] He frequently painted Europeans in Turkish costume (Fig. 6).[43] Other important French artists include Jean-Antoine Watteau (1684–1721), who created several paintings and drawings of women in faux-Polish dress, including *The Dreamer* (1712/14, Fig. 7).[44] François Boucher (1703–77) provided illustrations for Simon Francis Ravenet's *Recueil de diverses figures étrangères* (Collection

(*Left*) Fig. 6. This woman (probably French) wears the shirt, trousers, caftan, belt, and braided hair of Turkish dress. Jean Etienne Liotard, *Woman in Turkish Dress, Seated on a Sofa*, ca. 1752. (Drawing, pastel over red chalk underdrawing on parchment, 23 × 18⅝ in., the Metropolitan Museum of Art, New York. Bequest of Mrs. Charles Wrightsman, 2019.)

(*Right*) Fig. 7. A woman wearing "Polish" costume. Her short-sleeved, fur-trimmed caftan is more typical of Ottoman dress than Polish women's Western-influenced fashionable clothing. Jean Antoine Watteau, *The Dreamer (La Rêveuse)*, 1712/14. (Painting, oil on canvas, 9⅛ × 6¹¹⁄₁₆ in., Art Institute of Chicago. Mr. and Mrs. Lewis Larned Coburn Memorial Collection.)

18   DRESSING À LA TURQUE

of various foreign figures, 1730) and Jean-Antoine Guer's *Moeurs et usages des Turcs* (Mores and customs of the Turks, 1746), while his *Figures chinoises* series depicts Chinese characters wearing what looks more like Ottoman dress than authentic Chinese clothing.[45] Antoine de Favray (1706–98) lived in Constantinople from 1762 through 1771; in 1766, he painted the French ambassador and his wife wearing Turkish dress, seated on carpets and cushions in specifically Eastern poses.[46] Meanwhile, Élisabeth Vigée Le Brun (1755–1842) incorporated stylized elements drawn from Turkish dress in order to conjure a sense of timeless elegance in portraits of royal and aristocratic women.[47]

OTTOMAN MILITARY UNIFORMS

Beginning in the seventeenth century, French armies frequently met Eastern troops on the battlefield, while Polish and Hungarian regiments fought for the French.[48] Eastern European soldiers were celebrated for their bravery and flamboyant style, which included their military uniforms based on national dress: Hussar uniforms were based on Hungarian styles (Fig. 8), while Polish Lancers wore Polish headdresses and jackets.[49] French regimental uniforms incorporated Eastern European–styled garments, and references to uniforms that include garments styled

Fig. 8. The soldier on horseback is a hussar, and his uniform demonstrates the influence of Hungarian dress. *Gardes français et hussard trinquant. Evénement pendant la Révolution en juillet 1789* (French guards and hussar toasting. Event during the Revolution in July 1789), eighteenth century. (Print, 15 × 24.1 cm, Musée Carnavalet, Paris.)

CLOTHING PERSPECTIVES, EAST AND WEST   19

Fig. 9. One of Vien's published costume designs for the *Caravanne du Sultan à la Mecque*. Joseph Marie Vien, *Chef des Eunuques* [Chief Eunuch], plate 20 from *Caravanne du Sultan à la Mecque*, 1748. (Etching on ivory laid paper, 194 × 130 mm, Art Institute of Chicago. The Amanda S. Johnson and Marion J. Livingston Fund.)

à la polonaise (Polish) and *hongroise* (Hungarian) appear multiple times in the *État militaire de France* between 1758 and 1793, as well as in orders given by the king in 1761, 1762, and 1776.[50]

OTTOMAN DRESS IN MASQUERADES

Masquerades, both court functions as well as carnivals and subscription balls open to the masses, were a favored entertainment in this era. Ottoman costumes were especially popular but were frequently more impressionistic than accurate.[51] As Ribeiro writes of this phenomenon in England,

> There was a certain amount of confusion over the details of Oriental dress; the term an 'eastern habit' which occurs frequently in masquerade accounts, could cover any kind of costume that had easily recognizable features such as turbans, ermine facings to robes, and it was often extended to the dress of those countries, like Greece, which were subject to Turkey and whose costumes were 'oriental' in certain aspects. Distinguishing characteristics of the various eastern countries were often lacking.[52]

One particularly influential example is the 1745 *Bal des ifs* (Yew Tree Ball). Cochin the Younger's famous drawing of the event prominently displays a group dressed in comically oversized Ottoman costumes, complete with semigrotesque masks.[53] Meanwhile, the *Caravanne du Sultan à la Mecque* (Sultan's caravan to Mecca) was organized by the French Academy in Rome during the 1748 carnival. French artist Joseph-Marie Vien (1716–1809) designed costumes (Fig. 9) that emphasized theatricality over verisimilitude, basing these on Van Mour's *Recueil de cent estampes* (Collection of one hundred prints) and Guer's engravings (after Boucher) in *Moeurs et usages des Turcs* (Mores and customs of the Turks).[54] Engravings of these costumes were published the same year and widely circulated.[55]

20 DRESSING À LA TURQUE

THEATRICAL REPRESENTATIONS OF OTTOMAN DRESS

Of all the various means by which French people encountered representations of Ottoman dress, none was so pervasive or wide-reaching as the theater.[56] Plays, operas, and ballets were the foremost public entertainment in cities and towns throughout the country.[57] Elites certainly patronized the theater, but so did the bourgeois and working classes, and all of these in growing numbers.[58] Actors and actresses were celebrities, their public and private lives fascinated the French, and actresses functioned as fashion leaders.[59] From the 1680s through the 1820s, Turkish themes were the most popular theme for theatrical productions, and costumes were a large part of their appeal (Fig. 10).[60] Theater presented visual representations of Ottoman dress to a wide audience, provided a tangible embodiment of "the Turk," created a sense that differences between Ottomans and Western Europeans were mainly cosmetic, and supplied direct inspiration for mainstream fashions.[61] Charlotte Jirousek finds these costumes emphasized the elements of Turkish dress that Europeans considered attractive and/or characteristic: layering, asymmetrical draping, loose garments, turbans, feathers, and veils; to this list should be added tassels, fringed trims, and striped

Fig. 10. Costume designs for a "*polonoise*" and "*polonois*" from an unspecified production. Note the fur trims, open-front garments, and on the female figure, the slashed oversleeves, crossover front, and slightly tucked-up overskirt. Louis René Boquet, *Polonoise, polonois (maquette de costume)* (Polish woman, Polish man [costume design]), eighteenth century. (Drawing, iron gall ink, 255 × 325 mm, Bibliothèque nationale de France, Paris.)

fabrics.[62] Significant theatrical productions with Ottoman themes and costumes included *Le Bourgeois gentilhomme* (The bourgeois gentleman, 1670), *Les Indes galantes* (The gallant Indies, 1735), *Scanderberg* (1735), and *Soliman second ou les trois sultanes* (Soliman the second or the three sultanas, 1761), all of which were popular enough to be performed for decades.[63]

Probably no theatrical production was more influential in terms of *turquerie* than *Soliman second ou les trois sultanes,* first performed in Paris in 1761 and continuing in popularity across Europe for several decades.[64] In this story, three wives (Circassian, Spanish, and French) of sixteenth-century Ottoman Sultan Soliman "the second" (actually sixteenth-century Sultan Suleiman I) compete for his attention. In the end, Frenchwoman Roxelane wins the sultan's love, in the process domesticating and "civilizing" him and representing French culture's triumph over Turkish.[65] *Trois sultanes* was particularly impactful in terms of dress, most especially because of its claims of authenticity. Traditionally, stage performers wore costumes based on ceremonial court dress, but a new interest in verisimilitude was changing this practice and electrifying audiences.[66] Marie-Justine Favart (1727–72) played the role of Roxelane in *Trois sultanes,* and according to a contemporary publication,

> In the Comedy of the *Sultanes,* for the first time was seen authentic clothing of Turkish Ladies, they had been made in Constantinople with fabrics from that country; this dress, at once decent & voluptuous, still induced complaints. When the Parody of the *Indes Galantes* was given to the Court, Madame Favart had to appear in the ridiculous and fantastic Costume, which custom had required [the traditional style based on court dress]. Some time later, however, the Scanderberg Opera was presented there, and Madame Favart's *Sultane* costume was borrowed as a model. [Actress] Mademoiselle Clarion, who also had the courage to introduce authentic costume at the Comédie Françoise, had a costume made on almost the same pattern, which she used at the Theater.[67]

The play's director and author Charles Simon Favart (1710–92, husband of Madame Favart) championed this new wave of authenticity in theatrical costumes. Designer Louis-René Boquet's watercolor (Fig. 11) of Roxelane's costume illustrates a naturalistic silhouette: Madame Favart wears a loose, short-sleeve, ermine-trimmed caftan; underneath is an inner caftan, whose crossover front was more typical of Ottoman menswear than women's. Her slashed sleeves are evocative of Ottoman

Fig. 11. Madame Favart in her costume from *Trois sultanes,* consisting of layered caftans with ermine trim, sash and large buckle, trousers, and veil. Louis-René Boquet, *Mme Favart dans* [in] *"Les Trois Sultanes,"* 1760. (Ink and watercolor on paper, Bibliothèque nationale de France, Bibliothèque-Musée de l'Opéra, Paris.)

dress, but also look very similar to the *engageante* sleeve ruffles worn by Frenchwomen in this period. The actress also appears to be wearing *şalvar,* the full trousers worn by Turkish men and women. A sheer, striped veil hangs from her hair, which is arranged in the French style.[68]

Stage costumes directly inspired those worn for masquerades and portraiture, like when the Marquise de Broglie wanted to wear a "sultana's costume" in her 1742 portrait by Nattier, so sent to the *Comediennes* for a theatrical costume to borrow.[69] Moreover, this was a period when prominent actresses led fashion.[70] Some of the century's favorite styles were inspired by and/or named after individual actresses (or, less frequently, actors), characters, and titles.[71] By the late 1770s, theatrical costumes were so influential that the fashion magazine *Gallerie des modes* published three *cahiers* of theatrical costumes, in which its editors declared:

> It was not long ago that the costume of various Peoples was not known . . . The costume of Each Nation, & proper to each character, did not begin to appear with such authenticity until the *Comédie Italienne,* under Favard [*sic*], spared nothing to obtain knowledge about the true costume of Nations, endeavoring to ensure that their Clothes conformed to the costume consecrated for their role, & rejecting those fripperies that are as expensive as they are useless.[72]

CLOTHING PERSPECTIVES, EAST AND WEST   23

French fascination for *turquerie* found expression in multiple cultural domains, one of the most significant being dress. Accurate and fantastical Turkish images, stories, and garments were frequently in the public eye. The French appetite for the exotic found expression in fashion, as women's styles named for the Ottoman Empire and incorporating elements from its clothing led French fashion from the late seventeenth through the late eighteenth centuries.

POPULARITY AND DEMOGRAPHICS

The influence of Eastern dress aesthetics on French women's fashion from the late seventeenth through the mid-eighteenth century is generally accepted by historians and will be explored in chapter 2. However, despite having received comparatively less scholarly focus, Ottoman inspiration was also the most prominent and popular theme in French fashion from the late 1760s through the mid-1780s. Although these styles will be defined and their connections to Turkish dress explained in chapter 3, here I will set the stage by demonstrating their fashionability and broad reach across French society. Ottoman-influenced gowns and jackets dominated the pages of fashion magazines from the mid-1770s through the mid-1780s and remained significant through the end of the century, and they made up a considerable portion of elite wardrobes. Moreover, *turquerie* in dress was not just an elite Parisian phenomenon: the *robe à la polonaise* particularly appears to have been worn by bourgeois and working-class women, while all the major Turkish-inspired styles can be documented in the provinces and colonies. The fashionability of Ottoman-themed dress meant it was associated with the young and fashion-forward, and it had effects on children's dress. An examination of these styles' popularity and reach across class, geography, and age demonstrates the broad impact of Ottoman dress aesthetics on French culture in the late eighteenth century.

THE POPULARITY OF TURKISH-INSPIRED DRESS

The conventional narrative of eighteenth-century fashion history proclaims that the leading styles from the turn of the seventeenth through the mid-eighteenth century were initially inspired by Eastern dressing gowns: the *manteau* (coat, 1670s–1720s), followed by the *robe volante* (flying dress, 1720s–1730s) and *robe à la française* (French-style dress, 1740s–1770s). English, Caribbean, and working-class/rural styles dominated the last decades of the century: the *robe à l'anglaise* (English-style dress, 1770s–1780s); a multiplicity of styles, particularly jackets and the *chemise à la reine* (queen's shift, 1780s); derivations of the *anglaise*, jackets, and the chemise (1790s), leading up to neoclassical, high-waisted gowns (1790s–1810s). What this narrative fails to include is the massive popularity of Ottoman-inspired fashions, particularly the *robes à la polonaise* (Polish, a country whose dress was considered part of the broader Ottoman cultural sphere), *circassienne* (Circassian, a region controlled by the Empire), *turque* (Turkish), as well as the *lévite* (whose name referenced ancient Jewish dress, but was modeled after Ottoman dress), from the 1760s through the 1780s.[73] The *polonaise* appears to have been *the* most popular dress of its era, while the others garnered substantial favor. Turkish-inspired fashions were, indeed, surpassed by those with English and Caribbean influence in the mid-1780s, but the prominence of Ottoman dress and its connections to the styles that followed has thus far been underestimated.

Contemporary observers noted the progression of fashion with striking regularity, and generally included Ottoman modes as important milestones, specifically the *robes à la polonaise, circassienne, turque,* and *lévite*. In 1786, the *Cabinet des modes* recounted, "From the *robbes Françoises* they [French-women] followed with the *Polonoises,* from the *Polonoises* the *Lévites,* from the *Lévites* the *robbes à l'Angloise* [English] & *à la Turque.*"[74] In 1787, the *Tableau mouvant de Paris* declared, "The reign of the *Polonaises* was succeeded by that of *Lévites,* the

Circassiennes; women were not afraid to go out in *chemise* [*à la reine*]."[75] The following year, the *Tableau de Paris* reported, "We see the *chemise* today, which succeeded the *Angloise* which succeeded the *Lévite* which succeeded the *Polonoise* which was preceded by the *Françoise.*"[76]

The consistent publication of French fashion magazines beginning in 1778 documents the ubiquity of Ottoman themes. Of course, these periodicals were reporting what was new and innovative, but the repetition of specific styles demonstrates their ongoing fashionability. Notably, the editors of the landmark *Gallerie des modes* chose the *robe à la polonaise* for their first plate depicting a full ensemble (the initial six *cahiers* focused on women's hairstyles and headwear).[77] The *polonaise* continued to be the most frequently illustrated dress in the *Gallerie* through 1781; in fact, the supposedly dominant *robe à l'anglaise* does not appear in substantial numbers until that year.[78] Although illustrations of the *anglaise* would quickly multiply, its supremacy lasted only until 1784. Afterwards, the English-influenced redingote took the lead from 1785 to 1788, followed by the theatrically and working-class-inspired pierrot jacket from 1788 to 1791.[79] Also substantially popular were the *robes à la circassienne, turque,* and *lévite.* The *circassienne* reached its height in 1779, disappearing by 1783; the name was revived in the early 1790s, but by then it had merged with the *turque* in terms of cut. The *turque* was never featured in fashion plates as often as the *polonaise* or *circassienne,* but it lasted the longest: it was popular from 1779 through 1789, with its zenith in 1786, and continued to appear in smaller numbers throughout the 1790s.[80] Finally, the *lévite* achieved its greatest popularity from 1778 through 1782, appearing only occasionally in plates after that date through 1785, although dressmakers continued to advertise the style as late as 1794.[81]

Fashion publications can be compared to wardrobe inventories, which demonstrate the actual ownership of dress. Pascale Maillard's study of the inventories of 110 Parisian nobles (54 female, 56 male) from 1775 to 1789 corroborates the popularity of Ottoman fashions.[82] Most of these inventories were taken after death to value and distribute the owner's estate, and thus do not necessarily show what was worn but rather what was owned. Furthermore, if the owner was elderly at the time of their death, their wardrobe may have been somewhat conservative or out-of-date. In Maillard's study, 21 of the 54 female inventories listed specific dress style names. Whether the person who created the inventory recognized a particular style could vary, so much that within one inventory, some might be identified while others not. With these cautions in mind, it is significant that most of the inventories listing specific styles include large numbers of *lévites* and *robes à la polonaise.* Less frequently recorded styles are, in decreasing order, the chemise, *anglaise, turque, fourreau,* redingote, *circassienne,* and riding habit (these styles will be defined in chapters 3 and 4). Even more fascinating is the percentage of *polonaises* and *lévites* within individual wardrobes: *robes à la polonaise* are the most numerous style in ten wardrobes from 1775 through 1782, then again in one from 1784 and another from 1786. The style does not appear in inventories of the next few years, but a few are noted in 1787 and 1789. Meanwhile, the *lévite* is the most frequently listed style in six wardrobes spanning 1783 to 1786, and second in most others from 1780 to 1789. The composition of these inventories further demonstrates the omnipresence of Turkish-influenced fashions. For example, in one 1782 inventory, the owner's gowns are simply listed as "*polonaise* or *lévite* or others."[83] In another inventory from that year, which was not included in Maillard's study, the "State of the *robbes* and *polonoises* of Madame la Comtesse de Riocourt," the *polonaise* was significant enough to be placed on par with the generic "*robe.*"[84] The inventories of the bourgeois Madame Trousseau (1775), as well as noblewomen including the Comtesse de Riocourt (1782), Vicomtesse de Podenas (1786), and Princesse de Conti

(1792), show *polonaises*, *lévites*, and *robes à la turque* making up smaller percentages of their wardrobes than unspecified *robes* and *deshabillés*, but they are the only named gowns listed.[85] By comparison, the *robe à l'anglaise* does not appear in any of the inventories Maillard studied before 1784, and then only in three (1784 and 1789). The *chemise à la reine* appears in five inventories (one from 1784, three from 1786, and one each from 1787 and 1789). The *circassienne* and *turque* appear much less frequently than the *polonaise* and *lévite* and in smaller numbers. The *turque* appears in only three of Maillard's inventories (1784 and 1786); the *circassienne* is present in just one (1780), where it represents only a minor fraction of the wardrobe.

Obviously, the wardrobes of the French royal family were unusually grand and their contents quite numerous, but the preferences of elite style leaders were influential. The 1771 wedding trousseau of the Comtesse de Provence included eleven *polonaises*, compared to three unspecified *robes*. An incomplete list of Queen Marie-Antoinette's wardrobe from 1779 is entitled, "State of the *Grands habits* [ceremonial court gowns], *Robes* and *Polonoises* necessary each year for the Service of the Wardrobe of The queen," reinforcing the idea that *polonaises* were fundamental.[86] The only complete inventory of the queen's wardrobe to survive, comprising spring and summer 1782, demonstrates that her fashionable gowns consisted primarily of *lévites* (57 percent) and *polonaises* (35 percent), while *anglaises* (6 percent) and *turques* (1 percent) were minimally represented. The queen had a separate mourning wardrobe set aside in case of need; that year, it included *polonaises* and *lévites* for *grand* mourning (the most formal option) in winter and summer. These styles were not included in the queen's *petit* or half-mourning wardrobe, but they were notable (and expected) enough that more than one comment indicates "no *Polonoises* nor *Levites*." These royal wardrobes will be discussed at more length in chapter 6.

DEMOGRAPHICS

Who wore Turkish-inspired fashions? Roche's study of wardrobe inventories proves that in the late eighteenth century, even the working classes experienced a growing accumulation and diversification of dress-related goods; in the century's final decades, at least five all-purpose "gowns" are mentioned in two-thirds of the inventories he studied across all classes. Roche found more diversification in the wardrobes of women from professional families compared to the working classes. At the top of the social scale, only 8 percent of the inventories he studied included gowns like *lévites, chemises à la reine,* redingotes, "and all the new styles being elaborated by modest and elegant dressmakers."[87] Focusing on the noble Baronne de Schomberg, Roche found that beginning in 1775, "she increasingly bought lighter garments and adopted the fashionable simplicity popularised by the queen: polonaises, lévites and caracos [jackets] appearing in her wardrobe."[88]

These high-fashion styles were worn by the French aristocracy, appearing in numerous documents related to the queen and royal family, while the wardrobe inventories previously discussed prove the Parisian nobility's preference for *polonaises* and *lévites*. According to Roche, "informal garments, fantasy and exoticism" appeared only in upper-class wardrobes.[89] However, he does not include the *polonaise* in this category, and the bourgeoisie and even the working classes do appear to have adopted that style in particular.[90] The *Gallerie des modes* illustrates the *polonaise* not only on "ladies of quality," but also middling class women, including *marchandes de modes* and "*bourgeois* women."[91] Although this could be more indicative of marketing than reality, Roche found two *polonaises* in the wardrobe of a lawyer's wife, writing, "She is a good example of the way in which women of the liberal professions had acquired luxurious wardrobes and succumbed to fashion."[92] Similarly, revolutionary prosecutor Antoine Quentin Fouquier de Tinville's wife owned "one *polonaise* and its petticoat" when she died

in 1782.[93] In de Boissieu's painting of a Lyonnaise bourgeois family, two young women wear *polonaises* (Fig. 12). Even more intriguing are the several sources mentioning or depicting working-class women wearing the *polonaise*, including *grisettes* (young working women) in dressmaking shops, prostitutes (Fig. 13), a fishmonger, and a fruit seller.[94] Roche notes that the second-hand garment trade was an important method of obtaining clothing among what he calls the "popular" classes of Paris.[95] In fact, Marie-Victoire Monnard, apprenticed to a Parisian linen merchant, recalled in her memoirs how her grandmother gifted her a too-large *robe à la polonaise* purchased second-hand.[96]

Those who lived in the French provinces followed Parisian and court fashions; in fact, the advent of fashion magazines facilitated this process. The *polonaise, circassienne, turque,* and *lévite* can be found in inventories and bills from Champagne, Guyenne, Limoges, Honfleur,

Fig. 12. The young woman on the left wears a *camisole à la polonaise*, while the woman with the parasol (probably the artist's wife) wears a *robe à la polonaise*. Jean-Jacques de Boissieu, *La Danse des enfants* (The Children's dance). (Painting, oil on canvas, 30 × 38.5 cm, Petit Palais, Musée des Beaux-arts de la Ville de Paris.)

Fig. 13. A prostitute (fighting with the hairdresser who has just shaved her head) wears a *robe à la polonaise*. Naudet (publisher), *Fille de joie se battant avec le coiffeur qui l'a tondue* (Prostitute fighting with the hairdresser who shaved her), 1778. (Engraving, Bibliothèque nationale de France, Paris.)

and Seine-et-Oise, while dressmakers advertised their ability to make these styles in provincial newspapers from Bordeaux, Bretagne, Guyenne, Orléans, Mans, Poitiers, and even the French Caribbean colony of Saint-Domingue.[97] Antoine Raspal's paintings and drawings of the people of Arles, in Provence, illustrate numerous well-to-do ladies wearing *robes* and jackets *à la polonaise*.[98] Meanwhile, his circa 1785 painting *The Couturier's Workshop* (Fig. 14), depicting Arlésienne seamstresses at work, includes a *robe à la polonaise* among their projects. Other paintings documenting life outside of Paris that portray Ottoman-inspired styles include de Boissieu's *Danse des enfants* (Fig. 12), probably set in Lyon; Wertmüller's portrait of Madame Claudine Rousse, painted in Lyon; and Watteau de Lille's record of a hot-air balloon flight that took place in 1785 in Lille.[99]

Adult women were not alone in wearing Turkish-inspired fashions. For centuries, very young children had worn age-specific clothing that was relatively confining and bulky. However, Enlightenment ideas, particularly Rousseau's writings, had some of their first effects on children's dress, which in this period was becoming lighter and allowing more freedom of movement.[100] Given the connections between Ottoman modes and Enlightenment precepts, which will be explored in more depth in chapter 5, it is logical that young girls adopted these styles. Fourteen plates in the *Gallerie des modes* feature or include children, but only six show girls old enough to be put into dresses; four of these are wearing Turkish-inspired dress: three hybrids mixing the *fourreau* and *polonaise*, as well as one *lévite*.[101] The *polonaise* brought practical elements to girls' clothing, as its lifted skirts meant they could move more easily while their gowns would stay clean longer. Although paintings of young girls of this era generally show them wearing the *fourreau* or *chemise* gowns, several do depict them in Ottoman-influenced gowns, most frequently the *polonaise* and *turque*.[102] Roche notes that aristocratic Cecile de Schomberg "had her first polonaise at nine," while

28   DRESSING À LA TURQUE

the Comtesse d'Artois's wardrobe accounts include an order for a "girl's *polonaise*" in 1780, possibly meant for her daughter, Sophie, age four.[103] Some boys' styles were influenced by Ottoman and Eastern European military uniforms, and several paintings depict boys wearing clothing that includes elements such as the short oversleeve also seen on the *turque* and *circassienne*.[104] By the mid-1780s, fashion plates featuring young girls replaced Ottoman-inspired gowns with English (*robe à l'anglaise* and redingote), French (*fourreau*), and Caribbean (*chemise à la reine*) gowns, demonstrating the increasing influence of these cultures and the eclipsing of Turkish modes in this decade.

Given their fashionability, Turkish-inspired styles were most frequently associated with women in their teens and twenties.[105] Anne

Fig. 14. A red *robe à la polonaise*, distinguished by its distinctive cut without waist seam and two white ribbon rosettes at the lower back, hangs on a peg second from left on the wall. The seamstresses are wearing the *drolet* jacket, a regional Provençal style. Antoine Raspal, *The Couturier's Workshop*, ca. 1785. (Painting, oil on canvas, Musée Reattu, Arles, France. Bridgeman Images.)

Fig. 15. The mother (*left*) wears a *robe à la française*, while her daughter (*right*) is in a *polonaise*. Anne Vallayer-Coster, *Portrait of an Elderly Lady with Her Daughter.* (Painting, oil on canvas, the Bowes Museum, Barnard Castle, County Durham, UK. © Bowes Museum/Bridgeman Images.)

Vallayer-Coster's painting perfectly captures the generational divide: the older woman wears a traditional *robe à la française*, while the younger is in a *polonaise* (Fig. 15). Fashion magazines promoted the idea that Ottoman styles were youthful, like when the *Gallerie des modes* declared the *circassienne à l'enfant* ("child," but worn by an adult woman) was not "compatible except with the elegance of the size and the freshness of youth. This is also the cause of its name."[106] When older women selected these high-fashion styles, they sometimes met with criticism. As Marie-Antoinette approached her thirtieth birthday, she announced plans to give up fashionable dresses, specifically chemises, *circassiennes, lévites, polonaises*, redingotes, and *turques*, as well as pierrot jackets, in favor of what the *Mémoires secrets* calls "serious, pleated *Robes*."[107] The decision appears to have been short-lived, as these fashionable styles would continue to be found in sizable numbers in the queen's wardrobe in future years—something further explored in chapter 6. Nonetheless, she was right to be concerned, as older women who followed the latest fashion trends were sometimes satirized. The *Journal helvétique* mocked the stereotype of the elderly fashionable woman, writing of a (probably apocryphal) marquise: "Tell me if it is possible to look at her without laughing; this old *coquette* who has counted sixty years well, & has almost all the ugliness of old age, wears *robes à la polonaise, à la lévite,* hats, & all the paraphernalia of a young girl; which makes her so ridiculous, that there is no one who, in seeing her, would not write: ah, the old fool!"[108] In her study of the Princesse de Conti's wardrobe, Aurélie Chatenet-Calyste notes that the older woman (age thirty-nine in 1770) was conservative in adopting new styles, including *robes à la polonaise* and *lévites,* while mostly ignoring *robes à l'anglaise* and *à la turque.*[109]

Turkish-inspired fashions were extraordinarily popular in the final decades of the eighteenth century, and penetrated the wardrobes of the nobility, bourgeois, young, and fashion-forward throughout Paris and the provinces. These styles emerged from widespread interest in the Middle East and Asia, which included the dress of the Ottoman Empire and areas under its cultural influence. Real and fantastical depictions of Ottomans and their clothing were pervasive across French society in the stories told and written by travelers; images created by those who had visited the Empire or simply imagined it; and masquerade and stage costumes that ranged from authentic to fanciful. There were several significant differences between the clothing traditions of the Ottomans and the French, and these are critical to understanding the French attraction to Turkish dress.

Western and Eastern Approaches to Dress

French and Ottoman approaches to garment construction originated in a common tradition, in which garments were made from simple shapes and designed to be worn loosely. However, these traditions diverged in the medieval era, as technological innovations in the West allowed for new construction methods whereby clothing became increasingly complex, fitted, and structured. In the sixteenth and seventeenth centuries, French clothing reshaped the bodies of both genders but particularly that of women, whose fashionable ensembles consisted of two-piece gowns that stiffened the torso and obscured the contours of the legs. Meanwhile, clothing worn in the Ottoman Empire emphasized ease and comfort as men and women wore soft, layered ensembles consisting of shirts, trousers, and multiple caftans. The differences that emerged in dress traditions and garment construction between West and East partially explain the appeal of Turkish dress for the French.

Until the early medieval era, the peoples of Western Europe, the Middle East, and Asia approached clothing construction in similar ways: textiles were cut into rectangular shapes, with triangular inserts added to accommodate curves and movement, so that expensive textiles could be used with little waste. Naomi Tarrant uses the term *tunic* to describe the basic shape found in traditional garments of many cultures: "lengths of cloth draped over the shoulders without a shoulder seam . . .

As we live very comfortably today in France, we are rarely dressed [formally], & we no longer wear almost anything but what are called *Manteaux. Robes* are only for ceremonial Visits, or for those that we give to People of a more elevated rank than that which we hold, & we do not wear them to familiarly see Friends, nor for Promenade Parties.

—*Extraordinaire du mercure galant*

A simple tunic can be made by joining up the side seams leaving two holes for the arms."[1] When sleeves are added, the garment resembles a *T*, with the body forming a vertical rectangle and the sleeves a horizontal one. This tunic shape was common to many cultures across Eurasia and was preserved in the West until the mid-nineteenth century as the men's shirt and women's shift.[2]

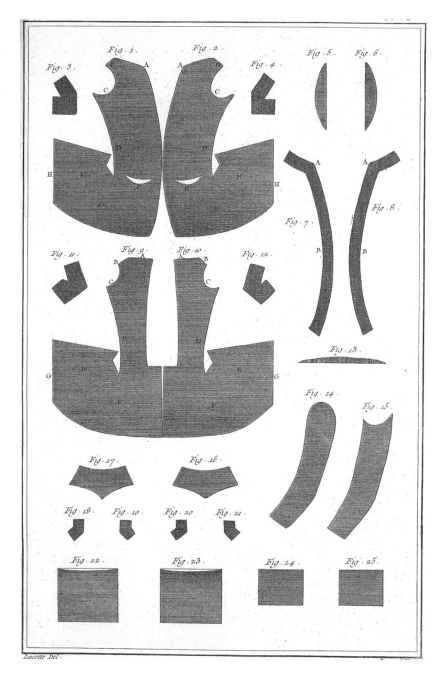

Fig. 16. Patterns for men's coats demonstrate the complex shapes used in Western tailoring. "Tailleur d'Habits, Pieces d'étaillées d'un Habit [Tailor of Suits, Detailed pieces of a Suit]," Denis Diderot and Jean Le Rond d'Alembert, eds., *Recueil de planches, sur les sciences, les arts libéraux, et les arts méchaniques: avec leur explication* (Collection of plates, on the sciences, the liberal arts, and the mechanical arts: with their explanation) . . . (A Paris: Chez Briasson . . . David . . . Le Breton . . . Durand, 1762). (Biodiversity Heritage Libraries, Smithsonian Libraries and Archives.)

However, the invention of the wide horizontal loom in thirteenth- and fourteenth-century Western Europe led to new approaches to garment construction that impacted dress. Wider textiles meant tailors could cut garments with curved and/or bias seams, allowing them to make tight-fitting clothing and also experiment with volume (Fig. 16).[3] In the sixteenth century and seventeenth centuries, garments followed the upper body's contours more closely (Figs. 17, 23, 24).[4] At the same time, the introduction of stiffened garments supported by whalebone molded women's torsos, eventually developing into what were called *corps de baleine* (literally *boned body;* called first *bodies* and then *stays* in English) and becoming more sophisticated over time.[5] The overall silhouette was cone-shaped rather than curved; contrary to nineteenth-century corsets, which emphasized waist reduction, bodies and stays of earlier eras reshaped the torso into a fashionably smooth line.[6] Meanwhile, petticoats, pads, and hoops augmented the lower half of women's bodies beyond the natural form, while these and skirts obscured the legs.[7] Writing of similar trends in England, Sarah A. Bendall notes that by the late sixteenth century, "Bodies and farthingales [hoops] had come to define the socially recognizable female body."[8] Although

(*Left*) Fig. 17. A well-dressed couple in 1620s French style. Both are wearing clothing that is stiffened in some areas and voluminous in others. Jean de Saint-Igny, Jean Picart (print maker), Etienne Dauvel (publisher), *Couple Wearing the Latest French Fashion,* 1628. (Engraving, 167 × 121 mm, Rijksmuseum, Amsterdam. Gift of L. Brender à Brandis.)

(*Right*) Fig. 18. An Ottoman woman's caftan made of simple, rectangular pattern shapes. *Robe d'intérieur de femme* (Women's indoor dress), Istanbul, eighteenth century. Silk and cloth of gold, 2.05 × 1.6 m, Musée du quai Branly, Paris, 71.1947.9.1 D. (Photo © musée du quai Branly—Jacques Chirac, Dist. RMN-Grand Palais / image musée du quai Branly—Jacques Chirac / Art Resource, NY.)

WESTERN AND EASTERN APPROACHES TO DRESS   35

men did not wear stays or hoops, their clothing was frequently padded and/or stiffened to create structure and volume (Fig. 17).[9]

By contrast, throughout these periods and well into the nineteenth century, clothing construction in the Middle East and Asia continued to be based on the rectangular, tunic-style approach (Figs. 3, 18).[10] Richard Martin and Harold Koda deftly summarize this method when they write that Eastern clothing "emphasizes the flat terrain of cloth, the looping and wrapping of the garment, and the integrity of the untailored textile."[11] Commonly recognized examples include the Japanese kimono, a long garment made of rectangular shapes; and the Indian sari, an uncut fabric length wrapped around the body. The natural contours were maintained in this tradition, without stiffened understructures like corsets or hoops, which reshaped the figure's lines. Thus, in the sixteenth and seventeenth centuries, Western Europeans wore tight, restrictive, and structured garments, while the peoples of the East wore comparatively looser and softer clothing.[12]

OTTOMAN DRESS

In the period under study, dress in the Ottoman Empire encompassed a wide variety of garments worn by a range of classes, from urban elites to rural farmers and herders, as well as multiple ethnicities and religious groups. The Empire not only covered a massive geographic area but also was a center for global trade routes, importing and exporting textiles and other goods from Europe, Asia, and Africa.[13] This initial summary will focus on the clothing of Constantinople, which was best known to Western Europeans and worn throughout the Empire by ruling elites.[14] Although the eighteenth-century French often thought of Middle Eastern and Asian clothing as timeless and unchanging, the history of dress demonstrates this is patently false.[15] The fashions worn in the Ottoman Empire evolved gradually over time, maintaining certain characteristics, most notably layering garments of different shapes, textures, and colors. Because inspiration for French women's fashions drew equally on men's and women's clothing, both will be discussed here.

The foundation of Ottoman dress was the layering of multiple garments in a way that was designed to display each individual layer through open fronts, slashed sleeves, and garment hems tucked up into the sash. Gender distinctions existed but were less prominent than in the West, being characterized by accessories like headwear and jewelry as well as specific garment layering techniques.[16] Both men and women wore loose, front-opening caftans that were closed with sashes in multiple, voluminous layers. *Caftan* is frequently used as a generic term for the long robes worn in Islamic cultures. The word derives from the Turkish *qaftan* (from Persian *xaftân*), where it referred to an outerwear cloak.[17] Despite its lack of precise applicability, I will employ it in this book as a catchall term for Ottoman fashion and outerwear garments due not only to its widespread recognition among modern readers, but also because it handily differentiates from the French *robe*, meaning *dress* in the Western sense. Ottoman caftans were front-opening garments made in the tunic style without a waist seam. Some were short sleeved, some long; some varieties were belted at the waist with a sash, others hung open. One of the most typical effects shown in eighteenth-century images was for the outermost caftan to fasten at the neck, then fall away from that point into a triangular-shaped opening that displayed the ensemble's underlayers. Outwear caftans frequently had short sleeves, revealing the longer sleeves of the garments worn underneath.[18]

Men's dress (Figs. 2, 4, 19, 47, 51, 133) began with the *gömlek*, a loose shirt made of white linen or cotton, worn with ankle-length, baggy trousers (*şalvar*) of white, diaphanous fabric.[19] Over this was worn one (or more, depending on the season) caftans, which had a variety of names, including *dolman* (a long-sleeved coat) and *hirka* (a loose coat that could be short or long).[20] Muslim men wore turbans (*tülbent*) consisting of one or two caps covered by a long length of fabric that wrapped around the head; those worn by courtiers were more structured than those of commoners.[21] Women (Figs. 3, 5, 6, 18, 20, 47, 119, 138) also wore the *gömlek* and *şalvar*, but their inner caftans were called *anteri* (or *entari*).[22] These were front-opening garments that could be short or full-length and buttoned from bust to hip, with narrow, tight sleeves that were slashed from wrist to elbow, falling back over the lower arm.[23] Multiple *anteris* were frequently layered on top of each other. The *yelek* (a sleeveless jacket) could be worn under the *anteri*.[24] Women's ensembles created a soft, fluid line,

Fig. 19. Turkish men wore several layered caftans over shirt and trousers, with a sash. Workshop of Jean Baptiste Vanmour, *Choadar, Servant of the Ambassador*, 1700–37. (Painting, oil on canvas, 39.5 × 30 cm, Rijksmuseum, Amsterdam.)

WESTERN AND EASTERN APPROACHES TO DRESS   37

Fig. 20. Turkish women display a range of softly draped clothing worn in layers, some with crossover bodices and/or short sleeves. Jean Baptiste Vanmour, *Lying-in Room of a Distinguished Turkish Woman* (detail), ca. 1720–37. (Painting, oil on canvas, 55.5 × 90 cm, Rijksmuseum, Amsterdam.)

without boned or stiffened garments, and the desired silhouette was streamlined but curvaceous.[25] A *kuşak* or *kemer*, initially a stiff belt that eventually became a sash, completed the ensemble.[26] Outdoors, women wore outer caftans, including the *ferace*, *kirk*, and *kürdiyye*, long coats analogous to male outerwear, while a *yaşmak* (veil) covered the face.[27] The construction of both men's and women's garments was based on the rectangular method, with full lengths of narrow fabrics slashed and seamed where needed, and triangular insets added to accommodate curves and movement.[28]

EASTERN EUROPEAN DRESS

French fascination with *turquerie* included Eastern European dress—that of Hungary, Poland, and western Russia. Irena Turnau's research on dress in this area shows its similarities and differences from Turkish clothing, the variations existing among regions, and the influence of Western tailoring models.[29] Nonetheless, what is important for this study is that the eighteenth-century French perceived strong commonalities between Eastern European and Ottoman clothing, viewing them

as part of a larger family and more alike than different, particularly in contrast with Western European dress.[30] Adam Jasienski argues that Polish and Hungarian noble dress was "strongly influenced by Ottoman, and more broadly Eastern fashion," causing Westerners to use "their knowledge or idea of what was Ottoman, or 'Oriental,' to understand the clothing" of these countries.[31] In Russia, the aristocracy followed French court styles, but ordinary men and women wore Turkish-influenced ensembles featuring layered caftans, often belted at the waist.[32] Some of the shared fundamental characteristics included rectangular garment construction and layering multiple long, voluminous caftans designed to show wealth through textiles (Fig. 21).[33] Finally, Ottoman and Eastern European fashion changed more slowly than that of Western Europe, giving it a timeless aura to French observers.

Poland particularly interested the eighteenth-century French due to its political upheavals and elected monarchy, both of which touched on issues of importance to Enlightenment thinkers. Furthermore, Louis

Fig. 21. This sixteenth-century plate illustrates a range of Eastern European dress, including Hungarian, Wallachian, and Polish. All wear layered knee- or ankle-length caftans, the outermost frequently with short sleeves; most have passementerie trimmings. Turbans, hats, and standing feathers feature prominently. Abraham de Bruyn (print maker/publisher), *Twaalf Polen en Hongaren, gekleed volgens de mode van ca. 1580* (Twelve Poles and Hungarians, dressed in the fashion of ca. 1580), on or before 1581. (Engraving on paper, 265 × 360 mm, Rijksmuseum, Amsterdam.)

Fig. 22. Augustus III of Poland (1696–1763) wears a long, red *kontusz* with front opening, slashed oversleeves, and sash. Louis de Silvestre, *Portrait of Augustus III of Saxony (1696–1763), King of Poland*. (Oil on canvas, 246 × 164 cm, Muzeum Narodwe, Krakow, MNK I-327. Laboratory Stock National Museum in Krakow.)

XV's queen (Marie Leszczyńska, 1703–68) hailed from that country, while her father King Stanisław Leszczyński (1677–1766) settled in France after being deposed from the Polish throne. The ethnocultural ideology of Sarmatism—the legend that Polish nobility were descended from the Sarmatii, an Iranian tribe who were considered the ancient rulers of Eastern Europe—led many elite Polish men to dress in clothing that had much in common with that of the Ottoman Empire.[34]

Sarmatism looked more to Byzantine, Ottoman, and Persian cultural influences than Western. Significantly, noble and well-to-do Polish men demonstrated their Sarmatic affiliation primarily through clothing.[35] Although a growing number of upper-class Polish men adopted French dress over the century, Poland's partition in 1772 encouraged a renewed interest in Sarmatic dress.[36]

The key Sarmatic men's garment was the *kontusz* (Figs. 21, 22), a short or long outerwear caftan made in the Turkish style (a similarly styled women's outer coat was called *kontusik*, but by and large, bourgeois and noble Polish women dressed in French styles).[37] It featured a fold-over fur collar and intricate passementerie trimmings. Initially worn with tapered sleeves and a fur lining, over the course of the eighteenth century that lining was omitted, and the sleeves were slashed and folded back to display underlayers. Underneath the *kontusz*, men wore a *zupan*, a buttoned, knee-length caftan that was often trimmed with fur, also of Turkish (or possibly Arabic) origin.[38] Over all was a decorative sash (*pas kontuszowy*), which was among the most celebrated elements of Polish dress.[39] It was usually made of metallic brocaded fabric with knotted, fringed ends. The earliest sashes were imported from the Ottoman Empire and Persia, while later ones were made in Poland and, interestingly, France.[40] The construction of these garments was based on the rectangular method typical of Eastern dress.[41]

SEVENTEENTH-CENTURY FRENCH FEMALE DRESS

While Ottoman and Eastern European dress was made up of simply cut garments worn in soft, comfortable layers, French fashion, particularly for women, had become comparatively structured and restrictive. During the sixteenth and seventeenth centuries, French women's fashions were founded on a relatively consistent silhouette: structured bodices were worn with long, trained skirts.[42] Although variations certainly existed, during the seventeenth century the foremost style for upper-class French women was the robe, a gown made of bodice, sleeves, and skirt (Figs. 17, 23, 24).[43] While separate stays were sometimes worn under a gown or jacket, most formal gowns were made with structure built into the bodice through whalebone and stiffened fabric.[44] Whichever option was employed, the torso was almost always controlled by a heavily boned garment with a long center-front panel supported by a busk (a shaped piece of baleen, wood, or ivory) that pushed the stomach in and the bust up.[45] Hoops mostly went out of fashion in this century,

(*Left*) Fig. 23. The French robe was founded on a structured bodice and full skirts; sleeves were full in the early part of the century. Abraham Bosse (printmaker), François Langlois (publisher), *Franse edelvrouw gekleed volgens de Franse mode van ca. 1630* (French noblewoman dressed in French fashion from around 1630), 1629. (Engraving on paper, 143 × 93 mm, Amsterdam, Rijksmuseum.)

(*Right*) Fig. 24. Near the end of the century, the robe's sleeves and skirts narrowed and the overskirt's train lengthened, but the rigid bodice remained. Nicolas Arnoult (print maker/publisher), *Marie Anne légitimée de France, fille de Louis le Grand* (Marie Anne of France, legitimized daughter of Louis le Grand) ca. 1685. (Engraving, watercolor, 300 × 200 mm, Amsterdam, Rijksmuseum. Purchased with the support of the Flora Fonds/Rijksmuseum Fonds.)

although pads and petticoats provided volume and support to skirts. By the century's end, the prevailing mode was for rigid, boned bodices with restrictive necklines placed at the shoulder point, elbow-length wide sleeves whose armscyes forced the shoulders back, and one or more full, often trained, skirts supported by petticoats and pads (Fig. 24).[46] This style's apogee can be seen in court dress, which Louis XIV stipulated in an effort to control his courtiers and therefore to exert his royal privilege. Based on current modes, the *robe de cour* featured a heavily boned bodice with a wide, off-the-shoulder neckline, puffed sleeves, and one or more full, trained skirts.[47] Writing of the eighteenth-century *grand habit* that was essentially a fossilization of the same style, Pascale Gorguet-Ballesteros argues it "remodeled the feminine body, which then evoked a reversed cone, rigid bust with shoulders thrust backwards, [and] thin waist" (Fig. 170).[48]

It was into this structured fashion tradition that dressing gowns, either literally caftans imported from the East or simply inspired by them, would provide a welcome option for French men and women, first during private, at-home wear, and soon as part of everyday fashion. This led to significant changes in French women's wear beginning in the late seventeenth century, and laid the groundwork for a hybrid dress tradition that merged elements of West and East in the eighteenth century.

TURQUERIE AND FRENCH FASHION, 1670S–1750S: THE FIRST WAVE

In France, the tight fit and structured silhouette that had become fundamental to sixteenth- and seventeenth-century ideas of appropriate dress and self-presentation underwent an important shift in the late seventeenth century. The massive popularity of Eastern (or Eastern-inspired) dressing gowns (*robes de chambre*) among men and women resulted in substantial changes in French fashion, as the *robe de chambre* was adapted and refined into women's fashionable clothing. These new gowns began as loose, rectangular garments layered over separate understructures, over time becoming more Europeanized by incorporating more complex pattern shapes that enabled tighter fit.[49] Nonetheless, Eastern influence created tangible shifts in French dress from the late seventeenth century through the close of the eighteenth century: the ideas that clothing could (and sometimes should) be comfortable and loose-fitting, as well as layering for design purposes, became fundamental to middle- and upper-class fashion for both genders, but particularly for women.

First, women adapted the *robe de chambre* to create the fashionable manteau gown, initially the same garment worn with a sash, but over time pleated and stitched into a more defined shape. In the 1720s, a new style based on dressing gowns was introduced: the *robe volante*. This loose, pleated gown was popular through the 1740s, when its fit began to refine enough that it became considered a new style: the *robe à la française*. The *française* maintained the *volante*'s loose pleats in back but grew increasingly fitted in the torso through the front and side. By examining these transitions, we can observe the incorporation of Eastern garments into French high fashion and understand how Ottoman approaches became so fundamental to women's wardrobes that this last iteration was literally named the *French dress*.

It is important to note that definitions of "comfort" are variable across history and culture. As Sarah A. Bendall's research on undergarments in sixteenth- and seventeenth-century England demonstrates, we must pay attention to what she terms "the mental comfort that early moderns sought in their clothing."[50] After reconstructing various stiffened undergarments, she concludes, "Far from being a monolithic experience of pain and restriction, these garments spanned a wide spectrum of comfort and restrictiveness in the everyday lives of the women who wore them, allowing for a range of bodily activities and functions."[51] In our modern era, we prize physical comfort above many competing factors, but as Valerie Steele aptly points out of the twentieth century, "The change from the admiration for the ample, mature female body to that of the slim, young, active body meant partly that the corset was internalized in the form of dieting."[52] In the sixteenth through eighteenth centuries, women wore structured garments and undergarments for a variety of reasons, including the practical desire for clothes to fit smoothly; ideas about class, rank, and social status; modesty; and what Suzanne Scholz calls the "'defensive wall' around the female body . . . [Corsets] sartorially supply the rigid body boundaries that are the preconditions of proper subjecthood in the West but which are found to be lacking in the 'natural' bodies of women."[53] The desire for physical comfort that manifested in the late seventeenth century was proportionate to the experience and expectations of that period, and we should not assume that changing fashions represented a revolution but rather a gradual and relative transition.

THE *ROBE DE CHAMBRE*

First introduced in the sixteenth century, by the 1660s dressing gowns were popular among men and women across the class spectrum (Figs. 25, 26).[54] Historians have connected *robes de chambre* to many Eastern origins, including Turkish caftans, Japanese kimonos and *yukata*s, and Indian house gowns.[55] Soon, versions adapted for European tastes began to be manufactured domestically, usually in Indian or Indian-style fabrics that reinforced their Eastern associations.[56] Early *robes de chambre* were long, loose, simply cut, rectangular garments that opened from neck to hem in front.[57] Over time, more fitted versions were created with somewhat more complicated pattern shapes, but these continued to mimic Eastern garments in their front opening, length, and tunic cut (i.e., lack of a waist seam).[58] Whether imported or domestically produced, dressing gowns retained their Eastern associations, becoming an important status symbol and a sign of intellectualism and worldliness.[59] They were meant to be worn at home, by oneself, or among intimates.[60]

Figs. 25 and 26. Dressing gowns were made with little shaping and meant to be voluminous. *Robe de chambre* (dressing gown), 1701–50. (Cotton [toile de Jouy], Palais Galliera, musée de la Mode de la Ville de Paris, 1920.1.2039.)

44 DRESSING À LA TURQUE

SHORT DEFINITIONS

Style	Fashionable	Front	Back	Fit	Skirts	Sleeves
Robe de chambre	ca. 1660 into the nineteenth century	• Two rectangular pieces • Open from neck to hem	• Fronts extend over shoulders without seam • Seamed at center back	• Loose without waist seam • Later versions could be more fitted through sewn-down pleats and/or shaped side seams	Triangular gores could be added at side seams	One rectangular piece
Manteau	ca. 1670s–ca. 1720s	• Two rectangular pieces • Open from neck to hem, with stomacher and petticoat to fill the gap	• Fronts extend over shoulders without seam • Seamed at center back	• Sash defined the waist and created informal pleats • Later versions had stitched-down pleats with linen lining to create a closer fit	• Pinned up high on side-back hip • Short or long train • Later versions added gores and long train drawn up and back into complicated drapery	• One rectangular piece • Folded up to create cuff • Displayed chemise underneath
Robe volante	ca. 1720s–ca. 1730s	• Two rectangular pieces, box pleated at shoulder seam • Open from neck to hem with stomacher and petticoat, or closed	Wide rectangular pieces box pleated at back neckline	Loose and floating over fitted linen lining	Short train	• Elbow-length • Separate pleated cuffs
Robe à la française	ca. 1740s–ca. 1770s	• Two rectangular pieces with narrow vertical pleats along front opening edge • Open from neck to hem with stomacher and petticoat to fill the gap	Rectangular pieces box pleated at back neckline (pleats narrowed over time)	• Bodice front semifitted around torso to side • Later version fitted around torso to side back with waist seam or tuck	Short train	• Elbow-length • Separate pleated cuffs • Later versions with stacked ruffles

THE MANTEAU

Although structured gowns would continue to be required at court for more than a century, Frenchwomen began to wear their soft, flowing *robes de chambre* as public fashion.[61] The most popular style to emerge as a result was the manteau, a gown introduced in the 1670s that remained fashionable in France for the next few decades and was nearly ubiquitous among Parisian women of all social classes.[62] It was a loose, pleated gown cut as a rectangular, T-shaped tunic without waist seam; it opened from neckline to hem down the center front, where it displayed a stomacher (*pièce d'estomac*) and petticoat (*jupon*) (Figs. 27, 28, 29).[63] A sash pulled the gown in at the waist. Its short sleeves displayed the chemise's longer sleeves. The front hems of its long, trained overskirt were usually pulled up and attached high on the side back of the hip.[64] The manteau represented a fundamental shift in women's dress as casual, comparatively comfortable, simply constructed gowns began to be worn in public.[65] Furthermore, Clare Haru Crowston has demonstrated how the manteau's rectangular construction made it the perfect garment to be created by the newly formed (1675) female

Figs. 27 and 28. An English doll's manteau demonstrates the early style's simple cut. Fabric rectangles are pleated at the front, back, and sleeve heads. *Doll's mantua*, English, 1690–1700. (Silk damask lined with silk taffeta, Victoria & Albert Museum, London, T.846E-1974. Courtesy of Victoria and Albert Museum, London. Purchased by public subscription.)

46   DRESSING À LA TURQUE

seamstresses guild. They had been working unofficially for some time on draped garments and those based on rectangular construction, and the manteau continued those construction practices.[66]

Furthermore, the manteau's front opening, which deliberately revealed its underlayers, is highly reminiscent of the layering evident in Ottoman clothing, where multiple caftans were worn in a similar effect.[67] Connections in garment cut also exist: like caftans and *robes de chambre*, early *manteaux* were cut as simple tunic-style garments, with a long length of fabric folded in half at the shoulder without a seam, opened fully down the front from neckline to hem, and generally left unlined. All these approaches can be seen in garments worn throughout the Middle East and Asia, particularly the Ottoman Empire, and the sash and manner of tucking up the manteau's overskirt (Fig. 29) comes directly from Turkish dress (Figs. 19, 47).[68] Further evidence of the manteau's links to Ottoman dress comes from the *sultane*, a variant of the manteau popular in the late 1680s (Fig. 30).[69]

(*Left*) Fig. 29. The manteau was worn pulled up and back in a manner reminiscent of Ottoman dress. Denis Mariette and Etienne Jeaurat (publishers), *Dame met fontange, open waaier in de hand* (Lady with fontange, open fan in hand), 1715–20. (Etching on paper, 149 × 97 mm, Rijksmuseum, Amsterdam. Purchased with the support of the F. G. Waller-Fonds.)

(*Right*) Fig. 30. The *sultane* gown, whose pulled-up sleeves and passementerie trimmings read as "Turkish." Jean Dieu de Saint-Jean, *Femme de qualité en Sultane* (Woman of quality in Sultane), 1688. (Print, engraving, 32.5 × 24 cm, Musée Carnavalet, Paris.)

WESTERN AND EASTERN APPROACHES TO DRESS

Thus, in the late seventeenth century a process began that would be repeated multiple times over the following century: the introduction of a new woman's gown based on rectangular shapes and loose fit with Ottoman associations, which over time became Europeanized through more complex fit and construction.[70] When women wore the manteau outside the home, they did so over separate stays, providing a rigid torso silhouette and initiating the ensemble's Westernization.[71] Soon, the manteau's

(*Above*) Figs. 31 and 32. An English manteau demonstrates the fashionable style of the 1690s. The front has wide pleats, and the train is arranged in a waterfall in back. *Mantua*, British, late seventeenth century. (Wool, metal thread, the Metropolitan Museum of Art, New York, 33.54a-c. Rogers Fund, 1933.)

(*Right*) Fig. 33. *Manteaux* worn over hoops. These later versions are more fitted, and only vestiges of the back drapery remain. Jacques Chéreau (publisher), *Dames en Manteaux* (Ladies in *Manteaux*), 1720s(?). (Engraving with etching on laid paper, 23.6 × 33.5 cm, National Gallery of Art. Katharine Shepard and Alisa Mellon Bruce Funds.)

fronts and backs were pleated over the torso and shoulder (Figs. 31, 32); later, a fitted linen lining was added underneath, and the train draping became increasingly sophisticated.[72] When hoops came into fashion, these were added underneath (Fig. 33).

THE *ROBE VOLANTE*

In the 1720s, a new dress based on *robes de chambre* was introduced: the *robe volante* (flying gown), which was popular into the 1740s.[73] It was cut similarly to the dressing gown, with wide rectangles of fabric controlled through pleats at the shoulders in front and back (Figs. 34, 35).[74] The *volante* was characterized by its loose shape: it omitted the manteau's sash and therefore the fitted waist, instead floating away from the body, becoming even wider when hoops began to be adopted around 1718.[75] Like the manteau, it closed down the center front; it could be worn closed, or if left open, filled in with a stomacher and petticoat.[76] The *volante* was worn over boned stays, maintaining the rigid structure that had long been fundamental to French women's dress even as that was hidden under the floating silhouette.[77] The *volante*'s connection to Ottoman garments can be seen in its dressing gown–like cut as well as its

Figs. 34 and 35. A closed-front *robe volante*. Both front and back are pleated at the shoulders. *Robe volante,* French, ca. 1730. (Silk, the Metropolitan Museum of Art, New York, 2010.148. Purchase, Friends of the Costume Institute Gifts, 2010.)

WESTERN AND EASTERN APPROACHES TO DRESS 49

volume. Jirousek argues that in Turkish dress, "Fit was never exact and often very bulky and stiff, obscuring and adding mass to the body form."[78]

THE *ROBE À LA FRANÇAISE*

By the 1740s, the *volante*'s fit had been refined enough that it was deemed a new dress, the *robe à la française*, thus experiencing a Gallicization process similar to the development of the *robe de chambre* into the manteau.[79] The *française* maintained the *volante*'s loose back pleats but grew increasingly fitted in the torso through the front and sides (Figs. 36, 37, 38, 39).[80] Nonetheless, the gown was still made of rectangular pieces, although these were modified in the draping process to fit more closely (Fig. 40).[81] Eventually, the bodice front adopted influences from many other popular gown styles, like the *robe à l'anglaise*'s closed front or the cutaway front of the *robes à la polonaise, circassienne,* and *turque*.[82] Although the *française*'s name (meaning "dress in the French style") demonstrates just how fundamentally French this gown had become, Jirousek argues,

Figs. 36 and 37. By mid-century, the *française* was fitted in the front torso and loose in back. *Robe à la française et jupe de* [and petticoat of] *robe à la française,* 1755–65. (Palais Galliera, musée de la Mode de la Ville de Paris.)

50   DRESSING À LA TURQUE

Many elements of Turkish dress had . . . been in use for some time and had been fully appropriated into the fashion of the day . . . The robe *à la française* with its flowing back and open-fronted, attached bodice and skirt . . . seems to be simply an incorporation of the sacques [*robes volante*] of the early eighteenth century with the fitted manteau of the late seventeenth century . . . This form had been fully assimilated into the vocabulary of European dress, but it is also apparent that the fashionable world was aware of the [Ottoman] roots of these forms.[83]

In France, Western and Eastern clothing traditions merged in the late seventeenth century. The growing availability of information about Turkish dress led to the incorporation of Ottoman dress aesthetics and approaches in France, where dress became a cross-cultural mélange that mixed traditionally Western approaches with imported Turkish ideas. Beginning with the late seventeenth-century manteau and continuing through the early and mid-eighteenth-century *robes volante* and *française*, French dressmakers adapted Eastern *robes de chambre* into increasingly formal gowns. These processes would continue into

Figs. 38 and 39. Over time, the *française*'s back pleats narrowed so that more of the torso was fitted, while the bodice front frequently took on the look of other fashionable gowns—here the closed front of the *robe à l'anglaise*. *Robe à la française et jupe de* [and petticoat of] *robe à la française,* 1770–80. (Silk, taffeta, gauze, needle lace, trimmings, Palais Galliera, musée de la Mode de la Ville de Paris.)

WESTERN AND EASTERN APPROACHES TO DRESS 51

the final decades of the eighteenth century, as new Ottoman-inspired women's styles led fashion and Eastern aesthetics continued to fulfill the desire for comfort and exoticism in women's dress.

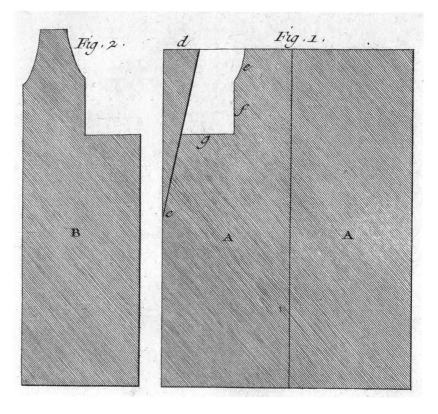

Fig. 40. The *robe à la française* was made from rectangular pieces, with pleats and a shaped side seam to provide fitting. (B) is the front piece, the center (A) is the side and side back, while the right-hand (A) creates the center-back pleats. The triangle from (c) to (d) is turned upside down to create a gore in the skirt's side seam. "Couturiere" (Seamstress) (detail), *Suite du recueil de planches sur les sciences, les arts libéraux et les arts méchaniques avec leur explication: deux cens quarante-quatre planches* (Continuation of the collection of plates on the sciences, the liberal arts and the mechanical arts with their explanation: two hundred and forty-four plates). (Paris: Panckoucke; Stoupe; Brunet, 1777, 117, Smithsonian Libraries.)

Defining Ottoman Influence, 1760–90

In dress, the *Polonoise* differs from the *Robe* [*à la française*], the *Robe* from the *Lévite*, & neither one nor the other can ever pass for a *Fourreau*.
—*Annonces, affiches, nouvelles et avis divers de la Province du Poitou*

In the final four decades of the eighteenth century, French women's fashion exploded into a dizzying number of variations, generally either a semifitted or fitted gown whose skirt was worn open in front displaying a petticoat, or a jacket and petticoat. Four of the most popular styles worn in this period were named, designed, and styled after Turkish garments: the robes and jackets *à la polonaise, circassienne, turque,* and *lévite*. Scholars have noted this decade's increasing fashion diversification, particularly in style terminology.[1] However, what has yet to be explored fully is the substantive distinctions that existed among these gowns and jackets in cut, as well as their real incorporation of dress aesthetics from the Ottoman Empire.[2] Fashion magazines' images and descriptions reveal variations that can be confirmed in extant garments. The *robes à la polonaise, turque,* and *circassienne* were all based on one common cut, so they will be discussed together. The *lévite,* however, was somewhat unique, and will be discussed separately in chapter 4 as it provides an excellent example of the cultural blending that typified this period. All four styles represent a continuation of the hybrid East/West approach to dressmaking begun in the late seventeenth century with the manteau, *robe volante,* and *robe à la française,* including the eventual Westernization of these Eastern-inspired fashions. This interest in Ottoman dress did not only impact fashion garments but also the structures worn underneath.

FRENCH WOMEN'S DRESS, 1760–99

In the final decades of the eighteenth century, numerous new gowns were introduced, as well as shorter jackets, which were themselves increasingly popular. Despite this diversification, the same cycle can be observed in which looser, Eastern-styled garments were introduced, then became more refined in fit over time; alternately, some were entirely replaced by more tailored, Western-identified styles. All were worn over some form of stays and (usually) hoops or pads, and can be sorted according to theme. The first theme was inspired by Ottoman dress, the most fashionable examples being the *robes à la polonaise, circassienne, turque,* and *lévite*. These emphasized layering and were initially based on loose silhouettes, although they used pleating and limited seaming to display the torso.[3] The next theme followed the English tradition: the *robe à l'anglaise,* as well as the riding habit (jacket) and redingote (gown). The *anglaise* was a French reinterpretation of the English mantua or nightgown, itself a stylized derivation of the manteau; its key feature was a closely fitted bodice, achieved through complex seaming and pleating.[4] The riding habit and redingote were styled after men's tailored garments.[5]

The third theme in women's fashion was primarily inspired by clothing worn in the Caribbean. The foremost example was the *chemise à la reine,* a dress made of lightweight fabrics gathered to fit the body.[6] The fourth group consisted of jackets modeled on peasant and working-class women's clothing.[7] Sometimes jackets were simply shorter versions of popular gowns, and sometimes a style in their own right, and so frequently overlapped with the other themes described here.[8] The fifth and final group was a dress that developed from the *fourreau,* a fitted gown originally worn by young girls, which may have had only one (drop-front) skirt.[9]

By the early 1790s, fitted gowns had become dominant, and many of these thematic groups converged to become a gown simply called *robe;* meanwhile, fashion's focus shifted to hats and headwear.[10] This robe was the preeminent gown, although jackets were arguably more popular. Over the decade, waistlines rose to become the high-waisted gown typical of the Directoire and Empire periods.

THE *ROBE À L'ANGLAISE*

Because so many studies have conflated the different gowns and jackets of the late eighteenth century, we must first define the *robe à l'anglaise,* or gown in the English style, as it has generally been presented as the prototypical gown of its era and thus confused with other styles. The *anglaise* began as the late seventeenth-century manteau, which was adopted in Britain as the mantua. The mantua was cut and styled similarly to the French version: a loose dressing gown, open entirely in front, cinched at the waist with a sash, with skirt pulled up high on each side hip; eventually, pleats at the shoulder in front and back were added. The gown was worn over a stomacher and petticoat, which filled the open front.

While the manteau went out of fashion in France, the mantua continued to be popular in Britain throughout the eighteenth century, where its details changed. An everyday version now called *nightgown* took on the *robe à la française*'s look in front, as the front pleats

Figs. 41 and 42. The mantua/nightgown's center back was fitted with stitched-down pleats and cut in one with the skirt, while the fronts and side backs were cut separately with the skirt knife-pleated to the bodice. *Robe à l'Anglaise,* British, 1770–75. (Silk, metal, the Metropolitan Museum of Art, New York. 2009.300.648. Brooklyn Museum Costume Collection at the Metropolitan Museum of Art, Gift of the Brooklyn Museum, 2009; A. Augustus Healy Fund, 1934.)

DEFINING OTTOMAN INFLUENCE, 1760–90

became narrower and stylized; it was worn open over a stomacher and petticoat, while hoops were added underneath (Figs. 41, 42). The bodice became increasingly fitted through the incorporation of a waist seam separating the bodice front and side backs from the skirt, and the skirt was pleated to fit.[11] The back treatment was distinct: the center back was cut in one piece from bodice to skirt. These center backs were pleated and stitched down from shoulder to waist, then released into the skirt, a style some historians have called *en fourreau* (a term used in eighteenth-century sources, but which then referred to a specific gown called the *fourreau*).[12] The *Gallerie des modes* described this pleated back as fundamental to the style: "True *robes à l'Anglaise* have in back small pleats, stopping at [stitched down until] the waist, that descend nearly to the ground."[13] The mantua became so ubiquitous in Britain that a formal version was adopted for court that maintained the looped-up train (increasingly narrowed and stylized), which was discontinued in the nightgown.[14]

Eventually, the English nightgown was adopted in France, where it was called *robe à l'anglaise*.[15] Determining exactly when this occurred is difficult. The earliest mention in French sources I have located is in the costume instructions for Beaumarchais's 1767 play *Eugenie*, set in England, in which multiple characters are dressed in robes "*Anglaise toute ronde* [all round, probably referring to its lack of train]."[16] The accompanying illustrations show gowns with fitted bodices worn open over V-shaped stomachers and pleated skirts. Michel-Barthélémy Ollivier painted two works in the mid-1760s that may depict *robes à l'anglaise*: a gown in *La Partie de dames* (1765) has long back pleats that appear stitched down to the waist, while *Le Thé à l'anglaise servi dans le salon des Quatre-Glaces au palais du Temple, mai 1766* includes one woman in what appears to be a gown with fitted bodice, among many others wearing *robes à la française*.[17] The *Courrier de la mode* reported in 1768, "The ballgowns most favorable to the figure are today the *habits* [suits] *Anglois*. The *fourreau* [i.e., robe] *Anglois* for the Ladies is the most gracious."[18] The following summer, its editors wrote that the "*deshabillé* [informal ensemble] *Anglois*, which garnered general favor for the last Carnival Masquerade, is become this summer the favorite *deshabillé* of our Ladies for the bedroom & for the country."[19]

Over time, the French redesigned the *anglaise*, cutting the entire bodice separately from the skirt and removing the stitched-down pleats from the bodice

(*Left*) Fig. 43. The bodice of the *robe à l'anglaise* had a fitted back, without pleats. Nicolas Dupin (print maker), Pierre Thomas Le Clerc (draughtsman), Esnauts & Rapilly (publisher), *Gallerie des modes et costumes français*, 1782, qq 230: Robe à l'anglais (. . .), 1782. (Engraving, 282 × 196 mm, Rijksmuseum, Amsterdam. Purchased with the support of the F. G. Waller-Fonds.)

(*Above*) Fig. 44. The skirt of the *anglaise* was cut entirely separate from the bodice and pleated to fit at the waistline. *Robe à l'anglaise,* 1770–90. (Taffeta, muslin, silk, Palais Galliera, musée de la Mode de la Ville de Paris, 1988.121.1.)

(*Below right*) Fig. 45. Some *robes à l'anglaise* retained the one-piece center back, although the English nightgown's stitched-down bodice pleats were omitted. *Robe à l'anglaise et jupe de* [and petticoat of] *robe à l'anglaise,* 1775–90. (Palais Galliera, musée de la Mode de la Ville de Paris, GAL 1969.59.3AB.)

(*Above right*) Fig. 46. The *anglaise* generally closed edge-to-edge with a pointed waistline in front. *Robe à l'anglaise,* 1770–90. (Taffeta, muslin, silk, Palais Galliera, musée de la Mode de la Ville de Paris, 1988.121.1.)

DEFINING OTTOMAN INFLUENCE, 1760–90   57

back (Figs. 43, 44), although sometimes a narrower version of the one-piece center-back cut continued but without pleating (a feature seen on many dress styles in this period, Fig. 45).[20] The *Gallerie des modes* recorded this change: "In France, we have removed the little [back] pleats of these dresses, we have given more width to the train; they have taken in front a more graceful form, and would be better named *robes à juste taille* [fitted figure] than *robes à l'Anglaise*."[21] Meanwhile, the center fronts were extended to meet edge-to-edge with a pointed waistline (Fig. 46).[22] The *Encyclopédie méthodique* referenced this separated bodice and skirt when it explained that the *anglaise* was "made separately out of several pieces, like stays used to be cut and *corsets* are still cut, it is boned very lightly; the skirt is pleated and sewn onto it."[23] Stomachers were no longer required, although in the 1780s the *anglaise* sometimes incorporated the cutaway front typical of the *polonaise*, *turque*, and *circassienne* (as did other styles), speaking more to the popularity of these Ottoman-influenced styles and hybrid approaches to dressmaking than any real fundamental change in the *anglaise*.[24]

THE *ROBES À LA POLONAISE*, *CIRCASSIENNE*, AND *TURQUE*

The *robes à la polonaise*, *circassienne*, and *turque* were cut in a way that connects the three, distinguishes them from the *anglaise*, and demonstrates their Ottoman inspirations. These three styles featured a layered effect created by fastening the gown at the breast, then allowing it to fall away, resulting in an opening that widened toward the waist and displayed a stomacher or underbodice, while the *anglaise* closed edge-to-edge at the center front. The bodice and skirt pieces were cut in one piece without the waist seam, which gave the *anglaise* a closer fit. These Turkish-inspired styles were made of two backs and two fronts, with the fronts vertically pleated to fit the torso at the side, while the *anglaise* used four, six, or more bodice pieces with curved seams to achieve a closer fit.[25] The *polonaise* and *circassienne*'s skirts were worn looped up, while the *turque* was always worn long and trained; the *anglaise* could incorporate looped-up overskirts but was more often depicted in fashion magazines as trained. Jacket versions of the *polonaise*, *circassienne*, and *turque* omitted the looped-up skirt, but maintained the other distinctive aspects of this cut.[26] The *polonaise* brought with it a new sleeve cuff, while the *circassienne* and *turque* featured short oversleeves displaying longer undersleeves. Many of these features can be connected to Ottoman dress and thus display a real incorporation of Turkish aesthetics.

SHORT DEFINITIONS

This summary focuses on these fashions as they were first introduced and popularized. However, it is important to note that none of these were fixed: while a style would usually include the characteristics listed below, they could vary, and designers clearly felt free to mix elements from different styles. This mixing and adaptation will be addressed at length in chapter 4.

Style	Fashionable	Bodice Front	Number of bodice pieces	Fit	Skirts	Sleeves
Robe à l'anglaise	ca. 1767–ca. 1784	Closed edge-to-edge with pointed waist	4 (2 fronts, 2 backs); 6 (2 fronts, 2 side backs, 2 center backs), or more (usually by adding more side back pieces)	Tight with waist seam	Trained	Usually just-past-the-elbow with *sabot* cuff, but sleeve styles were frequently mixed
Robe à la polonaise	ca. 1767–ca. 1781	Overgown effect: open in front in triangular shape displaying stomacher or underbodice	4 (2 fronts, 2 backs)	• Semiloose • No waist seam • Pleated at bodice side back	Looped up	Usually just-past-the-elbow with *sabot* cuff, but sleeve styles were frequently mixed
Robe à la circassienne	ca. 1777–ca. 1782	Overgown effect: open in front in triangular shape displaying stomacher or underbodice	4 (2 fronts, 2 backs)	• Semiloose or fitted • No waist seam • Pleated at bodice side back	Looped up	Short oversleeves over longer undersleeves (just past the elbow or wrist length)
Robe à la turque	ca. 1777–ca. 1789	Overgown effect: open in front in triangular shape displaying stomacher or underbodice	4 (2 fronts, 2 backs)	• Fitted • No waist seam (later versions with seam) • Pleated at bodice side back (later versions without pleats)	Trained	Short oversleeves over longer undersleeves (just past the elbow or wrist length)

DEFINING OTTOMAN INFLUENCE, 1760–90

OTTOMAN INSPIRATIONS

The characteristics distinguishing the *robes à la polonaise, circassienne, turque,* and *lévite* point to their Ottoman inspiration and demonstrate real incorporation of Turkish dress aesthetics. The specific details that late-eighteenth-century French designers took from Ottoman clothing (Fig. 47) varied, but usually consisted of one or more of the following characteristics: layering effects, looped-up skirts, soft silhouettes, and sashes.

Layering effects: A key element of Ottoman dress was layering, with multiple garments made strategically visible. Several caftans were usually worn, with the outermost fastened at the breast and falling open, or completely open in front, revealing the garments underneath. Short oversleeves and slashed sleeves also displayed underlayers. Similar layering is seen on *robes à la polonaise* in its overgown/undergown effect, with gown closed at center-front breast, then falling open toward the waist and into the skirt following the line seen on Ottoman outerwear caftans. This same layered overgown/undergown front was seen on the *circassienne* and *turque;* these also added short oversleeves that displayed longer undersleeves, mimicking Turkish short-sleeved outerwear caftans that revealed the long-sleeved garments worn underneath.

Fig. 47. Greek clothing, both male and female, displays many characteristics typical of Ottoman dress, including layering, looped-up caftans, soft silhouettes, and sashes. Jean Baptiste Vanmour, *Greek Men and Women Dancing the Khorra* (detail), ca. 1720–37. (Painting, oil on canvas, 44.5 × 58 cm, Rijksmuseum, Amsterdam.)

Looped-up skirts: The hems of Turkish caftans, usually one or both center-front corners, were frequently tucked up into the sash, displaying layers worn underneath. Both *robes à la polonaise* and *circassienne* may have adopted this element from Ottoman fashion, although if so, the effect was changed so the overgown was looped up at each side back with cords. Alternately, this effect may have been meant to suggest the swags seen on Turkish tents or may not be an Ottoman effect at all.

Soft silhouettes: Ottomans did not wear boned garments like stays, so their clothing could show more of the body's natural shape. The fashion for Turkish-inspired styles coincided with the introduction of new undergarments that displayed more of the natural figure. In particular, the *lévite* is sometimes depicted with a softer silhouette, possibly some kind of lightly boned or unboned stays. Furthermore, Ottoman outerwear caftans were generally worn loose and hanging. The *polonaise* adopted this aesthetic, with the robe fastened at the breast but otherwise floating away from the body.

Sashes: In Turkish dress, long fabric rectangles were tied around the waist as garment closure and storage for personal items, sometimes with long ends hanging down. Many Turkish-inspired French styles were worn with sashes; these appear to have been fundamental to the *lévite*.

Other elements drawn from Ottoman dress and used in French fashion that signified Eastern styles included crossover fronts, striped fabrics, wide collars, ermine and other fur trim, tassels and fringe, headwear mimicking turbans and veils, and feather plumes.[27]

THE CUTAWAY FRONT

The *polonaise, circassienne,* and *turque* emphasized a layered, overgown/undergown effect that is critical to contemporary definitions. All three usually closed at the center breast, then opened and widened from that point toward the waist.[28] This created a triangular-shaped bodice opening that extended into the skirt (Figs. 12, 13, 15, 48, 88, 122, 162, 165, 172), exactly the opposite of the modified V opening seen on the *robe à la française* and English nightgown (Figs. 15, 36, 41, 169). The *Gallerie des modes* declared that *polonaises* "are very narrow in front, leaving free the little waistcoat trimmed in its center and crowned by a large *contentement* [a decorative rosette]"; meanwhile the *robe à l'austrasienne* or *costume à la Jeanne d'Arc,* one of many variants of the *robe à la polonaise* further discussed in chapter 4, "is a type of *polonaise* that is very open in front, and which slopes entirely to the back."[29] The *circassienne* (Fig. 49) and *turque* (Figs. 50, 127, 173, 174)

(Left) Fig. 48. The *polonaise* closed at the breast, then sloped away into the skirt, highlighted here by the gathered white trim. "Jeune dame en robe à la polonnoise garnie de gaze" (Young lady in robe à la polonaise trimmed with gauze), *Gallerie des modes et costumes dessinés d'après nature, gravés par les plus célèbres artistes en ce genre, et colorés avec le plus grand soin par Madame Le Beau. (Ouvrage commence en l'année 1778* [Paris, 1778–81], view 193, Bibliothèque municipale de Lyon, France.)

(Right) Fig. 49. The *circassienne* also featured the cutaway front; here it is more closed at the top, but still angles open around the waist. Note the tassel trimmings, also considered typically Turkish. *Gallerie des modes et costumes français, 1778, K.55.* (Engraving on paper, 282 × 200 mm, Rijksmuseum, Amsterdam. Purchased with the support of the F. G. Waller-Fonds.)

were cut on similar lines to the *robe à la polonaise*, and so can be seen as later derivations.[30] The *Encyclopédie méthodique* described this cutaway effect when cataloging the *turque:* "Both fronts meet at the [neckline] top and then recede to the sides."[31] One of the most striking characteristics of Ottoman dress was designed, visible layering. Frequently, outerwear caftans were fastened at the neckline and then left to fall away (Figs. 4, 19, 20, 21, 51). This treatment is likely to have inspired the line of the *polonaise, circassienne,* and *turque.*

Two-thirds of the twenty-one fashion plates specifically identified as robes or jackets *à la polonaise* display the cutaway line. A smaller number do close further down toward the waist, but none have the *robe à l'anglaise*'s fully closed front with pointed waistline—nor do they have the *française*'s typical V-shaped opening. Instead, they close at or above the natural waist, while the skirt opening (or, in the case of jackets, the skirtings) still angles away from that point (Figs. 49, 110). Many of these more closed versions are jackets, about half of which close to the

62 DRESSING À LA TURQUE

waist; the *Gallerie des modes* differentiated these: "The difference of the *caracos à la polonaise* from the [*robe à la*] *polonaise négligée* [is] that [the *caraco*] only fastens to the middle of the waist, or only under the *contentement* [neckline rosette]."[32] Looking at the *circassienne* and *turque,* only two fashion plates do *not* feature cutaway, layered bodices, instead using closed, V-waistline bodices typical of the *robe à l'anglaise*. Unfortunately, the *Gallerie* does not record a reason for the difference, only that one is a "*robe à la Circassienne* in a new taste . . . closed in front to the bottom of the waist."[33] The *Magasin des modes* made clear that this fully closed front was more characteristic of the *anglaise*: "*Robes à l'Anglaise* close & are boned in front, very different from that of the *robes à la Turque,* which seem to only cover the back & the sides [of the torso]."[34]

Multiple surviving examples of late eighteenth-century dress reinforce the *polonaise, circassienne,* and *turque*'s unique cut. To create the cutaway opening of these styles, the front edge was angled from

(*Left*) Fig. 50. The *robe à la turque* had the same cutaway front line; here it is trimmed with fringe. Buisson (publisher), *Cabinet des modes ou les Modes nouvelles, 15 janvier 1786, 5e cahier, pl. 1.* (Engraving, 205 × 125 mm, Rijksmuseum, Amsterdam.)

(*Right*) Fig. 51. Ottoman outer caftans frequently closed at the neck, then widened toward the hem. Workshop of Jean Baptiste Vanmour, *The Capoudgi Bachi, Grandmaster of the Seraglio,* 1700–37. (Painting, oil on canvas, 39 × 31 cm, Rijksmuseum, Amsterdam.)

DEFINING OTTOMAN INFLUENCE, 1760–90   63

Figs. 52–54. The cutaway front of this *polonaise* was made by piecing and slashing. *Robe à la polonaise,* ca. 1778, silk and linen, Palais Galliera, musée de la Mode de la Ville de Paris, 62-108-14. (Courtesy of Palais Galliera, musée de la Mode de la Ville de Paris. Illustration by Michael Fleming. Author photos.)

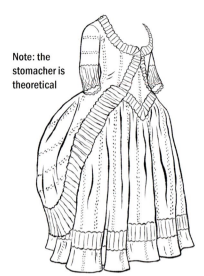

Note: the stomacher is theoretical

DRESSING À LA TURQUE

neckline to waist. A *robe à la polonaise* at the Palais Galliera was made with the fabric selvage forming the front opening (Figs. 52, 53, 54). To create the cutaway effect, a small triangle of fabric was pieced at the top, while the waist was slashed and turned in, narrowly at the top and bottom and more widely at the waist. Two pleats stitched down to the waist at the side and side back bring the gown in to the torso, while double box pleats at the center-back and side-back seams, just below the waist, release more fullness into the skirt. Another surviving example is the *polonaise longue*, a trained variation of the *robe à la polonaise*, at the Musée de la Toile de Jouy. To create the desired front opening, the bodice edge is cut on a curved slant in addition to side-back pleating (Figs. 55, 56, 57).

Figs. 55–57. The front opening of this *polonaise longue* was cut on a curved, angled line. Note how the stripes demonstrate the fabric grain. The museum currently identifies this gown as a *robe à la turque*, but as will be explored in the section on sleeves, that style always had short oversleeves over longer undersleeves. The identification of this dress as a *polonaise longue* is reinforced by another with a similar cut at the Museum of London (*Dress*, 1781–85, cotton, linen, metal, silk, Museum of London, 65.80/1). *Robe à la Turque [polonaise longue], manteau de robe, corsage et jupon ayant appartenu à Anne-Élisabeth Oberkampf* [gown, bodice and petticoat belonging to Anne-Élisabeth Oberkampf], ca. 1785. Cream silk pékin, Musée de la Toile de Jouy, Jouy-en-Josas, France, inv. 000.4.6, legs Feray et 001.1.13.2.a, 001.13.2.b, acquisition. (Courtesy of Musée de la Toile de Jouy. Second and third photos by author.)

DEFINING OTTOMAN INFLUENCE, 1760–90   65

In its early years, the *polonaise* was typically worn with the overgown unfastened other than at the center breast, allowing the gown to float away from the body.[35] The *Gallerie* proclaimed the *polonaise négligée* closed "simply on the breast like the usual *polonaises*, [and] is not fastened at the waist."[36] However, the flyaway feature is not generally seen on the *circassienne* and *turque,* indicating the bodice front edge was probably worn pinned, basted, or sewn in place. Either way, this open, cutaway line meant something must fill in the gap and cover the stays. Earlier gowns, notably the *robe à la française,* did so with a stomacher called *pièce d'estomac:* a separate, upside-down, triangle-shaped piece pinned or basted to the stays or gown. Some *polonaises, circassiennes,*

Fig. 58. This English *polonaise* has a false front stomacher sewn to the gown at the side and shoulder seams. *Polonaise dress,* 1775. (Linen, metal, muslin, silk, Killerton, Devon, UK, NT 1362010.)

and *turques* continued this practice, although their stomachers were now diamond-shaped to fit the new line. Alternately, these styles could be worn over sewn-in, front-opening false fronts, or separate sleeveless or sleeved underbodices.[37] *Polonaises* are most frequently described in fashion magazines with sewn-in false fronts called *compère*, or separate underbodices called *veste* (waistcoat).[38] *Circassiennes* and *turques* are generally listed as being worn over stomachers, reviving the term *pièce d'estomac*, or underbodices, although these were now called *soubreveste, corsage, corset,* or *sultane*—the last a specifically Turkish allusion.[39] The *Magasin des modes* wrote, "In order to cover the front of the stays & the arms, [the *robe à la turque*] uses sleeves, *pièces* [*d'estomac*], or *corsets* made of a different fabric & a different color, or of the same fabric, but a different color."[40] Even those *polonaises* closing at the waist still generally do so over a fill-in underlayer that extends into a pointed waistline.

The *polonaise*'s flyaway nature meant the sides of the stays could show, so it would have been practical to wear a full underbodice or to have the gown made with a false front. At least eight surviving *polonaises* include a sewn-in, center-front opening *compère*.[41] The false front of the circa 1770–75 English *robe à la polonaise* at Killerton is patterned as a full bodice front closing edge-to-edge, with a pointed waistline (Fig. 58). The robe is placed on top of this piece, and the two are sewn together at the side back, shoulder, and armhole, but not at the waist, neckline, or center front. Because this garment was difficult to photograph in its storage facility, a nightgown or *robe à l'anglaise* with cutaway front at the Museum of London, which uses a similar technique, provides a useful visual (Figs. 59, 60). A related approach was used on the *polonaise longue* at the Musée de la Toile de Jouy. In this case, the *compère* was whipstitched to the robe under one of the pleats (Figs. 61, 62, 63). The Killerton gown's underbodice has no clo-

Figs. 59 and 60. This English nightgown or *robe à l'anglaise* has a false waistcoat constructed similarly to the Killerton polonaise. It is cut as a full bodice piece, lined, and sewn to the rest of the dress, while the cutaway front is laid on top and unlined. Nonetheless, this gown's waist seam and lack of bodice pleats suggests a definition of an *anglaise. Dress,* ca. 1780. Pink silk lustring with white satin stripes and a self-colored pattern of small floral sprigs in the ground, Museum of London, 54.78/1. (Published with the permission of the Museum of London. Author photos.)

DEFINING OTTOMAN INFLUENCE, 1760–90   67

Fig. 61. The false front is stitched to the lining just under one of the robe's pleats. In this case, the gown front is lined. *Robe à la Turque [polonaise longue], manteau de robe, corsage et jupon ayant appartenu à Anne-Élisabeth Oberkampf* (gown, bodice and petticoat belonging to Anne-Élisabeth Oberkampf), ca. 1785. Cream silk pékin, Musée de la Toile de Jouy, Jouy-en-Josas, France, inv. 000.4.6. (Courtesy of Musée de la Toile de Jouy. Author photo.)

sures (presumably it would be pinned or sewn close), while the Musée de la Toile de Jouy dress has eyelets and laces closed, with a narrow whalebone strip at each front edge reinforcing the lacing. Seventeen extant *polonaises* have no accompanying underbodice or stomacher, implying a separate garment must have been worn underneath.[42] A rare example that survives with its separate stomacher is the post-1772 *robe à la polonaise* at the Musée d'Histoire de Marseille (Figs. 64, 65). The stomacher is cut in a diamond shape, extending into a semipointed waistline but clearly cut to fill in the gown's triangular opening given its narrow top and wide waist.[43] One *polonaise* survives with a coordinating sleeveless underbodice.[44] A similar garment exists as part of a 1780s Swedish jacket ensemble to fill its cutaway front (Fig. 66). Unfortunately, far fewer extant examples of the *circassienne* and *turque* have been located. Two feature a sewn-in false front, while three survive without whatever separate garment (stomacher or underbodice) was originally worn.[45]

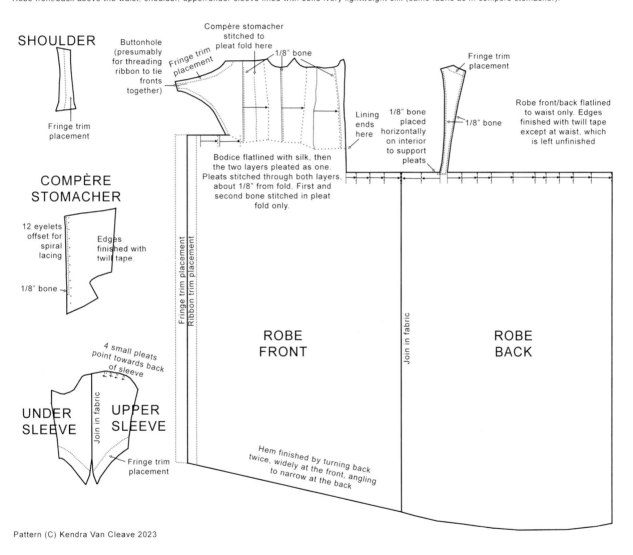

(*This page and overleaf*) Figs. 62 and 63. The pattern for the Musée de la Toile de Jouy *polonaise longue* and petticoat. (Courtesy of Musée de la Toile de Jouy. Author pattern.)

DEFINING OTTOMAN INFLUENCE, 1760–90

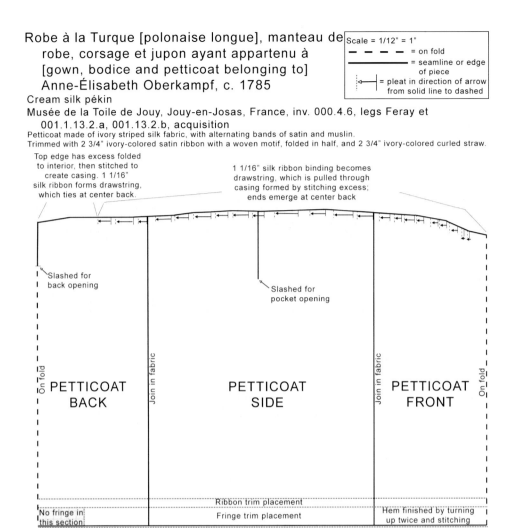

(*Top left and right*) Figs. 64 and 65. This stomacher suits the cutaway front of the *polonaise, circassienne,* and *turque* in that it provides coverage for the waist area, which could show under the flyaway robe. *Robe à la polonaise,* after 1772. Wool, silk, Musée d'Histoire de Marseille, France. (First photo by Claude Almodovar, © RMN-Grand Palais / Art Resource, NY. Second photo by author. Courtesy Musée d'Histoire de Marseille.)

(*Above*) Fig. 66. This sleeveless underbodice is worn under a cutaway jacket. The dual opening is unusual; more typical would be a closed-front, back-opening underbodice. *Klänning [dress],* 1782–1848. (Taffeta with silver embroidery, Nordiska Museet, Stockholm, NM.0222648A-E.)

DEFINING OTTOMAN INFLUENCE, 1760–90   71

THE TUNIC CUT

Another element critical to the eighteenth-century definition of the *polonaise, circassienne,* and *turque* was the tunic cut, with bodice and skirt pieces cut in one without waist seam (Figs. 14, 67, 87, 88, 99, 121, 123, 172).[46] To account for the skirts' fullness, inverted box pleats emerged at center and side-back seams, while the fronts were pleated vertically to fit the torso at the side; these pleats were stitched down to the waist, then released into the skirt.[47] This construction differs from most other gowns of the era. The *robe volante* and early versions of the *robe à la française* were cut without waist seam but were worn loose around the torso's front and sides. When a tighter fit became fashionable in the mid-century, the *française*'s front was cut with a waist seam or horizontal tuck separating the bodice from the skirt. While less usual, three extant *robes à la polonaise* do use the horizontal pleat technique, including the Galliera *polonaise* (Figs. 68, 69); one of these was remade from an earlier gown, probably a *française,* so the similar treatment is logical.[48] Meanwhile, the *robe à l'anglaise* had a separate bodice and skirt, except sometimes in the center-back pieces, with the skirt pleated and stitched to the waist. The *Encyclopédie* specified many of these variations: "The bodice of the . . . *angloise* is made separately out of several pieces, like stays used to be cut and *corsets* are still cut . . . The *polonoise* is cut out of four parts, two backs and two fronts; the two backs, which first fit gracefully at the waist, get wider to give fullness to the hips . . . The *robe turque* . . . is made as a *polonoise* in the back."[49] Ottoman caftans were usually cut from one fabric length without a waist seam. Triangular gores were inserted to allow the garment to flare as needed over the hips, and these as well as side slits and front openings allowed for movement. Each of the Turkish-inspired French styles began with a similar one-piece construction. Of course, these also recall the all-in-one cut of the *robe de chambre,* manteau, and *robe volante,* as well as the early *robe à la française,* but those gowns derived from Ottoman sources as well.

Extant gowns provide more information. Scholarly analysis of the differences between late eighteenth-century dress styles has only recently begun, so extant examples are still being identified and thus few. Consequently, this study will look beyond French examples to include others from Western Europe and the United States since their dress traditions were similar and these countries were strongly influenced by French fashion. A French

Fig. 67. The stripes' uninterrupted line demonstrates the lack of waist seam. "Femme en [Woman in] robe à la polonaise" [1778], *Gallerie des modes et costumes française dessinés d'après nature graves par les plus célèbres artistes nc e genre* (Esnauts & Rapilly: Paris, 1778–88), 1. (Muzeum Narodowe, Warsaw.)

robe à la polonaise at the Palazzo Mocenigo has three pleats at the side, two facing each other and thus forming the appearance of a side seam, but the gown's only actual seams are at the side- and center-back (Figs. 70, 71, 72, 73, 74). Lining techniques vary. Some extant *polonaises* are flat-lined, with the fashion fabric laid on top of the lining, then pleated together and stitched down, like the *robe à la polonaise* at the Musée d'Histoire de Marseille (Figs. 75, 76, 77, 78, 79).[50] More common is the treatment of the Swedish *robe à la turque* at the Nordiska Museet, which has its fashion fabric pleated and stitched down to a fitted lining (Figs. 80, 81, 82, 83).[51] While most of the gowns and jackets in this study are similarly constructed, a *polonaise* ensemble at the Worthing Museum & Art Gallery appears to have been altered from an earlier dress. A waist seam separates the bodice and skirt, but the skirt's pleating is different from the numerous small pleats typical of the *anglaise*, instead using several wide pleats to mimic the flat waistline sections seen on robes and jackets à la polonaise.[52]

More evidence for the *polonaise*'s seaming comes from the style's entrance into menswear, demonstrated by two informal *fracs* or frock coats and one more formal *habit* coat, all "à la polonaise," in the *Gallerie des modes*. One of these is specifically described as being "without a seam in the back."[53] In the accompanying illustration, side-back seams are present and highlighted with applied trim, while a faint line suggests a center-back seam. However, these are typical of any man's jacket

Figs. 68 and 69. This robe uses a horizontal pleat at the side front and back to fit the waistline. *Robe à la polonaise*, ca. 1778, silk and linen, Palais Galliera, musée de la Mode de la Ville de Paris, 62-108-14. (Courtesy of Palais Galliera, musée de la Mode de la Ville de Paris. Illustration by Michael Fleming. Author photo.)

DEFINING OTTOMAN INFLUENCE, 1760-90　73

(*This and facing page*) Figs. 70–72. What appears to be a side seam is actually a box pleat; the only seams are at the center and side back (closest to the center back). *Sopravveste femminile* [Woman's overdress] [robe or caraco à la polonaise], France, 1775–99. Cotton, Museo di Palazzo Mocenigo, Venice, Cl. XXIV No 0239.z. (Courtesy Museo di Palazzo Mocenigo. Author photos.)

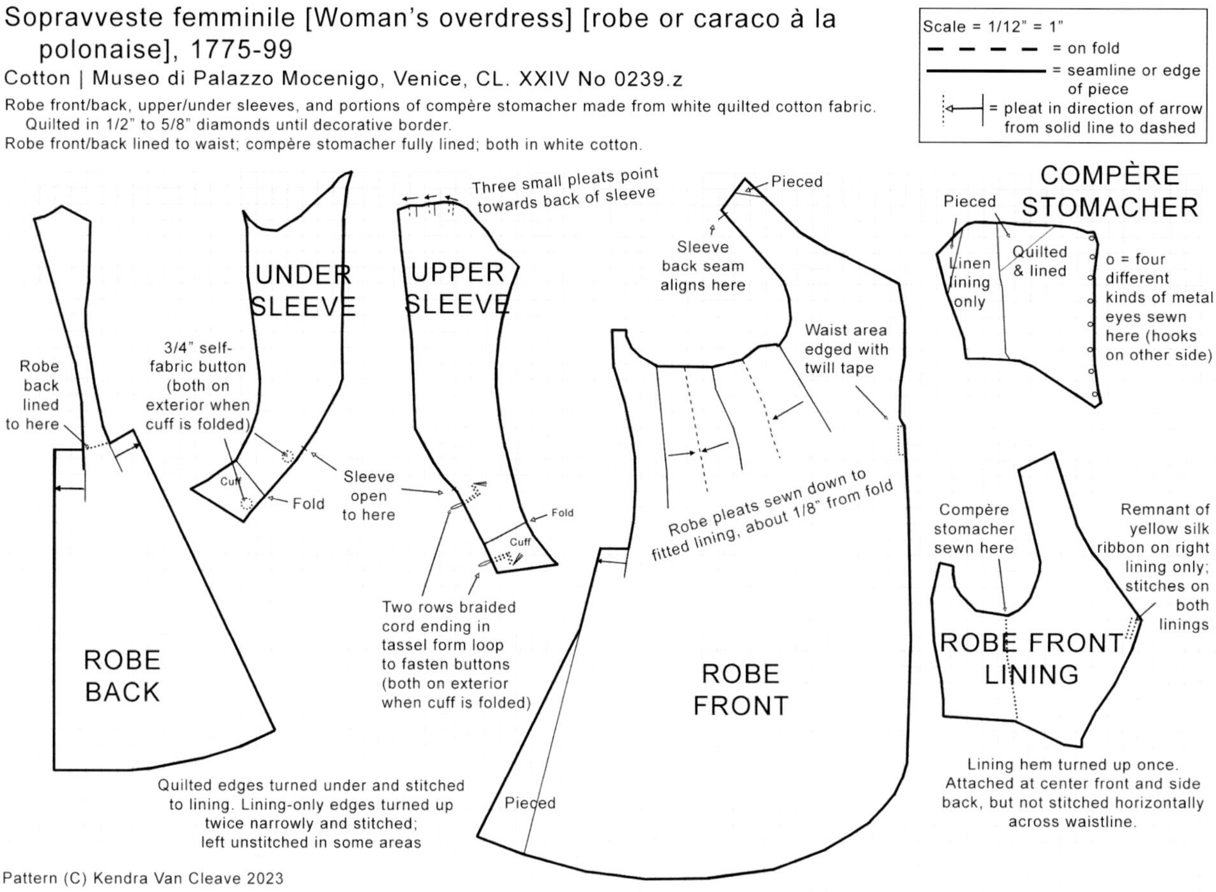

Sopravveste femminile [Woman's overdress] [robe or caraco à la polonaise], 1775-99
Cotton | Museo di Palazzo Mocenigo, Venice, CL. XXIV No 0239.z

Robe front/back, upper/under sleeves, and portions of compère stomacher made from white quilted cotton fabric. Quilted in 1/2" to 5/8" diamonds until decorative border.
Robe front/back lined to waist; compère stomacher fully lined; both in white cotton.

Scale = 1/12" = 1"
— — — — = on fold
———— = seamline or edge of piece
|⟵———| = pleat in direction of arrow from solid line to dashed

UNDER SLEEVE
UPPER SLEEVE — Three small pleats point towards back of sleeve
Pieced — Sleeve back seam aligns here
Waist area edged with twill tape
Pieced — COMPÈRE STOMACHER — Linen lining only — Quilted & lined — o = four different kinds of metal eyes sewn here (hooks on other side)

Robe back lined to here
3/4" self-fabric button (both on exterior when cuff is folded)
Fold — Cuff — Sleeve open to here — Fold — Cuff
Robe pleats sewn down to fitted lining, about 1/8" from fold
Compère stomacher sewn here
Remnant of yellow silk ribbon on right lining only; stitches on both linings

Two rows braided cord ending in tassel form loop to fasten buttons (both on exterior when cuff is folded)

ROBE BACK
ROBE FRONT
ROBE FRONT LINING

Quilted edges turned under and stitched to lining. Lining-only edges turned up twice narrowly and stitched; left unstitched in some areas.
Pieced
Lining hem turned up once. Attached at center front and side back, but not stitched horizontally across waistline.

Pattern (C) Kendra Van Cleave 2023

(*This and facing page*) Figs. 73 and 74. The pattern for the Palazzo Mocenigo *robe à la polonaise* and petticoat. (Courtesy Museo di Palazzo Mocenigo. Author pattern.)

of this era, so how this style differs is unclear. It is interesting to note that men's coats of this era, including the *polonaise,* were increasingly cut in such a way that the front opening sloped away toward the waist and into the tails. This is the same line seen on the women's *robes à la polonaise, circassienne,* and *turque,* and it echoes the line created in Ottoman caftans when they were closed at the breast and then allowed to fall away from that point.

However, by the mid-1780s, the *turque* and *circassienne* were sometimes made with a separate waist seam, with the skirt pleated to the bodice (Fig. 84). This change is likely due to the increasing popularity of the *robe à l'anglaise,* which featured a tight fit achieved through multiple curved seams and an entirely separate bodice and skirt. The *Cabinet des modes* wrote of the *anglaise,* "The merit of this ensemble is to slim the figure as much as possible. The *Robe* must fit closely and define the figure well."[54] Fashion plates specifically identified as a

DRESSING À LA TURQUE

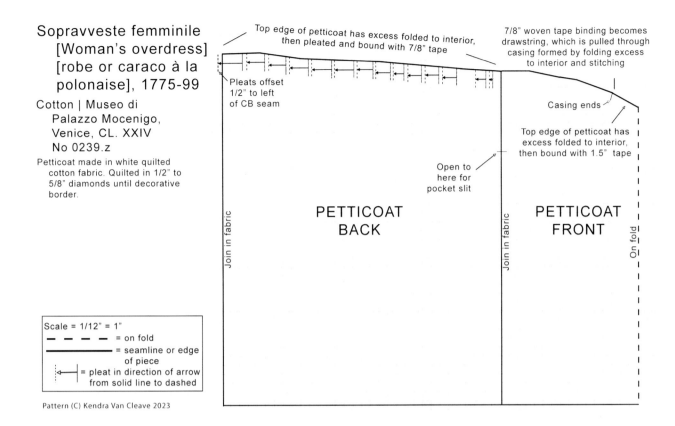

Sopravveste femminile [Woman's overdress] [robe or caraco à la polonaise], 1775-99

Cotton | Museo di Palazzo Mocenigo, Venice, CL. XXIV No 0239.z

Petticoat made in white quilted cotton fabric. Quilted in 1/2" to 5/8" diamonds until decorative border.

Pattern (C) Kendra Van Cleave 2023

polonaise, *circassienne*, or *turque*—and where the waist area is visible (unfortunately, the arm or a wrap frequently obscures it)—demonstrate they were nearly always cut in the one-piece tunic style until about 1781. Before that date, only one fashion plate (a *polonaise*) obviously features a waist seam, with the skirt knife-pleated to the bodice.[55] However, as the form-fitting *anglaise* grew to dominate French fashion in the 1780s, the *circassienne* and *turque*'s cut was adapted to copy the wholly separate bodice and skirt of the *anglaise*. Presumably, for those women still wearing the *polonaise* (which was no longer fashionable enough to feature in magazines or portraiture but still appears in inventories and other sources), the cut would have been similarly adjusted.[56] This would have been a relatively easy alteration to make to an existing gown to bring it up to date. A circa 1785–93 American *robe à la turque* (Figs. 85, 86) at the Philadelphia Museum of Art retains the all-in-one cut in the narrow center-back pieces, but the bodice and skirt are otherwise entirely separate.[57] The skirt is pleated to the bodice using numerous small knife pleats, as was the practice on the *anglaise*.

DEFINING OTTOMAN INFLUENCE, 1760-90   77

Figs. 75–77. The fashion fabric was laid on top of the lining, then the two were pleated together. *Robe à la polonaise,* after 1772, silk pékin lined in silk, Musée d'Histoire de Marseille, France, A/83/391. (Author photos.)

78   DRESSING À LA TURQUE

Robe à la polonaise, second half of the 18th c. (after 1772)
Silk, wool | Musée d'histoire de Marseille, Coll. MVM, inv. A/83/391

Robe made of silk taffeta with woven pink, white, yellow, & green stripes on a pale blue background.

Robe flatlined with unbleached lightweight silk. Robe back, robe front corner, shoulder, sleeve & stomacher also lined with ivory wool.

Robe neckline trim & cuff consists of pleated self-fabric ruche edged with woven, knotted, & tufted silk braid in coordinating colors. Robe fronts & hem trimmed with alternately pleated & gathered self-fabric ruches, edged with same braid. Portions of ruches lined with wool, others with unbleached lightweight silk.

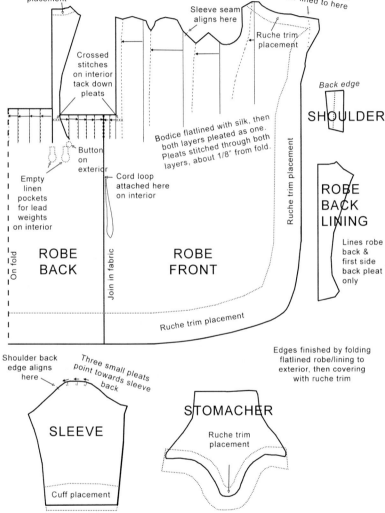

(*This page and overleaf*) Figs. 78 and 79. The pattern for the Musée d'Histoire de Marseille *robe à la polonaise,* stomacher, and petticoat. (Courtesy Musée d'Histoire de Marseille. Author pattern.)

DEFINING OTTOMAN INFLUENCE, 1760–90

Robe à la polonaise, second half of the 18th c. (after 1772)

Silk, wool
Musée d'histoire de Marseille, Coll. MVM, inv. A/83/391

Petticoat made of silk taffeta with woven pink, white, yellow, & green stripes on a pale blue background. Petticoat flatlined with ivory wool. Hem trim consists of wide self-fabric flounce, pleated horizontally across the top in three rows. This pleated portion alternates between flat & gathered sections. Flounce edged with woven, knotted, & tufted silk braid in coordinating colors. Pocket slit trimmed with gathered self-fabric ruche, edged with same braid. Flounce & ruche trim flatlined with ivory wool.

Scale = 1/12" = 1"
– – – = on fold
——— = seamline or edge of piece
|⇢⇠| = pleat in direction of arrow from solid line to dashed

Pattern (C) Kendra Van Cleave 2023

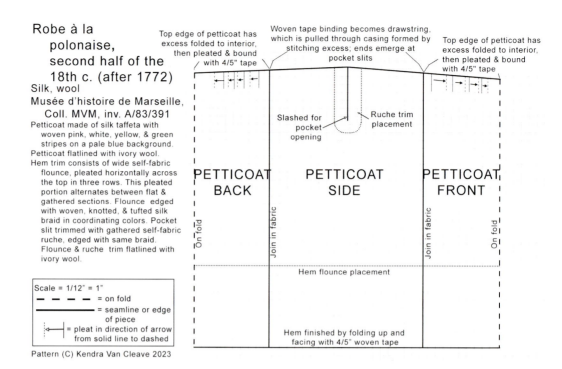

(This and following pages) Figs. 80–82. Those pleated to a fitted lining, like this *robe à la turque,* are generally stitched to the lining vertically along each pleat. However, the lining is not stitched horizontally across its hem, probably because those stitch marks would visually "break" the tunic cut. *Klänning* [dress] *[robe à la turque].* (Silk, Nordiska Museet, Stockholm, NMA.0052362.)

DEFINING OTTOMAN INFLUENCE, 1760-90

82　DRESSING À LA TURQUE

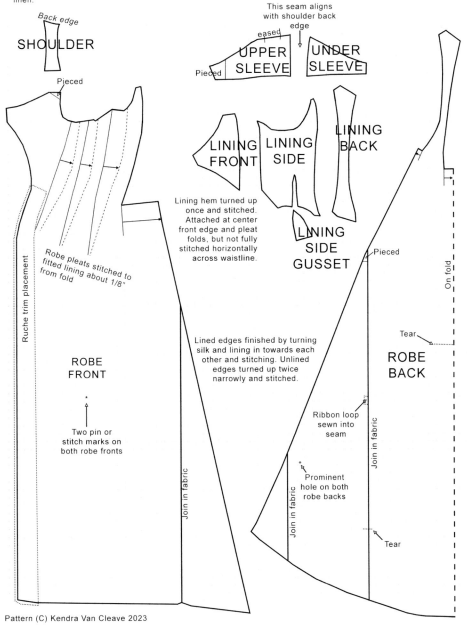

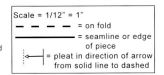

Fig. 83. The pattern for the Nordiska Museet *robe à la turque*. (Courtesy Nordiska Museet. Author pattern.)

DEFINING OTTOMAN INFLUENCE, 1760–90   83

Fig. 84. Based on the way the pleats fall, this *robe à la turque* appears to have its skirt knife-pleated to the separate bodice. The yellow lines on the bodice are trim highlighting the bodice seams. *Print (in colour) from "Magasin des modes nouvelles francoises et angloises" 1787–01–01* [April 30, 1787] (detail). (Print, Fashion Museum of Antwerp, Belgium.)

(*Bottom*) Figs. 85 and 86. An extant *robe à la turque* (so determined because its overgown, made of a sheer, embroidered material, has short oversleeves and cutaway front) with separate bodice and skirt. *Woman's Dress (Robe à l'anglaise) with Zone Front [robe à la turque],* American, ca. 1785–93. (Cotton and linen, Philadelphia Museum of Art, 1955-98-9. Gift of Thomas Francis Cadwalader, 1955-98-9.)

84 DRESSING À LA TURQUE

THE SILHOUETTE

Although vertical pleats allowed the *polonaise* to follow the figure, the style was still intended to skim rather than hug the torso and waist. Its only fastening was at the neckline, otherwise it floated away from the body. The *Gallerie des modes* described a *caraco* (jacket) *à la polonaise* as "detached & floating around the figure," and a *polonaise négligée* as closing "simply on the breast like the *polonaises courantes*, [and] is not fastened at the waist."[58] This fit can be seen in several fashion plates in the *Gallerie*, including two *robes à la polonaise* in which the drawing clearly indicates looseness around the side front waist (Fig. 67), and three *caracos à la polonaise* in which the jacket front hangs away from the body (Figs. 87, 165).[59] An image from the *Monument du costume* perfectly illustrates this silhouette. The front-facing woman's *robe à la polonaise* floats away from her torso near the waist, while the back-facing figure's opens out at the side and hangs away from the small of the back (Fig. 88).

The *polonaise*'s loose silhouette is reinforced by contemporary artworks, such as Robert's *Tapis Vert* (1774–75), in which Queen Marie-Antoinette wears a *robe à la polonaise* while bending forward.[60] Her position shows the looseness of her *polonaise* around her waist and the empty space between the gown and the stomacher or underbodice worn underneath. The same can be seen in another portrait of the queen by Mosnier, in which she sits in a gray or lavender *robe à la polonaise*; wrinkles beginning at the bustline and angled toward the side waist indicate it is similarly detached.[61] Vigée Le Brun's portrait of the Duchesse de Chartres (1777) shows the robe spread wide at the breast and only loosely tied, while it actually flips back on itself in Mosnier's 1781 portrait of the Duchesse de Fitz-James.[62] This detached, floating fit was characteristic of Ottoman clothing. Women's *anteris* followed the body's lines, but they did so softly, while the outer caftans of both sexes hung away from the body. Sometimes a sash would draw these garments in at the waist, but even then, they did so in a way that was relaxed. Thus, the *polonaise*'s soft fit represents a move away from the Western silhouette and a turn to Ottoman aesthetics.

The construction of extant gowns further emphasizes this changing silhouette. As previously discussed, many of these garments would have fastened with pins or basting, which were both common in the period. However, a 1770s white cotton *caraco* at the Palais Galliera has three interior ties sewn to the lining at the side front pleat (Figs. 89, 90, 91, 92). These would allow the jacket to fit closely at the back and sides, but fall open in front (the ties would presumably be covered

Fig. 87. The front of this *caraco à la polonaise* is detached and hangs open. Pierre Thomas Le Clerc (artist), Charles Emmanuel Patas (print maker), Esnauts & Rapilly (publisher), *Gallerie des modes et costumes français, 1779, cc 160: Jeune dame tenant son enfant (. . .)*, (Young woman holding her child), 1782. (Etching, watercolor, 290 × 207 mm, Rijksmuseum, Amsterdam. Purchased with the support of the Flora Fonds/Rijksmuseum Fonds.)

Fig. 88. Both women wear *robes à la polonaise* that drape away from the waist. Carl Gottlieb Guttenberg (printer) after Jean Michel Moreau, *Le Rendez-vous pour Marly, Le Monument du costume* (detail), 1776–77. (Etching, 410 × 318 mm, Rijksmuseum, Amsterdam.)

by a separate stomacher). A later *caraco à la polonaise* (or possibly a pierrot jacket) at the same institution demonstrates how dressmakers achieved the more fitted look desired in the 1780s (Figs. 93, 94, 95, 96, 97, 98). This jacket has a sewn-in stomacher with center-front opening. The cutaway edge of the *caraco* is sewn down to the stomacher pieces from neckline to waist, causing the jacket to fit closely around the entire torso. In addition, two extant *polonaises* have pleated trim around the petticoat's pocket slit (Fig. 79), indicating that the corresponding robe was expected to open widely enough to reveal the upper hip.[63] Finally, two *robes à la polonaise* have linen pockets for lead weights at the lower back, which would have helped to keep the dress fitted into the lower back (Figs. 78, 101).[64]

THE SKIRTS

For historians, the *polonaise*'s most noticeable feature has generally been its skirts worn lifted via cords or ribbons (Figs. 67, 88, 99, 121, 171, 172).[65] The skirt was drawn up at each side back, creating three swags, called the *ailes* (wings) or *côtes* (sides), and *queue* (train), often highlighted

Figs. 89–91. An extant *caraco à la polonaise* has three ties sewn to the lining at the side front pleat. There are also loops for a tie at the neckline, but otherwise the jacket would hang loosely from side front to center front. *Caraco [à la polonaise]*, 1770–80, cotton, Palais Galliera, musée de la Mode de la Ville de Paris, GAL1992.177.X. (Courtesy Palais Galliera, musée de la Mode de la Ville de Paris. Third photo by author.)

with a contrasting rosette or other decoration.[66] Some *polonaise* variations draped all three swags equally, while others differed in length. For example, the *Gallerie* indicates that on the *polonaise courante* or *en frac* (Fig. 67), "the wings, or sides of the *polonaise* should be small and the train very long," while the *polonaise aux ailes* featured the reverse, with the train or center swag shorter than the sides.[67] The term *retroussée* is frequently used in fashion magazines to refer to this technique, and can literally be translated as *to roll, fold,* or *lift up*.[68] Critically, wearing a gown *retroussée* was not limited to *robes à la polonaise*.[69] Many scholars

DEFINING OTTOMAN INFLUENCE, 1760–90   87

have confused the *polonaise* with the *robe à l'anglaise* and others due to the popularity of wearing any late-eighteenth-century gown with its skirts lifted up into swags. In fact, multiple dresses are featured in the *Gallerie des modes* with skirts worn *retroussée*, including a *habit de bal* whose "skirt is *retroussée* with tassels on the sides, a little in back, and in front unevenly into the pockets"; *robe à la Versaillaise*, whose "front is almost the same as that of the *polonaise;* but the back is cut in the bottom in three drapery falls" (that is, cut to shape rather than looped up); *robe à la reine*, which had "the double advantage of being either trained or *retroussée*"; four *robes à l'anglaise*, one specifically worn "*retroussée* to make dancing easier"; a *robe à la chinoise* (Chinese); and several *fourreaux*, some of which are "*retroussé à la Polonoise*," reinforcing the

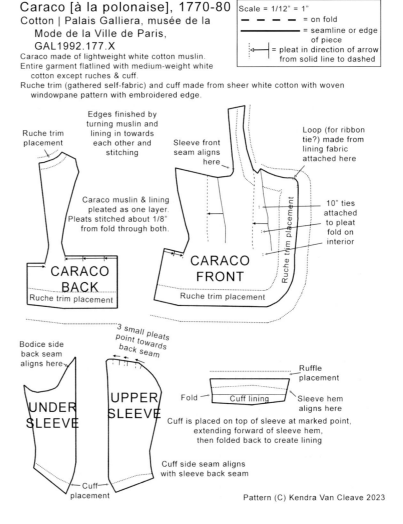

Fig. 92. The pattern for the Palais Galliera *caraco à la polonaise*. (Courtesy Palais Galliera, musée de la Mode de la Ville de Paris. Author pattern.)

Figs. 93–96. A later *caraco à la polonaise* or pierrot is sewn down to the false front, allowing for a closer fit. *Caraco [à la polonaise or pierrot] et jupe* [and petticoat], 1780–90. Cotton and linen, Palais Galliera, musée de la Mode de la Ville de Paris, GAL1920.1.2370. (Courtesy Palais Galliera, musée de la Mode de la Ville de Paris. First and fourth photos by author.)

DEFINING OTTOMAN INFLUENCE, 1760–90   89

Caraco [à la polonaise or pierrot] et jupe [and petticoat], 1780-90

Cotton & linen | Palais Galliera, musée de la Mode de la Ville de Paris, GAL1920.1.2370

Caraco made of medium-weight printed cotton with ivory ground & alternating stripes of red with floral vines in black, violet, red, & blue. Ruche trim and cuffs made of gathered self-fabric.

Caraco front/back above the waist has fitted lining in natural linen; caraco front/back below the waist flatlined with gray & black checked linen. Lining join at waist not stitched through caraco exterior. Shoulder, compère stomacher, & upper/under sleeve lined with natural linen.

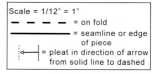

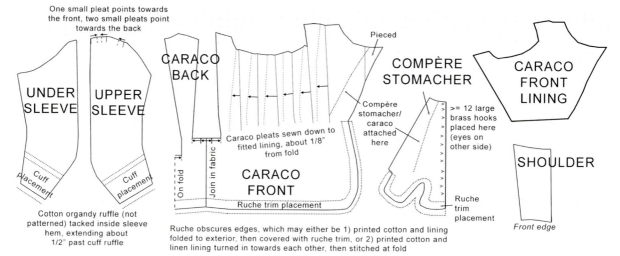

Figs. 97 and 98. The pattern for the Palais Galliera *caraco à la polonaise* or *pierrot* and petticoat. (Courtesy Palais Galliera, musée de la Mode de la Ville de Paris. Author pattern.)

Caraco [à la polonaise or pierrot] et jupe [and petticoat], 1780-90

Cotton and linen
Palais Galliera, musée de la Mode de la Ville de Paris, GAL1920.1.2370

Petticoat made of medium-weight printed cotton with ivory ground & alternating stripes of red with floral vines in black, violet, red, & blue.
Fully lined with natural linen.

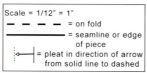

Pattern (C) Kendra Van Cleave 2023

origin of this particular style of drawn-up skirts with the *polonaise*.[70] Extant garments display a variety of methods of fastening up the skirt: the *polonaise* at the Musée d'Histoire de Marseille has cords sewn to the lower back interior, which are then looped over buttons at the side backs (Figs. 100, 101, 102). Meanwhile, a *polonaise* at Colonial Williamsburg has tapes stitched to the underside of the skirt (Figs. 103, 104, 105). These loop around the skirt, and the hooks sewn to the ends connect to thread loops at each side back just below the waist.[71] The Killerton *polonaise* (Fig. 106) has ribbons sewn at the lower side backs on the dress's interior and exterior; presumably these would tie, lifting the skirt's swags. Finally, a *robe à la circassienne* at the Metropolitan Museum of Art has five metal rings sewn at equidistant points along the robe's side-back skirt seam, through which a cord would be drawn.[72]

The *circassienne*'s skirt was also worn *retroussée* (Figs. 107, 120); initially, it was also lightly swagged at the side fronts (Fig. 49).[73] The *Gallerie des modes* writes of its first *circassienne* that the "*robe* or coat [is] tucked up in front, on the sides and behind," and the same treatment can be seen in its second plate (Fig. 49); one further *circassienne*, from 1780, has its skirt "lightly *retroussé* in the front."[74] Otherwise, the skirt was lifted only at the two side backs in the same manner as the *polonaise*. It appears that while variations of the *polonaise* could have swags of different lengths, the *circassienne*'s were always equal: "The back of the gown is *retroussée* like the *polonaises*, except that the train [center swag] must be of equal length to the very extensive wings [side swags]."[75] The key feature distinguishing the *robe à la turque* from the *circassienne* was the *turque*'s long, trained overskirt.[76] All the *robes à la turque* depicted in fashion plates are shown with trains (Figs. 50, 84, 123, 127, 173). Nevertheless, the *turque* at the Nordiska Museet includes loops sewn to the train, allowing it to be worn *retroussée* (Fig. 108); marks in the train, mirrored on both sides, suggest

Fig. 99. The *polonaise* was worn *retroussée* in three swags; the attachment point was frequently accented with ribbon bows (here in yellow) or rosettes. Pierre Thomas Le Clerc (designer), J. Pelicier (engraver), Madame Le Beau (possibly), Esnauts & Rapilly (publisher), *Gallerie des modes et costumes français*, 1780, jj 196: Polonaise vue par derrière (. . .), 1780. (Engraving, 280 × 195 mm, Rijksmuseum, Amsterdam. Purchased with the support of the F. G. Waller-Fonds.)

DEFINING OTTOMAN INFLUENCE, 1760–90

(*This and facing page*) Figs. 100–102. This *polonaise* has short cords sewn to the gown's interior that attach to buttons on the outside back, just below the waist. *Robe à la polonaise,* after 1772. Wool, silk, Musée d'Histoire de Marseille, France. (First and second photos by author. Courtesy Musée d'Histoire de Marseille. Third photo by Claude Almodovar, © RMN-Grand Palais / Art Resource, NY.)

DEFINING OTTOMAN INFLUENCE, 1760-90

the skirt may have been attached to something (a cord or trimming?) at that point (Fig. 109), although the marks may have been made later if the gown was worn for fancy dress. Trains had long been fashionable in French dress—the manteau's was long, those of court dresses were even longer, while short trains were seen on the *robes volante* and *à la française*. Ottoman outerwear caftans were sometimes, but not always, trained, so whether the *turque*'s train referenced Turkish or French dress is unclear.

(*Right and below left*) Figs. 103–105. This *robe à la polonaise* is looped up via tapes that hook to thread loops. *Robe à la Polonaise,* Europe, 1775–80 (altered later). (Silk and linen, Colonial Williamsburg, Williamsburg, VA, 2006-42. The Colonial Williamsburg Foundation. Museum Purchase.)

(*Below right*) Fig. 106. Silk ribbons are sewn to the exterior and interior of the gown at the lower back, which presumably would tie to lift the skirt. *Polonaise dress,* 1775. (Linen, metal, muslin, silk, Killerton, Devon, UK, NT 1362010.)

94 DRESSING À LA TURQUE

The *polonaise*'s jacket versions, none of which feature the *retroussée* skirts so typical of the gown, prove more exited to contemporary definitions of the style.⁷⁷ The skirting of the *caraco à la polonaise* (Figs. 87, 165) usually ended at mid-hip, while the camisole (Fig. 110) ended at the high hip. The *caraco* appears to have been the more popular of the two based on fashion plate distribution. Many extant garments exist that may have been considered *caracos* or *camisoles à la polonaise*, but confusingly, the later pierrot jacket style (very popular ca. 1786–92) often featured

(*Left*) Fig. 107. The *circassienne* was worn *retroussée* like the *polonaise*. Early examples such as this tended to create a gauzy, airy effect through gathered, sheer materials. Desrais (artist), Pelissier (engraver), *Circassian Style Dress [Gallerie des modes et costumes français: dessinés d'après nature: gravés par les plus célèbres artistes en ce genre, no. 47G]*, 1775 [1778]. (Engraving [print], colored, 11.5 × 15.75 in., Scripps College, Ella Strong Denison Library, Macpherson Collection, Costume Plates of Myrtle Tyrrel Kirby, box 1. Courtesy Scripps College.)

(*Right and below*) Figs. 108 and 109. Ribbon loops sewn close to the hem, as well as symmetrical marks on the upper skirt, indicate this *robe à la turque* may have been worn looped up. *Klänning* [dress] *[robe à la turque]*. (Silk, Nordiska Museet, Stockholm, NMA.0052362. Courtesy Nordiska Museet. Author photos.)

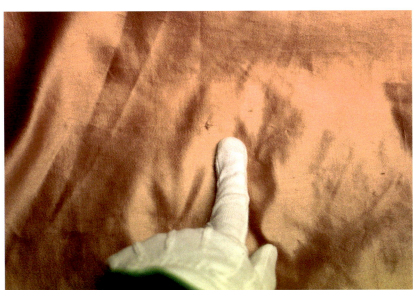

(*Left*) Fig. 110. The *camisole à la polonaise* had slightly shorter skirtings than the *caraco*. Claude Louis Desrais (designer), Jean Joseph Pelissier (engraver), Esnauts & Rapilly (publisher), *Gallerie des modes et costumes français, 1780, ee 172 (bis): Camisolle à la Polonoise (. . .).* (Engraving on paper, 282 × 193 mm, Rijksmuseum, Amsterdam. Purchased with the support of the F. G. Waller-Fonds.)

(*Center*) Fig. 111. The pierrot featured a similar cut but was more likely to fit tightly to the torso and feature long sleeves than the *caraco à la polonaise*. A. B. Duhamel (print maker), after drawing by Pierre Thomas Le Clerc, Buisson (publisher), *Cabinet des modes ou les modes nouvelles, 3e cahier, 15 décembre 1785, pl. I.* (Engraving on paper, 199 × 122 mm, Rijksmuseum, Amsterdam. Purchased with the support of the F. G. Waller-Fonds.)

(*Right*) Fig. 112. The *polonaise longue* was worn trained. This example appears to have a waist tuck along the sides, incorporating the influence of the *robe à l'anglaise;* the plate indicates that it is "made *à l'Anglaise.*" "Jeune elégante vétue d'une polonoise longue détroussée" [Young elegant woman dressed in a *Polonaise longue détroussée*], Claude-Louis Desrais et al., *Collection d'habillements modernes et galants: avec les habillements des princes et seigneur [Gallerie des modes],* 29 (Paris: André Basset, 1775–81). (Muzeum Narodowe, Warsaw.)

a strongly cutaway front and multiple small pleats at the side and back (Fig. 111). Based on the period in which it was fashionable, the pierrot would more likely feature a tight bodice fit with sewn-in stomacher and long sleeves, while the *caraco* or *camisole à la polonaise* would fit more loosely and have shorter sleeves.[78] One *caraco* at the Palais Galliera is certainly a *polonaise* given its loose-fitting front (Figs. 89, 90, 91, 92). The *robe à la polonaise* had many individual variations; one was the *polonaise longue,* with skirt worn trained (*détroussée*—"to detach that which was bundled, & let it hang down").[79] It was illustrated twice in the *Gallerie des modes,* but, unfortunately, no full description survives. One plate is front-facing and shows a gown like other *robes à la polonaise,* with cutaway front and a long skirt glimpsed in back.[80] Another is a back view and described as a "*Polonoise longue détroussée* made *à l'Anglaise* bordered by a Trimming in *Platitude* of another fabric. Sleeves *à la Circassienne*" (Fig. 112). This variant is reinforced by two extant examples, including the gown at the Musée Toile de Jouy, which shows no evidence of having been worn looped up (Figs. 113, 114).[81] Furthermore, its petticoat is only partially trimmed at the very center back, indicating that it was meant to be hidden from view by the long train (Fig. 63). The *circassienne* was more reliably worn *retroussée.* During its height of popularity (1778–82), only one fashion plate shows a *circassienne* with skirt worn down: the "*Circassienne Française,* so called because it is trained & floats like the *Robes Françaises.*"[82] A few jacket versions of the *circassienne* and *turque* existed, but not nearly as many as the *polonaise.*

Early *robes à la polonaises* were made with the gown's skirts ending just below the knees, a shorter length than most other styles. The *Encyclopédie méthodique* declared the *robe à la polonaise* should "only go down to about six inches above the petticoat's hem."[83] Several plates in the *Gallerie des modes* illustrate this length, including the "young *Bourgeois. . . .* in a morning *polonaise,* or *demi-polonaise,* composed of two wings and a train" as well as the "*Circassienne à l'Enfant* [child]."[84] These plates are reinforced by multiple artworks, like Carmontelle's portrait of Mademoiselle de Flinville in which she wears a knee-length *polonaise* gown.[85] Several extant *robes à la polonaise* survive in this shorter length, including the robe at Killerton (Figs. 58, 106).[86] The Palazzo Mocenigo *polonaise* (Figs. 70, 71, 72, 73) is another such example, although given that it does not show evidence of whether its skirts were looped up, it may have been considered a *caraco*. The ensemble is made of white cotton quilted into a diamond pattern with floral patterning at the edges—clearly the quilting was made to measure, demonstrating the length was a conscious choice. The skirts of the *polonaise* and *circassienne* were generally made with rounded front hem corners (Figs. 52, 58, 67, 71, 73, 78, 120, 121), unlike the squared shape seen on most other styles (Figs. 27, 34, 36, 38, 41, 51, 55, 81, 83, 86).[87] All three (*polonaise, circassienne,* and *turque*) were worn over the same petticoat or underskirt (*jupon*) worn with most other gowns and jackets of the period. However, the *polonaise*'s petticoat was often ankle length (Figs. 48, 110, 162), which was a few inches shorter than the traditional floor-length seen on most other styles.[88]

Figs. 113 and 114. This *polonaise longue* has been restored—the bodice and skirt had completely detached from each other (Patricia Dal-Prà, "Rapport d'intervention de restauration sur la robe à la turque appartenant au musée de la Toile de Jouy" [Musée de la Toile de Jouy, 2015]). It follows the usual cut of the *polonaise, turque,* and *circassienne,* and was clearly meant to be worn trained. *Robe à la Turque [polonaise longue], manteau de robe, corsage et jupon ayant appartenu à Anne-Élisabeth Oberkampf* (gown, bodice and petticoat belonging to Anne-Élisabeth Oberkampf), ca. 1785. Cream silk pékin, Musée de la Toile de Jouy, Jouy-en-Josas, France, inv. 000.4.6. (Courtesy Musée de la Toile de Jouy. Second photo by author.)

DEFINING OTTOMAN INFLUENCE, 1760–90 97

SLEEVES

The *polonaise* and *circassienne* each brought with them new trends in sleeves. The *robes volante* and *à la française* were worn with sleeves ending just above or at the elbow; from the 1720s they were trimmed with wide, pleated cuffs (Figs. 33, 35), then from the 1740s replaced by triple flounces called *engageantes* (Figs. 36, 37, 41, 42). By contrast, the *polonaise* was frequently worn with a sleeve ending just *past* the elbow, usually with a small dart or tuck to fit the elbow curve, and trimmed with a gathered, puffed cuff called *sabot* (Figs. 15, 48, 67, 87, 88, 99, 115, 121, 162, 165, 172) because the curve at the elbow resembled the wooden clogs (*sabots*) of peasants.[89] Meanwhile, an innovation key to the *circassienne* and *turque* was short, funnel-shaped oversleeves matching the robe, with longer undersleeves in the same fabric as the underbodice or stomacher and petticoat (Figs. 50, 84, 120, 123, 127, 173, 174).[90] Describing a *circassienne*, the *Gallerie des modes* wrote, "The sleeves very short, cut in cannon's mouth [shape], out of which appear to come the sleeves of the *soubreveste*."[91] Ottoman ensembles frequently featured short-sleeved outer caftans worn over longer-sleeved garments (Figs. 20, 21, 47, 51, 119), or outer layers with slashed sleeves falling back to display underlayers (Fig. 6). Thus, the purposefully designed display of over- and undersleeves in the *circassienne* and *turque* represents further incorporation of the layering so typical of Turkish dress, while the oversleeve length mimics that frequently seen on Ottoman outerwear.[92]

The first few *circassiennes* in fashion magazines have undersleeves made of sheer, puffed fabric extending just past the elbow (Figs. 49, 107). Meanwhile, the *turque*'s undersleeve was initially often wrist length (Fig. 123) and fitted to the arm. Sleeve styles were clearly interchangeable among dresses, and updating sleeves was one way to bring older gowns into current fashion. In the *Gallerie des modes*, the *polonaise*'s *sabot* cuff is worn with multiple styles, including the *caraco à la française, robe à la circassienne, robe à la Versaillaise, robe à l'anglaise, robe à la française*, a court gown called the *robe à la Lenoncourt*, and a *habit de bal*. However, *polonaises* were sometimes shown in fashion plates with longer, three-quarter cuffed sleeves; long sleeves called *amadis* (Fig. 110); just-past-the-elbow sleeves turned up *à la paysanne;* and sleeves *à la circassienne*, looped up like the skirts of the *robe à la circassienne* or the sleeves of the seventeenth-century *sultane*, having "tassels that hold up the sleeves of the robe, and leave uncovered second [that is, under] sleeves adorned with two rows of mesh as cuffs."[93] Similarly, the *circassienne* was sometimes illustrated with the long sleeves typical of the *turque* (Fig. 120), and from about 1786 onwards, the *turque* revived the just-past-the-elbow undersleeves previously characteristic of the *polonaise* (Figs. 50, 84, 127).

Fig. 115. This *sabot* cuff is made from the same fabric as the gown. The sleeve is cut to fit around the elbow bend. *Robe à la polonaise,* ca. 1778. Silk and linen, Palais Galliera, musée de la Mode de la Ville de Paris, Paris, 62-108-14. (Courtesy Palais Galliera, musée de la Mode de la Ville de Paris. Author photo.)

ORIGINS OF THE ROBES À LA POLONAISE, CIRCASSIENNE, AND TURQUE

The *polonaise*'s origins, the first of these late-eighteenth-century Turkish-inspired styles to appear in primary sources and thus likely the model on which the *circassienne* and *turque* developed, are unclear. Some scholars have repeated François Boucher's suggestion that the overskirt's three swags relate to the first partition of Poland between Russia, Austria, and Prussia in 1772.[94] However, Boucher's suggestion is simply that; he writes, "It seems that this gown *à la polonaise* was never worn in Poland, and in view of the eighteenth-century taste for symbolic translation, we may well *wonder* if the three swags represented the partition of Poland, which was a live issue in France in 1772; however *there are no texts to confirm this.*"[95] Certainly, Poland's political issues appeared frequently in French sources in the 1760s and 1770s, but thus far no documentation has suggested any such direct connection. Further complicating the issue is the dating. The first partition of Poland occurred in 1772, but contemporary sources date the *robe à la polonaise* to 1767, if not before.[96] As early as 1763, the *Gazette du commerce* announced, "In new fashions, *polonoises*, trimmings of *robes à la grecque* [Greek], and similar ensembles," although whether this refers to the robe, an earlier outerwear garment, or a trim is unclear.[97] The style must have emerged at a minimum by 1767 because on January 1 of the following year, a London newspaper carried the following advertisement in both English and French:

> MESDEMOISELLES GIGOT and D'AVION, who have for several Years worked with the Mantua makers of the King's Household in France, and for the greatest Part of the Nobility in Paris, are just arrived in this Metropolis, and offer their Service to the Ladies, being able to furnish them with every thing in the newest Fashion, either in Robe de Cour, en Deshabille, a la Reine, *a la Polonoise,* or a la Pompadour.[98]

Given the prominence of these seamstresses' French fashion knowledge, as well as the French terminology used for the gown, the style likely came to England (where it was generally called *polonese*, an anglicized spelling of the French) from France.[99] Only a week later, the same London newspaper published an article complaining that French dress, including the "deshabillie a la Polonoise," was too informal for England.[100]

The *polonaise* was firmly established in France by 1768.[101] In April of that year, the *Courrier de la mode* reported that it was part of a larger trend for informality in fashion:

For their part women have replaced large *paniers* [hoops] with simple *coudes* ["elbows," a smaller hoop], have renounced multiple flounces, the *robe* is tightened & trimmed with facings that allow the elegance of their figure to be seen; all the ornaments that are too embarrassing are removed, & several even have adopted the *négligé Polonois*, more noble & more gracious than the *Hollandoise* [Dutch] or the *Tronchine*.[102]

Jeanne Bécu, Comtesse du Barry (1743–93), purchased fabric for a "*robbe à la poloinoise* [*sic*]" in November 1769.[103] Some of the earliest artworks to feature the style are by French painters Carmontelle (*Madame de Sainte-Amarante*, ca. 1770; *Madame du Dreneuc*, 1771; and *Mesdames les comtesse de Fitz-James et du Nolestin*, 1771) and Vigée-Le Brun (*Study of a Woman*, ca. 1772).[104]

Many possible inspirations—but, unfortunately, no direct sources—exist for the *polonaise*. Polish-influenced garments do appear in France in earlier periods, but these were usually outerwear and/or involved fur trimming.[105] Turnau proves the *robe à la polonaise* did not originate in Poland, although it was eventually adopted there as noble and bourgeois women generally followed French fashion.[106] It seems most likely that the *polonaise* was modeled after the *kontusz*, the Ottoman-influenced caftan worn by Polish noblemen (Figs. 21, 22), although it was probably presented to the French via theater, art, costume albums, and/or military uniforms.[107] Inspiration for the French gown may have come generally from interest in Polish dress as well as costumes worn in theater, like Boquet's undated designs (Fig. 10).[108] More specifically, Madame Geoffrin, Parisian *salonnière*, sparked interest in that country when she visited Warsaw in 1766; she likely described Polish dress in her letters, which were widely read among Parisian intellectuals, and perhaps even brought home some examples.

Although tucked-up skirtings were a feature of Ottoman dress, generally these were lifted at the center-front opening; one or both front hem corners would then be tucked into the sash (Figs. 19, 21, 47).[109] This Ottoman-style technique was arguably used on the seventeenth-century manteau gown, but the side-back *retroussée* seen on the *polonaise* and *circassienne* appears to be specific to Western Europe. The technique could have various origins. The *Gallerie*'s first *circassienne* description states this overskirt style can be called "*à la musulmane*," so it could indeed be a reference to the tucked-up caftans seen in Ottoman dress, even if those created a different effect.[110] Ribeiro argues that the practice

Fig. 116. The "*lit à la polonaise*" featured swagged draperies. *Bed (Lit à la Polonaise),* French, about 1775–80. (Gessoed, gilded, and painted walnut; gilded iron; modern silk upholstery and passementerie; ostrich feathers, 118⅞ × 70½ × 89 in., Getty Museum, Los Angeles.)

references Rubens's seventeenth-century paintings of his wife, Helene Fourment, noting the popularity of English masquerade costumes based on her ensemble, but the same cannot be said of France, where the style most likely originated.[111] More convincing is Jean-François Solnon's argument that fashionable Turkish-inspired beds, like the *lits à la polonaise* (Fig. 116) and *à la turque*, had tied-back draperies creating swags reminiscent of Ottoman tents (Fig. 117); this effect could have been transferred to clothing (the bed predates the gown).[112] Possible native French origins also exist. Country and working women frequently tucked up their skirts for practicality's sake, a technique seen in numerous contemporary images. Higher up the class spectrum, women sometimes wore the *robe à la française* with the train *retroussée dans les poches* (tucked up into the pockets), whereby the front corners of the skirt hem were pulled through the pocket slits, resulting in a swagged overskirt (Fig. 118).[113]

The *robe à la circassienne* first appeared in the *Gallerie des modes* in 1778, although it was listed in the wardrobe inventories of the Comtesse d'Artois beginning in 1776 and advertised by a Bordeaux dressmaker the following year.[114] Circassia, a region under Ottoman control, interested Western Europeans because of the high status of Circassian slaves in Ottoman harems; this was in part because the Circassians were Christian and, therefore, enslaveable according to Islamic law.[115] The French translated this into the idea that Circassian women were more desirable because of their beauty, which they ascribed to their conception of Circassians as racially white.[116] Circassians do not figure much in costume albums by name, although many images of Ottoman wives and concubines are probably meant to depict them. Nonetheless, their dress was like that of Turkey, and since Circassia was under Ottoman control in the eighteenth century, the reference is clear (Fig. 119).[117] The *robe à la turque* (referring to

Fig. 117. Ottoman tents were usually depicted with swagged fabric. This was the "*tente Tartare*" (a Russian, and therefore Eastern, reference) at the Parc Monceau in Paris, where there were also "Turkish tents"; camel rides nearby reinforced the Ottoman theme. Louis de Carmontelle (designer), Jean Charles Delafosse (engraver), *Jardin de Monceau* (detail), 1779. (Engraving, 22 7/16 × 16 1/8 in., the Metropolitan Museum of Art, New York. Harris Brisbane Dick Fund, 1942.)

(*Above*) Fig. 118. The *robe à la française* could be worn with skirts pulled through its pocket slits, creating a swagged effect in back. Antoine Louis Romanet after Sigmund Freudenberger, *Le lever* [The waking], *History of Manners and Customs of the French* (detail), 1774. (Etching and engraving, National Gallery of Art, Washington, DC. Rosenwald Collection.)

(*Right*) Fig. 119. A woman in Circassian dress, which looks very similar to that of Turkish women. Jacques Grasset de Saint-Saveur, Labrousse, *Costumes de différents pays* (Costumes of Different Countries), "Circassienne," ca. 1797. (Print, hand-tinted engraving on paper, 10½ × 7⅞ in., Los Angeles County Museum of Art.)

Turkey, the Empire's heartland) first appeared in the *Gallerie des modes* in 1779, but it too was advertised by the same Bordeaux *couturière* two years earlier.[118]

The *robes à la polonaise*, *circassienne*, and *turque* were derived in part from Ottoman models and represented cross-cultural hybrids that mixed Western and Eastern dressmaking practices, thus continuing the processes established in the late seventeenth and early eighteenth centuries. Despite having been too often conflated with the English-inspired *robe à l'anglaise* by scholars, numerous details demonstrate their connection to Turkish dress. These styles came into fashion during a period in which French women's silhouettes were becoming more naturalistic, which may be a result of further incorporation of Ottoman aesthetics.

UNDERPINNINGS

While Turkish approaches can be seen in the cut and styling of women's fashionable gowns and jackets, it also may have affected the garments worn underneath. The unstructured approach of Ottoman clothing coincided with and likely encouraged a move toward softer, more natural body shapes for women. Despite the incorporation of more relaxed dress styles over the course of the late seventeenth through the mid-eighteenth century, Anne-Cécile Moheng argues that women's undergarments nonetheless continued to reconfigure the body as dresses like the *robe à la française* required stays and hoops to drape correctly; she writes, "Whalebone stays and panniers [hoops] were therefore a means of effacing a woman's natural shape and remolding it into a fashionable body entirely distinct from natural forms and anatomical curves."[119] However, as the *robe à la polonaise* entered fashion, hoops were becoming smaller and increasingly replaced by smaller pads, trends that only continued as new Turkish-inspired gowns entered fashion. Meanwhile, shifts in corsetry meant that women now had the option to wear stays that were more lightly boned than previously. These changes resulted in comparatively more naturalistic silhouettes both above and below the waist and may be a result of the influence of Ottoman aesthetics.

HOOPS

Hoops (*paniers*) rose to popularity in French fashion in the sixteenth century. Although they did not feature much in the seventeenth century, they were reintroduced around 1718. Initially rounded, in the 1740s *paniers* flattened in front and back to create the side-focused silhouette that predominated throughout the eighteenth century. *Paniers* could be wider or narrower depending on the current fashion or an occasion's formality, with court hoops generally being the widest. Women could also add crescent-shaped stuffed pads to their hips, but at the higher-class levels these were probably an addition to a *panier* rather than a substitute.[120]

The resurgence of Ottoman-inspired fashions in the 1760s and 1770s occurred as France was shifting toward increased informality and comfort in dress, and this extended to developments in underpinnings. As the *polonaise* came into style, so too did a smaller, rounder skirt silhouette.[121] By the early 1770s, most informal dresses and jackets were worn with narrower hoops than those previously fashionable; the *Encyclopédie méthodique* declared these were now more usually called *bouffantes* (puffings). Alternatively, the *Encyclopédie* explained, women could wear their gowns over the new pads called *culs* or *cus* (bums or rumps), which emphasized the hips and rear, or rear only, and were "nothing more than a doubled fabric lined with horsehair between its layers ... gathered at the waist, so that it puffs in back, & lifts the dress."[122] *Bouffantes* and *culs* may have been worn together, and garments existed combining features of both, like the padded and caned skirt supports in the collections of the Amsterdam Museum and Nordiska Museet.[123] Hoops may also have become rounded in the back, something suggested by the description of a *robe à la circassienne* in the *Gallerie des modes,* which was worn over a "large, very rounded *bouffante*" (Fig. 120).[124]

The *polonaise* and *circassienne* were generally worn with this smaller, rounder skirt silhouette, probably in part because skirts worn *retroussée* were shown to better advantage over rear, or rear and hip, fullness. The *Gallerie des modes* announced,

> Women not only have *bouffantes* under their Dresses, to seem bigger, but they have attached, in back, cushions, to give more roundness to the Dress, & feature the [*Polonaise en*] *Triton*'s curved train [Fig. 121]. This fashion is resurrected [from previous eras] in the *Polonaises*, & other *Robes retroussées*. It was to give grace to the looped-up skirts, to make

(*Left*) Fig. 120. This *circassienne* is described as worn over "a large, very rounded" *bouffante.* Claude-Louis Desrais or Desray (designer), Etienne Claude Voysard (engraver), Esnauts et Rapilly (publisher), *Gallerie des modes et costumes français. 13e. cahier des costumes français, 7e suite d'habillemens à la mode. N.78 "Jeune dame en circassienne de gaze d'Italie . . . ,"* ca. 1775 [1778]. (Colored engraving, Palais Galliera, musée de la Mode de la Ville de Paris.)

(*Right*) Fig. 121. The description implies this woman wears a *cul* (rump) under her *polonaise.* Pierre Thomas Le Clerc (designer), Charles Emmanuel Patas (engraver), Esnauts & Rapilly (publisher), *Gallerie des modes et costumes français, 1780, gg 181: Robe à la polonois (. . .),* 1782. (Engraving, 281 × 194 mm, Rijksmuseum, Amsterdam. Purchased with the support of the F. G. Waller-Fonds.)

draperies form pleasantly; & it did not find any better expedient, than to create a curved contraption, on which can feature, in back, the fabrics of which these *Robes* are composed."[125]

Alternatively, Turkish-inspired styles could also be worn over small *paniers* for more formal occasions. In the 1771 wedding trousseau of the Comtesse de Provence, some of her *robes à la polonaise* are listed as "with *panier*" or "with *consideration*" (another form of small hoop), while others are "without *paniers*."[126] In 1779, her sister-in-law, the Comtesse d'Artois, purchased both "a *bouffante* for *robe a lá* [sic] *polonese*" and "a *panier* for *robe a la polonaise*."[127]

Due to perspective, it can be difficult to determine exactly what shape is worn underneath the gowns and jackets seen in fashion plates, but most *polonaises* and *circassiennes* appear to be worn with hip and rear emphasis. A few gowns look wide enough at the hips to have hoops underneath, but all showing the rear have similar amounts of fullness, suggesting either these were worn over large rumps, rumps and hoops worn simultaneously, or a support merging both elements. Unfortunately, the skirt support is only occasionally specified, like the "young and plump lady" in the *Gallerie* who was "dressed in a *Polonaise* with blossoming train or a round rump."[128] Most artworks depicting the *polonaise* or *circassienne* demonstrate a similar range of silhouettes, although a few also illustrate these gowns worn over full, wide *paniers* for formal occasions, such as *La Reine annonçant à Mme de Bellegarde* (Fig. 122).

The *robe à la turque* appears to have been more frequently worn over hoops. Its first introduction in the *Gallerie des modes* helpfully includes views of the front and back (Fig. 123), and the silhouette is wide over the hips but relatively flat in back, indicating it is worn over a hoop. This idea is supported by a 1784 observer who recorded Queen Marie-Antoinette wearing a *robe à la turque* over "slightly exaggerated

Fig. 122. Queen Marie-Antoinette (leaning forward, *right*) and her ladies wear *polonaises* over medium-sized hoops. Charles Henri Desfossés (designer), Antoine Jean Duclos (engraver), Basan et Poignant (publisher), *Marie Antoinette: The Queen of Fashion: Marie Antoinette Visiting Mme Bellegarde / La Reine annonçant à Mme de Bellegarde, des juges, et la liberté de son mari; en mai 1777* (detail), 1779. (Etching and engraving, 375 × 485 mm, Rijksmuseum, Amsterdam.)

Fig. 123. This *robe à la turque* appears to be worn over hoops. "Cette robe dite [This gown called] à la turque" [1780], *Gallerie des modes et costumes française dessinés d'après nature graves par les plus célèbres artistes en ce genre* (Esnauts & Rapilly: Paris, 1778–88), 153. (Muzeum Narodowe, Warsaw.)

paniers."[129] By the mid-1780s, hoops were going out of fashion except for the most formal court ceremonies. Although the *Cabinet des modes* featured a *robe à la turque* over a hoop for formal dress in January 1786 (Fig. 50), it followed a few months later with another worn with a rump, as "Ladies do not wear the large Hoops which give them an immense width, and the Gowns with trains which trail one *aune* on the ground . . . In the grandest Full Dress, the Clothing is simplified."[130]

The *lévite* extended ideas of soft Ottoman dress further than any other style of its era. At least in its initial iteration, the gown appears to have been worn over little, if any, skirt supports. The first three examples in the *Gallerie des modes* (1779) do not show much lift at the hips or rear, suggesting nothing more than one or more petticoats were worn underneath (Fig. 135). In the description accompanying one of these, the *Gallerie* declared, "The first *Levites;* one wore them first plain, without *paniers,* or rumps."[131] Interestingly, the *Encyclopédie méthodique*'s entry on *paniers* describes a simple, unstructured horsehair half-skirt worn under the *lévite:* "The *bouffantes* for *lévite* are not quilted, but they are loosely stitched & lined in more horsehair than the *quilted bouffantes;* they are without a cane or frame, are worn only one & a quarter *aune* [wide?], & tighten in such a manner that they only cover the back & sides, without covering the front at all; this sort of *bouffante* is pleated like a petticoat, & cut about half an *aune* long." A 1784 English doll dressed in a *lévite* (Figs. 139, 140, 141) wears a three-quarter-length quilted petticoat underneath that is reminiscent of the *Encyclopédie*'s *bouffante,* although it does cover the front as well.[132] The doll is too delicate to be undressed, so it is unclear whether it is wearing any pads, but it is definitely not wearing hoops. Subsequent fashion plates show more shaping at the hips and rear, so much so that plates from 1780 and 1782 appear to feature small hoops (Figs. 136, 153).[133] Once again, the early *lévite*'s (comparatively) natural silhouette aligns with Ottoman dress silhouettes, while the later addition of hoops demonstrates an increasingly French approach.

Extant gowns show a similar mixture of silhouettes, although it can be difficult to be certain without measuring the petticoat, as museums sometimes display gowns over inappropriate supports and original petticoats are frequently missing. Furthermore, the many varieties of skirt support in this era complicates matters. Of those garments that have been measured, the *robe à la polonaise* at the Musée d'Histoire de Marseille (Fig. 79) appears to have been cut to fit over side-focused hoops. Meanwhile, the *polonaise* ensembles at the Palazzo Mocenigo (Fig. 74) and Musée de la Toile de Jouy (Fig. 63) both are better suited to a support with both hip and rear emphasis. The curved front angle of the skirt opening of the *robe à la turque* at the Nordiska Museet suits a hoop with side emphasis, but its train could fit over either a flat hoop in back or something with rear shaping as well (Figs. 81, 82, 83).[134] Finally, the *turque* at the Philadelphia Museum of Art (Figs. 85, 86) appears to have been designed to be worn over a rear-focused support, probably a *cul*.[135]

STAYS

The trend toward increased informality and comfort in dress affected corsetry as well. Since the mid-sixteenth century, French women had shaped and supported their bust and torso with heavily boned and stiffened bodices, or by wearing their gowns and jackets over separate stays. In the eighteenth century, it was typical to wear a gown or jacket, frequently in silk, cotton, or linen and lined with linen, over boned stays called *corps de baleine* (Figs. 124, 125), except for court gowns, in which the bodice itself was boned and stiffened. Sometimes the dress or jacket would include a few bones, but this was mostly to support the garment. However, in the last few decades of the century, lighter and slightly more curved stays came

Figs. 124 and 125. A fully boned *Corps à baleines,* 1725–75. (Silk taffeta, Palais Galliera, musée de la Mode de la Ville de Paris, 1920.1.1202.)

DEFINING OTTOMAN INFLUENCE, 1760–90

(*Right*) Fig. 126. These lightly boned stays are what the French would call *corset. Stays,* 1780s. Silk, Victoria & Albert Museum, London, T.188–961. (Courtesy of Victoria and Albert Museum, London.)

(*Below*) Fig. 127. The white underbodice is described as "busked." Buisson (publisher), *Magasin des modes nouvelles, françaises et anglaises, décrites d'une manière claire & precise, & represèntées par des planches en taille-douce, enluminées,* January 20, 1788, pl. 1 (detail). (Bibliothèque nationale de France, Paris.)

108   DRESSING À LA TURQUE

into fashion (Fig. 126).[136] According to the *Gallerie des modes,* "The *corset* is also an interior garment; it replaces the *corps de baleine,* and has the same usage; but it is more flexible: the two busks are the only whalebone with which it is trimmed."[137]

Most *robes à la polonaise, turque,* and *circassienne* were worn with stomachers or separate underbodices, implying a further *corps de baleine* or corset was worn underneath. However, a few sources specifically describe "busked" (referring to the wide piece of baleen or wood supporting the center front of a boned bodice or stays) corsets as underbodices, suggesting that here the underbodice may have been doing the work of the stays. The *Encyclopédie méthodique* writes the *robe à la turque* was worn with "a cut *pièce* [*d'estomac*], busked like the *corps* [*de baleine*] and of the same fabric as the petticoat . . . [which] closes with little oval steel buckles laid in a triangular pattern" (1785); while the *Magasin des modes* explains the visible white satin corset worn under a *robe à la turque* in 1788 is "busked" (Fig.

(*Left*) Fig. 128. Paintings depicting the *lévite* sometimes exhibit a natural bust curve. Marie-Victoire Lemoine, *Portrait de* [of] *Marie-Thérèse-Louise de Savoie-Carignan, princesse de Lamballe,* 1779 (oil on canvas). (Private collection, 61 × 49.5 cm. Photo © Christie's Images / Bridgeman Images.)

(*Right*) Fig. 129. Other illustrations of the *lévite* show a more typically smooth, cone-shaped torso. Alexander Roslin, *Marie Jeanne Puissant (1745–1828),* 1781. (Painting, oil on canvas, 74 × 59 cm, Rijksmuseum Twenthe, Enschede, Netherlands.)

DEFINING OTTOMAN INFLUENCE, 1760–90   109

127).[138] The Comtesse d'Artois's wardrobe accounts include several *robes à la circassienne* with boned corsets, while the Princesse de Conti ordered boned corsets to wear with *lévites,* among other dresses.[139]

Even more intriguing is the *lévite,* which is occasionally depicted in artwork with the kind of naturally curved bust not seen with most other styles, suggesting this gown may have been sometimes worn over lightly boned, or even unboned, corsets.[140] Ottoman women did not wear boned or stiffened garments (Figs. 5, 6, 20, 47, 119, 138). Intriguingly, several portraits in which the sitter is clearly wearing the *lévite*—including Lemoine's *Portrait de Marie-Thérèse-Louise de Savoie-Carignan, princesse de Lamballe* (1779, Fig. 128); Trinquesse's *Portrait of a Lady* (1780); Labille-Guiard's *Femme au Ruban Bleu* (1782) and *Portrait of a Lady* (1786); and Guttenbrun's *Ritratto di Giuseppina di Lorena-Armagnac* (1784–86)—show a definite bust curve not usually seen in French dress that suggests an Ottoman influence.[141] However, images exist in which women are definitely wearing fully boned stays under their *lévites,* like Roslin's portrait of Marie Jeanne Puissant (1781, Fig. 129) or Wille's *The Double Reward of the Merit* (1781).[142]

Women's garments considered "French" were in truth hybrid creations that drew on Western and Eastern (particularly Ottoman) dress traditions. *Robes à la polonaise, circassienne,* and *turque* were designed after Turkish and Eastern European garments and incorporated real references to the clothing of these cultures through characteristics such as designed layering and one-piece cuts. These styles demonstrate the incorporation of Turkish aesthetics into French fashion, which extended to new ideas about soft, comfortable silhouettes. This Ottoman influence was not limited to construction, but also included nomenclature, and the names given to these fashions demonstrate how fundamental national and cultural identity was to eighteenth-century French culture. Moreover, one particular example of Turkish-inspired fashions, the *lévite* gown, demonstrates just how fluid these concepts were becoming.

Fashion and National Identity

In an era when global connections were rapidly increasing, issues of national and cultural identity were central to French society. The vocabulary used in eighteenth-century French fashion provides clues to understanding these ideas. The last three decades of the century saw a massive rise in the use of specific name designations for clothing styles, in part precipitated by the invention of the fashion press, which illustrated and identified styles and circulated them widely.[1] An analysis of style nomenclature in eighteenth-century French fashion demonstrates its importance in and of itself, given trends in name construction and the references contained therein. Furthermore, most popular women's dress and jacket styles of this era were cultural hybrids, and, critically, were often further mixed and adapted. None provides a better example than the *lévite* gown, which began as a fusion between French and Ottoman dress, then merged with other popular styles with their own national references, including the English-inspired *robe à l'anglaise* and redingote, as well as the Caribbean-derived *chemise à la reine*. The *lévite*'s metamorphoses make it an excellent lens through which to examine how the French mixed and adapted various styles, as well as how they used dress to experiment with and redefine national and cultural identity in the late eighteenth century.

The Frenchman [who is] in the middle of his country, believes he is in distant countries; he assumes the French . . . are the Chinese . . . or rather he is not certain of which nation, nor which costume he sees; he asks: "Is it a *Turque* . . . a *Polonaise* . . . an *Anglaise*?" . . . It is not possible to decide, to recognize the Frenchwomen [as being French] in the center of Paris in this dress & in these accessories.

—Ch Remi, *Mon oisiveté*

NAMING CONVENTIONS

In 1781, a Poitiers dressmaker advertised that she made "*robes à la Polonoise, à la Lévite,* & other *foreign clothing, of all kinds, in the latest taste.*"[2] Despite her description, these "Polish" and "Levite" gowns were not literal recreations of the garments worn in other countries but French styles having strong global influences and representing hybrid East/West approaches to dress. In this era, style variations frequently were given specific names. Instead of generic dresses or suits, women wore *robes à la turque* and hats *à la Saint-Domingue,* while men wore jackets *à la polonaise* and overcoats called *redingotes* after the English riding coat.

Roland Barthes articulates how one garment can exist in multiple realities: the physical garment, the photographed or drawn image of the same garment ("image-clothing"), as well as its written description, what he calls the "written-garment."[3] Barthes lays out a detailed schema for understanding the language of dress, arguing, "The importance of the written garment confirms the fact that specific language-functions exist which the image... could not possibly assume."[4] Although Margaret M. Bryant writes about contemporary American fashion, her explanation that style names "fulfill a real need for accurate and precise description" holds true for the eighteenth century as well.[5] Daniel Miller argues the material culture field has demonstrated that taxonomies are important "precisely because being disregarded as trivial, they were often a key unchallenged mechanism for social reproduction and ideological dominance."[6] In this vein, some scholars have dismissed the denominations used in late-eighteenth-century French fashion, arguing that any relationship between the name and the referent was "only symbolic," or "there are simply too many of them to catalogue."[7] Anna König demonstrates the need for scholarly analysis of style naming, arguing that in the twentieth century,

While visuals, primarily in the form of photographs, dominate the presentation and representation of fashion in magazines and newspapers, text has a critical mediating role to play... Text contributes to an understanding of fashion by assigning descriptive or interpretive meanings to the objects and images presented on fashion pages, thereby mediating a cultural understanding of the phenomenon.[8]

Throughout French history, style variations often received specific designations distinguishing them from other iterations of the same garment, such as the gowns called manteau, *robe volante, robe à la polonaise,* etc. These appellations served as a shorthand—instead of having to use all the words, "a loose fitting, open-front dress with large pleats in front and back that extend from shoulder to hem," one could simply say "*robe volante*" or another term referring to this style. Fashion magazines and auxiliary sources provide multiple clues to defining and understanding the connections between these names and their corresponding garments.

In the seventeenth century, the dominant dress style was the robe or gown. The manteau and succeeding gowns were evidently different enough from this robe to require new names.[9] Significantly, the construction of these designations changed over the course of the eighteenth century: from *robe+* or *robe de+* to *robe à la+*. *Robe+* was used in cases like *robe volante* or *robe battante* to refer to descriptive aspects of the gown's appearance: the flying dress or swinging dress; while *robe de+* was used in cases like *robe de cour,* meaning a dress worn at court (robe of the court or court robe).[10] This construction changed in the middle of the century to *robe à la,* a phrase corresponding in this period to *à la mode de,* meaning *in the manner of.*[11] Contemporary dictionaries clarify this new construction. The *Dictionaire critique de la langue française* (1787) defined "*à la française*" as "in the manner of the French," giving the example of being "dressed *à la française*."[12] It further explained that references such as "*bonnet à la turque;* drawing *à la chinoise;* hairstyle *à l'antique*" meant "following the model or the resemblance."[13] A century earlier, the *Dictionnaire de l'Académie française* (1694) declared, "One also says, *Se vestir*, to mean, To be dressed in a certain manner. These people are dressed *à la Françoise, à la Turque*" (in the French style, in the Turkish style).[14]

Most of the fashions using the newer construction of *robe à la+*, which was common from at least the 1760s through the 1780s, referred primarily to geography and/or culture. First, that the *robe à la française* needed specifying is significant: a gown "in the French style" seems redundant because it should be self-evident that gowns worn in France were in the French style. However, contrasting the *robe à la française* with other *robe à la+* styles demonstrates why the French style needed specification, given that gowns existed in the Polish, English, Turkish, etc., styles. Three of the four fashions studied here follow this construction: *robe à la polonaise, robe à la circassienne, robe à la turque*. Over time, this construction would become increasingly abbreviated, with the *polonaise* and *circassienne* frequently referred to in that shorthand, although the *robe à la turque* was almost always referred to in its full form (or occasionally shortened to *robe turque*). At first glance, the *lévite* does not appear to follow this construction, but the *Gallerie des modes* does call it a *robe à la lévite* several times in its introductory year, shifting thereafter to simply *lévite* or occasionally *robe en lévite*.

When did this shift to *robe à la* [geography/culture] happen? Precision is difficult before the advent of fashion magazines. So far, the earliest documented uses of this construction date to the seventeenth century, but those writers were describing a particular country or culture's actual dress, like the Turkish ambassador who wore a *robe à la Turque* at a reception in Constantinople, or hostages living in Rome who obtained permission to wear the local *robe à la Romaine*.[15] These were not garments styled in a manner reminiscent or suggestive of that area but authentic to it. The earliest documented use of *robe à la française* is in 1760, suggesting gowns in the style of other countries or cultures also existed.[16] Other early applications include the *Gazette du commerce*, which in 1763 advertised a dressmaker or *marchande de modes* who made "*robes à la grecque*."[17]

While the style designations of earlier eras may have gone undocumented, the fashion press established in 1778 recorded and encouraged the creation of new names. In her study of late-eighteenth-century French fashion, Chrisman-Campbell argues, "The issue of naming fashions was one that the editors [of fashion magazines] took especially seriously ... The provincial subscriber to the journal did not want to know only what the women of Paris were wearing, but also what these fashions were called: *the fashion culture was clearly verbal as well as visual*, and the descriptions of the fashions in the journal were as important as the fashion engravings."[18] Lasic agrees, writing that "semantic appellations" were key to eighteenth-century French fashion's "commodification of the exotic," noting that "a significant feature of these sartorial trends was indeed their propensity to fuse and confuse geographical origins and adopt different, sometimes interchangeable names."[19] Jones argues there was an economic incentive to create novel fashions with different names, as consumers would then need to purchase future periodical issues (and the styles advertised therein), and style names helped create "a vision of a perpetually innovating Parisian fashion culture."[20] Introducing the *robe* "*à la Tippoo-Saïb*," the *Magasin des modes* declared, "We have to educate about names as well as things, & we have to put our Subscribers in a position to say that their clothing has such a name, & that it is, thus, in the newest fashion."[21] Contemporaries noticed and commented on the increased emphasis on style designations in this era. Writing in 1789, one author complained he had seen,

> Diverse Modes succeed each other with an inconceivable rapidity. Denominations of all kinds have been exhausted: *Robes à la Polonaise, à l'Anglaise, à la Circassienne, à l'Insurgente, à la Turque, à la Musulmane, à la Czarine, Demi-Négligente, Lévite, Fourreau à l'Àgnès, Chemise à la Jesus, Juste à la Suzanne, Caraco Zélandais* . . . Four Volumes would struggle to contain all the nomenclature of novelties that the spirit of Women has imagined since ten years ago.[22]

NAMING TRENDS

Looking more closely at these fashion naming trends demonstrates it as a phenomenon in and of itself, as well as developments over time. To analyze these trends, I cataloged the names given to fashion garments (dresses and jackets) worn by adult women in every plate of the major French fashion magazines of the period, specifically the *Gallerie des modes* (1778–87), *Cabinet des modes* (1785–86), *Magasin des modes* (1786–89), *Journal de la mode et du goût* (1790–92), and *Journal des dames et modes* (1797–99).[23] Several years occurred in which few issues and/or plates survive (1782, 1792, and 1797), and as the French Revolution interrupted fashion publishing, no sources exist for 1793–96, so gaps occur in the results. I chose to focus on adult women's garments, due in part to the comparative scarcity of plates featuring men or children in these magazines. This analysis looks at women's dresses and jackets made for public wear (that is, outside of the home), from casual to formal, and excludes costumes worn for theater or masquerade.

One problem inherent to undertaking this work is the tendency of eighteenth-century French writers to be free with their phrasing and spelling. Thus, style names needed to be grouped. Consider the *polonaise*'s many variations, which are referred to in fashion magazines by names including *polonaise longue, polonaise courante, polonaise en frac, demi-polonaise, polonaise à la liberté, polonaise aux ailes,* and *caraco à la dévote* (see the following section for more on these variations). All these appear to have been considered a robe or jacket called *polonaise*, but the *polonaise* had its own subvariants. Thus, both the variants and subvariants must be considered, and one dress or jacket can contain multiple simultaneous references.

The first thing the resulting analysis reveals is the popularity of style naming: during the period 1778 to 1791, most women's gowns and jackets were referred to with a designation beyond simply *robe, caraco*, etc. (Fig. 130). Unfortunately, the lack of fashion magazines from 1793 to 1798 means no data exist to analyze for those years. However, looking at 1797–99, unspecified "gowns" and "jackets" outnumbered those with distinct names, so it appears that a shift may have occurred over the course of the 1790s. Comparable data can be located in wardrobe inventories, which by and large do not use many designations before the 1770s except for the manteau, pointing to that gown's importance.[24] Grouping style names thematically, while allowing individual garments to fall into more than one category as appropriate, demonstrates that the most popular denominations referred to geography or culture, followed by theatrical references (Fig. 131), although it should be noted that some of those geographic allusions were inspired by theater. Less popular references, in decreasing order of occurrence, were to the French court, children's wear (the *fourreau* gown), history, peasantry, and finally politics. Moving to the last few years of the decade, historical references (specifically to ancient Greco-Roman culture) predominated.

What is considered "geographic," and which countries or regions predominated? The most frequent references were to France, the Ottoman Empire, England, and the Caribbean (Fig. 132). Looking more closely, Ottoman references were the most popular

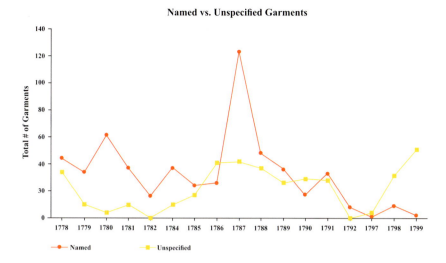

(*Left*) Fig. 130. Before the mid-1790s, robes and jackets with specific style names (orange) outstripped unspecified garments (yellow).

(*Center*) Fig. 131. Of those garments with specific style names, geographic references (orange) predominated until about 1790.

(*Below*) Fig. 132. Looking more closely at garments with geographic/cultural style names, references to the Ottoman Empire (orange) predominated until about 1784, after which English styles (light green) took the lead.

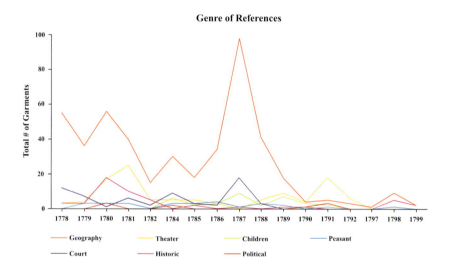

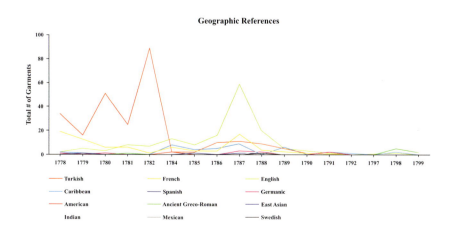

FASHION AND NATIONAL IDENTITY   115

until about 1784, peaking in 1782, after which the focus shifted to English styles, which emerged as significant in about 1781 and continued to dominate through 1789. Ottoman styles included references to Turkey, Poland, Circassia, the Levant, as well as typically Ottoman symbols like the sultana or seraglio. English styles included those literally called English (*anglaise*), as well as the riding habit and redingote. Secondarily popular styles were French and Caribbean. French styles generally referred literally to France—for example, *robe à la française*—or to the court, the queen, or other distinctly French symbols. Peasant styles, which were their own genre, were also counted as geographically French as they either carried an implied reference to French peasants, or denoted specific regions of France, like the *Cauchoise*, referring to the Caux region of Normandy.[25] Caribbean styles include the chemise as well as garments referencing *créole*.

By studying the construction of garment and style names in French fashion of the late eighteenth century, we can better understand the role and importance of foreign influences and references and the process of cultural amalgamation. No garment better embodies these peregrinations than the *lévite* gown, which began as an Ottoman import but went on to merge with English and Caribbean traditions, thus demonstrating the fluidity of cultural identity in the late eighteenth century.

THE LÉVITE

The *lévite* joins the *robes à la polonaise, circassienne,* and *turque* in being an Ottoman-inspired gown that was tremendously popular and demonstrates distinct influences from Turkish dress. The gown began as a stage costume, then was adapted for fashionable wear. In its first form, it looked much like an Ottoman caftan or *robe de chambre*: it was cut from full fabric widths, without a waist seam, and featured two wide, soft pleats at the back neckline continuing into the floor-length skirt. Its key characteristics were a shawl collar and sash, both directly referencing Turkish dress. Over time, however, the gown changed and merged with styles from several different cultures, including England and the Caribbean.

As a fashionable gown, the *lévite* was introduced in 1778. The *Gallerie des modes* introduces the style that year, recording it was directly copied from a costume worn in a staging of Racine's play *Athalie:*

> The first inspiration is due to clothing created for actresses of the *Théâtre Français,* when it presented the tragedy of *Athalie,* with the chorus. These clothes were copied from those of the *levites* and priests, consisting of a kind of *aube* [ecclesiastical gown], with a stole that crossed in front. That which was sacred was subtracted from this ensemble; the stole was transformed into a sash, and soon became a fashionable dress. These were the first *Levites;* one wore them first plain, without *paniers*, or rumps; but in time, they became far removed from the original simplicity, as we shall have occasion to notice later.[26]

Athalie is set in ancient Judah, now in modern Israel but in this era part of the Ottoman Empire. Levites are a Jewish priestly caste who in eighteenth-century France were particularly associated with the Ottoman Empire, the biblical period, and the clergy; the *Mémoires secretes* declared, "The latest fashionable dresses are the *Levites,* imitating those majestic dresses of the children of the tribe devoted to custody of the ark & to the service of the temple of Jerusalem."[27] Jirousek notes that biblical plays were often costumed in contemporary Middle Eastern dress, and examples of Jewish dress based on a coat and sash existed in those regions (Fig. 133).[28] Describing the dress of Georgian women, then part of the Ottoman Empire, one author explained that their "*Courdy*" (*kürdiyye*) caftan "is a type of short, sleeveless *justaucorps* [waistcoat], which is the summer dress of men

Fig. 133. Traditional Jewish dress worn in the Ottoman Empire featured layered caftans. Jacques le Hay and Bernard Baron after Jean Baptiste Vanmour, "Juif," plate 63 from *Recueil de cent estampes représentent differentes nations du Levant* (Collection of one hundred prints representing different nations of the Levant), 1714–15. (Etching and engraving, 16 7/16 × 12 in., the Metropolitan Museum of Art, New York. Bequest of Mrs. Charles Wrightsman, 2019.)

& women in Persia . . . It is much like the *Polonaises à la Lévite* of our Frenchwomen."[29]

Unfortunately, which production the *lévite* gown was drawn from is unclear; *Athalie* was performed at Versailles in 1770 for the future Louis XVI and Marie-Antoinette's wedding, but that is about eight years before the style became fashionable. Nonetheless, three costume designs from that staging give some sense of what the inspiration may have looked like. Each features a series of layered caftans, one meeting at the breast and then falling open over a soft silhouette.[30] Another is labeled as having been worn by Marie-Madeleine Blouin, called Mademoiselle Dubois

FASHION AND NATIONAL IDENTITY   117

SHORT DEFINITIONS

Style	Fashionable	Bodice front	Bodice back	Number of bodice pieces	Fit	Skirts	Sleeves	Other key characteristics
Lévite	ca. 1778–85	Closed edge-to-edge or open over stomacher or underbodice	• Two loose pleats, probably stitched down to waist and released into skirt • Multiple small pleats stitched down to waist and released into skirt • Later versions omit pleats	4 (2 fronts, 2 backs)	• Early version: loose, no waist seam, cinched with sash • Later versions with tighter fit and sometimes waist seam	Slight train or floor length	Usually wrist length with cuff	Fold-over collar and sash
Redingote	ca. 1779–98	Closed edge-to-edge or open over stomacher or underbodice	Fitted	4 (2 fronts, 2 backs); or 6 (2 fronts, 2 side backs, 2 center backs)	• Semiloose or fitted • Waist seam, except sometimes in the center-back pieces	Trained	Usually wrist length with cuff	Angular collar, often sectioned and/or layered
Fourreau	ca. 1781–91	Closed edge-to-edge	• Fitted • May sometimes have closed-in back	Unknown	Waist seam	Possibly only one drop-front skirt (no petticoat)	Usually wrist length	
Chemise à la reine	ca. 1783–98	• Gathered over drawstrings • Either pulled on over the head, or open down front but worn tied closed with drawstrings	Gathered or fitted	4 (2 fronts, 2 backs)	• Fitted with drawstrings at neckline and waistline • Sometimes another drawstring below the bust	Either round (no opening) or open down the front over petticoat	• Three-quarter length, gathered at cuff • Sometimes gathered around bicep	Sash at waist. Often featured 1–2 gathered collars at neckline.

(1746–79), in the role of Josabeth, and its handwritten description at the bottom of the drawing reads: "*Dolliman* [*dolman,* a Turkish outerwear caftan] of blue satin striped with silver lined in white. Garment of blue satin embroidered in silver and fringed in silver. *Amadis* [sleeves] in silver" (Fig. 134). Theatrical costumes were popular enough to be featured in the *Gallerie des modes* several times; a 1779 plate depicts the character Athalie wearing her costume, which it describes as a

> *Robe à l'Asiatique* [Asian], crossing across the front of the bodice with floating pagoda sleeves . . . The overskirt opens in front; the left side is lifted under the sash, forming a turnback. The right side is lifted in drapery. *Corset* and skirt, with the *pectoral* showing, and sleeves in *amadis,* revealing the pagodas of the dress . . . Over the whole, a mantle with trailing train, lined and furred with ermine. The crown on the head and veil draped & revealed in back.[31]

The actress wears a layered series of three caftans over wide *paniers,* the innermost with long sleeves and a richly embroidered hem trimmed with fringe; an outer caftan with crossover bodice, loose oversleeves slashed to display the layers underneath, skirt open in front and looped up to the waist on one side, just slightly on the other, all trimmed with fringe and tassels; and finally an outer cloak or caftan, worn mostly to the back but coming forward over one side of the *panier* to show its ermine trim. A sheer, striped veil forms a kind of turban on the actress's head, then drapes down her back, accented by various feathers. Although none of these designs depict the Levite characters/chorus, common to all was a series of layered Ottoman-style caftans, with swagged skirts and sashes. Finally, a plate depicting the "Costume of a high priest of the Hebrews attributed to [the character of] Joad in 'Athalie'" published in 1786–89 is described as

Fig. 134. A costume design for the 1770 staging of *Athalie.* Louis-René Boquet, *Josabeth // Mlle Dubois [maquette du costume],* 1770. (Drawing, 262 × 178 mm, Bibliothèque nationale de France, Paris.)

> A tunic of a double fine linen fabric that descends to the heels. It fits close & the sleeves go to the wrist. Above this tunic is a sleeveless *robe*, of hyacinth color, which descends two-thirds of the leg, & whose bottom edge is decorated with fringes with wool *grenades* [a kind of trimming] of different colors, interspersed with gold bells. It is secured by a belt laced with gold. Above is the *éphod*, a kind of *dalmatique* [liturgical robe] in different fabric & colors mixed with gilding. The sleeves stop at the top of the arms. It opens from the sides & descends a little lower than half-length; it closes on the shoulders with two pins enriched with precious stones.[32]

The earliest *lévite* gowns appear to have been cut similarly to *robes de chambre* and Ottoman caftans, from full fabric widths and in the tunic style without a waist seam.[33] The *Encyclopédie méthodique*

FASHION AND NATIONAL IDENTITY   119

(*Left*) Fig. 135. The early *lévite* gown looked much like a dressing gown. Note the pleats in the bodice back, as well as the tassels at the sash ends. Pierre Thomas Le Clerc (designer), Pierre Adrien Le Beau (engraver), Esnauts & Rapilly (publisher), *Gallerie des Modes et Costumes Français, 1779, V 124: Robe à la Levite (. . .)*. (Engraving on paper, 282 × 195 mm, Rijksmuseum, Amsterdam.)

(*Right*) Fig. 136. This *lévite* is cut without a waist seam. Pierre Thomas Le Clerc (designer), Nicolas Dupin (engraver), Esnauts & Rapilly (publisher), *Gallerie des modes et costumes français, 1780, dd 163: Habit en lévite (. . .)*. (Engraving on paper, 279 × 193 mm, Rijksmuseum, Amsterdam. Purchased with the support of the F. G. Waller-Fonds.)

declared the dress "was first almost like a loose men's dressing gown," these having been based on Middle Eastern and Asian garments as explored in chapter 2.[34] According to the *Gallerie des modes*, early *lévites* were cut with two pleats at the back neckline continuing into the floor-length, untrained skirt.[35] The first few plates illustrating the style show long, open-front, caftan-like gowns whose bodices either meet edge-to-edge or are worn unattached and hanging open, with full-length sleeves.[36] One features cords looped around buttons on either side of the front closure.[37] Those worn more widely open display an underbodice, probably the same stomacher or separate bodice worn under the *polonaise, circassienne,* and *turque*. The *lévite*'s front edges merge into a fold-over collar, whose neckline, according to both the *Encyclopédie* and *Gallerie*, covered more of the bust than other gowns but over time lowered.[38] Only one of these early *lévite* plates displays a glimpse of the back, seen in profile, and it very much resembles the *robe à la française* in its flat, wide pleats providing volume, although these do not appear to be as full as those of the *française*, which were generally made of multiple stacked box pleats; the *Gallerie* described the *lévite*'s as "two pleats in back, straight, ending at [stitched down until?] the waist" (Fig. 135).

The *Encyclopédie* recorded that the *lévite*'s first iterations did not separate the bodice and skirt with a waist seam, but were instead cut in one, with a sash "bringing it in close to the body."[39] Viewing the waist area is difficult in most fashion plates and portraits, as this is usually obscured by the sash, but at least one plate in the *Gallerie* illustrates this one-piece cut (Fig. 136).[40] This design mimics the construction of Ottoman caftans, as well as the early *polonaise, circassienne,* and *turque,* lending further credence to the idea that this tunic cut was considered evocative of Ottoman clothing. The robe's skirt was worn open in front over a petticoat, occasionally with a slight train, which the *Encyclopédie* described as "descending to the feet all around, but not sweeping the floor."[41] The figures in fashion plates do not appear to be wearing much, if any, skirt supports—no hoops or rumps. The sleeves are nearly always wrist length in these early versions, a longer length than most Turkish-inspired French styles excepting the *robe à la turque.* The majority had cuffs made in a contrasting color that matched the shawl collar. However, as with other gowns, sleeve styles were interchangeable; for example, one *lévite* in the *Gallerie des modes* included short oversleeves "like the *Circassienne*" over the usual long, cuffed undersleeves.[42]

Critical to the *lévite*'s definition was the collar and sash.[43] Almost all *lévites* illustrated in the *Gallerie des modes* include a fold-over (also modernly called shawl) collar (Figs. 135, 136, 152, 153, 167, 168).[44] The English-inspired redingote also featured a collar, but the *lévite*'s was generally cut in one piece in a rounded crescent, while those on redingotes were more angular, sectioned, and/or layered with turnback revers (Fig. 154). The *lévite*'s collar style was similar to that sometimes worn with the *polonaise* and other Ottoman-inspired styles (Figs. 122, 123, 162), which usually matched the wide, flat bands of contrast-colored fabric that often trimmed these gowns (Figs. 87, 121). Both the collar and trimming bands simulated the effect of the wide fur trims seen on so many Ottoman outerwear caftans (Figs. 4, 20, 47, 51, 119).[45] The sash was an item of clothing that had not been popular in French women's fashion since the manteau and was directly drawn from Ottoman dress (Figs. 4, 5, 6, 19, 21, 22, 47, 51, 119, 133). Initially, the sash was used to draw the robe in at the waist and provide torso definition.[46] Nearly all contemporary labeled images of the *lévite* include a sash, and that (and the rounded collar) are critical to identifying this style in portraiture (Figs. 128, 129, 137). In fashion plates, these sashes are generally worn over the gown, but occasionally they are laid underneath the gown and/

or underbodice in front; they almost always have long ends left trailing, sometimes with tassels or fringe, trims that were considered typical of Turkish dress. The collar and sash were so important that when other gowns were worn with these elements, they were frequently described in reference to the *lévite*, like a *robe à la turque* that "had a collar like a *robe en Lévite*," or a "New *Robe* called *la Longchamps*" with a "sash *à la Lévite*."[47]

A fascinating example of the early *lévite* can be found in Duplessis's portrait of the Duchesse de Chartres, exhibited at the Paris Salon in 1779 (Fig. 137).[48] Louis Petit de Bachaumont's *Lettres sur les peintures . . . exposés au sallon du Louvre* identified and described the duchess's gown: "well draped, but in the French manner [*à la françoise*] & in the most modern style, since we believe we recognize a *lévite*, with bare feet."[49] There is much to examine in this description and the

Fig. 137. The Duchesse de Chartres lounges in an Ottoman-styled *lévite*. The ship behind her is that commanded by her husband, Le Saint Esprit, which the Duc de Chartres led into the Battle of Ushant (1778) in the American Revolution. Joseph Duplessis, *The duchesse de Chartres in the presence of the vessel the Saint-Esprit, which is taking the duc de Chartres to the battle at Ouessant [westernmost island at Finistère, Brittany], 1777–78*. Painting, oil on canvas, 38.1 × 51.1 in., Musée Condé, Château de Chantilly. (Photograph by René-Gabriel Ojéda. © RMN-Grand Palais / Art Resource, NY.)

122 DRESSING À LA TURQUE

Fig. 138. The visual trope of the Ottoman woman lounging was considered erotic and luxurious. Jacques le Hay and Gérard Jean Baptiste Scotin after Jean Baptiste Vanmour, "Femme Turque, qui repose sur le Sopha sortant du bain" (Turkish woman, resting on the sofa after exiting the bath), plate 46 from *Recueil de cent estampes représentent differentes nations du Levant* (Collection of one hundred prints representing different nations of the Levant), 1714–15. (Etching and engraving, 14 1/16 × 9 3/16 in., the Metropolitan Museum of Art, New York. Bequest of Mrs. Charles Wrightsman, 2019.)

image itself. The duchess wears a cream silk satin gown, open completely down the front, that is full and loosely draped. The blue sash tied at the waist creates shaping. It is impossible to tell whether she is wearing a boned *corps de baleine*, but the silhouette is soft. A rounded shawl collar is trimmed with gathered lace, which extends down the dress's front edges and encircles the cuff of the elbow-length sleeves. Under her gown, the duchess wears a matching cream silk petticoat and a stomacher or underbodice, similarly trimmed in lace. She is not actually barefoot but wearing sandals with straps looped around her toes and ankles. The sash, sandals, and loose fit all reference Ottoman

FASHION AND NATIONAL IDENTITY

Figs. 139–141. A rare example of a contemporarily identified and dated *lévite,* with shawl collar and sash. The sides and back of the gown are in multiple stitched-down pleats without waist seam. *Doll, in a white linen dress with trimmings of muslin, silk ribbon and color-printed cotton ("Fashionable Undress called a Levette, 1784"),* wax over composition; dressed by Powell family, English. (Victoria & Albert Museum, London, W.183:1–1919. Courtesy of Victoria and Albert Museum, London. Third photo by Dr. Serena Dyer.)

dress, and the duchess's pose reclining on the ground is reminiscent of the way Turkish women were frequently depicted (usually lounging on sofas, carpets, or cushions, Fig. 138). Moreover, her petticoat is tucked between her legs in a manner suggesting the full trousers worn by Ottomans of both genders, but which Western women never adopted in this period (Fig. 119).[50] Thus, the dress in the painting has multiple indicators of an Ottoman aesthetic, but Bachaumont considers the ensemble to be in the *French* style, thus demonstrating just how deeply rooted Turkish references were in French culture of this period.

The *lévite* underwent several significant changes, the first of which was a more tightly fitted bodice. According to the *Encyclopédie méthodique*, the early, loose *lévite* "went up the neck above the shoulders, and covered up the bosom in the front . . . Soon the neckline got deeper, the collar went further down, and the dress became pleated to cinch the waist."[51] Three extant gowns reinforce these developments. Most important is an English doll that its owner specified was dressed in a "Fashionable Undress [informal ensemble] called a Levette (1784)" (Figs. 139, 140, 141).[52] Having an extant *lévite* that is both named and dated is truly remarkable. The dress and petticoat are made of white linen; the edges of the gown are folded back and trimmed with borders of printed cotton and muslin flounces. The collar is squared-off in front and pointed in back with a center-back seam. It has long sleeves with self-fabric cuffs, which are similarly trimmed with gathered muslin. Significantly, the gown is cut in one piece, without waist seam, with stitched-down pleats in the bodice that release into the skirt.[53] A ribbon forms a sash, while more folded ribbon suggests a stomacher. Two extant gowns are cut similarly, one of which is in the historical garment collection of Tirelli Costumi.[54] This dress features the fold-over or shawl collar so key to the *lévite,* with long, cuffed sleeves. The skirt is cut separately from the bodice in front, but importantly the back bodice and skirt are made as one piece, with the bodice piece pleated and stitched down around the torso back.[55] A similarly styled gown at the Muzeum Narodowe, Krakow features the one-piece tunic cut, box pleats at seams, and embroidered bands, but omits the fold-over collar.[56] All three examples feature a tightly fitted bodice accomplished through multiple stitched-down pleats, reinforcing the connection between Ottoman-inspired gowns and the one-piece tunic cut.

In this period, French people were not wearing exact recreations of foreign dress but instead prided themselves on redesigning, combining, and reinventing styles. As Geczy cautions, "Wearing orientalist clothing is rarely an act of assimilation or complete conciliation, it is rather the obverse. Since clothes become part of the individual, they are the very avatars of that individual's power."[57] The *Magasin des modes* declared, "Have they [French women] not borrowed, in less than two years, Polish, English, Turkish, Chinese [dress]? . . . It is true that they improve these styles . . . & they give things [in return]. When they copy, they correct, they embellish. When they imitate, they create."[58] Indeed, the history of Turkish-inspired fashions demonstrates how each began its life closer to its Ottoman model, then became increasingly French in cut and styling.[59] This process was recorded by the *Gallerie des modes* when its editors declared the *robe à la circassienne*, "in coming to Paris, was a bit Gallicized: the skirt *en musulmane* [Muslim] or full trousers was not adopted; the use of fur was moderated, the under bodice received cuffs . . . but despite these changes, it has lost almost none of its grace and lightness."[60]

Fashion magazines prove that differently named styles had specific characteristics distinguishing them from each other. However, eighteenth-century trendsetters and dressmakers clearly felt free to mix these elements together. Numerous individual garments depicted and described in fashion magazines are declared to be one style but include components from others. For example, the *Gallerie des modes* described a *robe à la turque* "or type of *Circassienne*, but different from others: it has a collar like a *robe en Lévite*, and a very large white sash tied at the waist"; while the description of a "*Polonoise* with sleeves *à la Circassienne*" argued such mixing was fashionable:

> The Naturalists, and with them experience, have taught us that the mixture of different types only produces monsters; it is not the same within the costume kingdom, or empire of Fashion. The combination of different genres of costumes, of diverse types, often gives birth to very pleasant creations; this is what happened when we were notified of the mixture of the *polonaise* with the *circassienne;* it resulted in a very graceful *robe*, which one can see in the engraving. The wings and the train [of the skirt] are from the *polonaise*, the body and the sleeves are *à la circassienne*.[61]

Several extant gowns demonstrate similar design mixtures, like the robes at the Metropolitan Museum of Art and Centre de Document-

Figs. 142 and 143. This gown features the cutaway front, vertical pleating, and lack of waist seam typical of the *polonaise* or *turque* in front, but the separate bodice and skirt at side back of the *anglaise*. Its sleeves were removed and repurposed as straps, probably for fancy dress, but otherwise the gown is unaltered. *Dress*, probably French, ca. 1780s. (Silk with linen lining, private collection. Courtesy Lisa VandenBerghe.)

ació i Museu Tèxtil that are cut as *circassiennes*, with short oversleeves over long undersleeves, looped-up skirts, and tunic-style bodies, but also feature closed-front bodices typical of the *robe à l'anglaise*.[62] Two gowns, one at the Musée d'art et d'histoire de Provence, Grasse, the other in a private collection (Figs. 142, 143), have front pieces that are pleated and stitched down without waist seam, but the skirts are cut separately from the bodices in back and pleated to fit.[63] Altering a gown to include newly fashionable design elements was a popular practice in the period, and many surviving garments have likely been remade, like the English nightgown at the Museum of London whose flounce was repurposed to add a cutaway bodice front overlay mimicking the *polonaise*.[64] Similarly, a dress at the Palais Galliera appears to have been originally closer to a 1770s-style *polonaise*, but was probably remade in the later 1780s. It still features the tunic cut and torso pleating of the *polonaise*, but several of its pleats have been released, probably to fit a larger size; whether it was once made with a cutaway front is unknown (Figs. 144, 145, 146, 147, 148, 149).

FASHION AND NATIONAL IDENTITY

Figs. 144–148. This gown has been altered, including releasing one of its back pleats and reshaping the bodice front. Robe à l'anglaise, eighteenth to nineteenth century. *Dress probably made from an eighteenth-century robe à la française,* [or *polonaise*] possibly eighteenth century with later alterations. Pink-and-cream silk taffeta; mechanical silk lace (nineteenth century). (Palais Galliera, musée de la Mode de la Ville de Paris, 1987.1.20. Courtesy Palais Galliera, musée de la Mode de la Ville de Paris. Third and fifth photos by author.)

128 DRESSING À LA TURQUE

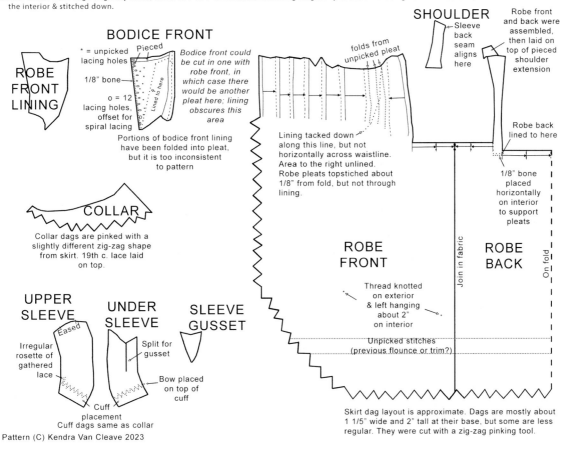

Fig. 149. The pattern for the Palais Galliera altered *robe à l'anglaise*. (Courtesy Palais Galliera, musée de la Mode de la Ville de Paris. Author pattern.)

FASHION AND NATIONAL IDENTITY   129

VARIATIONS ON THE *ROBES À LA POLONAISE, CIRCASSIENNE,* AND *TURQUE*

The *polonaise* appears to have had numerous variations, at least according to fashion magazines.[65] To what degree these were clear style designations is unclear; fashion magazines may have created variations as a marketing ploy. Nevertheless, the sheer number of variations speaks to the *polonaise*'s overwhelming fashionability and fluidity:

- *Polonaise longue* (long)—*Gallerie des modes* (1778; n.d. but probably ca. 1778–81, Fig. 112): undescribed.[66] Likely the same trained polonaise mentioned by the English *Lady's Magazine* in 1780 and described in March 1781:

  Long polonese, or Cumberland gown, first worn by that accomplished duchess—this dress is made profusely long, the train near five yards on the ground . . . The stomacher buttoned quite tight to the shape—two small scarves are fastened to the shoulders—sash around the waist—which is the length of the petticoat . . . This is esteemed a dinner dress . . . Long sleeves, cut in 4 quarters, with a silk braid down every seam—Turkish stomachers.[67]

- *Polonaise courante* (current), or *polonaise en frac* (frock coat, a man's informal jacket)—*Gallerie des modes* (1778, Fig. 67): "The wings, or sides of the *polonaise* should be small and the train very long."[68]
- *Polonaise d'hiver* (winter)—*Gallerie des modes* (1778): "With pocket and hood . . . These dresses are very narrow in front, leaving free the little waistcoat trimmed in its center and crowned by a large *contentement* [rosette]. The wings and the rounded train, rise very high . . . with ribbons, or with cords and tassels."[69]
- *Demi-polonaise* (half-, referring to a semiformal gown) or *polonaise à la liberté* (liberty)—*Gallerie des modes* (1778):

  This is a kind of shortening of the trains that the Ladies of the Court, obligated by etiquette to appear in public in the morning, have adopted for a long time . . . The *demi-Polonaise* consists of a skirt, on which one attaches a *bas de polonaise,* or simply a *polonaise* train as usual; it . . . provides the dual benefit of giving the appearance of being dressed [formally] when one is not.[70]

- *Polonaise aux ailes* (wings)—*Gallerie des modes* (1778): "The *retroussée* train with ribbon rosettes, or made of cord tassels, must be shorter than the two wings, and very puffy."[71]
- *Caraco à la devote* (devout)—*Gallerie des modes* (1778): "Type of *Caraco à la Polonaise,* closed completely, and with very little bust showing."[72]
- *Polonaise coupée* (cut)—*Gallerie des modes* (1778): "Made like ordinary *polonaises;* they differ only in the skirt, which is without flounce, without trimming, but a large apron acts as a veil and completely eclipses the front: a large flounce or demi-flounce is the ornament of this apron of which the top hides under the wings of the *polonaise.*"[73]
- *Polonaise à la Jean-Jacques* (philosopher Jean-Jacques Rousseau)—*Gallerie des modes* (1778, Fig. 162): "These *polonaises,* as well as the *polonaises courantes* or *en frac,* close under the *contentement* [rosette], have small wings, and diverge on the sides, revealing the little waistcoat that is tabbed on the bottom and without trimming."[74]
- *Costume à la Jeanne d'Arc,* which includes a *robe à l'Austrasienne*—*Gallerie des modes* (1778): "A type of *polonaise* that is very open in front, and which pulls back sharply in back, where it [the *retroussée* skirt?] is very high."[75]
- *Polonaise négligée*—*Gallerie des modes* (1778): "These dresses close simply on the breast like the usual *polonaises,* are not fastened at the waist, have long wings and very short trains."[76]
- *Polonaise à deux fins* (dual purposes)—*Gallerie des modes* (1779): "So named because by removing the *troussis* [a tuck used to shorten a skirt] of the back, it floats to the ground and provides the dual satisfaction of a short dress and a trained dress."[77]
- *Robe à la Cleophile*—*Gallerie des modes* (1780): "This is a *Polonaise,* remarkable by its manner of being lifted with olives [a kind of passementerie] & tassels, in a manner that the two seams of the body clip to the lifted portion [of the skirt?]."[78]
- *Polonaise en triton*—*Gallerie des modes* (1780, Fig. 121): Undescribed.[79]

The *circassienne* had fewer variations cited in fashion magazines:

- *Circassienne à l'enfant* (child)—*Gallerie des modes* (1779): "Sleeves *à la paysanne,* skirt the same fabric as the *robe* . . . This coquettish costume can only suit an elegant figure and the freshness of youth. This is also the cause of its name."[80]
- *Circassienne française*—*Gallerie des modes* (1780): "So called because it is floating & trained like the *Robes Françaises.*"[81]
- *Circassienne à la Provençale*—*Gallerie des modes* (1780, Fig. 107): Undescribed.[82]
- *La Grenadiere*—*Gallerie des modes* (1780): "Type of *Circassienne,* which owes its name to the capture of the Isle of Grenada from the English by the Count d'Estaing . . . It leaves the breast completely exposed; Symbol of the bravery of the French troops, who seized Grenada."[83]
- *Caraco à la circassienne*—*Magasin des modes* (1788): "*Caraco* with long skirtings, covering all the body in front, as would be if it were a *redingote,* & being stripped of collars (no longer worn)."[84]

Finally, a few variations of the *robe à la turque* are mentioned in fashion magazines:

- *Robe de cour à la turque*—*Gallerie des modes* (1787, Fig. 164): Undescribed.[85]
- *Caraco à la turque*—*Magasin des modes* (1787): "The skirtings are pulled more sharply towards the back, and which one wears with a *sultane* (type of waistcoat) underneath, in place of a stomacher, & which one attaches with large buttons, instead of attaching them with ribbons."[86]
- *Robe demi-Turque*—*Magasin des modes* (1788): "The sleeves & the first collar are the same [fabric/color] as the *robe.*"[87]

ADAPTING THE *LÉVITE*

The *lévite* is a particularly illuminating example of how French fashion adapted and combined styles with different geographic connotations. Sources indicate that over time, the *lévite* merged with two different English-inspired gowns, the *robe à l'anglaise* and redingote, as well as the Caribbean-derived *chemise à la reine*.[88] In this period, many foreign cultures fascinated the French. England appealed because their constitutional monarchy was so different from France's autocratic system, and they were believed to have a more casual way of life, both of which were attractive to the French, who were increasingly influenced by Enlightenment precepts of democracy and naturalism.[89] Meanwhile, profits from French colonies in the Caribbean, including Saint-Domingue (modern Haiti), Martinique, and Guadeloupe, as well as debates over slavery kept these islands in the forefront of the French mind. In particular, the popularity of cotton grown in the Caribbean was important to French fashion and brought colonial culture to public attention.[90]

ENGLISH INFLUENCE

The *Encyclopédie* helpfully documented the process whereby the *lévite* and *anglaise* took on characteristics from each other. Because the pleating discussed previously

> seemed to make it [the dress] look wider; the bodice was cut off and made to fit at the waist, and the skirt was pleated over the hips and attached to it; it had a train, and the sleeves that first went down to the wrist became gradually shorter; they got narrower and decorated with trim; they went up the arm and now only go to below the elbow; while straying away from its original plainness, this dress slowly turned into a fancier one; the belt, which wasn't needed anymore over such a close fitting gown, remained as a decorative element.

These were all changes that made the dress "close in terms of shape" to the *anglaise*.[91] The accompanying plate illustrates a *lévite* (Fig. 150), and it looks much like the *anglaise*—fitted bodice, center-back pieces cut in one between the bodice and skirt, while the rest of the skirt is cut separately and pleated to the waist from the front to the side-back seams. This one-piece center back, which scholars frequently call *en fourreau*, is not specific to the *lévite*. Multiple gown (and jacket) styles commonly included this feature, such as the *anglaise* and redingote;

Fig. 150. The *Encyclopédie méthodique* illustrates a *lévite* with closed front, pointed waistline, bodice cut separately from the skirt except in the center back, and three-quarter sleeves; it is trimmed with ruffles. The usual collar or sash are not depicted. "Couturiere" (Seamstress) (detail), *Recueil de planches de l'encyclopédie, par ordre de matières* (Collection of plates from the encyclopedia, in order of subject), vol. 6 (Paris: Panckoucke; Liège: Plomteux, 1786), pl. 24. (Centre de Documentació i Museu Tèxtil, Terrassa, Spain.)

FASHION AND NATIONAL IDENTITY   131

Fig. 151. The *fourreau* was a fitted gown whose details are unclear. Mitan (designer), A. B. Duhamel (engraver), Buisson (publisher), *Magasin des modes nouvelles françaises et anglaises*, 30 octobre 1787, 35e cahier, 2e année, Pl. 3. (Engraving on paper, 191 × 124 mm, Rijksmuseum, Amsterdam. Purchased with the support of the F. G. Waller-Fonds.)

English nightgowns did as well, although those center-back pieces were generally pleated and stitched down. The American *robe à la turque* at the Philadelphia Museum of Art (Figs. 85, 86), which demonstrates the strong influence of the *anglaise* in the mid-1780s, similarly has its center-back pieces cut in one with the skirt.

The *Encyclopédie* description frustrates attempts to differentiate this new version of the *lévite* from the *anglaise*. It does specify that the *lévite* was more fussily trimmed, making it "something very different from the elegant and noble plainness of the *robe à l'anglaise*." Otherwise, however, "The only thing that is different in an *anglaise* [compared to the *lévite*] is that the three back seams always get closer to the small of the back, almost like a *fourreau*."[92] The *fourreau* (sheath) was originally a girl's dress, "fitted at the waist & untrained," that was becoming fashionable for adult women (Fig. 151).[93] The *fourreau* is also difficult to separate from the *anglaise* and other styles, particularly since it could be worn *à l'anglaise* or *retroussée à la polonaise*, and because the term was sometimes used interchangeably with *robe* in this period. Scholars suggest it may have had only one, drop-front skirt, in which case it corresponds to what has been called in English a "roundgown," but several *fourreaux* in fashion plates have open-front skirts over petticoats.[94] The young girl's *fourreau* had a back opening, but the extent to which this practice continued in the adult woman's gown is unclear; in her memoirs, the Marquise de la Tour du Pin recalled wearing gowns "laced in back that very much marked the waist and which were called *fourreaux*," but this detail is not illustrated or described in fashion magazines nor seen on extant roundgowns or other fitted gowns of the period.[95] One 1779 *lévite* in the *Gallerie* is made with bodice *en fourreau*, meaning "as a *fourreau*" (Fig. 152); a *robe à la Levantine* in the *Gallerie* is made "*en fourreau* in back: that is to say where the skirt only forms pleats on the back and sides" (Fig. 166); and a "*Grande Robe à la Française*" is "boned like a *fourreau*."[96]

Fashion plates illustrating this *anglaise*-like *lévite* reveal a more fitted silhouette than the prototypical style, with bodice fronts meeting edge-to-edge and seams at center back and side back, which the *Gallerie* described as "made *à l'Anglaise*" (Fig. 153).[97] In fashion magazines, the *lévite* is sometimes referred to as "fitted" (*ajusté*), which may signify it is one of these more *anglaise*-like styles.[98] Over time, the bodice front opened to display an underbodice, prob-

132   DRESSING À LA TURQUE

(*Left*) Fig. 152. This *lévite*'s bodice is made "*en fourreau*," meaning "in the style of a *fourreau* gown." It clearly opens in front over a petticoat. "Robe à la lévite à corsage en fourreau" [1779], *Gallerie des modes et costumes française dessinés d'après nature graves par les plus célèbres artistes en ce genre* (Esnauts & Rapilly: Paris, 1778–88), 119. (Muzeum Narodowe, Warsaw.)

(*Right*) Fig. 153. A *lévite* with bodice "made *à l'anglaise*," probably referring to the fitted bodice and waistline separating it from the skirt. This dress must open in front as no back closure is shown. Pierre Thomas Le Clerc (designer), J. Pelicier (engraver), Madame Le Beau (possibly), Esnauts & Rapilly (publisher), *Gallerie des modes et costumes français, 1780, jj 197: Lévite simple vue par derriere (. . .)*. (Engraving on paper, 283 × 195 mm, Rijksmuseum, Amsterdam. Purchased with the support of the F. G. Waller-Fonds.)

ably the same stomacher or sleeveless bodice worn with other open-front styles. All the *anglaise*-like *lévites* shown in fashion magazines include the sash and wide fold-over collar, both of which appear to be critical to the *lévite*'s definition; however, neither is included in the *Encyclopédie* plate, although the text does specify that the sash remained an integral part of the ensemble. These new *lévites* appear to have been worn with more substantial skirt supports than the prototypical version, so much so that gowns in plates from 1780 through 1782 could even be worn over small hoops (Figs. 136, 152, 153). Since this version of the *lévite* is so indistinguishable from the *anglaise*, at least in this later form, identifying extant examples is difficult.[99]

Although the *lévite* was initially a soft, loose style, over time another variant became associated with the structured redingote, which had primarily English associations.[100] The term *redingote*, a Gallicization of the English *riding coat*, was used from the 1720s to refer to a man's overcoat.[101] Soon after the *lévite* came into women's fashion, a longer version of the man's redingote was introduced under that same name (*lévite*). Determining what makes these men's coats into *lévites* is difficult. Comparing the two in

FASHION AND NATIONAL IDENTITY 133

(*Left*) Fig. 154. A redingote, with layered collars and revers (turnbacks). A.-B. Duhamel (print maker), Claude-Louis Desrais or Desray (Draughtsman), *Robe jaune d'or et redingote gris-bleu, grand chapeau blanc à rayures dorées* (Golden yellow dress and gray-blue frock coat, large white hat with golden stripes), *planchet* (plate) no 1, *Magasin des modes, 16e cahier, 2e année, avril 1787, Fonds d'estampes du XVIIIème siècle* (Collection of prints from the eighteenth century), 1787. (Engraving, 19.7–12.2 cm, Palais Galliera, musée de la Mode de la Ville de Paris.)

(*Right*) Fig. 155. This *lévite* is nearly indistinguishable from a redingote. Jean-Antoine Lebrun-Tossa, *Journal de la Mode et du Goût, Trente-deuxième Cahier, 5 Janvier 1791* [January 5, 1791] (detail). (Text with engravings, 8¼ × 10 in, Minneapolis Institute of Art. The Minnich Collection. The Ethel Morrison Van Derlip Fund, 1966.)

the *Gallerie*, the only noticeable difference is that the redingotes are knee-length, while the three *lévites* end at mid-calf. These *lévite* overcoats appear to have retained the redingote's English associations.[102] For example, the *redingote à la lévite* is also called a *Redingote Angloise*, while the "Elegant Young man of the *Palais Royal* in *lévite Angloise*" makes no mention of *redingote* yet is still considered English.[103]

Some women's *lévites* of this era are suggestive of overcoats, like the *lévite pelisse* featured in the *Gallerie des modes* made of fur and meant to be worn as a cold-weather gown/coat hybrid.[104] In the late 1780s, a woman's dress version of the redingote was introduced (Fig. 154).[105] This was styled like the man's overcoat, with seams at the side and center back and one or more wide collars, differing from the *lévite*'s in being more pointed and usually sectioned and layered.[106] Following the same pattern observed in menswear, a few years after the introduction of the redingote dress, the term *lévite* appeared as an alternative. In 1791, the *Journal de la mode et du goût* announced that many were wearing the "*redingote* or *lévite* . . . as the cold is beginning to be felt" (Fig. 155).[107] Although the depicted gown has two collars, no sash remains, making it difficult to differentiate this style from the redingote. Queen Marie-Antoinette appears to have ordered several redingote-style *lévites* from Madame Éloffe, one of her *marchandes de modes*, between 1787 and 1789. Gustave

Armand Henri de Reiset, who edited Madame Éloffe's account books, argues that the frequently mentioned trimming called *mari* was "without a doubt a trimming that ornamented the lapels of the *robe,* or a sort of lace *jabot* related either to an open *redingote,* or a *lévite* with lapels," and this trimming is mentioned with several of the queen's *lévite* orders.[108]

CARIBBEAN INFLUENCE

The connection between the *lévite* and the *robe en chemise* (or *chemise à la reine* as it would often be called after becoming associated with Queen Marie-Antoinette, Fig. 175) is similarly intriguing, especially given the furor that later garment caused.[109] Thus far, historians have connected the chemise's origins to dresses worn in the French colonies in the West Indies, as well as to *robes de chambre*.[110] However, contemporary sources suggest the *lévite* also played more than one role in the chemise's evolution, adding a previously unexamined Ottoman layer to its cultural meanings.

The *chemise à la reine* (Figs. 156, 160, 175) was a gown made of extremely fine, lightweight cotton—usually white—that was tightly gathered in front and back via cords at the neckline and waist. It was cut full-length, without waist seam; some opened in front, while others were pulled on over the head; its sleeves were full and gathered, generally both above and below the elbow.[111] Later extant versions have fitted backs, one with the fabric stitched down in tiny vertical pleats across the bodice back, the other with a diamond-shaped center-back piece.[112] Like the *lévite,* the chemise was invariably worn with a sash at the waist.

Most historians argue the chemise gown derived from the lightweight cotton clothing worn in the Caribbean. However, the *Encyclopédie méthodique* records that the chemise was in part a development of the *lévite,* which, "in its first form [the loose, prototypical version of the gown] was so practical for travelling and getting dressed that it came back, this time under the name of *quinzevine;* the collar and the wrists are gathered over a drawstring. The dress has known another incarnation, with some slight variations, in the *robes en chemise.*"[113] Given the chemise's Caribbean origins, it is particularly interesting that the *Gallerie des modes* described a 1779 ensemble featuring a *caraco* or jacket *à la lévite* as being "called *à la Créole,* because it was used in the *Ballet des*

Fig. 156. The *chemise à la reine* was made of full widths of gathered sheer material (usually white cotton); note the sleeve gathering above the elbow, accented with ribbons. Pierre Thomas Le Clerc (designer), Nicolas Dupin (engraver), Esnauts & Rapilly (publisher), Madame Le Beau (possibly), *Marie Antoinette: The Queen of Fashion: Gallerie des modes et costumes français, 1784, xx 261: Chemise à la reine ouverte par le bas* [open at the bottom] (. . .). (Engraving on paper, 276 × 198 mm, Rijksmuseum, Amsterdam. Purchased with the support of the F. G. Waller-Fonds.)

(*Left*) Fig. 157. The loose, salmon-colored jacket is the *lévite;* the sheer, white, striped undergown is the *simarre*. The sash was typical of both the *lévite* and *robe en chemise*. "Vêtement dit [Clothing called] à la Créole" [1779], *Gallerie des modes et costumes françaises dessinés d'après nature gravés par les plus célèbres artistes en ce genre* (Esnauts & Rapilly: Paris, 1778–88), 135. (Muzeum Narodowe, Warsaw.)

(*Right*) Fig. 158. This *lévite* has the sheer materials and puffed, gathered sleeves of the *chemise à la reine*. "La Galante Flore indiquant à l'homme prudent [The Gallant Flora indicating to the prudent man] . . . ," *Collection d'habillements modernes et galants avec les habillements des princes et seigneurs* (Collection of modern and gallant clothing with the clothing of princes and lords) *[Gallerie des Modes]* (Paris, 1781), No. 47 G. (Bunka Gakuen University Library, Tokyo.)

Créoles, in a fairground Theater . . . [It is] composed of that which our French Ladies wear in America" (Fig. 157).[114] The loose jacket is the *lévite* portion of the ensemble. It is completely open and unattached in front, with the wide, short oversleeves frequently seen in Turkish dress. Underneath is worn a *simarre*, referencing the loose overgown worn by sixteenth-century Italian women (*zimarra* in Italian) that was itself based on Turkish caftans.[115] Here it is made of a loose, sheer, striped gauze, and it looks much like a *chemise à la reine* without all the gathers and the extra fabric needed to accommodate them: "The *robe* is a bit fitted to the figure and detached around the neckline in the taste of a *chemise* . . . [and has] a sash with a ribbon like the *Lévite*." Another chemise in the *Gallerie* is described as "open at the bottom [that is, the skirt] like a *lévite*" (Fig. 156).

Other sources suggest that a later iteration of the *lévite* existed that was nearly identical to the *chemise à la reine*. Specifically, one plate in the *Gallerie des modes* depicts a *lévite* made of cotton gauze fabric that has the sheer fabric and gathered sleeves typical of the chemise gown (Fig. 158). The main difference is the widely open skirt front (its fitted, sleeveless overbodice is, unfortunately, not described in the plate's caption). Another contemporary fashion plate illustrates a "*Lévite* with three collars" (Fig. 159) that looks exactly like a *chemise à la reine* published two years earlier in the *Gallerie des modes* (Fig. 160): a loose, gathered gown tied at the waist with a sash; the sleeves are full and gathered above the elbow by a ribbon; three layered collars are gathered at the

(*Left*) Fig. 159. This *lévite* looks exactly like a *chemise à la reine* with its gathered body and sleeves, plus its collars. "Lévite à trois collets" (Three-collared *lévite*), in *Album Maciet, gravures* [Engravings]. *Modes* [Fashions]. *Louis XVI. Vol. 2* (ca. 1785–92), pl. 15, Paris, bibliothèque du MAD. (© Les Arts Décoratifs.)

(*Right*) Fig. 160. It seems likely that the *lévite* illustrated in fig. 159 was copied from this fashion plate. "Chemise à la reine vue par derriere" (viewed from behind) [1784], *Gallerie des modes et costumes française dessinés d'après nature graves par les plus célèbres artistes en ce genre* (Esnauts & Rapilly: Paris, 1778–88), 283. (Muzeum Narodowe, Warsaw.)

FASHION AND NATIONAL IDENTITY 137

neckline.[116] Furthermore, while nearly all contemporary commentators call the gown famously worn by Marie-Antoinette in Vigée Le Brun's 1783 painting (Fig. 175) a "*chemise*," Grimm's *Correspondance littéraire* refers to it as a "*lévite*."[117]

However, multiple sources differentiate between the two styles. As mentioned above, the *Encyclopédie méthodique* states the *lévite* was reinvented, first as the *quinzevine* and then the *robe en chemise*.[118] Rose Bertin's accounts show that she began making chemise gowns under that designation in July 1782.[119] Meanwhile, in 1788 the *Tableau de Paris* noted the progression of "the *chemise* which succeeded the *Angloise* which succeeded the *Lévite* which succeeded the *Polonoise* which was preceded by the *Françoise*."[120] Both styles are listed concurrently in the Parisian noblewomen's wardrobe accounts studied by Maillard.[121] The last *Gallerie* plate featuring a *lévite* is from 1782, while plates for gowns named some variation of *chemise* span 1784 through 1787. However, the *Cabinet des modes* included a *fourreau à la Lévite* in 1785, while *lévites* were specifically mentioned in dressmakers' advertisements in Guyenne in 1784 and 1790, and by one particularly enterprising Parisian dressmaker repeatedly from 1790 through 1794.[122] One source merging elements of the *lévite* and chemise is Baudin's *Portrait de femme au livre* (1789), auctioned at the Coutau-Bégarie auction house in 2011.[123] The sitter wears a white dress in a lightweight cotton or linen fabric with a pink sash. The gown has multiple vertical gathers across the entire bodice front, as would a chemise gown, but smoothly fitted sleeves and a wide, flat pink collar extending around the entire neckline, elements that better suit the *lévite*.

Changing trends in the construction of fashion nomenclature provide important clues to French conceptions of national and cultural identity and their expression in fashion, as well as the importance of foreign influences. The *lévite* gown demonstrates just how flexible concepts of national and cultural identity were considered in late-eighteenth-century France. The *lévite*'s evolution suggests the Gallicization process was not necessarily a straightforward path from "foreign" to "French," and the practice of redesigning, reinterpreting, and mixing different cultural styles was a key part of that process. These styles would play an important role in Enlightenment debates around fashion, based on conceptions of the physical and moral characteristics of Ottoman clothing and the "correct" way to dress and, therefore, to live.

Turquerie, Enlightenment Thought, and the French Fashion Press

The intellectual movement of the Enlightenment had considerable effects on French culture, particularly in the second half of the eighteenth century. Philosophes (philosophers) debated how best to restructure society as well as the most beneficial ways of living, which included issues related to fashion and appearance. The intellectual leader in this area was Franco-Genevan philosopher Jean-Jacques Rousseau (1712–78), who was concerned about the negative effects of luxury and artifice in dress on society, as well as clothing's physical and moral effects, especially on women and children, and who argued in favor of more "natural" clothing forms. Many Enlightenment writers developed his ideas, such that by the late eighteenth century, naturalism, simplicity, comfort, health, and morality became the bywords of dress.

Historians have long connected Rousseau's ideas about dress to the English fashion trend that took place in France in the second half of the eighteenth century, as well as the neoclassical styles of the Revolutionary (1789–94), Directoire (1795–99), and Empire (1800–1815) periods. However, a further avenue bears investigation: Ottoman-inspired fashions. In the newly emerging fashion press of the late eighteenth century, editors adopted the arguments of philosophes to resolve potential conflicts between consumption and Enlightenment ideas. However, they did so primarily with Turkish-themed styles, rather than with the English fashions that have thus far been the scholarly focus.

Jean-Jacques Rousseau . . . having declaimed strongly against the practice of swaddling infants, and against the manner they are dressed, has finally had the satisfaction of making converts; children are raised, dressed according to the method he indicated; but the simplicity he sought to introduce to the clothing of men and women did not have the same success. It was not until 1778 . . . one ventured to make gowns analogous to the principles of the Author, and it was on the *polonaises* that this was attempted; they are known under the name of *polonaises à la Jean-Jacques.*

—*Gallerie des modes,* "Demoiselle en polonoise unie en buras"

Turquerie allowed the creators of these magazines to connect fashion to Enlightenment principles while reinforcing consumption through more subtle promotion of luxury, and unlike the democratic subtext of Anglomania, *turquerie* did not challenge France's autocratic monarchy. The fashion press's adoption of Enlightenment thought contributed to the assimilation of Turkish design elements into French fashion and connected Ottoman-inspired styles with progressive Enlightenment thought.

THE ENLIGHTENMENT

The eighteenth century was a period of intellectual exploration across Europe as men and women of letters debated and analyzed the world around them through politics, science, and literature in a movement that has been called the Enlightenment. In France, the most notable thinkers were Voltaire (1694–1778), who was concerned with civil liberties, religious freedom, and free trade; Jean-Jacques Rousseau, whose writings focused on creating an ideal society; and Denis Diderot (1713–84), who used scientific methods to catalog and categorize human society, particularly through his *Encyclopédie* project. These debates and discussions had important impacts beyond the world of writing, as people across Europe read these authors and participated in debates through salons, letters, and conversations.

Fashion and dress attracted Enlightenment thinkers' attention as they explored interconnected ideas about commerce, display, and performance in urban public life.[1] Rousseau's writings underpin most Enlightenment thinking on dress. His response to perceived social ills was to search for a mythical "state of nature" that would be more appropriate, healthful, and constructive to well-functioning societies. Although Rousseau's writings about dress were quite general, his advocacy of naturalism had a major influence on contemporary ideas about fashion.[2] His book *Émile, ou De l'éducation* (1762) was influential, leading to fundamental changes in children's clothing, while his promotion of simple, comfortable lifestyles more subtly affected adult dress.

Subsequent philosophers and physicians based their specific recommendations for women's and children's dress on Rousseau's ideas. Writers like François Fénelon, Etienne de La Font de Saint-Yenne, Louis-Joseph Plumard de Dangeul, and François Véron Duverger de Forbonnais articulated concerns about what they understood to be artifice and luxury's negative impacts, partly as expressed through fashion, on individuals and society. Meanwhile, physicians like Jacques Ballexserd (1726–74), Pierre Brouzet, Jean Charles Desessartz, Alphonse LeRoy (1742–1816), Joseph Raulin, and Charles Augustin Vandermonde focused public attention on the health effects of children's and, sometimes, women's dress. Several important philosophers joined in these medical discussions, including John Locke (1632–1704), Rousseau, and the Comte de Buffon.[3]

THE ENLIGHTENMENT AND ENGLISH DRESS

Beginning in the 1730s, the writings of English philosophers became influential in France as the Enlightenment's more radical elements questioned the existing social order, particularly regarding religion and science. The ideas of Francis Bacon, John Locke, and Isaac Newton were supportive of theology and existing political structures and thus offered a less threatening avenue of philosophical thought.[4] Meanwhile, Britain's constitutional monarchy provided a more democratic model than absolutist France.[5] The result, according to Josephine Grieder, was that all things British, including food, clothing, and sport, became increasingly fashionable in Paris and Versailles.[6]

Connections between Enlightenment ideas and English and neoclassical fashions have long been established in historical scholarship, and the resulting transition to a simpler dress mode is generally placed in the 1780s.[7] English-inspired dress was indeed highly fashionable in late eighteenth-century France due, in large part, to its Enlightenment associations. Grieder argues that by the 1760s, it became fashionable to imitate the "dress, demeanor, [and] amusements" of the English, and this was expressed in fashion via smaller hoops, lower hairstyles, and wearing the *robe à l'anglaise* and redingote gowns for women and the *frac* coat and redingote greatcoat for men.[8] Chrisman-Campbell demonstrates that the English passion for outdoor, physical activities led to their creating "functional, comfortable garments"; these styles became popular in France, first in menswear, as "the restrained, sober elegance of English menswear—so different from the brightly colored, heavily embroidered suits worn in France—made a powerful impression."[9] Eventually English influence reached the wardrobes of both sexes in France, where they were associated with the ideas of progressive Enlightenment writers who championed naturalism and constitutional government.

In fact, English influences in French fashion appear to date from the 1760s: the earliest usage of the terms *frac* (the less formal, English-style frock coat) and *robe anglaise* thus located are from 1765 and 1767, while the *Courrier de la mode* reported on the popularity of English gowns from winter 1768 through summer 1769.[10] Both Boucher and Chrisman-Campbell argue Anglomania in fashion intensified in the eighteenth century's last quarter.[11] This is borne out in the fashion press, in which English styles did not become dominant until about 1782; before that date, it was Turkish-inspired dress (particularly the *robe à la polonaise* and *lévite*) that was more frequently presented. It could be that English modes were experiencing a lull, and no fashion magazines were published between the *Courrier de la mode*'s fold in 1770 and the first issue of the *Gallerie des modes* in 1778. Furthermore, as the *Gallerie* began publication, the American Revolution and the resulting war between France and England temporarily dampened enthusiasm for *anglomanie*.[12] Grieder argues that after the war's end, Anglomania became so integrated into French culture as to be second nature; thus, magazine editors may not have felt the need to persuade readers to embrace these styles. However, the idea that English-inspired fashions really achieved popularity only *after* the reign of Turkish-inspired styles is borne out in Parisian noblewomen's wardrobe inventories, which demonstrate a preponderance of Ottoman-inspired styles like the *polonaise* and *lévite* in the period before English styles took the lead.[13]

French fashion periodicals occasionally presented English-inspired styles using Enlightenment language, but they did so primarily with *men's* fashion—of which there is little coverage.[14] For example, the transition from the *justaucorps* (the traditional, full-skirted men's coat) to the more streamlined *frac* (frock coat) was attributed by more than one publication to English influence. In a 1768 discussion of menswear, the *Courrier de la mode* declared, "French clothing seems to be getting closer day by day to *natural* beauty," something particularly seen in the "reform" of the "*frac* [which is] borrowed from English simplicity."[15] Ten years later, the *Gallerie des modes* argued the traditional French suit (the *habit à la française*) was becoming "simpler," but noted the *fracs à l'anglaise* were still more casual.[16] The *Monument du costume* is the most explicit in promoting English-inspired women's dress, connecting the *robe à l'anglaise* to the newly popular practice of women nursing their own children (something many philosophes recommended for moral and health benefits).[17] Fashion magazine editors did highlight the *robe à l'anglaise*'s grace and simplicity but also its majesty and magnificence, which derived from its long train. Both the *anglaise* and the redingote gown tend to be simply trimmed in fashion plates, but otherwise, no extensive discourses about Enlightenment ideas related to either style are present in the texts of these magazines.

THE ENLIGHTENMENT AND OTTOMAN DRESS

By contrast, fashion magazines extolled the Enlightenment virtues of Ottoman-inspired women's styles from their earliest issues in the late 1760s. Chrisman-Campbell articulates how despite being "outwardly distinct," the fashion trends of Orientalism, Anglomania, and neoclassicism were "philosophically related," explaining, "Eastern dress was considered morally superior to western dress as it was more practical, more comfortable, and less susceptible to whims of fashion."[18] *Turquerie* was familiar to Enlightenment thinkers because, as a facet of Orientalism, it provided a focal "other" to compare against French society as well as symbols through which French writers could critique their own culture while avoiding government censors.[19] Rousseau's writings partly fueled this interest: although he usually pointed to indigenous North Americans as exemplars, his search for more "natural" models encouraged others to look at non-Western cultures.[20] By the 1770s, Rousseau's ideas had achieved widespread popularity across French society, leading to a growing desire for naturalism and simplicity in appearance that had real effects on fashion.[21] Chrisman-Campbell argues that by the following decade, fashion became obsessed with the idea of naturalism, which then took the form of finding inspiration in "cultures and peoples perceived as being closer to nature—whether physically or ideologically—than the French elite."[22]

Rousseau himself went so far as to adopt "Armenian" clothing as his everyday dress from 1762 to 1767 while living in a remote town in Switzerland. His primary motivation was medical (he suffered from a urinary illness), but wearing Ottoman dress also allowed Rousseau to assume the *robe de chambre*'s exotic, intellectual, and classical associations.[23] Armenia was then under direct Ottoman control, and that region's clothing was "Turkish" in the French mind. Rousseau may have chosen the dress of Armenians because of their status as the most visible *oriental* in France, which derived from their long history in international trade.[24] On a practical level, he was able to obtain information about the region's clothing, including fabric swatches and required yardage, from an Armenian tailor's son.[25] Rousseau described his costume in his *Confessions:* "I put on the coat, the caftan, the fur cap, the belt . . . and I no longer wore any other clothes."[26] He also discontinued wearing a wig, something considered essential for French men of this era.

Although Rousseau did not write specifically about his Armenian dress "experiment" in his published work, it was widely viewed on his person in Paris and London, and reported in the press.[27] Furthermore, he was painted in his Armenian dress by Maurice Quentin de la Tour in 1763 and Allan Ramsay in 1766, images reproduced by printmakers (Fig. 161). The philosophe eventually gave up his Armenian costume due

Fig. 161. Rousseau in his "Armenian" caftan and fur cap. Jean-Baptiste Michel, *Philosophe, éloquent, sensible / Il nous a peint l'humanité* [Philosopher, eloquent, sensitive / He painted humanity for us] [. . .], ca. 1765. (Print, etching, 22.8 × 17.1 cm, Musée Carnavalet, Paris.)

142   DRESSING À LA TURQUE

to public criticism and because he felt he was losing control of his appearance's meanings.[28] Although he never publicly advocated that others wear non-Western dress, his experiment did have larger effects: it made Middle Eastern culture "an intimate element" of what Ian Coller calls Rousseau's "cultural repertoire," which then "shaped both his discursive production and his self-fashioning"; meanwhile, Chakè Matossian argues it allowed Rousseau to fashion a timeless personal identity existing outside of history.[29]

Although Rousseau's experiment with Armenian dress was ultimately unsuccessful, Enlightenment writers who built on his work overwhelmingly recommended children and, occasionally, adult women replace French dress with non-Western, usually Ottoman, clothing.[30] For example, Genevan doctor Jacques Balexert's *Dissertation sur l'education physique des enfants* (Essay on the physical education of children, 1762) argued the "Turks of Constantinople" were "the strongest & most robust men in Europe" because they did not swaddle their babies or wear restrictive clothing like boned stays.[31] Lawyer and author Guillaume Grivel held similar opinions, writing, "The ancient Greeks & [the modern] Turks who occupy their country, have never worn the *maillot* [swaddling clothes] . . . The Turks are tall, more rested than us, & their strength is so famous that it has become proverbial."[32] Physician Alphonse LeRoy's *Recherches sur les habillemens des femmes et des enfans, ou examen de la maniere dont il faut vêtir l'un et l'autre Sèxe* (Research on the clothing of women and children, or examination of the manner in which both should be dressed, 1772) recommended faux-Turkish costumes worn with the "simple [unboned] *corset*" instead of the "*robes françoises*" that, when worn with boned stays, "work together without a doubt to obscure the charms of the most powerful women."[33] In physician Guillaume-René Le Fébure's 1777 manual for pregnant women, he specifically recommended dressing children between three and four years old in "Muslim" clothing that was literally Ottoman, including trousers, caftans, and the "*doliman*"(*dolman*, a Turkish outerwear caftan), as well as turbans for boys. According to Le Fébure, the benefit of these Ottoman styles was that they could be "simple or decorated with magnificence" and avoided the dreaded "constraint" that "opposes growth & blood circulation."[34]

Enlightenment thinkers extended these supposed advantages to Ottoman-inspired French women's fashions, frequently endorsing the *robes à la polonaise* and *turque* as well as the *lévite*. Swiss doctor Jean-Andre Venel's *Essai sur la santé et sur l'éducation médicinale des filles destinées au mariage* (Essay on the health and medicinal education of girls destined for marriage, 1776) recommended women wear "*robes Turques* & those *à la Polonoise*, which snugly mark the natural contours of the torso" and are "an infinitely more pleasant illusion in the eyes of sensible & tasteful men," citing Balexert's argument regarding the healthful effects of Turkish dress.[35] Similarly, abbot, mathematician, and historian Nicolas Halma endorsed the *lévite* as a dress for young girls that avoided "luxury and worldly distinction so blamed & so justly proscribed by Religion."[36] Novelist Restif de la Bretonne declared, "Any honest girl will wear a dress like those that are called *à la polonaise*, which show the figure," with correspondingly understated accessories.[37] Three years later, he wrote with approbation about what he called "a general revolution in the manner of dressing, especially that of Women. One can only approve of *robes-à-la-polonaise, à-l'anglaise, à la-levite*, finally, all that suits" (and so becomes the only of these writers to include an English style in his list of recommended fashions).[38] In a 1782 work, Bretonne specifically endorsed the "*robe* called *à-la-lévite*" for young girls; following marriage, women should wear the "*robe à-la-polonaise*, without wings [side swags]."[39] Similarly, Riballier advocated for the *lévite* as it was similar to the clothing worn by the "fierce" ancient Greek Lacedaemonians, who valued "modesty & decency."[40]

TURQUERIE AND ENLIGHTENMENT THOUGHT IN THE FRENCH FASHION PRESS

Fashion magazine editors responded to these Enlightenment recommendations by promoting women's fashions named and styled after foreign locations and cultures, the majority of which referred to the Ottoman Empire and areas under its influence. At their most essential, these publications were designed to generate profit. To do so, they needed to create demand for future issues, and more generally, for fashion by advertising new styles, garments, and accessories.[41] At the same time, fashion existed in a culture in which Enlightenment philosophers' ideas were hugely influential. The press could not simply ignore changing ideas about the correct way to dress, or fashion's proper role in society, if they wanted to resonate with their audience. However, taking the philosophes' recommendations at face value would not make for much profit, so the French fashion press winnowed and reshaped Enlightenment ideas about women and consumption to encourage the luxury and fashion trades.[42]

CLASSICISM

A primary reason for Enlightenment enthusiasm for Ottoman clothing was the mistaken assumption that dress there had not changed since ancient times, which these writers believed precluded the need to purchase new clothing for stylistic reasons.[43] The philosopher Sylvain Maréchal declared, "Costume, in Turkey, is not subject to the caprices of fashion; if variations are allowed, they are so small that they are scarcely perceived," while Montesquieu quite literally stated the "mode of dress" was "the same to this day in Eastern countries as they were a thousand years ago."[44] This idea of ageless dress extended to other areas of the East, such as Eastern Europe. Jones argues that when neoclassicism did become the overriding fashion theme in the late 1790s and 1800s, magazines positioned these "seemingly 'timeless'" styles as "susceptible to the vicissitudes of *les modes,* [such] that they were in fact just another in a seemingly ceaseless succession of styles."[45] However, in preceding decades, editors did not really promote any classical origins for Ottoman-inspired styles. Only the *lévite* referenced any ancient source, but its description made clear it was copied from contemporary stage costumes and the style went through several obvious developments. Editors were focused on inventing new modes to create demand for future issues and fashion goods and thus appear to have avoided promoting styles that could be considered classical until compelled by cultural forces. That being said, scholars argue that the artistic tradition of painting French people in Ottoman costume was meant to conjure the same timeless qualities of antique costume.[46] Thus, the transition from *turquerie* to neoclassicism is not as abrupt as might be imagined.

NATURALISM AND SIMPLICITY

In sixteenth- and seventeenth-century France, luxury was foundational to conceptions of fashion: one should dress in appropriately expensive, sumptuous garments corresponding to one's status.[47] When intellectuals condemned luxury, they focused on dressing or otherwise consuming *above* one's social station. However, by the second half of the century, Enlightenment philosophes transformed this debate into one focused on concerns about conspicuous consumption—buying goods to demonstrate wealth—and shifted their admonitions to the upper classes.[48] Intellectuals also expressed concern about female consumption, arguing women's supposedly inherent desires for luxury goods meant they were in danger of wasting the family's income on dress, deceiving men through appearance, and trading their virtue for goods.[49]

Another of the philosophes' key anxieties regarding fashion centered on artifice.[50] Rousseau in particular

144 DRESSING À LA TURQUE

was troubled by what he understood to be contradictions between appearance and character in French society. According to his argument, clothes could not be separated from a person's inner spirit because they were worn on the physical body and played a role in how others responded to the wearer. He feared an individual's dress more frequently masked his or her social position, lifestyle, occupation, and morality rather than demonstrating truth.[51] Rousseau wrote,

> The real self can only be seen in private life... History shows actions far more than men, because it grasps the latter only in certain selected moments, in their parade clothes. It exhibits only the public man who has dressed himself to be seen. It does not follow him in his home, in his study, in his family, among his friends. It depicts him only when he plays a role. It depicts his costume far more than his person.[52]

According to Charles Ellison, Rousseau was concerned that artifice would lead to moral and aesthetic corruption, which would in turn cause "a lack of authenticity, of emotional honesty and inward-turning creativity, in artistic and performing work."[53] The philosophe focused his disapproval on the fashion industry, which he felt was a key promoter of artifice: "Love of fashion is in bad taste, because faces do not change with the fashion, and while the face remains the same, what suits it at one time will suit it always."[54]

When it came to specific advice on how to dress, Rousseau emphasized simplicity, comfort, and consistency. His most literal recommendations can be found in *Émile* (1762), a hugely influential book that led to fundamental changes in children's clothing but also had more subtle effects on women's dress. In this treatise, Rousseau described the ideal education of a girl named Sophie, touching on dress throughout his narrative and demonstrating how Sophie's manner of dressing was central to her moral character. Sophie loves dress, but Rousseau demonstrated her good taste through simplicity:

> She hates rich garments, and in what she wears we always see simplicity united with elegance; she does not love what glitters but what is becoming; she does not know what the fashionable colors are, but she knows perfectly which are becoming to her. There is no young woman who seems dressed with less study, yet whose attire is more elegant; there is not a single article of her clothing chosen at random, yet in no one of them is there the appearance of art. Her attire is very modest in appearance but very coquettish in effect; she does not display her charms, she covers them; but in covering them she knows how to suggest them.[55]

Rousseau's concerns focused on what he saw as clothing's harmful effects on a child's morals and character: "But from the moment that children prefer a material because it is rich, their hearts are already abandoned to luxury, to all the whims of opinion; and this taste surely did not come to them from themselves."[56] To encourage what he considered proper dress for young girls, Rousseau recommended parents "never praise her so much as when she is most simply dressed" and warned against using "coarser and simpler costume as a punishment."[57] Instead, he suggested parents make certain a child's "richest costumes were his most uncomfortable" to ensure "the simplest garment, the most comfortable, the one which subjects him the least, is always the most precious for him."[58] Numerous eighteenth-century philosophes built on Rousseau's advice, suggesting people—in particular, women and children—dress in a "natural" style.[59]

Fashion periodicals responded to these condemnations of luxury and artifice by promoting Ottoman-inspired styles as more "natural" and "simple"—literally smaller and minimalist but also thematically informal, unpretentious, and sincere—than preceding fashions, which were portrayed as overly complicated and cumbersome. For example, describing a *robe à la turque*, the *Cabinet des modes* declared, "Women no

Fig. 162. The *polonaise à la Jean-Jacques,* a literal reference to the philosopher Rousseau. "Demoiselle en polonoise unie en buras" (Lady in plain polonaise in buras) [1778], *Gallerie des modes et costumes français dessinés d'après nature, gravés par les plus célèbres artistes en ce genre, et colorés avec le plus grand soin par Madame Le Beau. Ouvrage commence en l'année 1778* (Paris, 1778–81), view 193. (Bibliothèque municipale de Lyon, France.)

longer wear those *large hoops* which give an immense width, or those *robes* with trains that trail an *aune* on the ground ... In the most formal dress, the clothes are similarly simplified."[60] Editors gave clear instructions for coordinating overall ensembles to create a modest effect, as when the *Gallerie* informed its readers that when wearing the *polonaise,* "one should not ... adopt a very elegant coiffure ... The shoe should be simple and matching with the rest of the costume."[61] Both the *robe à la turque* and *lévite* were minimally trimmed,

if at all, when they were first introduced, something editors repeatedly highlighted. The *lévite* gown was so associated with this simplicity it spawned a shoe of the same name; the *Gallerie* reported, "The latest fashion consists of not wearing buckles nor rosettes, & it is the shoes *à la Lévite* which created this revolution."[62] Responding to Rousseau's overwhelming influence, the *Gallerie* even integrated a literal reference to that philosophe into the name of one variant of the Ottoman-inspired *robe à la polonaise:* the *polonaise à la Jean-Jacques,* which the editors proclaimed was the first adult women's style to fulfill Rousseau's precepts (Fig. 162).[63] A few years later, another *Gallerie* plate illustrated a young girl wearing a "*Foureau* of painted Cotton trimmed in Bands and *retroussé à la Polonoise,*" which it claimed followed the "beneficial principles" of Rousseau's writings.[64]

One reason for the supposed simplicity of Turkish-inspired dress was the drawn-up skirt of the *robes à la polonaise* and *circassienne* in contrast to the usually trained *française.*[65] The *demi-polonaise* or *polonaise à la liberté* had a separate train attached to the petticoat that could be lifted with the *polonaise*'s usual cords. The *Gallerie des modes* declared this style was "as convenient as it is agreeable" because it gave women the option to lift the train when it was not needed, providing "the dual benefit of giving the appearance of being [formally] dressed when one is not."[66] Walking, in parks or the countryside, was a newly popular leisure activity that was considered very healthful. The *polonaise* dress facilitated park and country walking through its raised overskirt and styling. In plates featuring *robes à la polonaise,* the *Monument du costume* implied that women undertook "the exercise of the Promenade" because it was fashionable, but also praised it for being "pleasant & healthy." Indeed, the doctors advising the Princesse de Conti urged her to take up walking, and her father's abbot specifically recommended she wear the *polonaise* for this purpose.[67] Interestingly, although the *robe à l'anglaise* was also praised for its naturalism and simplicity, one part of its appeal was the grandeur its train offered.[68] The *Gallerie* recommended the *anglaise* as the choice for "Women who murmur against the *Polonaises*, because they leave idle your trainbearers . . . The *robe à l'Anglaise* satisfies all. It combines both grace and majesty, magnificence and simplicity."[69] Indeed, wearing a dress with a long train can be seen as impractical and therefore luxurious.

Although fashions *à la paysanne* (peasant) were their own trend, they sometimes overlapped with Turkish-inspired styles. While the "noble savage" was the Enlightenment's primary ideal, writers including Rousseau argued French peasant clothing was comparatively more natural and healthful: "It is in the rustic clothes of a laborer and not beneath the gilt of a courtier that strength and vigor of the body will be found."[70] Rousseau's search for man's "state of nature" meant interest was growing in rural areas, which were viewed as more healthful and happy. Examples of Ottoman-inspired styles that merged with the peasant trend include the *circassienne à la provençale* (Fig. 107), a variant of the *robe à la circassienne*, named after the Provence region.[71] Meanwhile, jacket versions of these modes incorporated Turkish designs into the short garments long worn by bourgeois, working, and rural women. The *caraco à la polonaise* "originated in Nantes in Bretagne where the Bourgeois women of this city wore it," according to the *Gallerie*, while the *Magasin des modes* declared the "*caraco à la Arlaise* [*sic*]" (Fig. 163), referring to Arles and styled like the regional *drolet* jacket (Fig. 14), was essentially "the bodice and sleeves of the *robes à la turque*."[72] Similarly, the *Gallerie* declared the trend for decorative aprons was partly due to the *polonaise*'s popularity; although these were frothy, fashionable confections, they referenced a practical element of rural and working women's wardrobes.[73] Even when Turkish-inspired fashions did not specifically reference the provinces themselves, they were suggested as appropriate for wearing in the countryside. The *polonaise* was particularly singled out for

Fig. 163. The *caraco à la Arlaise* was styled after the *drolet* jacket (fig. 14) worn by lower-class and bourgeois women in the area around Arles, and cut similarly to the *robe à la turque*. A. B. Duhamel (designer) after Defraine, *The First Fashion Magazine/Magasin des modes nouvelles françaises et anglaises*, 10 février 1788, 3e Année, 9e cahier, Pl. 1,2 et 3 (Paris: Buisson, 1788) (detail). (Rijksmuseum, Amsterdam. Purchased with the support of the F. G. Waller-Fonds.)

being "so convenient, especially in the country" and "very comfortable ... in the countryside."[74]

Despite this emphasis on naturalism and simplicity, a coded theme of luxury emerges in magazines' descriptions of Ottoman-inspired styles. Jones has demonstrated how editors responded to luxury's critics by emphasizing "taste," different from ostentation and positively associated with morality and religion.[75] Nonetheless, as Roche emphasizes, "natural" styles were no less artificial than preceding modes, and dressing fashionably remained expensive; the benefit of less expensive fabrics like cotton was balanced by the increased pace of fashion change.[76] Moreover, informal dress, and the Eastern lounging wear that inspired it, was understood to be luxurious: only the rich could afford clothing specific to that activity.[77] Some of the names used for Ottoman-inspired styles had patrician associations: robes and other garments *à la sultane* placed French women in the position of the Empire's first ladies, while the *circassiennes* for whom that gown was named had prominent positions in the Ottoman harem hierarchy.[78] The *Gallerie* declared that a French woman wearing the *robe à la circassienne* invoked these elite concubines: "Of all the beauties that adorn the seraglio of the sultan, there is none that match those from Circassia.... Their clothing matches their charms."[79] Almost a decade later the *Cabinet des modes* praised the *robe à la turque* for originating "in the Orient," where clothing had "nobility," declaring that in this gown, "A pretty woman ... won more confident and enjoyable triumphs than those of a Georgian or Circassian in the harems of Constantinople. Not even the *sultane* was immune from jealousy of her elegance, her grace, and the tributes afforded her."[80] In the mid-1780s the *robe à la turque* evolved into the principal dress for elegant occasions like balls and weddings. In fact, Turkish details were so fashionable they eventually found their way into ceremonial court attire (Fig. 164).[81] Both the Ottoman Empire and France were absolutist regimes, unlike England with its constitu-

Fig. 164. A court dress based on the *robe à la turque.* Note the stripes, swagged fabrics, and tassels, all associated with Ottoman dress. Augustin de Saint-Aubin (designer), Nicolas Dupin (printer), Esnauts & Rapilly (publisher), *Gallerie des modes et costumes français, 1787, sss384: Robe de cour à la turque; (. . .).* (Engraving on paper, 295 × 227 mm, Rijksmuseum, Amsterdam. Purchased with the support of the F. G. Waller-Fonds.)

tional monarchy. Although democratic ideals would win out in the French Revolution, *turquerie* may have been less threatening than Anglomania in preceding decades because, despite concerns about despotism, the Empire's regime did not serve as a conceptual or practical challenge to the French monarchy.[82]

COMFORT

The idea that material surroundings, including clothing, should be comfortable was relatively new, but it gained significant traction during the eighteenth century. In clothing, from the mid-sixteenth century women had generally worn constricting stays (or equivalently stiffened bodices), unwieldy hoops, heavy fabrics, and structured garments to create a fashionable appearance. However, as physical comfort became increasingly valued in and of itself, and philosophers and physicians connected it to health and morality, fashionable dress for women became comparatively lighter and less restrictive. Geczy argues the idea of comfortable garments was connected with liberal thought, and philosophers looked to Turkish dress for examples of clothing "sympathetic to the body."[83] Indeed, Enlightenment writers often highlighted Ottoman clothing's ease, as when Rousseau argued the "comfort" of ancient Greek dress, which "did not cramp the figure, preserved in both sexes . . . beautiful proportions," or when dramatist Louis-Sébastian Mercier declared, "Oriental clothing is made for the human form."[84] Although John E. Crowley's research focuses on Britain and North America, his argument that physical comfort had become highly desirable and a sign of liberation holds true for France as well.[85]

In response to these ideas, French fashion magazines promoted comfort as a significant benefit of Turkish-inspired women's dress.[86] From the late-seventeenth-century manteau through the *robes volante* and *à la française* that dominated the eighteenth century, fashionable dresses had been inspired by Ottoman clothing. Although generally worn over boned stays and, in the eighteenth century, hoops, the gowns themselves usually began as loose and flowing garments analogous to Turkish caftans. In the century's last quarter, the overall desired look in women's fashion was lightness, which translated into thin fabrics and gauzy, floating silhouettes. It therefore seems appropriate that fashion should turn again to the Ottoman Empire to discover styles that fulfilled this vision for women's clothing.

Compared to the previously reigning *robe à la française*, the *polonaise* ushered in an era of lighter fabrics, looser fits, and smaller silhouettes, not to mention the practicality offered by its lack of train.[87] Many of these same characteristics persisted in the *circassienne*. While the *turque*'s train removed one element of ease, the *lévite* returned to the manteau's easy caftan silhouette. Although most French fashion plates featured standing figures, the few presenting more comfortable poses primarily did so with Ottoman-inspired styles. One such plate features a lady wearing a *caraco à la polonaise* while "carelessly" half-sitting, half-lying on a sofa (Fig. 165).[88] Turkish-inspired fashions were less imposing than the *française*, a style that had coincided with the trend for heavy silk brocades and damasks, which, combined with the gown's long back pleats and train,

Fig. 165. A lady lounges in a *caraco à la polonaise.* Her hand between her legs may be meant to suggest Turkish trousers, or it may be an erotic gesture. *Femme en déshabillé rosé et caraco olive allongée sur un sofa* (Woman in pink déshabillé and olive jacket lying on a sofa), *Galerie des modes, Fonds d'estampes du XVIIIème siècle* (Collection of eighteenth-century prints), ca. 1780 [1778]. (Colored engraving, Palais Galliera, musée de la Mode de la Ville de Paris.)

created what seemed to contemporaries a more substantial appearance. The *Monument du costume* argued the *polonaise* "has substituted wide & carelessly placed pleats, for the stiff and constraining manner which one formerly folded the fabrics in the *robes* [*à la française*] of Women."[89] Magazines praised Ottoman-inspired styles for their comfort, as when the *Gallerie* declared the *lévite* "another one of those... dresses that the desire to banish any constraint in clothing has led us to adopt."[90]

One Turkish-inspired style that does not appear to have gained much traction is nonetheless notable for how much physical comfort is emphasized in its description. The *robe à la Levantine*—a reference to the Levant, the Ottoman-controlled eastern Mediterranean area—was among the most directly Turkish in cut and silhouette of all the late eighteenth-century French styles (Fig. 166). It was essentially a caftan, cut in one piece from shoulder to hem, open all the way down the front, draped loosely over an undergown, and it featured the short oversleeves, long undersleeves, and fur trim so associated with Turkish clothing.[91] Despite appearing only once in the *Gallerie*, the *Levantine* is nonetheless notable for how its description emphasized physical comfort:

> The desire to empower women with those clothes, in which the figures are revealed... has made imagined, in recent years, various dresses no less convenient than graceful. It was felt it was ridiculous how, under the pretext of decorating nature, it is stifled, so to speak, under pompous ensembles, it is true, overwhelming by their weight, their figure and their lines. Any discomfort was outlawed, and the French, free in their clothes, have finally recovered the ease, no less necessary for health, which supports the development of beauty. The *Levantine* is among the number of these new clothes. It is so easy and requires so little preparation, whether in dressing or undressing, that it has earned the nickname of *Négligé* of Pleasure.[92]

Fig. 166. The *robe à la levantine* looks nearly identical to an Ottoman outwear caftan with its short oversleeves, ermine trim, and tunic cut. "Robe à la Levantine" [1780], *Gallerie des modes et costumes française dessinés d'après nature graves par les plus célèbres artistes en ce genre* (Esnauts & Rapilly: Paris, 1778–88), 43. (Muzeum Narodowe, Warsaw.)

The Turkish trend coincided with a period of exponential growth in the popularity of cotton textiles, which were fashionable both for their practicality and affordability, but also their exotic, Eastern associations, being primarily imported from India and Persia.[93] Cotton was lighter, more breathable, and easier to wash than the heavy silk brocades and damasks previously in fashion, or even the lighter silk taffetas currently *à la mode*. However, cotton's popularity negatively affected the French silk industry based in Lyon. Writer Pierre Jean-Baptiste Nougaret complained in 1781, "The fashion of *robes à la Polonaise,* & those of the *robes à la Lévite . . .* absolutely brought down all our [French silk] Manufactures . . . If our great Ladies, if those who enjoy a splendid fortune, continue to engage in the odd taste for shabby clothing that is now in vogue, all is forever ended for a branch of work, that made so much honor to French industry."[94] In fashion magazines, a small but nonetheless significant number of Turkish-inspired styles were described as being made in cotton or linen, another lightweight and breathable fabric, and many of their descriptions emphasize these characteristics, like the *polonaise courante,* or *polonaise en frac:* "This gallant dress, lithe and informal . . . is only made of light materials."[95] Gathered trims made of sheer materials added to the overall effect and, according to the *Gallerie des modes,* could be directly traced to "the fashion of *polonaises,* or *robes retroussées,*" which "achieved the expansion of the empire of flounces: as trim, they became an essential part of the ensemble."[96]

HEALTH AND MORALITY

Turkish women did not wear boned or stiffened garments, and their clothing gently skimmed the torso and hip, characteristics that Enlightenment authors approved for both aesthetic and health reasons. LeRoy argued Turkish women's dress was "the most modest, and at the same time the most charming, because it displays the body's [natural] contours."[97] Balexert connected Turkish clothing's softness with health, declaring, "The Turks of Constantinople . . . are so strong & so vigorous because in that country they do not know the swaddling bands, the boned stays, & all the clothes that can hinder different parts of the body."[98] While French women never abandoned stays, new versions coming into fashion were more lightly boned than those of earlier decades. These combined with more body-conscious Ottoman-inspired styles to create a significant change from the *robe à la française* with its heavier fabrics, back pleats, and corseted torso and hoops underneath. Fashion magazines enthused that Ottoman-inspired French styles revealed the "natural" figure, using language strikingly similar to that used by philosophes to praise Turkish dress. Describing the *polonaise,* the *Courrier de la mode* declared, "Women have made simple small hoops [*coudes*] succeed the large hoops, renounced the multiplied frills, the tight dress and trimmings in order to reveal the elegance of their figure."[99] Some Ottoman-inspired gowns featured trim along the back seams called *nervures* (veins; Figs. 68, 69, 84, 87, 88, 107, 112, 123, 153), further drawing attention to the line of the figure.[100] These modes were also frequently accented with a sash, an element drawn from Ottoman dress that, by cinching the waist, allowed "a glimpse of the figure in all its lightness" and "liberated the figure and gave it grace," according to the *Gallerie.*[101] The English-inspired *robe à l'anglaise* also received praise, although more for fitting tightly ("The merit of this Ensemble is to slim the body as much as is possible. The *robe* must hold and define the figure well"), while Ottoman styles were commended for skimming the body ("the bodice detached and floating on the figure").[102]

Philosophers and physicians were concerned about clothing's supposedly damaging effects on bodies, particularly for mothers and children, arguing comfortable clothing promoted health and morality (ideas that were frequently linked in this era).[103] Rousseau claimed illness, deformity, and—for women—infertility could result from constricting garments.[104] Later authors developed these ideas, recommending the clothing of other cultures, particularly the Ottomans. For example, writer Claude Etienne Savary asserted that whalebone and busks, corsets' supportive elements, caused "the martyrdom of European youth"; as these were unknown in "Oriental" dress, "it is in the Eastern countries that man rises in all his majesty, and that woman deploys all the charms of her sex."[105]

Fashion magazines never promoted abandoning stays, which were considered necessary for women to be suitably attired for public display. However, corsetry's health and aesthetic aspects had for decades been a cause for concern for Enlightenment writers, so magazine editors eagerly endorsed the lightly boned corsets coming into fashion as an improvement over traditional, heavily boned *corps de baleine*.[106] Many Ottoman-inspired styles are described in fashion magazines as being worn over corsets as visible underbodices. Unfortunately, it is difficult to determine whether in these cases the corset was worn over separate stays, like other underbodices worn under open-front gowns appear to have been, but if the corset replaced the stays, that would be significant. One fashion plate featuring the *robe à la turque* suggests such a substitution, as the woman is described as wearing "a busked corset" (Fig. 127).[107]

Given philosophers' concern for maternal health and their elevation of maternity to a noble cause, the links between motherhood and Ottoman-inspired modes in fashion magazines is important.[108] The *Gallerie* wrote that *robes à la polonaise* "are ideal for those who nature has bestowed with a good roundness or whose pregnancy is beginning to show."[109] Although most fashion plates feature a solitary adult woman, a small number include a baby or child along with a declared or implied mother or governess, the majority of whom wore *polonaises* or *lévites*. Rousseau particularly encouraged the health and moral benefits of mothers nursing their own children instead of using wet nurses, so the *Gallerie* plate depicting a mother nursing a child while wearing a *lévite* is striking; the magazine declared she was "fulfilling the sublime functions of motherhood," and that "the elegant dress of this tender mother can prove that pure morals are not incompatible with the taste for the most graceful, newest fashions" (Fig. 167).[110]

Based on the recommendations of philosophers and physicians, children's clothing underwent significant changes over the course of the eighteenth century, from the abandonment of swaddling for babies to less usage of boned stays and structured garments.[111] Rousseau recommended clothing "which leaves all limbs free and [is] neither heavy enough to prevent movement nor hot enough to prevent it [the child] from feeling the impressions of the air."[112] Balexert promoted the supposedly healthier Ottoman example when he argued against restrictive clothing for children, while Le Fébure recommended both boys and girls wear unstructured Turkish clothing for its health benefits.[113]

Fig. 167. A mother nurses while wearing a *lévite*. Pierre-Thomas LeClerc (designer), Charles Emmanuel Jean Baptiste Patas (engraver), Esnauts et Rapilly (publisher), *Gallerie des modes et costumes français, 32e. Cahier des costumes français, 25e suite d'habillemens à la mode en 1780. hh.187 "Jeune dame se faisant porter son enfant . . ."* (Young lady carrying her child . . .). (Hand-colored engraving on laid paper, 17⅜ × 11⅛ in., Museum of Fine Arts, Boston. Photograph © 2023 Museum of Fine Arts, Boston.)

Fashion magazines embraced these connections, assuring readers that the few items of children's clothing they promoted were based on Enlightenment precepts. The *Courrier de la mode* announced that children's clothing could be made in various exotic styles, including "*Polonois, Espagnols, Turcs, Chinois*" (Polish, Spanish, Turkish, Chinese), and that "some of these clothes correct for small deformities that some children have."[114] In particular, the one *cahier* of the *Gallerie des modes* dedicated solely to children's clothing addressed "the revolution made in recent years regarding the manner of clothing Children." The degree to which the editors used scientific language is striking: "Hardly a Child is out of the *laboratory of nature*, when the overloading of clothes is hastened."[115] In the accompanying plates, young girls are depicted in various styles of Turkish-inspired dress: one "*fourreau relevé en Polonaise*," two *fourreaux* "*retroussé à la Polonoise*," and one *lévite* (Fig. 168); the other two plates feature a plain *fourreau* and a "*juste* [jacket] *à la Paysanne*."[116] The *Gallerie* described the girl's *lévite* as "simple, plain, [and] truthful," while one of the *fourreaux retroussé à la polonaise* used direct reference to Rousseau's writings:

> Jean-Jacques Rousseau undertook to combat and rectify the eloquent and sensitive physical education, his writings did germinate in the heart of the fathers desiring to ensure education for the first tender tokens of their love. Women felt all the value of becoming mothers and fulfilling their duties. She adopted the fashion of breast-feeding her own children. Diapers, *bandes*, *maillots* [both making up swaddling clothes] were rejected. Children had the absolute right to live and breathe: *corps baleinés* were ordered to disappear: a different costume, but led by beneficial principles, distinguished both sexes and a new generation arose under the banner of freedom.[117]

Fig. 168. The young girl (*right*) wears a *lévite* with shawl collar and sash. The older boy wears the *matelot* or skeleton suit. Le Clerc (designer), Nicolas Dupin (engraver), Esnauts & Rapilly, *Gallerie des modes et costumes français . . . Le plus petits de ces enfans . . .* (The smallest of these children . . .), . . . (Engraving on paper, 31 × 26 cm, Rijksmuseum, Amsterdam. Gift of Jonkvrouw C. I. Six, 's-Graveland.)

Not every French person of the late eighteenth century was necessarily a scholar, or even a direct supporter, of the Enlightenment, but the values the philosophes promoted—naturalism, simplicity, comfort, health, and morality—were broadly accepted, even if only on a surface level, as the proper way a modern French person should live and dress. According to French fashion magazines of the era, it was Ottoman-inspired fashions that fulfilled this vision of up-to-date, progressive women's clothing. These ideas would play out in consequential ways in the life of one significant French person: Queen Marie-Antoinette.

Marie-Antoinette *à la Turque*

The connections between French Queen Marie-Antoinette (1755–93) and fashion have become legendary. In the modern popular mind, she is the vapid queen whom detractors (inaccurately) claim dismissed the poor with, "Let them eat cake," while she shopped for dresses to wear to opulent parties.[1] Scholars have analyzed how the queen used fashion to create public and private identities, particularly as this relates to Enlightenment ideas and debates about luxury. Current research connects the Caribbean-inspired *chemise à la reine* to Marie-Antoinette's desire for a "simple" life, as well as to public criticism of her expenditures, sexuality, and lifestyle. However, Ottoman-inspired styles also functioned similarly in her public and private life. *Robes à la polonaise* and *turque* as well as *lévites* formed a significant portion of the queen's fashionable wardrobe. Marie-Antoinette probably chose to wear these styles for their fashionability, elegance, and alignment with the Enlightenment ideas she supported. Nonetheless, the public's suspicions about the queen's profligacy as well as her political and sexual indiscretions were likely reinforced by the associations that surrounded Turkish dress.

It is believed that neither *Polonoises* nor *Levites* are needed except a few articles to augment those in Silks, having in the Wardrobe 14 *Polonoises* whereof 6 in Silks and 8 in muslin and Percale, and 28 *Levites* whereof 5 in Silks and the Surplus in *Perse, Bazin,* muslin, two white quilted *florences* [all cotton fabrics]. Plus 22 *Pierrots* or *caracos.*

—"Comptes de la maison du roi," "Choix a faire du Printemps 1782 par madame La Comtesse d'Ossun," Mémoires & Quîttances d'ouvriers pour differns ouvrages, Comptes de la maison du roi, K//505

MARIE-ANTOINETTE AND FASHION

Austrian Archduchess Marie-Antoinette married the future Louis XVI (1754–93) in 1770, becoming queen when he ascended the throne in 1774. She was initially popular with the French public, but over time opinions soured as she was increasingly viewed as a symbol and cause of royal and aristocratic excess.[2] Fashion played a particularly important role in Marie-Antoinette's life, both in terms of her daily interests as well as her public reputation. In her book *Queen of Fashion,* Caroline Weber demonstrates that only by understanding the queen's relationship to fashion can we truly understand Marie-Antoinette and the complexities of the reactions she engendered.

In her early years, the dauphine tended to dress conservatively, wearing what Weber calls "carefully selected, unconventional outfits and accessories" (Fig. 169).[3] However, after meeting famed *marchande de modes* Rose Bertin and becoming queen, dress became a form of personal entertainment and self-expression.[4] Madame Campan, the queen's lady-in-waiting, wrote in her memoirs that before being introduced to Bertin, "The queen, until this moment, had not developed more than a simple taste for dress; [afterwards] she began to make it a principal occupation; she was naturally imitated by all women."[5] By increasingly focusing on new and varied dress designs as personal entertainment, the queen as a style leader contributed to the escalating speed of the fashion cycle in the late eighteenth century.[6] Instead of a rarified court existing outside of time, her love of fashion meant she reigned over one that was ever-changing and constantly seeking novelty.[7]

This change in the queen's approach to fashion resulted in public criticism. Her predecessors, most notably Louis XV's wife Queen Marie Leszczyńska (1703–68), dutifully followed court protocol, wearing formal attire and living physically removed from the populace. Challenging these traditions, Marie-Antoinette led fashion and mixed with Parisian

Fig. 169. Dauphine Marie-Antoinette wears the conventional *robe à la française.* Joseph Hickel, *Marie Antoinette, 1755–1793, Archduchess of Austria, Queen of France,* ca. 1773–74. (Painting, oil on canvas, 65 × 50 cm, Nationalmuseum Stockholm.)

society, roles previously the purview of the king's mistress, thereby shattering the image of a semidivine queen.[8] She became all too real when she was seen at popular establishments like the Paris Opéra dressed in the same clothes as other fashionable women, including actresses and others of questionable reputation. The public saw a woman who was, in their minds, "Much prouder of the Title of *petite Maistresse* [women who were on the bleeding edge of fashion] than of Queen of France."[9] She was blamed for the growing sums women spent on fashion, as well as diminishing class distinctions in dress.

However, Marie-Antoinette's fashionability was not only founded on luxurious fabrics, expensive

jewels, and ornate gowns (Fig. 170).[10] Following elite intellectual trends, she was among the first to adopt what were deemed simpler, more natural styles inspired by Enlightenment ideals.[11] She was not a scholar, nor did she have a reputation as a reader, but she valued the lifestyle that philosophers advocated, including the dress they promoted.[12] Chrisman-Campbell argues the queen increasingly followed the precepts of "Rousseau, whose writings on dress . . . advocated a return to a state of nature, free from the physically and spiritually confining bonds of fashion . . . Marie-Antoinette began to edit her wardrobe . . . simplifying her style of dress."[13] The queen's comparatively minimalist dress is frequently associated with the Caribbean-inspired *chemise à la reine* (Fig. 175), English-derived *robe à l'anglaise* and redingote, and working-class and bourgeois-inspired jackets.[14]

(*Left*) Fig. 170. Marie-Antoinette in opulent court dress. Pierre Adrien Le Beau (engraver), *Marie-Antoinette archide d'Autriche / sœur de l'empereur, reine de France, / Née à Vienne le* [archd(uchess) of Austria / sister of the emperor, queen of France / Born in Vienna on] *2 novembre 1755. (IFF 90),* 1778. (Print, etching, 40.9 × 27.8 cm, Musée Carnavalet, Paris.)

(*Right*) Fig. 171. In later years, the queen preferred to dress in simple styles; here she is wearing a *polonaise* in the gardens of the Petit Trianon. Elisabeth Louise Vigée Le Brun, *Marie Antoinette in a Park,* ca. 1780–81. (Black, stumped, and white chalk on blue paper, 23 3/16 × 15 7/8 in., the Metropolitan Museum of Art, New York. Bequest of Mrs. Charles Wrightsman, 2019.)

However, she also embraced Ottoman-influenced fashions—*lévites* as well as *robes à la polonaise* (Figs. 122, 171) and *turque* (Fig. 174)—with similar motivations.[15] While her enthusiasm for these styles contributed to their popularity, their associations with her supposed indiscretions, both personal and political, meant they became symbolic of those transgressions and attracted public criticism.[16] Ariane James-Sarazin and Régis Lapasin explain: "The desire to liberate her body [through dress], like her occupations and her movements, from the yoke of etiquette (more Paris and its spectacles than the Court and its ceremonies, more [Petit] Trianon than Versailles) was interpreted as a sign of the moral disorders of which the queen was considered guilty)."[17]

The locus for this restrained dressing was the Petit Trianon, Marie-Antoinette's small, private palace on the grounds of Versailles, where only she and her guests were allowed, and where she specifically requested visitors join her in dressing "like we are in the country."[18] First the *robe à la polonaise*, and later the *lévite* and its Caribbean cousin, the *chemise à la reine*, became expected dress at the Trianon. As these fashions grew in popularity, they were increasingly adopted by the broader court in general. The *lévite* and chemise were particularly associated with the queen: the *Encyclopédie méthodique* records the *lévite*'s earliest iteration was the gown "the Queen wore during her first pregnancy."[19] Meanwhile, what was first called the *robe en chemise* became more popularly known as the *chemise à la reine* after the exhibition of Vigée Le Brun's 1783 portrait of the queen wearing that style (Fig. 175).[20] Public reaction to the queen's informal dress was mixed. On the one hand, Marie-Antoinette's adoption of "natural," Rousseauean fashions played a large role in their popularity.[21] On the other hand, the queen's taste for casual dress was a focal point for criticism, one she herself did not anticipate.

DRESS AND OCCASION

Eighteenth-century France was an era of distinct dress categories separated by occasion, although these began to blur near the end of the century. Chrisman-Campbell explains the term *court dress* signified "the opposite of fashionable dress, which was worn in town"; specific ceremonial dresses were required for presentation at Versailles, Sunday court, as well as *les grands jours,* which included royal weddings and baptisms, mass, court balls, and major holidays.[22] These required the *grand habit* (Figs. 164, 170), an opulently trimmed gown consisting of rigid, boned, cone-shaped bodice that forced the shoulders back; petticoat worn over wide *panier;* and long, removable train.[23] Partially because *grands habits* were uncomfortable to wear, smaller gowns began to be allowed for less formal occasions, beginning in 1773 with the *grande robe à la française*, a larger, more embellished version of the gown that was becoming old-fashioned.[24] Spanning both court and fashionable dress was *parure,* also called *robes parées* (ornamented robes), which were fashionably cut gowns worn at court for evening entertainments, semiformal balls, and suppers in the *petits appartements* of Versailles, as well as outside of court for elegant events.[25] Fully outside the realm of court dress were fashionable, informal ensembles called *deshabillé* and *négligé*.[26] All these categories could be made more elegant with the terms *grand* (e.g., *grande parure*) and *demi* (e.g., *demi-négligé*).[27] Trimmings were important in determining the formality of an ensemble. The *Gallerie des modes* explained that *camisoles à la polonaise* must be richly trimmed to be considered "*deshabillés pares*" (dressed *deshabillés,* ensembles suitable for wearing in public), otherwise, "they remain in their former state of *dishabille,* or *camisole de nuit* [technically, a *camisole* worn as sleepwear, but meaning a style that should be worn only at home]."[28] In a similar vein, an American visiting Paris explained, "The robe à l'angloise if trimm'd either with the same [fabric] or with gauze is dress [*parure*], but if intirely [*sic*] untrimm'd must be worn with an apron & is undress [*deshabillé*]."[29]

Most new styles entering French fashion in this era did so as informal *deshabillé* or *négligé*. Early descriptions of the *polonaise* mention the style being appropriate for morning wear or walking for exercise and pleasure.[30] The *demi-polonaise* was specifically made for this second activity: "The skirt and train are of white fabric, [and] as trim and flounces are very inconvenient on walks, [they] are replaced by bands of painted cotton with borders."[31] Multiple artworks illustrate women wearing *polonaises* in gardens, such as Hilaire's *Promenade dans un parc* (Fig. 172), Lespinasse's *The Château de Versailles Seen from the Gardens*, Dugourc's *The Garden Façade of Bagatelle*, and

Fig. 172. Ottoman-inspired fashions (here, *robes à la polonaise*) were frequently depicted in garden settings. Jean-Baptiste Hilaire (attr.), *Promenade dans un parc* (Walk in a park) (detail), second half of the eighteenth century. (Painting, 40.5 × 32.5 cm, Musée Cognacq-Jay, Paris.)

Fig. 173. "A Woman in *parure* . . . dressed in a *robe à la Turque* of green-black satin, trimmed with gauze & with a garland of roses. The *robe* is laced loosely in front with a medium pink ribbon. Under this *robe,* a *corset* of white satin, which the sleeves, coming out from underneath those of the *robe,* are trimmed with undersleeves of two rows of lace; & a petticoat of the same satin, trimmed, at the bottom, with a very large flounce of gauze same as that which trims the *robe,* &, at the head of this flounce, with a garland of roses." Defraine (designer), A. B. Duhamel (printer), Buisson (publisher), *The First Fashion Magazine; Magasin des modes françaises et anglaises, 30 novembre 1787, 3e année, 2e cahier, p1.1,2,3* (detail). (Engraving on paper, 210 × 354 mm, Rijksmuseum, Amsterdam. Purchased with the support of the F. G. Waller-Fonds.)

Robert's *Terrace of the Chateau de Marly*.[32] The *Gallerie des modes* provides less information about the formality of *robes à la circassienne, turque,* and *lévite,* but these likely began as informal gowns as well. Contemporary artworks depict them as such, like Wille's "Young Woman with Miniature" (1778), in which the sitter wears a *robe à la circassienne* or *turque* and lounges comfortably on cushions in an Ottoman pose; and Lemoine's drawing of artist Vigée Le Brun wearing the *lévite,* sitting in a garden reading a letter (1783).[33]

As Ottoman-inspired styles gained popularity and their cuts refined and became more French, they could be worn for more formal occasions. While visiting Paris in 1775, Lady Mary Coke recorded a fellow Englishwoman who attended the theater and then supper in "a *polonaise,*" although she qualified that Parisians considered the style "as much undressed [that is, informal] as an English nightgown."[34] In 1778, the Marquise de Bombelles recorded that "everyone assembles in the salon in hat and *polonaise*" during the regular breakfasts given by a court lady-in-waiting in her Versailles apartment.[35] Meanwhile, in 1780, the *polonaise* was deemed appropriate for "a ball without ceremony" given by Marie-Antoinette, whose invitation declared, "Ladies should be in *petite robe* or *polonaise.*"[36] By the mid-1780s, the *robe à la turque* had become elegant enough to be worn for court and fashionable *parure,* and in fact replaced the long-standing *robe à la française* in this role. In 1786 and 1787, the *Cabinet des modes* repeatedly declared the *turque* was the most frequently worn style for court ceremonies such as "Wedding Assemblies, formal Balls, formal Meals, & other similar [events]" (Fig. 173).[37] It eventually influenced the *grand habit,* evidenced by three *cahiers* of the *Gallerie des modes* from 1787 featuring "*grandes robes d'etiquette de cour de la France*" (formal robes required by French court etiquette) including *robes de cour à la turque* (Fig. 164), *à la sultane, au grand Orient,* and "in the Asian taste," worn over *grands paniers* and styled like the *grand habit*.[38]

TURKISH-INSPIRED DRESS IN THE QUEEN'S WARDROBE

According to the few surviving records of the queen's wardrobe, Ottoman-inspired styles represented a significant portion of Marie-Antoinette's fashionable, nonceremonial clothing. The 1771 inventory of gowns belonging to the Duchesse de Villars, who oversaw the dauphine's wardrobe, has recently been discovered to include many gowns that Marie-Antoinette had removed from her wardrobe and given to her lady-in-waiting as etiquette required.[39] The most precise wardrobe records span from 1779 to 1782 and include written inventories as well as the fascinating *Gazette des atours,* a register made of fabric swatches from her dresses. Some records also survive from the period when the royal court was trying to economize in 1783–84; *marchande de modes* Rose Bertin was asked to reduce some of her bills, and the details of some of these reductions still exist. Finally, the account book of Madame Éloffe (d. after 1789), one of the queen's *marchandes de modes,* records purchases made by the queen and others from that specific milliner between 1787 and 1790. These records can be compared to those of her sisters-in-law, the Comtesse de Provence, Comtesse d'Artois, and Madame Elisabeth. All these inventories are incomplete at best, but they provide useful information about the styles worn by the queen and those closest to her in status.

In the 1771 inventory, which includes gowns Marie-Antoinette had given to her lady-in-waiting, the only fashionable dresses listed are *robes à la française* and *caracos;* the rest are formal court gowns.[40] However, later records demonstrate the queen's changed focus to the modish styles seen in fashion magazines. In 1779, Marie-Antoinette owned twenty-three *grands habits* for official court occasions, fifty "*robes,*" and thirty-two "*polonoises* or *circassiennes.*"[41] *Lévites* and *robes à la turque* feature prominently in the *Gazette des atours* (1782, with a few later entries), a partial inventory made of fabric swatches taken from the queen's dresses.[42] A written inventory for 1782 demonstrates *lévites, polonaises,* and pierrot jackets were most numerous among the queen's fashionable wardrobe. These were made in a range of silk, cotton, and linen fabrics, including four *polonaises* "in Percale with colored borders," a *lévite* in "imperial color," and three pierrots "in *Basin* recovered in plain muslin and trimmed in striped muslin." This inventory included only four *robes à l'anglaise* and one *turque,* "of Linen with large stripes."[43] Bills from Rose Bertin prove the queen continued wearing the *polonaise* through 1782, having had "the Collars of old *Polonoises*" retrimmed that year.[44] Bertin's (very incomplete) bills also show orders for trimming *lévites* and "*Robes Turques*" in 1782 and 1783, and "*Robes turques*" again in 1784. One of these *turques* was "in blue satin the skirt bordered in marten [fur]," and its trimmings included ribbon, lace, *sabot* cuffs "for the first *corset*" and another pair "for the second *corset,*" indicating the gown was worn over sleeved underbodices, as well as "Trimming of steel buckles for *corset.*"[45] The queen would wear the same kind of dresses should she need to go into mourning. Mourning gowns held in reserve included court gowns as well as *lévites* and *polonaises;* significantly, when in some seasons these were not present, the phrase "no *Polonoises* nor *Levites*" was expressly noted, indicating the extent to which these gowns were expected.

In February 1785, the queen announced she would no longer wear fashionable gowns, specifically no "*Pierrots,* nor *Chemises,* nor *Redingotes,* nor *Polonnoises,* nor *Levites,* nor *Robes à la Turque,* nor *Circassiennes,*" and no lady wearing these would be admitted to ceremonial visits without permission, indicating these styles were being worn for court *parure*.[46] The *Mémoires secrets* records that Marie-

Antoinette instead meant to wear "serious, pleated *Robes*," probably referring to the *française*. The *Mémoires* ascribes this decision to the queen's advanced pregnancy, as well as her desire to dress more soberly given her approaching thirtieth birthday. Nonetheless, *marchande de modes* Madame Éloffe's accounts prove that the queen continued to purchase fashionable dress from 1787 through 1792, including a variety of Turkish-inspired clothing. These included lining the mantle of a blue *"habit de musulmane,"* retrimming a *turque* made of iced violet *peau de soie* with white petticoat embroidered in violet, trimming a *"robe turque"* in striped pink and white satin with violet velvet flowers, and making a pair of *"mirfas"* sleeve ruffles in wool gauze for a striped black *"robe turque."*[47] She also ordered Alençon lace trimmings for multiple *lévites*, including one in white satin with "a pair of two-row *maris*," indicating this may be a redingote-style *lévite;* another in striped violet and green satin, trimmed with lace at the neckline and cuffs; and one in striped blue and white taffeta, trimmed with a gauze flounce and lace and ribbon trimmings at the neckline, cuffs, front edges, and flounce.[48]

The wardrobe records of Marie-Antoinette's sisters-in-law, whose status was eclipsed only by the queen, similarly demonstrate the prominence of Ottoman-inspired styles for royal French women. In 1771, Marie Joséphine of Savoy (1753–1810) became Comtesse de Provence by marrying the future Louis XVIII, Louis XVI's younger brother and thus next in the line of succession. Mademoiselle Alexandre, Parisian *marchande de modes,* made her wedding trousseau, which included two *grands habits* as well as fourteen fashionable gowns of differing formality.[49] These included twelve for *parure* and *deshabillé:* one unspecified robe and three *polonaises* to wear over *paniers,* the widest hoops, one of which was meant to be worn at the palace of Choisy; two unspecified robes and one *"polonnoise"* to wear over *considérations,* slightly smaller hoops; and five *polonaises* to wear "without *panier,"* presumably over rumps or small pocket hoops, two of which were for suppers. Also included were two *polonaises* to be worn as *"robes a peigner,"* meaning gowns to be worn for *négligé,* while dressing (*peigner* means *to comb,* as in one's hair) or otherwise in a semiprivate context.

Marie-Thérèse of Savoy (1756–1805) married Charles Philippe, Comte d'Artois (the future Charles X, youngest brother of Louis XVI) in 1773. Her wardrobe accounts are more extensive than those of her sisters-in-law, but they are still incomplete and thus difficult to summarize.[50] Partial records exist for each year from 1773 to 1780, 1783, and 1785–87, and these document numerous examples of Ottoman-inspired styles that reflect many of the details discussed in fashion magazines. *Polonaises* were present from 1773 to 1780, although most numerous before 1777, and many were listed with coordinating *compère* or *pièce* stomachers. From 1777, the comtesse favored *robes à la circassienne,* which were numerous through 1779. *Circassiennes* were usually listed along with a separate corset, although sometimes with *pièce* or *compère* stomachers; many include *"polonnaises"* among their trimmings, which were a passementerie ornament.[51] In 1776, the comtesse paid Rose Bertin for "The trimming of a *noisette* [nut-colored] *Circassienne . . .* Furnished for the said *robe.* 11 *polonnaises,* 8 tassels."[52] *Lévites* were introduced in 1779 and quickly became a favorite; these persisted until 1786, although they were few in the last two years. Most *lévites* were not listed with any stomacher or underbodice, although in a few instances they were accompanied by corsages, like when the comtesse purchased "6 *aunes* Batiste [cotton] for the *corsages* of 3 *pierrots* [jackets] and one *Levitte."*[53] *Robes à la turque* appear from 1783 to 1787 and competed only with pierrots in prevalence. Some *robes à la turque* had coordinating corsages, but many did not mention any underbodice.

Finally, the 1791 *Gazette des atours* of Madame Elisabeth (1764–94), the king's youngest sister and close companion to the queen, survives. In this inventory, her fashionable wear included only pierrot jackets and unspecified robes, which could be due to style names going out of fashion, as well as the fact that the royal family was then living under the control of revolutionaries at the Tuileries Palace.[54]

Marie-Antoinette's preference for Turkish-inspired gowns, including the *polonaise, lévite,* and *turque,* was obvious enough to be noted by contemporaries. In 1775, Englishwoman Lady Clermont reported from the French court, "The Queen . . . desir'd me to wear the uniform [of the court, that is, nearly ubiquitous], which is a *polonaise, couleur de puce* [flea colored]."[55] The queen was so associated with the *lévite* that the *Encyclopédie méthodique* mentioned her in its description of the gown ("the *lévite* the queen wore during her first pregnancy").[56] In 1785, Englishwoman Lady Sarah Napier wrote, "A lady who left Paris last autumn told me that the *Queen & everybody* wore white linnen levettes [*lévites*] & nightgowns [*robes à l'anglaise*] all day long."[57]

These Ottoman-inspired styles played an important role in the queen's wardrobe simplification and her attempts to live a private, country life at Petit Trianon.[58] Madame Campan recalled, "The queen sometimes stayed a month in a row at the petit Trianon, and had established there all the customs of [country] chateau life . . . A *robe* of white percale, a gauze scarf, a straw hat, were the only adornment of princesses; the pleasure of browsing all the workshops in the hamlet, of seeing the cows milked, of fishing in the lake, enchanted the queen."[59] Writing of the period around 1780, Campan further explained:

> The taste for adornment, in which the queen indulged during the first years of the reign, had given way to a love of simplicity carried even to an impolitic degree, the brilliance and magnificence of the throne not being to a certain degree separated in France from the interests of the nation. Except for the days of very formal ceremonies at the court . . . the queen wore only *robes* of percale or white Florence taffeta. Her headdress was limited to a hat: the simplest ones were preferred, and the diamonds only came out of the cases for the [formal] etiquette ensembles dedicated to the days I have just indicated.[60]

This preference for understated dress eventually included the *chemise à la reine,* but it first focused on the *robe à la polonaise* and then the *lévite.* Multiple artworks depict the queen in these Ottoman-inspired fashions.[61] Several of these represent her at Trianon wearing the *polonaise,* including a circa 1780–81 drawing by Vigée Le Brun (Fig. 171) and a 1784 gouache by Dumont in which she stands next to the Trianon's balustrade.[62] She may be wearing the *lévite* in a 1780 painting where she sits in the Trianon gardens holding a riding crop, as well as in Dumont's 1790 miniature seated with her children.[63] Also of interest are Châtelet's *Illumination of the Belvédère of the Petit Trianon* (1781) and Robert's *Evening Party Given by the Queen Marie-Antoinette* (ca. 1782), both documenting the queen's evening parties in the Trianon's gardens.[64] Although the figures are small, most of the women's gowns in these paintings suggest the raised skirts of the *polonaise* and *circassienne.* Meanwhile, Lafrensen's painting of an evening party given by the queen for Gustav III at the Petit Trianon include a mix of fitted-back gowns, some of which may be *robes à la turque* or *l'anglaise,* along with at least one *robe à la française.*[65]

Perhaps most significant for this study, Marie-Antoinette was painted by Adolf Ulrik Wertmüller in the Trianon's gardens wearing a *robe à la turque* in a portrait exhibited at the Paris Salon of 1785 (Fig. 174).[66] The queen probably chose to wear a *robe à la turque* for its fashionability, elegance, and alignment with the Enlightenment ideas she supported as she attempted to repair her now tarnished reputation. Nonetheless, the style's associations with fashionable dress, as well as Ottoman luxury and sexuality, appear to have reinforced the public's suspicions about the

Fig. 174. Marie-Antoinette wears a *robe à la turque* in this 1785 portrait. Adolf Ulrik Wertmüller, *Queen Marie Antoinette of France and Two of Her Children Walking in the Park of Trianon,* 1785. (Painting, oil on canvas, 108.6 × 76.3 in., Nationalmuseum, Stockholm.)

queen's profligacy as well as her political and sexual indiscretions; the painting caused a minor scandal analogous (if less extreme) to that of her 1783 portrait by Vigée Le Brun in *chemise à la reine* (Fig. 175). That earlier portrait drew widespread condemnation, and the queen's chemise gown was the particular focus of public ire.[67] The chemise was informal and fashionable, not ceremonial court wear; and it was associated with the queen's private realm at the Petit Trianon.[68] Vigée Le Brun's painting reminded the public of the place within the French court where

Marie-Antoinette held primary power, inverting a queen's traditional submissive role to the king.[69]

Observers confirm that when Marie-Antoinette wore Ottoman-inspired styles, they were considered restrained and understated. When the queen's brother Joseph, Emperor of Austria, visited Versailles in 1781, the *Correspondence secrète* reported, "Whenever the queen appeared in public, in the company of her august brother, her dress was of the utmost simplicity. On Tuesday, when their majesties went with each other from Versailles to Trianon . . . the Queen was dressed in a *lévite* of muslin with a blue sash, her hair high with a simple ribbon, without *rouge* and without diamonds."[70] Marie-Antoinette wore a *robe à la turque* to a ceremonial event at the

Fig. 175. The queen wears the *chemise à la reine* in this portrait from two years earlier. After Élisabeth-Louise Vigée Le Brun, *Marie-Antoinette,* after 1783. (Oil on canvas, 36½ × 28¾ in., National Gallery, Washington, DC. Timken Collection.)

MARIE-ANTOINETTE À LA TURQUE 165

Tuileries Palace during the Swedish king's visit in 1784. Despite this being an occasion where the queen was in elegant court *parure,* Englishwoman Anna Cradock nonetheless emphasized the unpretentiousness of the queen's dress: "Her ensemble, full of distinction, was very simple. Unexaggerated hoops, a *robe à la turque* in pigeon's throat brown (clear brown shaded with blue) taffeta, bordered all around with a narrow white ribbon; the underbodice trimmed with very small agate buttons. Hair dressed a bit simply, disappearing in part under an elegant mix of gauze and blue ribbons. Little *rouge*."[71]

Although the reaction to the Wertmüller portrait of Marie-Antoinette in *robe à la turque* in 1785 was less extreme, commentators and the queen herself—perhaps having been given advance notice of the public reaction—disliked the Wertmüller portrait, and criticism focused on the informality of the queen's dress.[72] In this period, the Enlightenment associations surrounding Turkish-inspired fashion were in tension with negative images of decadence and licentiousness, and these connections would have reminded the public of their worries about the queen's supposedly unchecked spending and sexuality. The *robe à la turque*'s conflicting associations help explain the reactions to the Wertmüller portrait: instead of depicting Marie-Antoinette in the regally maternal role to which she now aspired, her detractors saw the frivolous, seductive schemer they had long presumed her to be.[73]

For one, the fact that court *parure* had become mixed with fashionable dress with all its associations negatively affected Marie-Antoinette.[74] She was accused of devaluing the monarchy and social order when she dressed down and mingled with the populace at the Paris Opéra or her palace of Saint-Cloud.[75] The abbé Jean-Louis Giraud-Soulavie (1751–1813) would later connect these two faults in his memoirs:

> Wealth in clothes . . . marked the degrees of society, prevented confusion in the hierarchy, supported the variety and the prominence of ranks. Marie-Antoinette was the first to destroy this conservative principle of the monarchical state . . . She did not realize that she was playing the role opposite that of a great sovereign, seeking courtiers instead of allowing, as a favor, to be sought after the old ways . . . She showed herself in the middle of coarse town festivals and celebrations of the people and populace of Paris . . . The queen only came to Saint-Cloud, a castle known by the orgies of the house of Orléans; by the mass meetings of Parisians, and no one has yet forgotten that she placed herself in the jousts and other games of the boatmen as a simple spectator, alongside the bourgeoisie, who every Sunday flocked to Saint-Cloud. The queen took advantage of all these circumstances to change and simplify our costumes.[76]

Despite their comparative minimalism when compared to court gowns, fashionable dress was criticized as debates about luxury raged.[77] Women were accused of profligacy as the pace of fashion change increased due to advances in manufacturing, trade, and communication. Consumption's critics condemned the same styles that fashion magazines lauded for simplicity. For example, dramatist and scholar Beffroy de Reigny complained that provincials' conspicuous consumption was minimizing class distinctions and wasting money on trivialities like "a *robe à la turque* & a thousand other things of equal importance, which are as useless to happiness as to merit."[78] A significant portion of blame was placed on Marie-Antoinette; purportedly, her lavish and frequently changing wardrobe encouraged French women to spend themselves into penury.[79] Furthermore, Turkish-inspired clothing had opulent associations, which derived from perceptions of the Ottoman Empire as a decadent country where people spent their time in indolent pleasure.[80]

To complicate matters, concerns about Marie-Antoinette's dress were not limited to her vast expenditures. She also came under repeated fire for not adequately promoting the French silk industry.[81] In December 1779, commercial representatives from Lyon, the silk fabric manufacturing center of France, traveled to Versailles to report on the financial difficulties occurring in that city due to the massive popularity of cotton fabrics. As a result of the Lyonnais visit, Marie-Antoinette announced that no ladies should appear before her in the *polonaise* gown.[82] When another deputation made similar complaints several months later, the king responded by ordering "rich fabrics" for his clothes, and the court ladies (presumably including the queen) followed suit by abandoning "*les polonoises, les circassiennes, les turques, les lévites.*"[83] However, clearly neither of these decisions lasted long given these incidents' repetition, and the queen's wardrobe inventories continued to include these gowns. As a result, she persisted in being accused of personally destroying the silk industry until the Revolution. According the Abbé Soulavie's memoirs, the queen's wardrobe simplification meant "thousands of families, busy with our arts, fell into inaction and misery, and discontent broke out."[84]

Finally, the strong suggestion of sensuality associated with Ottoman-inspired fashions may have damaged Marie-Antoinette. Ottoman women had long been connected with the idea of sexual licentiousness in the French cultural imagination, based on fascination with the practices of polygamy and harems.[85] Solnon argues that when French women were painted in costume as desirable *sultanes*, their costume was meant to display their beauty and "talents as major lovers."[86] When Louis XV's mistresses, the Marquise de Pompadour and Comtesse du Barry—derogatively called "*la Sultane française*"—were painted in costume as *sultanes*, they referenced their unauthorized, yet powerful, positions founded on sexuality and luxury consumption.[87] Marie-Antoinette was not called "*sultane*," but was similarly criticized for her sexual hold over the king, which her critics declared gave her unofficial, and therefore uncontrolled, political power; she was further accused of multiple affairs with men and women of the court, signaling her supposed moral and political corruption.[88]

Chrisman-Campbell contends the "perceived eroticism of the dress of the Near and Far East remained a large part of its enduring appeal," and the French styles they inspired were considered "more sensual than western."[89] Fashion magazines drew on this eroticism, promoting Turkish-inspired modes by invoking the myth of the Ottoman harem's seductive *sultanes*, desirable wives, and beautiful concubines.[90] For example, the *Cabinet des modes* declared that, wearing a *robe à la turque*, "A pretty woman, whether at the Theatre, or in an Assembly, wins more certain & more agreeable triumphs than those of a Georgian or Circassian woman in the Harems of Constantinople. Even the *Sultane* is jealous of her elegance, her grace, and the homage rendered to her."[91] These and other fashionable styles were associated with the trope of the "*petite maitresse*," what we might call today a "fashionista," whose love of novelty was thought to make her susceptible to seduction.[92] One author cautioned,

> Fashions have lost more young girls than all the vices put together. What should the little bourgeois girl whose parents raise with decency think, who is only dressed formally on ceremonial days, and whose very adornment is modest? . . . Will she dare look at her pretty plain *fourreau*, when she sees a *robe à la turque*, green, made with a pink silk petticoat? . . . The fatal instant arrives, the seducer appears . . . Virtue falters, & the victim lets herself be drawn into the trap that vanity & fashion have set for her.[93]

The eroticism of Turkish dress was thought to indicate a moral corruption that threatened to break down the social order, just as Marie-Antoinette's assumed dissipation was supposed to endanger the monarchy and French society.[94] These fashions brought together criticisms of the queen's spending and sexuality, two themes that Crowston argues operated in similar ways, as both "carried similar implications of illegitimate female networks of exchange and expenditure sapping the heart of a corrupt realm."[95] Jones concurs, explaining,

> At the heart of critiques of the queen's relationship with Rose Bertin [that is, fashion] lay anxieties about women's *commercial* as well as *political* prominence, concerns about women's material as well as sexual longings, and fears of the disorder that might result if working-class women controlled the buying habits of upper-class women. If the public role of aristocratic women was increasingly called into question on the eve of the Revolution, surely this was connected to the growing conviction among contemporaries that all women were innately frivolous consumers of the material goods available in the public commercial spaces of Paris as well as of the political ideals available in the public sphere of salons and assemblies; female incapacity to rule—either in the realm of commerce or in the realm of politics—was increasingly believed to be grounded in women's enslavement to the despotism of *la mode*.[96]

When Marie-Antoinette chose to wear fashionable dress influenced by that worn in the Ottoman Empire, she likely hoped to counteract her reputation for extravagance and demonstrate her morality through her commitment to Enlightenment ideals. Instead, by dressing not as a queen but rather like other fashionable women, she did exactly the opposite. The French people did not want a stylish, enlightened queen with political agency; they wanted one who dutifully provided the country with heirs and otherwise lived an irreproachable, ceremonial, secluded life. In this way fashionable dress, particularly Ottoman-inspired styles with their connections to luxury and female licentiousness, reinforced ongoing criticism against the French queen. These connections established between Turkish and French dress would continue to play out through the French Revolution and beyond.

CONCLUSION

OTTOMAN-INSPIRED FASHIONS, 1785–1810

By the mid-1780s, English-inspired styles dominated French fashion. As the decade ended and the Revolution loomed, the *robe à l'anglaise* and other English gowns and jackets seemed more appropriate to the national mood. Chrisman-Campbell argues these became "inexorably entwined with the radical ideas that would soon erupt in the French Revolution."[1] Nonetheless, Ottoman and Eastern European references continued to exist as a secondarily significant theme in French fashion. Robes, *caracos, bonnets, capotes,* and poufs *à la turque* appear in the *Magasin des modes* in the second half of the 1780s, as well as garments styled *à la Polonoise, à la Czarine, à Sultane, à la Grecque, du serrail, à la Circassienne, à la Samaritaine,* and *à la lévite*.[2] The names of these styles all referenced the Ottoman Empire or culturally related regions and symbols, and most of the gowns and jackets featured cutaway front bodices. The *robe à la Tippoo-Saïb,* as well as the redingote and *caraco à l'Indienne,* were inspired by the 1788 ambassadorial visit from Mysore (in modern India).[3] These gowns were essentially variations on the *turque* and *anglaise,* as the *Magasin*'s editors explained: "Does it differ much from the *robes à la Turque,* or *à l'Angloise,* or even *à la française* (these are no more than *robes à l'Angloise*)? No; since it only differs in the length of the train, which is much wider than that of those dresses."[4] Furthermore, the emphasis in fashion magazines of the late 1780s and early 1790s turned toward headwear; increasingly, robes or jackets were mentioned only briefly before turning to extensive

Fig. 176. A *robe à la circassienne*, which looks identical to the *robe à la turque*, in revolutionary colors. *Journal de la mode et du goût*, March 5, 1790, pl. 1 (detail). (Bunka Gakuen University Library, Tokyo.)

descriptions of hats, caps, and other accessories for the head.[5] As gowns receded in importance, their variations were minimized. In 1789, the *Magasin des modes* introduced a *robe à la turque* as

> not cut too high, nor too *décoletée* [*sic*], nor too long, nor too wide, but made in the right proportions. This form, [which] we could say is already old, is recognized as so agreeable, so perfect, that we do not change it *anymore,* and instead try variations for the colors of the bodice, or the sleeves, or the petticoat, or the collars, which are different from those other parts of the *robe*. The different names that we give to *robes,* does not mean that their shape is different. It is *no longer so,* because the sleeves are of one color, and the bodice of another.[6]

The French Revolution that began in 1789 accelerated many of the changes that were already underway in French society. After the storming of the Bastille in July, Chrisman-Campbell explains, "The upper classes . . . had to give up their habitual finery or risk being branded counterrevolutionaries. Fashion and luxury became synonymous with tyranny."[7] Lynn Hunt argues that once the Revolution began, "A body was no longer defined by its place in a cosmic order cemented by hierarchy, deference, and readily readable dress; each individual body now carried within itself all the social and political meanings of the new political order, and these meanings proved very difficult to discern."[8] Many traditional symbols of social status became suspect, and for men, the dress of the working-class *sans culottes*, the tricolor cockade, and the *bonnet rouge* (also called Phrygian cap) all came to symbolize republican sentiment and the active role of the new citizen.[9] Female republican dress was not so straightforwardly defined, and women's efforts to adopt these same symbols, particularly the *bonnet rouge,* met with resistance.[10] The Revolution interrupted the fashion cycle, and slightly dated styles appear to have been reintroduced and nationalized

170   CONCLUSION

as magazine editors scrambled to create news. In 1790, the *Journal de la mode et du goût* announced, "The beginning of the revolution has not given birth to many new fashions, and on this chapter the Ladies are dressed rather indifferently."[11] English styles continued to be associated with republican sentiment; simple, informal dress was essential; and revolutionary symbols like the Bastille and the national colors of red, white, and blue became stylish.[12] The *Journal*'s editors explained, "Today their [ladies'] taste begins to awaken, and a great number become patriots, adopting the colors of the Nation." Interestingly, this discussion of patriotic fashion is regarding a "satin *robe à la circassienne* striped in the three colors of the Nation" (Fig. 176). Despite its name, this "*circassienne*" looks more like a *robe à la turque*, with cutaway front bodice, short oversleeves, and long train, which is the same cut seen again on subsequent *circassiennes* in this magazine two years later.[13]

No fashion magazines were published in France between 1794 and 1797, during which the Terror's violence interrupted many aspects of daily life.[14] Nonetheless, we can look to English sources for clues about French fashion. Although the English had their own trends, they also had a long-standing tradition of following French modes, and London was a center for French émigrés who became style leaders.[15] Ottoman-inspired fashions are mentioned in English sources in this period, possibly reflecting what was being worn in France (or by French émigrés), although they may have been a distinctly English phenomenon. The *Times* of London reported that one of summer 1793's new styles was a "Polonese," whose cut appears to be similar to the earlier version in that it included the cutaway front, but now omitted the looped-up skirt: "the robe sloped away at the sides, so as to leave a slip of scarcely a foot broad, which falls over the petticoat behind."[16] Meanwhile, illustrations of Ottoman-inspired gowns surfaced multiple times in the English *Gallery of Fashion*, which began publication in 1794. These include a "Circassian robe" (1794); four "robes à la turque" (1794 and 1796); five "robes à la Polonoise," one with "Circassian sleeves" (1795); two "Russian robes" (1795 and 1796); an "Armenian robe" (1796); a "Persian robe" (1796); a "robe with a Turkish front" (1797); a "Hungarian robe" (1797); and more of the same in following years.[17] Most of these were worn fully open in front, some with a narrow sash closing the dress at the (now high) waist, over an undergown; a few have crossover fronts, an element drawn from Ottoman and Persian menswear. Intriguingly, in 1798 *The Fashions of London and Paris* featured a *polonaise* shown clearly from the back that was cut in the tunic style without waist seam, with inverted pleats opening at the waist—just like the 1770s *polonaise* (Fig.

Fig. 177. The figure on the right wears a "Blue muslin polonese and petticoat; gold or lace trimming. Blue puckered epaulets; white satin short sleeves." Note the lack of waist seam and box pleats opening from the bodice seams. (*Fashions of London & Paris,* March 1798, Plate 1, Bunka Gakuen University Library, Tokyo.)

177). Several extant gowns in this style exist. One particularly interesting example is a 1795–99 English gown made from a cashmere shawl (Figs. 178, 179), which in this period would have been imported from India, reinforcing the gown's Eastern associations, at the Victoria & Albert Museum. The body is made without waist seam, with multiple vertical stitched-down pleats to fit the torso.[18] It has the kind of shawl collar seen on the *lévite* and *polonaise*, as well as the short oversleeves and longer undersleeves associated with the *turque* and *circassienne;* the collar and oversleeves are in green silk satin, and undersleeves in cream silk. It also has a sewn-in, front-opening stomacher made only from the linen lining, which crosses over to close (it was probably covered by a separate stomacher in the fashion fabric or meant to be covered by the tails of a fichu). According to Alexandra Palmer, the construction of another similarly styled English gown from this period at the Royal Ontario Museum shares many connections with Turkish garments.[19] However, none of these 1790s iterations featured looped-up overskirts; instead, the defining component was the robe, generally worn open over an underdress, likely with bodice and skirt cut in one.

As the French economy stabilized in 1797, the *Journal des dames et des modes* (Journal of ladies and fashions, 1797–1839) began publication, followed by the *Tableau général du goût, des modes et costumes de Paris, par une société d'artistes et gens de lettres* (General table of taste, fashions and costumes of Paris, by a society of artists and men of letters, 1797–99) and *L'Arlequin, ou Tableau des modes et des goûts* (The Harlequin, or Table of fashions and tastes, 1798–99). The dominant theme in Directoire (1795–99) and Empire (1800–1815) fashion was neoclassical (called "ancient" or "antique" in the period), referencing ancient Greco-Roman dress.[20] High-waisted muslin gowns with comparatively narrow silhouettes styled *à l'antique* predominated among upper-class and bourgeois women, and these were associated with ancient Athenian democracy and thus modern republican sentiment.[21] These gowns had their roots in a number of styles, including "classical" costumes worn for portraiture and theater, the *chemise à la reine* and *fourreau* gowns, and the ancient Greek peplos and chiton.[22] This dress, generally called "*robe*" or "*tunique*," was associated with the antiquity and nature cults, and was seen as appropriately patriotic and revolutionary as it was considered modest,

liberating, simple, and egalitarian. Moreover, it allowed women to assume what E. Claire Cage calls the "ennobling language of arts and of the virtues and glory of antiquity" and, through its simple silhouette, sheer fabrics, and reduced undergarments, encouraged a new visibility of the female body, which had been deemphasized during the masculine Jacobin period of the Revolution.[23]

Despite the rhetoric promoting the neoclassical mode, Ottoman and other Eastern references continued to be a prominent theme that was subsumed into the new aesthetic.[24] Naomi Lubrich argues that although the *Journal des dames* did ascribe ancient Greek inspiration to stylish gowns, "Neither Greece nor Rome provided the dominant context for the dress. Rather, *Journal des dames* most often depicted *exotic* accessories to go along with the dress."[25] Among the most important was the turban, which entered French fashion in the 1770s. In the Ottoman Empire, headwear was a key identifier of gender, religion, ethnicity, and status, and thus a focus for French interest.[26] The men's turban (Figs. 2, 4, 19, 133) consisted of fabric wrapped around a brimless hat, although Westerners often failed to notice the hat base, while women wore various wrapped and draped veils, frequently over hats.[27] Since the medieval era, Western Europeans had drawn on the intricate headwear worn in Turkish dress to create and adapt their own styles, and with the advent of eighteenth-century *turquerie*, turbans became fashionable female accessories.[28]

Figs. 178 and 179. This gown may be a late 1790s iteration of the *robe à la turque*, given its one-piece construction and short oversleeves over longer undersleeves, as well as the lack of waist seam. Meanwhile, the shawl collar suggests the *lévite*. Gown, England, 1795–99, wool, silk, linen, Victoria & Albert Museum, London, T.217-1968. (Courtesy of Victoria and Albert Museum, London. First photo by author.)

CONCLUSION 173

Fig. 180. The "*Pouf à l'Asiatique,*" referring to the puffed gauze headdress accented with pearls, flowers, and feathers. The stripes, swagged pearls, crescent-shaped brooch, and tassel all reinforce the headdress's Ottoman associations. Esnauts et Rapilly (publisher), *Gallerie des modes et costumes français . . . coiffure à la Flore . . .* (detail), ca. 1776–87. (Engraving on paper and cardboard, 310 × 260 mm, Rijksmuseum, Amsterdam. Gift of Jonkvrouw C. I. Six, 's-Graveland.)

According to Landweber, Marie-Antoinette and her ladies adopted a version of the turban after seeing the ambassadors from Mysore (India), but that visit took place at least a decade after the turban entered French fashion.[29] Multiple references to turbans as women's headdress exist in the *Gallerie des modes* from its first issues as well as the later *Magasin des modes* and *Journal de la mode et du goût*, like the "*turban à la turque,*" "*turban* or *toque à la Levantine,*" and "cap *à la* High-Priestess of white gauze, tied with a large ribbon with wide blue & white stripes, forming a sort of turban cap *à la Turque.*"[30] Moreover, wrapped, bouffant headdresses imitating the look of turbans were fashionable in this period.[31] In the first half of the century, women's caps (*bonnets*) worn for fashionable daywear tended to cover closely the top, back, and sides of the head, and were made from a fabric circle gathered to a frilled band. However, from the early 1770s, the fashionable *bonnet* transitioned to a gathered, puffed shape sitting primarily on top of the head, often without any kind of visible band, which echoed the silhouette of the turban (Fig. 180). By the late 1770s, these caps were also called "*poufs,*" which seem to be a distinctive variation of the *bonnet* (for example, the *Magasin des modes* writes of one: "the *Bonnet* represented is a *Pouf* . . . made of blue Italian gauze"), although *bonnets* and *poufs* had similar silhouettes.[32] Veils, including those covering the face, were much more typical of Ottoman female dress; however, French women never embraced the practice of covering the face, which was generally considered oppressive, although a few efforts occurred in the Directoire and Empire periods.[33] Nonetheless, *bonnets*, *poufs*, and turbans frequently included long hanging back pieces evoking Turkish veils.

The fashion for turbans reached its apogee in the Directoire and Empire periods. Both by design and now by name, they were nearly ubiquitous in the *Journal des dames et des modes* from its first issues in 1797 through the 1830s (the Greek War of Independence, 1821–30, gave the turban a later boost).

Intriguingly, several of the first turbans illustrated in the *Journal des dames* include the structured base that formed part of the Ottoman man's turban but was usually omitted in later Western adaptations (Fig. 181).[34] These fashionable women's turbans carried with them Turkish connotations. The *Journal*'s editors warned, "The turban today enjoys a favor all the better deserved, since no hairstyle adapts more elegantly to cropped heads . . . Our charming *odalisques*, assuming the costume of the followers of the Koran, seem to presage the necessity where we will soon have to treat them according to the laws of Mohammed, if the number of women continues to increase as that of men decreases."[35]

Jirousek connects the fashion for turbans to Napoleon's campaign in Egypt (1798–1801), and indeed Egyptian references in fashion did follow.[36] Most popular were gowns and other garments referring to the Mamluks, the Egyptian military ruling class who were Ottoman vassals, and who French troops understood superficially to be Turkish.[37] Beginning in Year X of the French Republican calendar (circa 1801–2), the *Journal des dames* illustrated several "*tuniques à la Mameluck*," all short, front-opening overgowns, as well as gowns with "Sleeves *à la Mameluck*" and at least one "Turban *à la Mameluck*."[38] These styles were simultaneously cast as French, Eastern, and colonial; observing English newspapers reporting on their own country's trend for Egyptian-inspired styles, the editor of the *Journal des dames* countered, "I do not know how the English fashions appropriated names over which we should have exclusive privilege, since they belong to us by right of conquest. Egypt is ours; therefore only we can dispose of the Nile, the pyramids and the crocodiles. So our milliners are busy claiming this property."[39]

Turkish-inspired gowns continued to be fashionable well through the neoclassical era, and were increasingly employed as outerwear. In 1806, the Ottoman Empire established a permanent embassy in Paris. According to the journal *Le Miroir*, this led to

Fig. 181. This "spiral turban trimmed with jet beads" is wrapped around a structured base, as were Ottoman turbans. Sellèque (publisher), Pierre de la Mésangère (publisher), *Journal des dames et des modes, costume parisien, 11 mai 1798, An 6, (19): Turban en spiral (. . .)* (detail). (Engraving on paper, 177 × 118 mm, Rijksmuseum, Amsterdam. Purchased with the support of the F. G. Waller-Fonds.)

CONCLUSION 175

a resurgence of Turkish-inspired fashions, including the *robe à la turque:* "The *Journal des dames* announces officially that Turkey will pay the tribute of its fashions to France. The makers are only occupied with making *bonnets turcs, chapeaux à la sultane. Robes à la turque* already exist. Mme T . . . n [Thérésa Cabarrus, Madame Tallien, 1773–1835, according to one source] wore one the day before yesterday at the Odéon ball."40 When the Turkish ambassador visited Marseille, the *Journal de Marseille*'s editor wrote of a resulting "revolution in our fashions . . . Is it Turkey that pays its tribute to our fashions, or is it our elegant women who become tributes to *oriental* taste?"41 The *Journal des dames et modes* included multiple dresses and outerwear garments with Turkish names and stylings in this period, including the "*doliman*" and "*douillette*" (a "type of *doliman*" [Fig. 182], several specifically "*Lévantine*"); "spencer [a short jacket] *à L'algérienne*"; *robe* and *pelisse* "*en Demi-Turque*" and "*à la Turque*"; "Russian *Tunique*"; "*Polonnoise*"; "*redingote à la Polonaise*"; and robe, redingote, spencer, and *pelisse* "*de Lévantine*."42 Several "*Juive*" or Jewish gowns also appear, which Lubrich connects conceptually to the *lévite*.43

French fashion magazines had some difficulty explaining the pairing of Eastern elements with neoclassical modes. The *Tableau général du goût* commented on the incongruity of a "French costume imitating the antique" worn with a "*Coiffure à l'Egyptienne*":

> The artist would have liked not to place an oriental-style hairstyle on a woman's bust draped in Roman style; but obliged to give an account of the costume followed in Paris, he had to sacrifice his taste for the truth, and retrace the fashion as it is, however ridiculous it may seem. Our elegant women in general adopt without reflection the fantasies which flatter them by their novelty. Little is known about the analogy that one kind of adornment can have with the rest of the clothing, and the advantages which must result from the harmonious agreement of the parts with the whole.44

Discordant Ottoman themes could be reconciled by recasting them with French or ancient Greco-Roman associations. The *Journal des dames* observed, "At the balls, most of the outfits derive from antiquity; if fashion had rules, this would mean establishing conventions; but capriciousness unscrupulously associates a Greek tunic with a *Parisian* turban."45

Fig. 182. The "*Douillette*" was "a kind of *doliman*," dolman being a Turkish outer caftan. The short sleeves, fur trim, and front opening are characteristic of Ottoman dress. Sellèque (publisher), Pierre de la Mésangère (publisher), *Journal des dames et des modes, costume parisien*, 29 janvier 1799, An 7 (87): *Capote de satin rose* (. . .) (detail). (Engraving on paper, 177 × 114 mm, Rijksmuseum, Amsterdam. Purchased with the support of the F. G. Waller-Fonds.)

The *schall* (shawl, from the Persian *chal* or *shaal*) was another Eastern garment that achieved widespread popularity in France in this period.[46] Although it was taken from Indian dress, it also brought with it Ottoman associations: cashmere shawls found their first fashionability after French soldiers returned with them from Egypt, and they were imported through Constantinople among other ports.[47] In fact, several early examples in the *Journal des dames* are specifically called "*schall turc.*"[48] The *Arlequin* recast these Indian and Ottoman associations by connecting shawls to their ancient Greco-Roman analogues:

> Greek women, as well as the Romans, wore over their clothing, a type of light coat which almost entirely covered them. Often they tied it on the shoulders, and raised the end of it in their sashes; often, they fixed it up under the breast, by a knot, or with a pin. Our French women, in their dress, ancient costumes, have replaced the *peplum* of the Greeks, and the *palla* of the Romans, by a very ample and very transparent *schall.*[49]

Their floral motifs added decoration to the generally plain, white textiles used for gowns in the early nineteenth century, added grace to arm gestures, and warmed women dressed in lightweight Empire gowns.[50] Empress Joséphine (1763–1814), a key style leader of the period, was an early adopter of shawls and many Frenchwomen followed suit.[51] Shawls became a central feature of French (and, more generally, Western) female fashion from this period through the middle of the nineteenth century, and were associated with both the domestic and female as well as colonial and exotic. Several reasons existed for this garment's staying power: Susan Hiner demonstrates that the shawl was exotic, expensive, and considered simultaneously erotic yet virtuous, while Geczy argues that it "articulated the beauty and profits of colonization."[52]

A few Ottoman-inspired styles existed in the mid-nineteenth-century fashion, generally fur-

Fig. 183. The lady wears a one-piece *polonaise* in black over a pink waistcoat and gray petticoat. The skirts are drawn up in back following the influence of the Dolly Varden. Jules David, A. Bodin (engraver), Ad. Goubaud et Fils (publisher), Bruyant-Christophe et Compagnie (publisher), *Journal des dames et des demoiselles, 15 Novembre 1872, no. 1809B* (detail). (Engraving on paper, 295 × 200 mm, Rijksmuseum, Amsterdam. Purchased with the support of the F. G. Waller-Fonds.)

CONCLUSION 177

trimmed outerwear, which is reminiscent of the early eighteenth-century application of the term *polonaise*.[53] This practice continued sporadically throughout the first half of the nineteenth century until the late 1860s, when a major renaissance of the *polonaise* occurred as part of a general eighteenth-century fashion revival.[54] Fashion magazines began to promote a gown called "*polonaise*" (Fig. 183) along with styles referencing Madame de Pompadour and Marie-Antoinette. This reimagined *polonaise* was a gown, generally cut without a waist seam, initially with a crossover front.[55] It combined with an English trend for dresses worn *retroussée*, inspired by a painting of Dolly Varden—Charles Dickens's heroine from *Barnaby Rudge* (1841)—that circulated after Dickens's death in 1870.[56] The novel was set during the 1780 Gordon Riots, and Varden was painted by William Powell Frith in a printed cotton dress worn *retroussée*. This spawned a vogue across the West for a gown called the "Dolly Varden," which was inspired by the eighteenth-century *polonaise*. This new iteration featured an overskirt, open or with an apron drape in front, with the skirt drawn up in back. The *polonaise* and Dolly Varden styles were frequently combined, and aspects of both lasted throughout the decade, particularly the *polonaise*'s tunic-style cut and Varden's looped-up overskirts. Both went out of style in the late 1870s, although the (frequently one-piece) *polonaise* resurfaced occasionally in fashion magazines through the Edwardian era.

The scarcity of extant examples of Ottoman-inspired garments in museums may be because they have yet to be identified. Furthermore, the late eighteenth century was a period when styles changed quickly while textiles remained costly, so dressmakers and wearers had incentive to alter existing garments to suit changing modes.[57] Of the four key styles studied in this book, extant robes and jackets *à la polonaise* are the most numerous; fewer examples of the *circassienne*, *turque*, and *lévite* have been identified, although these do exist (see appendix 2 for a full list of extant Ottoman-inspired garments). This may have contributed to scholars' sense that these fashions were relatively insignificant, but written and visual sources prove just the opposite.

The history of French and Ottoman dress was not a one-way street. Scholars have demonstrated Turkish interest in Western European fashion, their importation of Western goods, and the effects of Western designs on Ottoman clothing.[58] Fatma Koç and Emine Koca trace the first impacts to the eighteenth century, when they find a more Westernized ornamentation aesthetic in textile motifs and trims, while women's traditional coats and veils became more of "a dressing and ornament style rather than a way of covering the body."[59] Scarce observes that French textiles were imported for use in Ottoman clothing from the early eighteenth century.[60] Jirousek clarifies that while imported textiles were fashionable in the Empire, only about 20 percent of silks came from France in this period, with the rest coming from Persia and India.[61] Interestingly, she also notes that the hats used as the turban's base, which were primarily manufactured in Tunisia, were also fabricated by newly created factories in the French cities of Marseilles and Bearn.[62] Ottoman men's dress did not evolve much in this period, but Jirousek finds multiple aesthetic changes to women's dress that she traces to Western influence, including deeper necklines, closer fits, and oversized headdresses.[63] More significant impacts would be felt in the nineteenth century, as interactions with Europeans increased and the government reorganized and oriented more toward the West.

More than a century of *turquerie* in dress—from the 1670s through the 1800s—gave exoticism a firm hold on French fashion and national identity. As trade routes opened, and travel and communication methods improved, a wider world became available for fashion inspiration—and for colonialism. The French had already established colonies in North America, as well as smaller settlements in India and Africa. In the nineteenth century, France became the second largest colonial empire after the British, with territories in Africa and Southeast Asia. Did French *turquerie* help pave the way for the nineteenth- and twentieth-century colonialist mindset? The eighteenth-century relationship between France and the Ottoman Empire was one of relative equals, although a tone of condescension and appropriation is sometimes present in French adoption of Turkish dress, and generally the meanings of these fashions speak more about French culture than Ottoman. In the nineteenth century, the power balance was more unequal as France held political and military control over its colonial possessions. According to Marie-Cecile Thoral's study of colonial Algeria, cultural cross-dressing "served to highlight the progress of French colonial expansion and the western appropriation of Algerian resources."[64] Given current discussions of the problematic aspects of cultural appropriation and commodification, understanding the historical systems from which these processes originated is important.[65] However, Thoral demonstrates how for native Algerians, "dress ... became one of the most powerful channels of expression of growing anti-colonial grievances and the flowering of an independence movement in the early decades of the twentieth century."[66] Thus, we must be conscious of the multiplicity of possible meanings and power dynamics, and ready to understand dress as a means of *active* communication and negotiation. Just as condescension and appropriation existed in eighteenth-century French *turquerie*, so did admiration, respect, and varying levels of comprehension.

Scholars have tended to focus their studies not only by field, subfield, and period but also by geography. The history of consumption, including dress, demonstrates the need for larger cross-cultural and/or global perspectives. If we study one geographic area in isolation, we miss the opportunity to understand just how connected people were across region, country, continent, and even hemisphere. Why has knowledge of the overwhelming cultural influence of the Ottoman Empire on the West in the early modern period faded? One critical factor may be that looking back from a contemporary viewpoint, we are too aware of the Empire's decline and end. Thus, cross-cultural approaches to history are necessary if we are to fully understand the perspectives of historical individuals and communities, and to redress the history of Eurocentric scholarship. So long as the West is considered in isolation, we perpetuate the myth that it has always been superior, only playing the influencer and never the influenced. Turkish-inspired French fashions brought with them real, tangible changes to women's dress and thus to concepts of how clothing *should* operate on a material level. At the same time, *turquerie* in dress played critical social functions, allowing the French to negotiate changing understandings of personal, national, and cultural identity as well as the social roles of dress and fashion. By taking a global perspective, more nuance is visible in the power relationships of previous eras—and perhaps we can even move beyond a focus on power to instead consider world views in all their complexity.

APPENDIX 1

Other Ottoman-Influenced Styles, 1775–92

Numerous styles referenced Ottoman fashions and culture, but some are harder to catalog due to their more fleeting nature. It is unclear whether these were commonly worn or were failed attempts to introduce new styles. Nonetheless, they demonstrate the overwhelming popularity of Turkish themes in French fashion during the late eighteenth century.

"Déshabillé à la Henri IV"*—Nouveau Mercure de France*, 1775:

> We strongly applaud a gallant *négligé*, named, the *déshabillé à la Henri IV*. This is a type of *robe,* or Turkish *simarre,* without pleats, & where the sleeves are large & ample. They are made in plain taffeta in the desired color, they are trimmed entirely with plain or brocaded gauze, with a flounce trimming all around. These *robes* are tied at the neck with a ribbon, which brings together a double ruff in gauze, thus the effect is charming. This *déshabillé* has the advantage of repairing, or at least hiding the most *négligée* toilette. They are worn when getting out of bed, over a morning *robe, caraco* & even a *peignoir*. It joins a true ease, an elegance, & yet is very noble.[1]

Simarre comes from the Italian *zimarra,* a sixteenth-century Italian loose overdress modeled on Turkish caftans.[2] In eighteenth-century France, the term generally referred to academic or ecclesiastical dress. The 1762 *Dictionnaire de l'académie française* defines it as, "A long and trained garment that women used to use . . . Today it is used for a type of robe that Presidents, Prelates, etc. wear sometimes when they are at home."[3] No plate.

"*Robe à la Levantine*"—*Gallerie des modes*, 1779 (Fig. 166):[4]

> The petticoat and the *soubreveste* named *l'Assyrienne* [the Mesopotamian kingdom of Assyria, located in what was then the Ottoman Empire] . . . This is a *robe* with sleeves, cut *en fourreau* in back: that is to say that only the skirt forms pleats at the back and sides: it closes as preferred on the chest, and must appear rather placed on the body where attached. This *robe* covers part of a *soubreveste* open in front, which is cut to size. The sleeves *en amadis* emerge from the oversleeves of the *Levantine*, and end by a wide facing.[5]

Levantine refers to the Levant, the area of the eastern Mediterranean then under Ottoman control.

Sultane: Multiple iterations of garments called "*sultane*" were introduced throughout the eighteenth century.[6] These include:

- *Journal de Paris*, 1780: Femme Guedon, Maîtresse Couturiere, wrote to the journal to announce,

> After much research, I have created a new type of *Robe* which combines the advantages of those known under the names of *Polonoise* & *Lévite*, & removes the inconveniences. The first is too short, & the second does not sufficiently reveal the beauty of the figure. That of my invention, which I call *à la Sultane*, can be trained or can be *retrousser* in an elegant & always favorable manner, even to people who have some defects in their hips. The front takes the shape of the man's *veste*, & holds the *Robe* to the body, at the top of which is an elegant, though simple collar. I have adapted to this *Robe* a new trim that I dare to find beautiful, in which I hope not to be alone in my opinion.[7]

No plate.

- *Gallerie des modes*, 1781: "*Grande robe à la Sultane* the bodice closed in front and draperies *retroussée* on the side with knots and tassels, it has sleeves like the *robes à la Circassienne*, it differs from the ordinary *robe à la sultane*, which is totally open in front and without oversleeves like a *Polonaise*, the skirt is cut, the coiffure in turban."[8] A typically shaped court bodice with wide *paniers*. Fur trims the edges of the short oversleeves and long undersleeves. An overskirt is swagged in front asymmetrically, as is a flounce on the petticoat; both are trimmed in fur and tassels. A short standing ruff recalls the fashions of the sixteenth and seventeenth centuries. The puffed cap has a standing feather placed asymmetrically in front.

- *Gallerie des modes*, 1782: "Simple *robe à la Sultane* that which is actually worn except in full dress. This robe is unattached in front and displays the skirt entirely. In back it forms the *polonaise détroussé* [detached from being *rétroussée*] and hangs to the ground like the *Lévite*."[9] An overgown that is open widely in front; instead of fastening at the center front, it opens from the side bust. It has long sleeves, and is worn over a stomacher or underbodice, with petticoat over wide *paniers*.

- *Encyclopédie méthodique*, 1785: "The *sultane*, which existed before all these dresses [the *polonaise*, *turque*, *anglaise*, etc.], also had the shape of a *robe de chambre*, but was not loose. It had a single pleat below the waist in the back, and one on each side of the hips, over the *poches* [small hoops]. It descended to the floor, covering the breast and all of the arm down to the hand; it only had little success."[10] No plate.

- *Gallerie des modes*, 1787: "*Robe à la Sultane*," a closed-front gown whose bodice and long sleeves feature ruffled accents. The whole gown is trimmed with swagged fabric that has bows at each attachment point. The neckline is cut low enough for most of the breast to be exposed.[11]

- *Magasin des modes*, 1787: "a *sultane* (type of vest), instead of a stomacher" worn with the *caraco à la turque*.[12] No plate.

- *Magasin des modes*, 1789:

> *Juste à la Sultane*, of which the front, the skirtings & the shoulders are sky blue satin, & of which the backs & sleeves are white satin. From the shoulders, silver fringes fall on the long sleeves. The sleeves, which only descend to the elbows, are trimmed with cuffs of linen trimmed with sharp teeth [i.e., triangular points]. The *juste* is laced in front by a ladder of white ribbons, over the stomacher, of white satin. It is tied with a large sash of blue satin, trimmed with large silver fringes at points, which forms a large knot on the right side where it falls.[13]

A jacket whose front bodice pieces and short oversleeves are made in one color, with the back pieces and elbow-length undersleeves are in another. A swag of fabric trims the petticoat. A wide sash is tied at the waist. Everything is trimmed with gathered or pleated ruches that are cut in triangular points.

- *Magasin des modes*, 1789:

Caraco à la Sultane, of light purple satin, with long sleeves similar to the *caraco*, trimmed with gauze cuffs cut in points, with very long skirtings cut in diamonds, & with two collars, the first of which, narrower, is of violet satin like the *caraco*, & the second, very large, is of white satin. Under this *caraco*, a stomacher & a very long petticoat, all the same fabric, of white satin . . . It is tied with a wide sash of black velvet, where are fastened two large medallions with subjects, enameled backgrounds & circles of gold."[14]

A long-sleeved jacket with wide open front in the typical triangular shape, and with short skirtings. It has a wide fold-over collar. The black belt has two medallions at the front closure, mimicking Turkish belt buckles.
- *Magasin des modes*, 1789: "*Caraco à la Sultane*, with long sleeves split *à la Marinière*, of green satin, & stomacher of pink satin, tied with a very wide black satin sash fastened by a broad medallion made of black satin *surrounded by a very wide circle of worked steel*."[15] The figure is only shown from the neck up; she wears an overbodice that fastens at the breast and then opens widely at the waist, with matching green oversleeves. Underneath is a stomacher and long sleeves. A wide sash with a center medallion is worn at the waist.
- *Journal de Paris*, 1790: "*Robe à la Sultane*. This one is also beautiful for full dress."[16] No plate.

"Robe à l'Asiatique"—*Gallerie des modes*, 1787: "*Robe à l'Asiatique* in blue satin, pink petticoat and pink collar."[17] The gown is shown from the back; it has a fitted bodice with a waist seam. The overskirt is very unusual: it is cut short over the hips and then graduates to full length in the center back. The sleeves are three-quarter length. A wide collar matches the petticoat.

Court gowns:
- *Gallerie des modes*, circa 1786–87: "*Grande robe de cour* in the Asian taste, trimmed with gauze and oak garlands."[18] A typically shaped court bodice with wide *paniers*. There are at least two skirts, possibly three, all trimmed with swags of ruffled material accented with bows; some of the swags are made in a spotted fabric; others are in the form of oak leaves. The neckline is trimmed with a ruffle, and the sleeves have gathered *sabot* cuffs.
- *Gallerie des modes*, circa 1786–87: "*Robe de cour au grand Orient*." Worn with a "coiffure in the asian fashion."[19] A typically shaped court bodice with wide *paniers*. The bodice has the triangular opening typical of the *polonaise*, *circassienne*, and *turque* over a stomacher or underbodice with center-front buttons. The sleeves are in multiple puffs. The overskirt has wide bands of contrasting fabric along its edges, which are turned back near the hem. Swags of drapery trim the overskirt, with rosettes at the attachment points. A long, striped scarf is draped around the neck, hanging down to about knee-length.
- *Gallerie des modes*, circa 1786–87: "*Robe de Cour à la Turque*" (Fig. 164). Worn with an "Oriental coiffure with aigrettes & plumes &c."[20]
- See also "*Grande robe à la Sultane*," above.

"Robe à la Czarine"—*Magasin des modes*, 1788:

Russia is the latest country to appear in Fashion; the *robes à la Czarine* derives from there. The *robe à la Czarine* . . . is adorned with a *colerette montante* [a small collar that grows taller toward the back of the neck] with two rows of cut gauze, like the cuffs. This *colerette montante* seems to be the only difference of this dress to the others we have shown. It must be the only one, since Russia follows the fashions of France . . . It is tied with a very long sash . . . tied on the side. This kind of sash was the first that our Ladies tied . . . [The *robe* is worn over a] *pièce d'estomac*.[21]

A gown that closes at the neckline, then slopes open toward the waist, worn over a contrasting stomacher and petticoat. Layered ruffles cut in spiky points form a collar and cuffs. A wide hanging sash is tied around the waist. *Czarine* refers to Catherine the Great, empress of Russia, a country whose commoners' dress was influenced by Ottoman styles. In the late eighteenth century, Russian court dress took on the look of the *robe à la turque*.[22]

"Robe à la Tippoo-Saïb"—*Magasin des Modes*, 1788:

See, in this Plate, a *robe à la Tipoo-Saïb*. Does it differ much from the *robes à la turque*, or *à l'angloise*, or even *à la Françoise* (these are no more than the *robes à l'Angloise*)? No; since it differs only in the length of the train, which is much longer than that of these dresses. It differs still by name . . . to come to descriptions, the *robe à la Tippoo-Saïb* worn by the Woman represented in

APPENDIX 1   183

this Plate, differs from the *robes à l'Angloise, à la Turque* and *à la Françoise*, by the name and the length of the train, is made of green-lemon taffeta with pink spots. We ourselves find a third difference with the *robes* that have appeared so far; but, rather, we will say that it is a new fashionable color. The long sleeves of the *redingote* are trimmed with cuffs of two rows of plain gauze, cut in points. Under this *robe*, the woman wears a petticoat of pink taffeta, plain, cut at the bottom edge. It has the *corps* tied with a sash of the same taffeta, trimmed, at points, with knots of green ribbon, & a fringe of silver at the ends, forming a large knot behind.[23]

A gown with fitted bodice, three-quarter sleeves, and short train made of spotted fabric, over a contrasting petticoat. A wide sash is tied in back, which hangs down to almost the ankle; it is gathered at multiple points with a trimming. Inspired by the visit of the ambassadors of Tipu Sultan, King of Mysore (now in modern-day India); thus, it is not technically Ottoman, but draws on Turkish dress to create a "foreign" style.[24]

"*Redingote à l'Indienne*"—*Magasin des modes*, 1788:

> Tippoo-Saib is chief of the *Marattes* & Lord of a rather vast Empire in India; his Ambassadors in paying their tribute to fashion, must not have given birth to only one form; but no single name could be given to each form, it was impossible to name every dress *à la Tippoo-Saïb;* the second form the Ambassadors gave has been named the *redingote à l'Indienne*. The *redingote à l'Indienne*, worn by the Woman represented in this Plate, is of apple-green taffeta: it is serrated on the fronts, & its train is very long. It is caught in front with a very large ladder of pink ribbons. We can feel that the difference of this *redingote* from the others is the length of the train of the *redingote*, the serration & the ladder of ribbons which catches it or attaches it. The Woman wears under this *redingote* a petticoat of linen gauze, trimmed with two ribbons of the same linen gauze; &, on the first furbelow, bouquets of pink ribbons.[25]

A gown with fitted bodice and long sleeves. The bodice front features a "ladder" of bows. The overskirt front edges are cut in scallops. The petticoat has two rows of spiky gathered flounces, the topmost trimmed with pink ribbon. Inspired by the visit of the ambassadors of Tipu Sultan, King of Mysore (now in modern-day India); thus, it is not technically Ottoman, but draws on Turkish dress to create a "foreign" style.

"*Caraco à la [sic] Arlaise*"—*Magasin des modes*, 1788 (Fig. 163):

> The *caracos*, which are almost the only dress of our Ladies today, as we have said, it is necessary to create infinite variations. A prodigious quantity have been created; presently they are in the shape of the *corsages* and sleeves of the *robes à la Turque;* & they are called *à la [sic] Arlaise*, because the women of Arles dress like this. The one worn by the young person represented in the Plate I, is in *souci chiné* black colored satin, bordered with a black & marigold fringe. Under this *caraco*, a white satin corset, tied with long ties in marigold silk, passed through polished steel buckles, fastened on the side, & whose sleeves of the same white satin, showing underneath those of the *caraco*, are a little slit on the side, & button with little matching buttons. These sleeves, are trimmed at the wrist with simple *découpé* Italian gauze cuffs. A petticoat also of white satin, trimmed with a double furbelow of the same *découpé* Italian gauze. This simple, but very elegant, ensemble is worn a great deal at balls.[26]

This references the *drolet* (Fig. 14), a jacket worn in Provence, particularly in and around the city of Arles; it was cut open widely in front in the same triangular line seen on many Turkish-inspired styles. When Englishwoman Mary Berry visited Provence in 1785, she recorded in her journal that the local women wore "a sort of loose robe, made behind like what we used to call in England a Polonaise or Circassian."[27] Similarly, Polish Count August Fryderyk Moszyński noted that the peasant women around Aix-en-Provence wore a garment almost "exactly the same" as the *robe à la circassienne*.[28]

"*Négligé du serrail*"—*Magasin des modes*, 1788:

> A woman in *négligé du serrail*. It is impossible that this fashion is not due to the Indian Ambassadors [of Tippoo-Saib]. Assuredly, it will be the *Marchandes* of *robes* who have conceived the *modes à l'Indienne*, & who have imagined the most agreeable fashions. And, in particular, it will be the Proprietor of the *Magasin de la rue de la Monnoie*, where our Draftsman drew the very elegant ones we gave, & which we give in this *cahier*,

who will have the honor of having invented all the dress fashions. This *négligé* is a *robe retroussée all round,* & revealing the petticoat, with a very long train, which develops & extends [in length]. The *robe,* whose back alone is in pink taffeta, is made of apple-green taffeta, & is trimmed with a white & green silk fringe. Its cuffs are in plain gauze, one row, scalloped. The petticoat has a very long train, is in pink satin, trimmed with a green silk fringe. The woman is tied with a sash *au Bramin,* in pink taffeta, trimmed at intervals, & at the bottom, with green silk fringe.[29]

The dress is illustrated in back view; the center-back portion is made in pink fabric, the rest in green. The bodice is fitted with elbow-length sleeves. The overskirt is pulled up high, to about hip length. The petticoat has a long train. A wide sash is tied in back. Inspired by the visit of the ambassadors of Tipu Sultan, King of Mysore (now in modern-day India); thus, it is not technically Ottoman, but draws on Turkish dress to create a "foreign" style. Furthermore, although Indian women could live in sequestered housing, *serrail* [seraglio] generally referred to upper-class Ottoman women's living quarters. *Bramin* refers to the Brahmin caste of India.

"À la Samaritaine"—*Magasin des modes,* 1789:

> A woman coiffed & dressed *à la Samaritaine.* We still do not know to whom [to give credit for] this new fashion. If it lasts a long time, & if the name of its author reaches us, we shall know it. Perhaps this fashion has been invented, because the beautiful season makes it possible to wear an ample *robe,* & because the winds suffer, in ceasing to blow, so one lets float a large veil falling from the head; perhaps it was invented to mark the difference of spring with winter, & to make a kind of allegory; perhaps it was seen on some theatrical character, thus one wanted to make this *habit* fashionable; perhaps it is no more than an idea, a caprice that has produced it; but, without giving in to our conjectures, here are the details of this *Samaritaine.* She is dressed in a long *robe* of dark green colored cotton cloth, with long sleeves in the same [fabric], trimmed, at the edge & false epaulettes, with pink gauze *hérissons* (hedgehogs), &, under this *robe,* a petticoat in plain white linen, trimmed with a similar pink gauze *hérisson.* A very long sash made of wide pink ribbon brocaded in gold is tied, & adorned with long silver fringe, which forms a large knot on the side, a little behind.[30]

The Samaritans are an ethnic group of the eastern Mediterranean (then controlled by the Ottoman Empire). A gown with a fitted bodice and round waistline, with a long, trained overskirt. Short oversleeves and the petticoat are trimmed with spiky ruffles called "hedgehogs." A wide sash with fringed ends is tied at the side and hangs down. The *bonnet* or *pouf* includes a very long veil that hangs in back.

"Robe au Doliment"—*Journal de Paris,* 1790: "Detached from the waist, it closes with a single buckle in front; this type is very elegant."[31] The name refers to the *dolman,* an outer caftan worn in Ottoman dress. No plate.

"Simarre à la Bérénice"—*Journal de Paris,* 1790: "For the morning, open in front, crossing as desired, & closing by two 'barriers.'"[32] The *simarre* refers to the sixteenth-century Italian *zimarra,* itself derived from Turkish caftans. No plate.

"Chemise a la Sultane"—*Journal de Paris,* 1790: "It is formed as desired the *caraco à la Guimard:* this *négligé* is charming for the apartment."[33] This *caraco* may relate to the *robe à la Guimard,* which, according to Grimm, was created in 1771 and named for famed dancer Marie-Madeleine Guimard (1743–1816). She

> danced in the third act [of *Jason et Medée*] as a simple shepherdess, in a dress so elegant that our ladies abandoned the carnival domino [cloak] to dance in *robes à la Guimard.* This is nothing more than a dress *retroussée* with elegance over a petticoat of a different color. The first invention is due to the actresses of the Comédie Italienne who played the roles of the comic opera in these clothes; mademoiselle Guimard, or her decorator, only added many *pompoms,* trimmings and garlands.[34]

The *Gallerie* also featured a *chemise à la Guimard* "of spotted linen" that looks very similar to other examples of the *chemise* gown.[35] No plate.

"Caraco a la Caravanne"—*Journal de Paris,* 1791: "Good for the country & horse riding, detached from the waist, sash, revers & collar *à la Jannissaire* [a type of Ottoman soldier], petticoat with hidden buttons, it is as light as it is elegant."[36] No plate.

APPENDIX 2

Extant Ottoman-Inspired Garments

ROBES À LA POLONAISE

COLONIAL WILLIAMSBURG FOUNDATION (WILLIAMSBURG, VIRGINIA)
Title: Robe à la polonaise
Date: 1775–80, altered later
Culture: Europe
Materials: Green-and-salmon-striped silk with ribbed and supplementary warp areas; linen lining.
Inventory number: 2006-42
Figures: 103–05

COUTAU-BÉGARIE & ASSOCIÉS (AUCTION HOUSE, PARIS)
Title: Robe à la polonaise
Date: circa 1780
Materials: Silk pékin *chiné à la branche* (multicolored warp-patterned fabric) in green and cream
Sale: Linge, dentelles, tissus, February 9, 2012
Lot number: 303
Notes: Matching petticoat

DROUOT (AUCTION HOUSE, PARIS)
Title: Robe à la polonaise
Date: circa 1778
Materials: Silk lampas, cream background in gros de Tours brocaded with flowers in shades of blue, yellow, pink, and purple; pink silk faille lining
Sale: Collections d'etoffes et costumes ancien, June 15, 2012
Lot number: 287
Notes: Matching petticoat

Title: Robe à la polonaise
Culture: France
Materials: Salmon pink silk moiré and damask; braided, fringed, knotted trim; tassels
Sale: Art islamique et indien, tableaux, mobilier et objets d'art, mode, October 31, 2018
Lot number: 269
Notes: Separate, unboned, back-closing, sleeveless underbodice

ENCHERES SADDE S. A. R. L. (AUCTION HOUSE) (MOULINS, FRANCE)
Title: Manteau à la polonaise
Date: circa 1770–80
Materials: Silk chiné taffeta, cream background with striped, mottled, and waved patterns in pink, green, purple, and yellow; linen lining
Sale: Collection Gilles Labrosse #1, September 22, 2020
Lot number: 95
Notes: Now in private collection
Pattern: In Arnold et al., *Patterns of Fashion 6*, 101–3

GEMEENTEMUSEUM, THE HAGUE
Title: Robe à la polonaise
Date: circa 1770–90
Materials: Cream-colored silk with red/yellow check, light blue silk ribbon trim and crocheted cord
Inventory number: 0556545

GÖTEBORGS STADSMUSEUM (GOTHENBURG, SWEDEN)
Title: Robe
Date: 1700s
Culture: Sweden
Materials: Silk taffeta with stripes of lighter and darker blue and white and woven pattern of scattered white petals; linen lining
Inventory number: GM:7703
Notes: Stomacher or underbodice (front-closing)

KELVINGROVE ART GALLERY AND MUSEUM (GLASGOW)
Title: Polonaise dress
Date: 1780–81
Culture: Scotland, United Kingdom
Materials: Silk, linen
Inventory number: 1932.51.I
Notes: Stomacher or underbodice (front-closing); matching petticoat; possibly a maternity dress

NATIONAL GALLERY OF VICTORIA (MELBOURNE)
Title: Robe à la polonaise
Date: circa 1772–80
Culture: France
Materials: Silk, silk (floss), linen, cotton, metal (fastenings)
Inventory number: 2018.321.a-b
Notes: Matching petticoat
Pattern: In Arnold et al., *Patterns of Fashion 6*, 104–7

KILLERTON, NATIONAL TRUST (DEVON, UNITED KINGDOM)
Title: Polonaise dress
Date: circa 1775
Materials: Linen, metal, muslin, silk
Inventory number: NT 1362010
Notes: Sewn-in, front-closing stomacher
Figures: 58, 106

KYOTO COSTUME INSTITUTE (JAPAN)
Title: Dress (robe à la polonaise)
Date: circa 1780
Culture: France
Materials: Silk taffeta
Inventory number: AC7620 92-34-1AB
Notes: Matching petticoat

THE METROPOLITAN MUSEUM OF ART (NEW YORK)
Title: Dress (Robe à la Polonaise)
Date: 1774–93
Culture: France
Materials: Silk
Inventory number: 34.112a, b
Notes: Stomacher or underbodice (closure unclear); matching petticoat

MUSÉE D'HISTOIRE DE MARSEILLE (FRANCE)
Title: Robe à la polonaise
Date: Second half of the eighteenth century (after 1772)
Materials: Silk pékin taffeta in pink, white, yellow, and green stripes on a blue background, trimmed with silk passementerie; lined in silk "toile"
Inventory number: A/83/391
Notes: Stomacher; matching petticoat
Figures: 64–65, 75–77
Pattern: Figs. 78–79

MUSÉE DE LA TOILE DE JOUY (JOUY-EN-JOSAS, FRANCE)
Title: Robe à la Turque [polonaise longue], manteau de robe, corsage et jupon ayant appartenu à Anne-Élisabeth Oberkampf
Date: circa 1785
Culture: France
Materials: Woven striped fabric alternating pékin silk and muslin, trimmed with curled straw
Inventory number: 000.4.6, Feray legacy; 001.13.2.a, 001.13.2.b, acquisition
Notes: *Polonaise longue;* sewn-in, front-closing stomacher; matching petticoat
Figures: 55–57, 61, 113–14
Pattern: Figs. 62–63

MUSEO DEL TRAJE (MADRID)
Title: Vestido [dress]
Date: circa 1775–80
Culture: Spain
Materials: Brocaded silk taffeta in salmon and green, trimmed with silk ribbon hand painted with leaf and stem motifs and braided silk cord; linen lining
Inventory number: CE001005
Notes: Matching petticoat
Pattern: In *Moda en sombras, Museo Nacional del Pueblo Español* (Ministerio de Cultura, 1991), back cover.

MUSEU DEL DISSENY DE BARCELONA (SPAIN)
Title: Vestido a la circassiana [robe à la circassienne]
Date: 1782–87
Culture: Spain
Materials: Blue silk taffeta ground with stripes in blue, white, and black, as well as brocaded flowers and lace in dark blue, white, green, greenish-brown, and two shades of pink
Inventory number: MTIB 88009-0
Notes: Stomacher or underbodice (front-closing); matching petticoat

MUSEUM OF FINE ARTS, BOSTON
Title: Robe à la polonaise
Date: About 1785, altered later
Culture: France
Materials: Block printed cotton (plain weave) in polychrome on white with Indian-style floral motifs; linen and cotton lining
Inventory number: 43.1619
Notes: Matching petticoat

MUSEUM OF LONDON
Title: Dress[1]
Date: 1781–85
Materials: Cotton, linen, metal, silk
Inventory number: 65.80/1
Notes: *Polonaise longue;* sewn-in, front-closing stomacher

PALAIS GALLIERA, MUSÉE DE LA MODE DE LA VILLE DE PARIS
Title: Robe à la polonaise
Date: circa 1778
Materials: Ivory silk taffeta with woven vertical lines in blue, pink, and green bouquets superimposed between various sinuous garlands, trimmed with *chiné à la branche*
Inventory number: 62-108-14
Notes: Matching petticoat, which has been heavily altered.
Figures: 52–54, 68–69, 115

PALAZZO MOCENIGO (VENICE)
Title: Sopravveste femminile [woman's overdress]
Date: 1775–99
Culture: France
Materials: White quilted cotton; cotton lining
Inventory number: CI. XXIV No. 0239
Notes: Sewn-in, front-closing stomacher; matching petticoat
Figures: 70–72
Pattern: Figs. 73–74

ROYAL ONTARIO MUSEUM (TORONTO)
Title: Dress
Date: 1770–80
Culture: England
Materials: Printed cotton in vermicelli ground with meandering tendrils and small flowers in yellow, red, green, blue, and black
Inventory number: 978.101.2
Notes: Sewn-in, front-closing stomacher

VICTORIA & ALBERT MUSEUM (LONDON)
Title: Polonaise
Date: circa 1780
Culture: Great Britain
Materials: Silk taffeta, trimmed pleated silk and braid; linen lining
Inventory number: T.20-1945
Pattern: In Waugh and Woodward, *Cut of Women's Clothes*, diagram XXI

WORTHING MUSEUM & ART GALLERY (UNITED KINGDOM)[2]
Title: Dress
Date: 1780
Materials: Cream figured silk with woven flowers and leaves (evenly scattered sprigs of mixed flowers and leaves in pinks, greens, and browns) on a self-colored stripe
Inventory number: 1972/59/1
Notes: Sewn-in, front-closing stomacher; matching petticoat; possibly a maternity dress; altered from an earlier style

CARACOS À LA POLONAISE

BAYERISCHES NATIONALMUSEUM (MUNICH)[3]
Title: Caraco à la Polonaise
Date: circa 1760–70
Culture: France
Materials: Plain weave silk; linen lining
Inventory number: 96/143

APPENDIX 2   189

Title: Caraco mit halblangen Ärmeln [*caraco* with half-length sleeves]
Date: 1786–90
Culture: France
Materials: Plain weave linen; linen lining
Inventory number: 96/178
Notes: Sewn-in, front-closing stomacher

Title: Mädchencaraco [girl's *caraco*]
Date: circa 1775–85
Culture: Italy
Materials: Plain weave silk with woven floral motifs; linen lining
Inventory number: 96/182

CENTRE DE DOCUMENTACIÓ I MUSEU TÈXTIL (TERRASSA, SPAIN)

Title: Casaca [jacket]
Date: 1760–70
Materials: Yellow silk taffeta; lined with linen (possibly)
Inventory number: 11732

Title: Casaca [jacket]
Date: 1760–70
Materials: Silk pékin taffeta, ecru background, stripes in red, yellow, and different colors with elaborate motifs; lined with linen (possibly)
Inventory number: 11819

PALAIS GALLIERA, MUSÉE DE LA MODE DE LA VILLE DE PARIS

Title: Caraco
Date: 1770–80
Materials: White cotton; cotton lining
Inventory number: GAL1992.177.X
Figures: 89–91
Pattern: Fig. 92

Title: Caraco and jupe [*caraco* and petticoat]
Date: 1770–80
Materials: Quilted silk taffeta, pink silk taffeta ribbon; cotton lining
Inventory number: GAL1966.33.1
Notes: Matching petticoat

NORDISKA MUSEET (STOCKHOLM)

Title: Embroidered jacket and skirt
Date: 1780s
Culture: Sweden
Materials: Silk, embroidery
Inventory number: NM MXC
Notes: Matching petticoat

ROBES À LA CIRCASSIENNE

MUSEO DEL TRAJE (MADRID)

Title: Polonesa [*polonaise*]
Date: circa 1775–85
Materials: Pink-and-green-striped silk, trimmed with braided cord and tassels; linen lining
Inventory number: CE000592

THE METROPOLITAN MUSEUM OF ART (NEW YORK)

Title: Robe à la circassienne
Date: circa 1787
Culture: Italian (probably)
Materials: Yellow brocaded silk
Inventory number: 1983.32
Pattern: In Arnold et al., *Patterns of Fashion 6*, 108–9

ROBES À LA TURQUE

NORDISKA MUSEET (STOCKHOLM)

Title: Klänning [dress]
Date: circa 1790
Culture: Sweden
Materials: Pink silk atlas
Inventory number: NMA.0052362
Figures: 80–82, 108–9
Pattern: Fig. 83; and in Arnold et al., *Patterns of Fashion 6*, 110–12

PHILADELPHIA MUSEUM OF ART

Title: Woman's Dress (Robe à l'anglaise) with Zone Front
Date: circa 1785–93
Culture: United States
Materials: White cotton mull embroidered with silver foils; ivory silk satin; linen lining
Inventory number: 1955-98-9
Notes: Sewn-in, front-closing stomacher; bodice and skirt separated by waist seam except at center back
Figures: 85–86
Pattern: In Arnold, "Cut and Construction of Women's Clothes," 131; and Arnold, *Patterns of Fashion . . . c. 1720–1860*, 2nd ed., 98–99.

PRIVATE COLLECTION
Title: Day dress worn by Hon. Mrs Graham
Date: circa 1790–92
Culture: Scotland
Materials: Yellow-brown silk, cream silk, trimmed with cream silk ribbon
Inventory number: see Belsey, *Gainsborough's Beautiful Mrs Graham*, 42
Notes: Sewn-in, front-closing stomacher; bodice and skirt separated by waist seam

LÉVITES

MUZEUM NARODOWE (KRAKOW)[4]
Title: Open gown (*lewitka?*)
Date: circa 1780–95
Culture: Unknown
Materials: Silk gauze with embroidered robings
Inventory number: MNK-XIX-2802
Pattern: In Arnold et al., *Patterns of Fashion 6*, 28–29

TIRELLI COSTUMI (ROME)[5]
Title: Closed gown (*lévite* or redingote?) & petticoat
Date: circa 1780–90
Materials: Green silk
Inventory number: MCCT-D20
Notes: Matching petticoat
Pattern: In Arnold et al., *Patterns of Fashion 6*, 124–27

VICTORIA & ALBERT MUSEUM (LONDON)
Title: Doll, in a white linen dress with trimmings of muslin, silk ribbon, and color-printed cotton; wax over composition
Date: 1784
Materials: Muslin, silk, cotton
Inventory number: W.183:1-1919
Notes: Owner noted one dress (of several) is a "Fashionable Undress called a Levette, 1784"; doll's dress
Figures: 139–41

GARMENTS WITH CHARACTERISTICS OF OTTOMAN-INSPIRED DRESS

BAYERISCHES NATIONALMUSEUM (MUNICH)
Title: Caraco eines zweiteiligen Mädchenkleides [*caraco* of a two-piece girl's dress]
Date: circa 1785
Culture: France
Materials: Silk; linen lining
Inventory number: 96/191.1
Notes: Possibly a *caraco à la polonaise* or pierrot

Title: Caraco eines zweiteiligen Frauenkleides [*caraco* of a two-piece women's dress]
Date: circa 1780–90
Culture: France
Materials: Silk and linen pékin; linen lining
Inventory number: 96/115.1
Notes: *Pet-en-l'air* (jacket version of the *robe à la française*) with cutaway front; matching petticoat

Title: Hüftlanger Caraco mit ovalem Halsausschnitt [hip-length *caraco* with an oval neckline]
Date: circa 1780–1800
Culture: Netherlands?
Materials: Plain weave silk; linen lining
Inventory number: 96/145
Notes: Possibly a *caraco à la polonaise* or pierrot

Title: Knielanger Caraco für ein zweiteiliges Frauenkleid [knee-length *caraco* for a two-piece women's dress]
Date: circa 1770–90
Culture: England
Materials: Plain weave silk; linen lining
Inventory number: 96/132
Notes: Nightgown with cutaway front; stomacher or underbodice; gown was cut shorter circa 1780

BRISTOL MUSEUMS (UNITED KINGDOM)
Title: Dress
Date: circa 1795
Materials: Cream taffeta with single floral print, trimmed with green tassels
Inventory number: TA2031
Notes: Late 1790s-style *polonaise* (no waist seam)

CENTRE DE DOCUMENTACIÓ I MUSEU TÈXTIL (TERRASSA, SPAIN)
Title: Vestit [dress]
Date: 1760–80
Materials: Green silk moiré, vertical stripes, woven motifs in florals and lace
Inventory number: 11779(b)(3)
Notes: Cut as a *polonaise* in back, but has closed front and pointed waistline typical of the *anglaise;* matching petticoat

APPENDIX 2   191

Title: Vestit [dress]
Date: 1795–1808
Culture: Spain
Materials: Purple silk satin with silver metallic embroidery and sequins
Inventory number: 12230
Notes: Late-1790s-style *turque* (no waist seam, short oversleeves); coordinating white cotton chiffon dress with silver metallic embroidery and sequins

CHERTSEY MUSEUM (UNITED KINGDOM)
Title: Dress
Date: circa 1790–95
Materials: White cotton, hand-painted with floral design in red, indigo, yellow, brown, and mauve, with green silk bodice front and sleeves
Inventory number: MT.2023
Notes: Late 1790s-style *polonaise* (no waist seam); matching stomacher or underbodice

FINE ARTS MUSEUMS OF SAN FRANCISCO
Title: Woman's dress: bodice and skirt
Date: 1789
Culture: United States
Materials: Pale blue-green silk
Inventory number: 58.10.1a-b
Notes: Late 1790s-style *polonaise* (no waist seam); sewn-in, front-closing stomacher; matching petticoat

HISTORIC DEERFIELD (MASSACHUSETTS)
Title: Gown; robe a la polonaise[6]
Date: 1795–1803
Culture: Ireland
Materials: Red, green, and brown brocaded silk; bleached (white) plain weave linen lining
Inventory number: HD 92.028
Notes: Late 1790s-style *polonaise* (no waist seam, possible crossover front)

THE HOPKINS COLLECTION (LONDON)
Title: Open gown
Date: circa 1785–92
Materials: Striped black silk satin, lined in silk
Inventory number: HC.D-1.82.2
Notes: Cut as a *polonaise*, with cutaway front and without waist seam, but worn trained; sewn-in false front with straps in fashion fabric
Pattern: In Arnold et al., *Patterns of Fashion 6,* 113–15

KENT STATE UNIVERSITY MUSEUM (OHIO)
Title: Robe à l'anglaise (dress)
Date: circa 1770–90
Culture: England
Materials: Ivory silk brocade woven with vertical stripes and small floral design; linen lining
Inventory number: KSUM 1983.1.10ab
Notes: Nightgown (sewn-down center-back bodice pleats, cut in one with the skirt, more typical of the English nightgown) or *robe à l'anglaise* with cutaway front; stomacher or underbodice (front-closing); matching petticoat

KYOTO COSTUME INSTITUTE (JAPAN)
Title: Dress (robe à la française)
Date: circa 1780
Culture: French
Materials: Pink silk taffeta with painted garlands
Inventory number: AC5312 86-8-1AC
Notes: *Robe à la française* with cutaway front; matching stomacher and petticoat

LEEDS MUSEUMS & GALLERIES (UNITED KINGDOM)
Title: Caraco
Date: 1770
Culture: United Kingdom
Materials: Silk, linen
Inventory number: LEEAG.1949.0008.0091
Notes: Redingote or *lévite?* Cut as a *polonaise* in back, either jacket or short *robe à la polonaise* length skirtings, front closes edge-to-edge with pointed waist like an anglaise, angular collar like a redingote
Pattern: In Waugh and Woodward, *Cut of Women's Clothes,* diagram XXIII.

LOS ANGELES COUNTY MUSEUM OF ART
Title: Dress (robe à l'anglaise)
Date: 1785–90
Culture: France
Materials: Silk twill and silk plain-weave stripes (purple and white)
Inventory number: M.2007.211.931
Notes: *Robe à l'anglaise* with cutaway front; stomacher or underbodice (front-closing); matching petticoat

MANCHESTER CITY GALLERIES (UNITED KINGDOM)
Title: Dress
Date: 1790–1800
Culture: United Kingdom

Materials: Brown silk satin, woven with a warp-printed (chiné) motif in green, cream, and red; linen lining
Inventory number: 1947.1613
Notes: Late 1790s-style *polonaise;* front-opening, crossover stomacher

THE METROPOLITAN MUSEUM OF ART (NEW YORK)

Title: Dress
Date: 1775
Culture: France
Materials: Silk
Inventory number: 2009.300.917a, b
Notes: Possibly a *caraco à la polonaise*

Title: Dress
Date: 1775–80
Culture: Probably Great Britain
Materials: Silk
Inventory number: C.I.61.33.1a,b
Notes: *Robe à la française* with cutaway front; matching petticoat

Title: Robe à la française
Date: 1778–85
Culture: France
Materials: Linen, silk
Inventory number: C.I.65.13.2a, b
Notes: *Robe à la française* with cutaway front; includes diamond-shaped stomacher that suits the cutaway front
Pattern: in Arnold et al., *Patterns of Fashion 6*, 96–98

Title: Robe à l'anglaise
Date: 1785–87
Culture: France
Materials: Silk
Inventory number: C.I.66.39a, b
Notes: *Robe à l'anglaise* with cutaway front; sewn-in, front-closing stomacher; matching petticoat

Title: Dress
Date: 1785–80
Culture: France
Materials: Silk
Inventory number: C.I.60.40.3a, b
Notes: Cut as a *circassienne* in back, with short oversleeves, but closed, pointed waistline bodice front of *anglaise*

Title: Dress
Date: 1795–1805
Culture: Great Britain
Materials: Cotton
Inventory number: 1981.352.5
Notes: Late 1790s-style *polonaise*

MUSÉE D'ART ET D'HISTOIRE DE PROVENCE (GRASSE, FRANCE)

Title: *Robe*
Inventory number: 2012.0.7
Notes: Fronts cut in one piece and pleated to fit; back cut separately from the skirt except in the very center back; ties demonstrate it was worn with skirts looped up

MUSÉE D'HISTOIRE DE MARSEILLE

Title: Robe à la française
Date: Second half of the eighteenth century (circa 1776)
Materials: Silk taffeta *chiné à la branche* in floral motifs and pink roses on ivory ground
Inventory number: M.V.M., inv. A/83/390
Notes: *Robe à la française* with cutaway front; matching stomacher and petticoat

MUSÉE DE LA TOILE DE JOUY (JOUY-EN-JOSAS, FRANCE)

Title: Robe à l'anglaise
Date: circa 1780
Culture: France
Materials: Printed Indian cotton
Inventory number: 977.11.1 a and b
Notes: *Robe à l'anglaise* with cutaway front; matching petticoat

MUSEO DEL TRAJE (MADRID)

Title: Vestido [dress]
Date: circa 1770
Materials: Silk pékin taffeta with polychrome floral motifs; linen lining
Inventory number: CE016036A
Notes: *Robe à la française* with cutaway front; matching stomacher and petticoat

MUSEU D'HISTÒRIA DE BARCELONA

Title: Caraco a la polonesa de seda azul celeste [*caraco à la polonaise* in sky-blue silk]
Date: 1770–89
Culture: France, Italy, Spain

APPENDIX 2   193

Materials: Blue silk with small floral motifs on a moiré background with embroidered decoration; linen (possibly) lining
Inventory number: MHCB-33403
Notes: Cut as a *polonaise* in back, but as an *anglaise* in front; possibly altered from an earlier cutaway style

MUSEUM OF FINE ARTS, BOSTON
Title: Woman's dress in two parts (*caraco* jacket)
Date: About 1785–90
Culture: French
Materials: Scarlet-and-yellow-striped silk satin; braid trim; linen lining
Inventory number: 43.703a
Notes: Possibly a *caraco à la polonaise* or pierrot; stomacher or underbodice; matching petticoat

MUSEUM OF LONDON
Title: Dress
Date: circa 1770s
Materials: Yellow cannellé ground silk on which is a white flowering stem with detached bunches of flowers in the curves formed by the stem
Inventory number: 85.553
Notes: Nightgown with cutaway front (later alteration); sewn-in, front-closing stomacher

Title: Dress
Date: circa 1780
Materials: Pink silk lustring with white satin stripes and a self-colored pattern of small floral sprigs in the ground
Inventory number: 54.78/1
Notes: *Robe à l'anglaise* with cutaway front; sewn-in, front-closing stomacher; matching petticoat
Figures: 59–60

NORDISKA MUSEET (STOCKHOLM)
Title: Klänning [dress]
Date: 1782–1848
Culture: Sweden
Materials: Light red silk with silver embroidery
Inventory number: NM.0222658A-E
Notes: Shares features of the *polonaise* (cutaway front, shorter length), *anglaise* (separate bodice and skirt), and Swedish national dress. Includes matching separate stomacher and front-closing underbodice, possibly intended to wear together
Figure: 66

PALAIS GALLIERA, MUSÉE DE LA MODE DE LA VILLE DE PARIS
Title: Caraco and jupe [*caraco* and petticoat]
Date: 1780–90
Materials: Cotton, white background, block-printed in four colors in dark red, blue, and purple stripes and flower garlands; linen lining
Inventory number: GAL1920.1.2370
Notes: Sewn-in, front-closing stomacher; matching petticoat; possibly a *caraco à la polonaise* or pierrot
Figures: 93–96
Pattern: Figs. 97–98

Title: Caraco and jupe [*caraco* and petticoat]
Date: circa 1785
Materials: Striped gros de Tours silk in yellow, white, and black, trimmed with pink silk taffeta ribbon; linen lining
Inventory number: GAL1977.80.3B
Notes: Stomacher or underbodice (front-closing); matching petticoat; possibly a *caraco à la polonaise* or pierrot

Title: Caraco et jupe
Date: 1780–90
Materials: Printed cotton percale
Inventory number: acquired 29-11-1962
Notes: Possibly a *caraco à la polonaise* or pierrot

Title: Robe à l'anglaise
Date: Eighteenth century with later alterations
Materials: Pink-and-cream silk taffeta; mechanical silk lace (nineteenth century)
Inventory number: 1987.1.20
Notes: *Robe à l'anglaise* or redingote, but the back cut as a *polonaise* and the front having been altered
Figures: 144–48
Pattern: Fig. 149

Title: Robe à l'anglaise et jupe de robe à l'anglaise
Date: 1775–90
Materials: Satin, silk, pink. Lining, taffeta, silk, white, and linen, white.
Inventory number: GAL 1969.59.3AB.
Notes: *Robe à l'anglaise* with cutaway front; stomacher or underbodice (front-closing); matching petticoat

Title: Robe et jupe de [and petticoat of] robe
Date: 1785–95

Materials: Changeable taffeta, silk, yellow. Lining, taffeta, silk, cream, linen, white. Ribbon, taffeta, silk, cream.
Inventory number: GAL 1988.121.4ab
Notes: Redingote with cutaway front; stomacher or underbodice (front-closing); matching petticoat

Title: Casaquin [jacket]
Date: 1787–90
Materials: White cotton printed with pink and blue
Inventory number: GAL2004.232.1
Notes: Possibly a *caraco à la polonaise* or pierrot; stomacher or underbodice

PRIVATE COLLECTION
Title: Dress
Date: circa 1780s
Culture: Probably French
Materials: Silk with linen lining
Notes: Fronts cut in one piece and pleated to fit over a sewn-in false front stomacher; back cut separately from the skirt except in the very center back
Figures: 142–43

ROYAL ONTARIO MUSEUM (TORONTO)
Title: Formal overdress
Date: circa 1801
Culture: England
Materials: Egyptian silk tabby brocaded in gold and silver filé
Inventory number: 2004.33.1 ROM2008_9949_8
Notes: Late 1790s *polonaise*

VICTORIA & ALBERT MUSEUM (LONDON)
Title: Gown
Date: 1795–99
Culture: England
Materials: Cream figured silk brocaded with blue roses and yellow and red floral motifs; linen lining
Inventory number: T.10-2005
Notes: Late 1790s *polonaise;* sewn-in, front-opening, crossover false front/stomacher

Title: Gown
Date: 1795–99
Culture: England
Materials: Cotton, dyed in a pattern of vertical trailing stems, bearing fruits, flowers, and leaves; linen lining
Inventory number: T.121-992
Notes: Late 1790s *polonaise*

Title: Gown
Date: 1795–99
Culture: England
Materials: Cream-colored shawl with a wool weft and silk warp, printed in pink and green with a floral sprig central design, and a border suggesting chiné stripe; collar and oversleeves in dark green silk satin; linen lining
Inventory number: T.217-1968
Notes: Late 1790s *turque* (no waist seam, contrasting short oversleeve); sewn-in, front-opening, crossover false front/stomacher in lining fabric only; shawl collar like a *lévite*
Figures: 178–79

Title: Gown
Date: 1795–99
Culture: England
Materials: Cream poplin with a silk warp and satin weft, figured with a diamond motif
Inventory number: 513-1902
Notes: Late 1790s *polonaise* (no waist seam); sewn-in, front-opening, crossover false front/stomacher
Pattern: In Arnold, *Patterns of Fashion . . . c. 1660–1860*, 45; Waugh and Woodward, *Cut of Women's Clothes*, diagram XXXIV

Title: Robe
Date: 1795–1800
Culture: England
Materials: White cotton, block-printed in red, green, brown, and blue vertical floral trails; linen lining
Inventory number: T.286-1968
Notes: Late 1790s *polonaise;* sewn-in, front-opening false front/stomacher

NOTES

INTRODUCTION

1. For example, although men's dress had been trending in that direction for decades, the late-seventeenth-century layered three-piece suit (coat, waistcoat, and breeches) was based on Ottoman theater costumes (de Beer, "King Charles II's Own Fashion," 105–15; Knauer, "Toward a History of the Sleeved Coat," 18–36; Kuchta, *The Three-Piece Suit and Modern Masculinity;* Landini, "Dress for the Body, Body for the Dress," 24–25; de Marly, "King Charles II's Own Fashion," 378–82; Pierre, "From the Doublet to the Justaucorps," 95–107).

2. For an excellent overview of these, see Chrisman-Campbell, *Fashion Victims*, particularly 6–7, 77, 151–55.

3. Lasic, "Ethnicity," 139.

4. Roche, *The Culture of Clothing*, 46.

5. Kaiser, *Fashion and Cultural Studies*, 1.

6. Eicher and Sumberg, "World Fashion, Ethnic, and National Dress," 302; Hollander, *Seeing through Clothes*, xv; Leeds-Hurwitz, *Semiotics and Communication*, 113.

7. Turner, "The Social Skin," 112.

8. Eicher and Higgins Roach, "Definition and Classification of Dress," 15.

9. Calefato, *The Clothed Body*, 16.

10. Crane, *Fashion and Its Social Agendas*, 1.

11. Geczy, *Fashion and Orientalism*, 3.

12. Geczy, *Fashion and Orientalism*, 60.

13. Davis, *Fashion, Culture, and Identity*, 16–17.

14. Kaiser, *Fashion and Cultural Studies*, 1.

15. Cavallaro and Warwick, *Fashioning the Frame*, 135.

16. Hayward, "Clothing," 172.

17. Geczy, *Fashion and Orientalism*, 4.

18. Geczy, *Fashion and Orientalism*, 41; Peck, "Trade Textiles at the Metropolitan Museum," 3.

19. Baird, "Introduction," 1–2.

20. Bevilacqua and Pfeifer, "Turquerie," 117.

21. Davis, *Fashion, Culture, and Identity*, 8, 25.

22. Miller, "Why Some Things Matter," 11.

23. Appadurai, "Introduction," 5; Lubar and Kingery, "Introduction," xii; Maquet, "Objects as Instruments, Objects as Signs," 35.

24. Kidwell, "Are Those Clothes Real?," 9.

25. Said, *Orientalism*, 55.

26. Landweber, "Celebrating Identity," 186; Landweber, "Turkish Delight," 20.

27. Avcıoğlu, *"Turquerie" and the Politics of Representation*, 15.

28. Geczy, *Fashion and Orientalism*, 11.

29. Martin and Koda, *Orientalism*, 12.

30. Said, *Orientalism*, 1.

31. Karen Culcasi notes that *Middle East* refers to the region that was midway between Great Britain and its colonies in India ("Constructing and Naturalizing the Middle East," 585). *Near East* refers to the East that is "nearer" to Western Europe; thus, both are Eurocentric terms.

32. Lewis, *Rethinking Orientalism*, 69–70.

33. Newton, *Images of the Ottoman Empire*, 7; *Trésor de la Langue Française informatisé* (hereafter *TLF*), s.v. "levant."

34. Boucher, *20,000 Years of Fashion*, 318; Chrisman-Campbell, "Minister of Fashion," 28–29; Chrisman-Campbell, *Fashion Victims*, 14; Ribeiro, *Art of Dress*, 30; Redondo, "Polonesa del Siglo XVIII," 4.

35. Carson, "'L'Economique de la Mode,'" 138.

36. Ribeiro, *Art of Dress*, 35.

37. Bohanan, *Fashion beyond Versailles*, 12, 32; Hayward, "Clothing," 178.

38. Bohanan, *Fashion beyond Versailles*, 13; Carson, "Economique de la Mode," 141; Fairchilds, "The Production and Marketing of Populuxe Goods in Eighteenth-Century Paris," 239.

39. Chrisman-Campbell, *Fashion Victims*, 8.

40. Coquery, "The Language of Success," 71–72; Roche, *The People of Paris*, 164.

41. Roche, *Culture of Clothing*, 142–45; Roche, *People of Paris*, 162, 168–72.

42. Crowston, *Fabricating Women*, 41; Roche, *Culture of Clothing*, 108.

43. Chrisman-Campbell, *Fashion Victims*, 19.

44. Chrisman-Campbell, *Fashion Victims*, 32, 155; Jones, "Repackaging Rousseau," 943; Jones, *Sexing la Mode*, 74, 193.

45. Crowston, *Fabricating Women*, 186; Kirillova, "Tailleurs d'habits et couturières à Reims en 1716," 86–99; Pellegrin, "Les Vertus de 'l'ouvrage,'" 747–69.

46. Crowston, *Fabricating Women*, 12.

47. Jones, *Sexing la Mode*, 193.

48. Jones, *Sexing la Mode*, xvii; Roche, *Culture of Clothing*, 220.

49. Delpierre, *Dress in France in the Eighteenth Century*, 18.

50. Crowston, *Fabricating Women*, 43; Roche, *Culture of Clothing*, 147.

51. Chrisman-Campbell, *Fashion Victims*, 16; Ribeiro, *Dress in Eighteenth-Century Europe*, 207.

52. Harvey, *The French Enlightenment and Its Others*, 8.

53. Chrisman-Campbell, *Fashion Victims*, 17.

54. Nevinson, *Origin and Early History of the Fashion Plate*, 87.

55. Benhamou, "Fashion in the Mercure," 27.

56. Ribeiro, *Fashion in the French Revolution*, 20–22; Roche, *Culture of Clothing*, 13–14, 187; Vittu, "Presse et diffusion des modes françaises," 129.

57. Bertrand, "'Le Monument du costume' de Rétif de La Bretonne," 389–90; Heller-Greenman, "Moreau le Jeune and the Monument du costume," 67. The *Monument* was first published as *Suite d'estampes pour servir à l'histoire des mœurs et du costume des François dans le dix-huitième siècle* (1775), *Seconde suite d'estampes pour servir à l'histoire des mœurs et du costume des François dans le dix-huitième siècle* (1776), and *Troisième Suite d'estampes pour servir à l'histoire des modes et du costume en France dans le dix-huitième siècle* (1783), then republished together in 1789 as the *Monument du costume*.

58. Chrisman-Campbell, *Fashion Victims*, 16; Gaudriault, *Répertoire de la gravure de mode française des origines à 1815*, 146–70; Ribeiro, *Art of Dress*, 76.

59. Tétart-Vittu, "La Gallerie des modes et costumes français," 16. No complete *Gallerie* collection exists. This study focused on Paul Cornu's 1912 published compilation and the collections of the Bibliothèque municipale de Versailles, Bunka Gakuen University Library, and Museum of Fine Arts, Boston.

60. Dandois, "Les Journaux de mode en France (1785–1792)," 13–15; Gaudriault, *Répertoire de la gravure de mode française*, 190; Ribeiro, *Art of Dress*, 76.

61. Gaudriault, *Répertoire de la gravure de mode française*, 196, 212.

62. Gaudriault, *Répertoire de la gravure de mode française*, 232.

63. Chrisman-Campbell, *Fashion Victims*, 77; Jones, "Repackaging Rousseau," 956.

64. Carson, "L'Economique de la Mode," 139; Kleinert, "La Révolution et le premier journal illustré paru en France (1785–1793)," 470; Vittu, "Presse et diffusion des modes françaises," 134.

65. Rimbault, "La Presse féminine de langue française au XVIIIème siècle," 119.

66. Kleinert, "Révolution et le premier journal," 286.

67. Jones, "Repackaging Rousseau," 953; Jones, *Sexing la Mode*, 183–84.

68. Chrisman-Campbell, *Fashion Victims*, 153; Lemire and Riello, "East & West," 888.

69. Dandois, "Journaux de mode en France," 19–21.

70. Tétart-Vittu, "Dessinateurs et diffusion de la mode par la gravure et la presse," 145–50; Sgard, *Édition électronique . . . dictionnaire des journaux*, s.v. "Galerie des modes."

71. Sgard, *Édition électronique . . . dictionnaire des journaux*, s.v. "Cabinet des modes."

72. Jones, "Repackaging Rousseau," 950.

1. CLOTHING PERSPECTIVES, EAST AND WEST

1. Said, *Orientalism*, 3.

2. Said, *Orientalism*, 40.

3. Carrière and Courdurié, "Un Sophisme économique," 16; Çırakman, *From the "Terror of the World" to the "Sick Man of Europe,"* 3, 183; Kugler, *Sway of the Ottoman Empire on English Identity*, 181–82; Mayer, "Cultural Cross-Dressing," 282; Schmidt, *Inventing Exoticism*, 3–5; Smentek, "Jean-Etienne Liotard, the Turkish Painter," 88–89; Tekin, *Representations and Othering*, 25–60.

4. Aravamudan, *Enlightenment Orientalism*, 5; Avcıoğlu, *"Turquerie" and the Politics of Representation*, 7.

5. Neumann, *Uses of the Other*, 40; Tekin, *Representations and Othering*, 26–29.

6. Bevilacqua and Pfeifer, "Turquerie," 77.

7. Chrisman-Campbell, *Fashion Victims*, 249; Egler, Ballesteros, and Maeder, "L'Orient et la mode en Europe au temps des Lumières," 62; Harvey, *French Enlightenment and Its Others*, 11.

8. Bevilacqua and Pfeifer, "Turquerie," 78–79; Eysturlid, "'Where Everything Is Weighed,'" 618, 622; Kugler, *Sway of the Ottoman Empire*, 2–3; Newton, *Images of the Ottoman Empire*, 8; Takeda, "French Mercantilism and the Early Modern Mediterranean," 14.

9. Lemire and Riello, "East & West," 888.

10. Göçek, *East Encounters West*, 72; Landweber, "Turkish Delight," 203.

11. Bevilacqua and Pfeifer, "Turquerie," 79; Landweber, "Turkish Delight," 203; Tekin, *Representations and Othering*, 38–40.

12. Bevilacqua and Pfeifer, "Turquerie," 75–76, 94; Fairchilds, "Production and Marketing of Populuxe Goods," 229–30, 238; Landweber, "Turkish Delight," 205; Landweber, "'This Marvelous Bean,'" 197; Leclant, "Le Café et les cafés à Paris," 8; Lemire and Riello, "East & West," 907; McCabe, *Orientalism in Early Modern France*, 189–90.

13. Landweber, "Turkish Delight," 175; Williams, *Turquerie*, 7.

14. Furetière, *Dictionaire universel*, s.v. "Turquerie," 759.

15. Saint-Beuve, "L'Abbé Prévost," 203–25; Solnon, *Le Turban et la stambouline*, 305.

16. Geczy, *Fashion and Orientalism*, 14.

17. Boucher, *20,000 Years of Fashion*, 329; Mansel, *Dressed to Rule*, 19, 43; Turnau, *History of Dress in Central and Eastern Europe*, 12.

18. Delpierre, *Dress in France in the Eighteenth Century*, 67; Lehnert, "Des 'Robes à la turque' et autres orientalismes a la mode," 189; Wolff, *Inventing Eastern Europe*, 5–7.

19. Borderioux, "La Presse française, miroir des 'modes russes' à Paris," 271–72; Boucher, *20,000 Years of Fashion*, 299; Chrisman-Campbell, *Fashion Victims*, 150; Delpierre, *Dress in France in the Eighteenth Century*, 67–68; Jirousek, "The Kaftan and Its Origins," 138; Tarrant, *The Development of Costume*, 38. That influence was reciprocal (Boucher, *20,000 Years of Fashion*, 329; Hill, "The Influences of Ottoman Culture," 66–68).

20. Apostolou, *L'Orientalisme des voyageurs français au XVIIIe siècle*, 277; Delpierre, *Dress in France in the Eighteenth Century*, 67; Geczy, *Fashion and Orientalism*, 63; Herbette, *Une Ambassade turque sous le Directoire*, 142, 169; Jirousek, "Kaftan and Its Origins," 136; Jirousek, *Ottoman Dress and Design in the West*, 166; Landweber, "Celebrating Identity," 176; Landweber, "How Can One Be Turkish?," 409–10; Neumann, *Uses of the Other*, 53–54; Sheriff, "The Dislocations of Jean-Etienne Liotard," 114; Solnon, *Turban et la stambouline*, 307; Tekin, *Representations and Othering*, 35–37; Van Dyk, "The Embassy of Soliman Aga to Louis XIV," 4; Williams, *Turquerie*, 39–43; Wolff, *The Singing Turk*, 61–62.

21. Chrisman-Campbell, *Fashion Victims*, 241, 250–55; Martin, "Tipu Sultan's Ambassadors at Saint-Cloud," 49–50; Thepaut-Cabasset, "Fashion Encounters," 165–69.

22. Breskin, "'On the Periphery of a Greater World,'" 101; Melman, *Women's Orients*, 79.

23. Konuk, "Ethnomasquerade in Ottoman-European Encounters," 394; Scholz, "English Women in Oriental Dress," 90; Solnon, *Turban et la stambouline*, 282.

24. Konuk, "Ethnomasquerade in Ottoman-European Encounters," 393–94; Pointon, *Hanging the Head*, 151; Scholz, "English Women in Oriental Dress," 90–92.

25. Inal, "Women's Fashions in Transition," 253.

26. *Robe*, Turkey, ca. 1720, Victoria & Albert Museum, London, T.225-1958. See Micklewright, *Encyclopedia of World Dress and Fashion*, s.v. "Ottoman Dress," 131.

27. Wolff, *Inventing Eastern Europe*, 243.

28. Aldis, *Madame Geoffrin*, 276; Goodman, *The Republic of Letters*, 42.

29. Boucher, *20,000 Years of Fashion*, 300; Lilti, *The World of the Salons*, 252.

30. Marianne Loir, *Marie Therese Rodet Geoffrin, saloniere française*, oil on canvas, ca. 1760, Private Collection. See Aldis, *Madame Geoffrin*, 285.

31. Apostolou, "L'Apparence extérieure de l'Oriental," par. 42; Geczy, *Fashion and Orientalism*, 67; Williams, *Turquerie*, 20. Ottoman-authored albums circulated in Western Europe as well (Fraser, "The Color of the Orient," 45).

32. Bevilacqua and Pfeifer, "Turquerie," 85.

33. Williams, *Turquerie*, 81.

34. Bevilacqua and Pfiefer, "Turquerie," 84; Bull, "The Artist," 28–29; Landweber, "Celebrating Identity," 181–83; Lasic, "Ethnicity," 149; Luebbers, "Documenting the Invisible," 5; Moronvalle, "Le Recueil Ferriol (1714) et la mode des turqueries," 425–26; Nefedova-Gruntova, *A Journey into the World of the Ottomans*, 11, 181; Ribeiro, *Art of Dress*, 222; Scarce, *Women's Costume of the Near and Middle East*, 58.

35. Bevilacqua and Pfeifer, "Turquerie," 84.

36. Moronvalle, "Le Recueil de cent estampes représentant différentes nations du Levant," 16–17.

37. Bull, "Artist," 57; Nefedova-Gruntova, *Journey into the World of the Ottomans*, 105, 117; Solnon, *Turban et la stambouline*, 290; Williams, *Turquerie*, 50–51.

38. Boucher, *20,000 Years of Fashion*, 300; Nefedova-Gruntova, *Journey into the World of the Ottomans*, 44; Sheriff, "Dislocations of Jean-Etienne Liotard," 100.

39. Braided hair was traditionally worn by Turkish brides (Delaney, "Untangling the Meanings of Hair in Turkish Society," 161; Williams, *Turquerie*, 90–93).

40. Boer and Bal, *Disorienting Vision*, 84; Hughes, "Fash-

ioning the Other," 55–56; Mayer, "Cultural Cross Dressing," 286; Solnon, *Turban et la stambouline*, 242.

41. Ribeiro, "The Elegant Art of Fancy Dress," 94.

42. Smentek, "Jean-Etienne Liotard," 85.

43. Denny, "Images of Turks and the European Imagination," 15; Sheriff, "Dislocations of Jean-Etienne Liotard," 97; Smentek, "Jean-Etienne Liotard," 89; Williams, *Turquerie*, 99.

44. Germann, *Picturing Marie Leszczinska (1703–1768)*, 184.

45. Wolff, *Singing Turk*, 83.

46. Apostolou, *Orientalisme des voyageurs français*, 296–97; Solnon, *Turban et la stambouline*, 298; Williams, *Turquerie*, 53.

47. Lasic, "Ethnicity," 153–54; Ribeiro, *Fashion in the French Revolution*, 39; Williams, *Turquerie*, 98.

48. Abler, *Hinterland Warriors and Military Dress*, 23–66; Scher, "Relations militaires entre la France et la Pologne," 68.

49. Abler, *Hinterland Warriors and Military Dress*, 23–66; Grüßhaber, *The German Spirit in the Ottoman and Turkish Army*, 5; Rodenbeck, "Dressing Native," 74; Scher, "Relations militaires entre la France et la Pologne," 70.

50. Montandre-Longchamps and Roussel, *Etat militaire de France*; Louis XV, *Ordonnance du Roi, concernant sa cavalerie: du 1er décembre 1761*; Louis XV, *Ordonnance du Roi, concernant la cavalerie: du 21 décembre 1762*; Louis XVI, *Règlement arrêté par le Roi, concernant l'habillement et l'équipement de ses troupes: du 31 Mai 1776.*.

51. Apostolou, *Orientalisme des voyageurs français*, 305; Chrisman-Campbell, *Fashion Victims*, 246; Geczy, *Fashion and Orientalism*, 60; Ribeiro, *Dress in Eighteenth-Century Europe*, 226–28; Ribeiro, *The Dress Worn at Masquerades in England*, 222; Ribeiro, "Elegant Art of Fancy Dress," 155–57.

52. Ribeiro, "Elegant Art of Fancy Dress," 139, 141.

53. Landweber, "Celebrating Identity," 183–86; Ribeiro, "Elegant Art of Fancy Dress," 142–43.

54. Apostoulou, *Orientalisme des voyageurs français*, 265; Hughes, "Fashioning the Other," 20–32.

55. Landweber, "Celebrating Identity," 177–81; Ribeiro, "Elegant Art of Fancy Dress," 141; Williams, *Turquerie*, 74–75.

56. Bevilacqua and Pfeifer, "Turquerie," 92–93.

57. Clay, *Stagestruck*, 2.

58. Berlanstein, *Daughters of Eve*, 479; Clay, *Stagestruck*, 164–65.

59. Berlanstein, *Daughters of Eve*, 478–79; Chrisman-Campbell, *Fashion Victims*, 32.

60. Apostolou, *Orientalisme des voyageurs français*, 305; Bevilacqua and Pfeifer, "Turquerie," 92–93, 102; Boulaire, "La Rencontre de l'Autre dans le théâtre français de la Saint-Barthelémy à la Révolution française," 103, 126; Geczy, *Fashion and Orientalism*, 43; Wolff, *Singing Turk*, 1.

61. Boulaire, "Rencontre de l'Autre," 136; Chrisman-Campbell, *Fashion Victims*, 246; Delpierre, *Dress in France in the Eighteenth Century*, 67; Williams, *Turquerie*, 63; Wolff, *Singing Turk*, 9.

62. Boulaire, "Rencontre de l'Autre," 105–6; Jirousek, "Ottoman Influences in Western Dress," par. 13; Wolff, *Singing Turk*, 9.

63. Boulaire, "Rencontre de l'Autre," 134; Landweber, "Turkish Delight," 203.

64. Elmarsafy, "Submission, Seduction, and State Propaganda," 22; Göçek, *East Encounters West*, 73; Moindrot, "The 'Turk' and the 'Parisienne,'" 427–28; Scarce, "Turkish Fashion in Transition," 144; Wolff, *Singing Turk*, 80; Yermolenko, *Roxolana in European Literature, History and Culture*, 40–42.

65. Moindrot, "'Turk' and the 'Parisienne,'" 431; Williams, *Turquerie*, 82; Wolff, *Singing Turk*, 4.

66. Apostolou, *Orientalisme des voyageurs français*, 305; Carlson, "The Eighteenth Century Pioneers in French Costume Reform," 37–41; Chrisman-Campbell, *Fashion Victims*, 203; Collins and Jarvis, "The Great Leap from Earth to Heaven," 187; Dotlačilová, "Costume in the Time of Reforms," 2–3; Mele, *Le Théâtre de Charles-Simon Favart*, 30.

67. "Éloge de Madame Favart," 22:20–21. See Hammerbeck, "Les Trois Sultanes," 76n42; Kurz, "Pictorial Records," 312; Moindrot, "'Turk' and the 'Parisienne,'" 434; Scarce, "Turkish Fashion in Transition," 144; Wolff, *Singing Turk*, 89.

68. Dotlačilová, "Costume in the Time of Reforms," 128–29.

69. Williams, *Turquerie*, 94n5; Wolff, *Singing Turk*, 83.

70. Berlanstein, *Daughters of Eve*, 56; Chrisman-Campbell, *Fashion Victims*, 32, 200; Geczy, *Fashion and Orientalism*, 74; Jones, *Sexing la Mode*, 190.

71. Chazin-Bennahum, *The Lure of Perfection*, 47; Foster, *Choreography & Narrative*, 87.

72. *Gallerie des modes et costumes français*, introduction to 24e, 25e, and 26e *cahiers* (1780).

73. It also fails to include the *fourreau* (chap. 4), which was clearly very popular but on which more research is needed.

74. *Cabinet des modes*, Jan. 15, 1786, 34.

75. Nougaret, *Tableau mouvant de Paris, ou variétés amusantes*, 3:50.

76. Mercier, *Tableau de Paris*, 9:80.

77. By contrast, it is not until the thirteenth *cahier* (1778) that the *robe à l'anglaise* makes an appearance in the *Gallerie des modes*.

78. Other sources documenting the *polonaise* post-1781 (its final appearance in fashion magazines) include bills for retrimming "the Collars of old *Polonaises*" in 1782 ("Relevé des mémoires de Mlle Bertin, Quartier de Janvier 1782," Comptes de la maison du roi, 1730–91, K//506), for the making of a *polonaise* between 1782 and 1784 ("Memoire en Ouvrage faire pour Madame Bernier par Mme Verjon Depuis le 26 mars 1782 jusqu'au premier aoust 1784," Bernier d'Archet [famille],

1755–85, Papiers de famille, FR/FR-AD078/E 112), and another for the bleaching of a *polonaise* in 1785 ("Memoires du blanchisage de robe que jay [*sic*] fait pour Madame la Duchesse De lorge," duchesse de Dufort de Lorge, eighteenth century, Papiers de famille, E/SUP 523). This list does not include wardrobe inventories, as these could include older clothes that were no longer worn.

79. Chrisman-Campbell, *Fashion Victims*, 212; Coulomb, "L'Empire des modes," 66; Pietsch, "On Different Types of Women's Dresses in France in the Louis XVI Period," 408.

80. Chrisman-Campbell, *Fashion Victims*, 243.

81. *Supplement au Journal de Paris*, Mar. 16, 1794, 1–3. Other sources documenting the *lévite* post-1785 (its final appearance in fashion magazines) include a bill for the making of a *lévite* for the daughter of opera singer Henri Larrivée ("Memoire pour mes demoiselle larive [*sic*]," Oct. 14, 1786, Henry Larrivée, *5 mémoires fournis à Monsieur Larrivée, à ses filles et à Madame de Granville, 1777–1786*, Bibliothèque nationale de France, département Bibliothèque-musée de l'opéra, NLAS-256), many made by marchande de modes Mme Éloffe between 1787 and 1792 (Éloffe, *Modes et usages au temps du Marie-Antoinette*, 1:70, 79, 88, 91–92, 136, 167, 264, 297, 347–48, 360, 442, 448, 2:123, 161, 272, 309, 319, 320); and advertisements by Parisian couturière Mme Teillard from 1790 to 1794 (*Journal de Paris*, Oct. 5, 1790, 2; Feb. 7, 1791, iii; Mar. 23, 1791, iii; Apr. 18, 1791, 4; Oct. 12, 1792, 3; and Mar. 16, 1794, 3). This list does not include wardrobe inventories as these could include older clothes that were no longer worn.

82. Maillard, "Contributions à l'histoire du costume."

83. Maillard, "Contributions à l'histoire du costume," appendix, Mme la Comtesse de Montenay, Mar. 27, 1782.

84. "La Garde-robe d'une champenoise au XVIIIe siècle," 17:413–15.

85. "La Garde-robe d'une champenoise au XVIIIe siècle," 413–15; Le Gouil-Bauzin, "Inventaire de François Guillaume Claude Trousseau"; Péage, "Inventaire après décès de Madame de Podenas," 175–86.

86. "Garderobe depuis 1779," Comptes de la maison du roi, 1784–92, K//505 no. 25.

87. Roche, *Culture of Clothing*, 146–47.

88. Roche, *Culture of Clothing*, 199.

89. Roche, *Culture of Clothing*, 146.

90. Van Cleave and Welborn, "'Very Much the Taste and Various Are the Makes,'" 19–20.

91. Lasic, "Ethnicity," 156.

92. Roche, *Culture of Clothing*, 145–46.

93. Lenotre, *Mémoires et souvenirs sur la Révolution et l'Empire*, 43.

94. Panckoucke, *Recueil de planches de l'encyclopédie*, s.v. "Couturiere," 6:pl. 24; Desrais, *Filles publiques chassées par ordonnance de police*, 14; Desrais, *Petits métiers, cris de Paris*, 1:63.

95. Roche, *People of Paris*, 164, 183.

96. Monnard, *Les Souvenirs d'une femme du peuple*, 14–16.

97. *Les Affiches americaines*, Sept. 16, 1772; May 11, 1774; June 1, 1774; July 24, 1776; Aug. 31, 1779; Feb. 26, 1783; *Affiches de Bordeaux*, July 24, 1777; Mar. 4, 1779; Mar. 8, 1781; Aug. 30, 1781; Oct. 11, 1781; *Affiches du Poitou*, July 12, 1781; *Affiches Generales de la Bretagne*, Oct. 27, 1780; Nov. 17, 1780; *Annonces, affiches, nouvelles et avis divers de l'Orléanais*, Mar. 1, 1776; Nov. 10, 1776; Jan. 23, 1778; May 29, 1778; July 10, 1778; Mar. 26, 1779; Apr. 2, 1779; Nov. 26, 1779; July 21, 1780; Mar. 9, 1781; Apr. 20, 1781; Jan. 25, 1782; *Annonces, affiches et avis divers pour la ville du Mans et pour la province*, Nov. 2, 1778; Bonnaud, "La Mode féminine à Limoges il y a deux cents ans," 202–5; "La Garde-robe d'une champenoise au XVIIIe siecle," 413–15; Figeac, *La Douceur des Lumières*, 154; Bénet, "E. 112., Serie E," 10:18; Bénet, "H. Suppl. 1814-H. 96," 10:311; *Journal de Guienne*, Oct. 24, 1784; Sept. 20, 1786; May 27, 1787; Mar. 5, 1790; *Journal de l'Orléanais ou Annonces, affiches et avis diver*, Feb. 7, 1783; May 2, 1783.

98. For example, Antoine Raspal, *Intérieur de Cuisine*, ca. 1780; Antoine Raspal, *Portrait de Madame de Privat et Ses Enfants*, 1780–81. See Tétart-Vittu, "Incidence de la mode française à Arles," 17–18.

99. L. J. Watteau, *La 14ème expérience aérostatique de M. Blanchard*, 1785; Adolf Ulrik Wertmüller, *Portrait de Mme Claudine Rousse, née Morin*, 1780, in Lundberg, *Le Peintre suédois*, 4.

100. Biernat, "Whalebone Stays and Corsets for Children from the Seventeenth to the Nineteenth Centuries," 129–41; Chrisman-Campbell, *Fashion Victims*, 46; Crowston, *Fabricating Women*, 47.

101. In "*Fourreau relevé en Polonaise*": "Habillemens d'enfans dans le nouveau goût" (1780), *Gallerie des modes et costumes français, dessinés d'aprés nature, Gravés par les plus Célèbres Artistes en ce genre, et colorés avec le plus grand soin par Madame Le Beau*, 1778–81 (hereafter *GDM*), 30e cahier, pl. 5 (hereafter abbreviated as cahier/plate, e.g., 30/5). In *fourreau* "*retroussé à la Polonaise*": "Cette petite Fille est vétue d'un Foureau" (1780), *GDM*, 25e suite, hh.191; "Le petite Fille vue de face est vétue d'un Foureau" (1780), *GDM*, 25e suite, hh.190. In *lévite*: "Le plus petit de ces enfans est vétu" (1780), *GDM*, 25e suite, hh.189.

102. In *polonaise*: Louis Carrogis, called Carmontelle, *Monsieur N., fermier général, avec sa fille*; Peter Adolf Hall, *La femme et les enfants*, in Gauffin, "A Propos de l'exposition de l'art Suedois à Paris," 63; Hubert Robert, *L'entrée du Tapis vert*, 1777; Pierre Alexandre Wille, *La Famille malheureuse*, 1777. In *lévite*: Louis-Marin Bonnet after Jean-Baptiste Hüet, *Les Échasses, jeux des enfants*, ca. 1790. In *turque*: Antoine

Vestier, *Portrait présumé de la famille de Bergeret de Grancourt*, ca. 1785; François Louis Joseph Watteau (called Watteau de Lille), *Père de famille donnant la Saint Nicolas à ses enfants*, 1788; François Louis-Joseph Watteau (called Watteau de Lille), *Gathering in a Park*; Pierre Alexandre Wille, *Portrait d'un Amateur et de sa famille*, 1786.

103. "Memoir: Des ouvrages et fournitures fait pour le service de "Memoir: des Ouvrages et fournitures fait pour le service de madame la Comtesse d'Artois à l'ordre de madame la comtesse de Bourbon Busset," July 1780, cotte 20, Papiers Bourbon-Busset, T//265/4-T//265/5; Roche, *Culture of Clothing*, 201.

104. Carmontelle, *Madame Millin du Perreux and Her Son, with a Painted Portrait of Monsieur Jérôme-Robert Millin du Perreux*, ca. 1760; François-Hubert Drouais, *Le Comte de Nogent, enfant*, 1765; Marie-Victoire Lemoine, *Portrait of a Young Boy Feeding Two Birds*, before 1820; Louis-Rolland Trinquesse (attr.), *Portrait d'un enfant tenant des fruits*, 1782. See Delpierre, *Dress in France in the Eighteenth Century*, 30; Landini, "Dress for the Body," 18.

105. Van Cleave and Welborn, "'Very Much the Taste and Various Are the Makes,'" 20.

106. "Circassienne de taffetas à bandes" (1779), *GDM*, 21/6.

107. Bachaumont, *Mémoires secrets*, 34:176–77.

108. "Theatres, Comedie Francaise," 63.

109. Chatenet-Calyste, "Une Consommation aristocratique et féminine à la fin du XVIIIe siècle," 255. For reference, Amanda Vickery argues that English women in this era were considered beyond youthful fashions by their late twenties ("Mutton Dressed as Lamb?," 859–61), while Englishwoman Lady Crewe observed that Parisian women "leave off wearing Flowers and Feathers on their heads at the Age of Thirty" (Crewe, *An English Lady in Paris*, 87).

2. WESTERN AND EASTERN APPROACHES TO DRESS

1. Tarrant, *Development of Costume*, 30.
2. Tarrant, *Development of Costume*, 32.
3. Boucher, *20,000 Years of Fashion*, 191; Tarrant, *Development of Costume*, 49; Turnau, *History of Dress in Central and Eastern Europe*, 9.
4. Boucher, *20,000 Years of Fashion*, 191; Jirousek, *Ottoman Dress and Design in the West*, 42–43; Jirousek, "Ottoman Influences in Western Dress," 41–43.
5. Hayward, "Clothing," 176; Landini, "Dress for the Body," 26–27; Moheng, "Whalebone Bodies and Panniers," 109–27; Moulinier and Vesin, "Women's Undergarments," 57–61.
6. Tarrant, *Development of Costume*, 64.
7. Moulinier and Vesin, "Women's Undergarments," 61–63; Tarrant, *Development of Costume*, 56.
8. Bendall, *Shaping Femininity*, 36.
9. Aschengreen, Albukhary, and Landini, "Men's Dress, the Invention of the Tailored Shape," 62; Bruna, "Puffed out Chests and Paunched Bellies," 39–45.
10. Aschengreen, Albukhary, and Landini, "The Costumes of the Islamic Peoples," 82; Scarce, *Women's Costume of the Near and Middle East*, 51, 56.
11. Martin and Koda, *Orientalism*, 13.
12. Martin and Koda, 17–18.
13. Calvi, "Imperial Fashions," 159–65; Faroqhi, "Women, Wealth and Textiles in 1730s Bursa," 219; Jirousek, *Ottoman Dress and Design in the West*, 156; Vogelsang, "History of Dress and Fashion," 17–18.
14. Scarce, *Women's Costume of the Near and Middle East*, 14.
15. Jirousek, *Ottoman Dress and Design in the West*, 5; Vogelsang-Eastwood, "Introduction to Dress and Fashion in Central and Southwest Asia," 5:5.
16. Jirousek, *Ottoman Dress and Design in the West*, 13, 18.
17. Grehan, *Everyday Life and Consumer Culture*, 202; Kallander, *Women, Gender, and the Palace Households*, 236. The term *caftan* was used in this period in Russia (Turnau, *History of Dress in Central and Eastern Europe*, 161).
18. Jirousek, "Kaftan and Its Origins," 135.
19. Tezcan and Delibaş, *The Topkapı Saray Museum*, 25.
20. Jirousek, *Ottoman Dress and Design in the West*, 12–15; Micklewright, "Ottoman Dress," 127–30; Tezcan and Delibaş, *Topkapı Saray Museum*, 25.
21. Jirousek, *Ottoman Dress and Design in the West*, 16–17.
22. Scarce, *Women's Costume of the Near and Middle East*, 46, 49, 60.
23. Scarce, *Women's Costume of the Near and Middle East*, 56.
24. Micklewright, "Ottoman Dress," 130–31; Scarce, *Women's Costume of the Near and Middle East*, 46, 49, 53, 56.
25. Landini, "Dress for the Body," 19; Scarce, *Women's Costume of the Near and Middle East*, 56, 59–60.
26. Scarce, *Women's Costume of the Near and Middle East*, 53, 62.
27. Scarce, *Women's Costume of the Near and Middle East*, 49, 60, 62.
28. Jirousek, "Kaftan and Its Origins," 135.
29. Turnau, *History of Dress in Central and Eastern*; Turnau, "The Main Centres of National Fashion in Eastern Europe," 47–65; Turnau, "The Dress of the Polish Jews in the 17th and 18th Centuries," 101–8; Turnau, "Pour une histoire du costume," 1127–37.
30. Solnon, *Turban et la stambouline*, 247; Turnau, *History of Dress in Central and Eastern Europe*, 128, 130.
31. Jasienski, "A Savage Magnificence," 174. See also Ribeiro, *Dress in Eighteenth-Century Europe*, 97–104.

32. Boucher, *20,000 Years of Fashion*, 329; Korshunova, *The Art of Costume in Russia*, 7.

33. Turnau, *History of Dress in Central and Eastern Europe*, 124, 128.

34. Solnon, *Turban et la stambouline*, 246; Taszycka, "Symbols of Nationhood," 73.

35. Straszewska, "Poland," 222.

36. Straszewska, "Poland," 226.

37. Biedrońska-Słota and Molenda, "The Emergence of a Polish National Dress," 114–23; Borchard, "Reflections on the Polish Nobleman's Attire," 14; Boucher, *20,000 Years of Fashion*, 329; Mansel, *Dressed to Rule*, 39; Solnon, *Turban et la stambouline*, 246; Straszewska, "Poland," 226; Turnau, *History of Dress in Central and Eastern Europe*, 160.

38. Solnon, *Turban et la stambouline*, 246.

39. Taszycka, "Symbols of Nationhood," 73.

40. Solnon, *Turban et la stambouline*, 246; Taszycka, "Symbols of Nationhood," 76.

41. Turnau, *History of Dress in Central and Eastern Europe*, 10.

42. Aschengreen, Albukhary, and Landini, "The Woman's Cuirass," 72–73; Crowston, *Fabricating Women*, 37; Hart, "The Mantua," 95–96; Landini, "Dress for the Body," 24–25.

43. Boucher, *20,000 Years of Fashion*, 255, 260. This is not to say there were not other, less formal garments. For example, the *justaucorps* was a woman's jacket, while the *hongreline* was an informal jacket with long skirtings (there was a men's version as well). Interestingly, the *hongreline* was styled and named after Hungarian clothing and thus is an earlier example of Eastern influence (Boucher, *20,000 Years of Fashion*, 254–55).

44. Tiramani et al., *Seventeenth-Century Women's Dress Patterns*, 9.

45. Hart et al., *Historical Fashion in Detail*, 96.

46. Boucher, *20,000 Years of Fashion*, 260; Gorguet-Ballesteros, "Caractériser le costume de cour," 59. See patterns for robes in Arnold, *Patterns of Fashion . . . c. 1660–1860*, 23; Arnold, *Patterns of Fashion 5*, 50–51, 54–55, 60–62, 66–67, 72–73, 78–79; Tiramani, *Seventeenth-Century Women's Dress Patterns: Book 2*, 66–70; Waugh and Woodward, *The Cut of Women's Clothes*, diagram VI.

47. Gorguet-Ballesteros, "Caractériser le costume de cour," 58–59; Mansel, *Dressed to Rule*, 2; Ribeiro, *Art of Dress*, 36, 128; Trey, *La Mode à la cour de Marie-Antoinette*, 51. See patterns for court dresses in Arnold, *Patterns of Fashion 5*, 96–98; Waugh, *Corsets and Crinolines*, 36; Waugh and Woodward, *Cut of Women's Clothes*, diagram XXVII.

48. Gorguet-Ballesteros, "Caractériser le costume de cour," 58.

49. Tarrant, *Development of Costume*, 64–65.

50. Bendall, *Shaping Femininity*, 162.

51. Bendall, *Shaping Femininity*, 187. My own experiences wearing reconstructed eighteenth-century garments mirrors Bendall's analysis.

52. Steele, *Fashion and Eroticism*, 241.

53. Scholz, "English Women in Oriental Dress," 89. See also Bendall, *Shaping Femininity*, 252; Crowley, *The Invention of Comfort*, 392; Landini, "Dress for the Body," 22–23; Moheng, "Whalebone Bodies and Panniers," 109–27; Stobart, "Introduction," 6–7.

54. Kirkness, *Le Français du Théâtre italien*, 201; Lasic, "Ethnicity," 146; Raveux, "Spaces and Technologies in the Cotton Industry," 54; Roche, *Culture of Clothing*, 170. The *robe de chambre* was alternately called *indienne* (Indian, a reference to the printed Indian cottons from which it was frequently made), *manteau de lit* (bed coat) or *de nuit* (night), or *robe d'intérieur* (interior gown).

55. Blum, *Eighteenth-Century French Fashion Plates*, vii; Boucher, *20,000 Years of Fashion*, 294; Crowston, *Fabricating Women*, 32; Cunningham, "Eighteenth Century Nightgowns," 2–4; Delpierre, *Dress in France in the Eighteenth Century*, 10; Fennetaux, "J'étais pittoresque et beau," 269; M. Hollander, "Vermeer's Robe," 180, 186; Jirousek, *Ottoman Dress and Design in the West*, 130–31; Lasic, "Ethnicity," 145; Lemire, "Fashioning Global Trade," 373; Martin and Koda, *Orientalism*, 35; Raveux, "Fashion and Consumption of Painted and Printed Calicoes," 11; Swain, "Nightgown into Dressing Gown," 10; Tarrant, "Lord Sheffield's Banyan," 65–66; Thunder, "New Object in Focus," 1–2.

56. Schoeser, "Oriental Connections," 176; Swain, "Nightgown into Dressing Gown," 11–12.

57. Tarrant, "Lord Sheffield's Banyan," 92–97; Thoisy-Dallem, "La Robe de chambre d'Oberkampf," 82–85.

58. Cunningham, "Eighteenth Century Nightgowns," 2.

59. Cunningham, "Eighteenth Century Nightgowns," 9; Geczy, *Fashion and Orientalism*, 49; L. E. Miller, "An Enigmatic Bourgeois," 52–53; Swain, "Nightgown into Dressing Gown," 12–13; Thoisy-Dallem, "La Vieille robe de chambre de Diderot," 69–74.

60. Egler, Gorguet-Ballesteros, and Maeder, "L'Orient et la mode en Europe," 64; Fennetaux, "Du boudoir au salon," 72; Urbain, "'Dans un instant, la toilette aura tout gâté,'" 243.

61. Gorguet-Ballesteros, "La Double vie de la robe volante, 1700–1735," 194; Lister, "La Mantua," 58.

62. Hart, "Mantua," 95; Roche, *Culture of Clothing*, 120–22.

63. Arnold et al., *Patterns of Fashion 6*, 14; Arnold, "The Cut and Construction of Women's Clothes in the Eighteenth Century," 126–28; Arnold, "A Mantua c. 1708–9," 26; Crowston, *Fabricating Women*, 36–37; Ribeiro, *Dress in Eighteenth-Century Europe*, 34; Lister, "La Mantua," 58. See patterns for *manteaux* in Andersen, *Moden in 1700-årene*, 221–23; Arnold, "Mantua c. 1708–9," 30–31; Arnold, *Patterns*

of Fashion . . . c. 1660–1860, 23, 71; Arnold et al., *Patterns of Fashion 6*, 34–36, 40–41, 56–59, 60–63; Waugh and Woodward, *Cut of Women's Clothes*, diagrams IX and XII.

64. Hart, "Mantua," 98–99.

65. Boucher, *20,000 Years of Fashion*, 261; Crowston, *Fabricating Women*, 37, 40; Hayward, "Clothing," 178.

66. Arnold et al., *Patterns of Fashion 6*, 21; Crowston, *Fabricating Women*, 40–41.

67. Jirousek, *Ottoman Dress and Design in the West*, 137; Schoeser, "Oriental Connections," 170, 176.

68. Jirousek, *Ottoman Dress and Design in the West*, 137–38; Schoeser, "Oriental Connections," 172.

69. Jirousek, *Ottoman Dress and Design in the West*, 138–39; Landweber, "Turkish Delight," 5.

70. For an excellent visual overview of this process, see Arnold et al., *Patterns of Fashion 6*, 8–9.

71. Aschengreen, Albukhary, and Landini, "Woman's Cuirass," 72; Crowston, *Fabricating Women*, 37; Landini, "Dress for the Body," 26–27; Lister, "La Mantua," 58; Pfiefer, "Undressed" 39.

72. Arnold, "Cut and Construction of Women's Clothes," 128; Arnold, "Mantua c. 1708–9," 26; Arnold et al., *Patterns of Fashion 6*, 12.

73. The style had many names, all of which referred to its loose silhouette: *manteau volant*, *robe flottante* (floating), *robe ballante* (swinging), *robe battante* (or *à battante*, flying), or the older term *robe de chambre* (Crowston, *Fabricating Women*, 41; DeJean, *The Age of Comfort*, 259n194; Gorguet-Ballesteros, "Double vie de la robe volante," 193–99; Ribeiro, *Dress in Eighteenth-Century Europe*, 37).

74. Ribeiro, *Dress in Eighteenth-Century Europe*, 35–37. See patterns for *robes volante* in Arnold et al., *Patterns of Fashion 6*, 80–82, 84–87; Waugh and Woodward, *Cut of Women's Clothes*, diagrams X and XI.

75. Crowston, *Fabricating Women*, 42; Gorguet-Ballesteros, "Double vie de la robe volante," 196–97; Leloir, *Histoire du costume de l'Antiquité à 1914*, 11:44–48; Ribeiro, *Art of Dress*, 35–38.

76. Ribeiro, *Dress in Eighteenth-Century Europe*, 37.

77. Delpierre, *Dress in France in the Eighteenth Century*, 10; Landini, "Dress for the Body," 27; Moheng, "Whalebone Bodies and Panniers," 112.

78. Jirousek, *Ottoman Dress and Design in the West*, 15.

79. Boucher, *20,000 Years of Fashion*, 294; Crowston, *Fabricating Women*, 41; Jirousek, *Ottoman Dress and Design in the West*, 171; Ribeiro, *Dress in Eighteenth-Century Europe*, 35.

80. Arnold, "Cut and Construction of Women's Clothes," 129; Boucher, *20,000 Years of Fashion*, 296; Crowston, *Fabricating Women*, 42; Delpierre, *Dress in France in the Eighteenth Century*, 14–16; Landini, "Dress for the Body," 27; Leloir, *Histoire du costume de l'Antiquité à 1914*, 11:48; Pietsch, "On Different Types of Women's Dresses," 399; Ribeiro, *Art of Dress*, 57; Ribeiro, *Dress in Eighteenth-Century Europe*, 35, 38–39, 136–38, 219–22. See patterns for *robes à la française* in Arnold, "Cut and Construction of Women's Clothes," 130; Arnold, *Patterns of Fashion . . . c. 1660–1860*, 29, 33, 35; Arnold et al., *Patterns of Fashion 6*, 88–91, 96–98; Baumgarten, Watson, and Carr, *Costume Close-up*, 17; Waugh and Woodward, *Cut of Women's Clothes*, diagrams XV, XVIII, XIX, XX.

81. Arnold et al., *Patterns of Fashion 6*, 15.

82. Delpierre, *Dress in France in the Eighteenth Century*, 18.

83. Jirousek, *Ottoman Dress and Design in the West*, 171.

3. DEFINING OTTOMAN INFLUENCE, 1760–90

1. Boucher, *20,000 Years of Fashion*, 300; Chrisman-Campbell, *Fashion Victims*, 77; Crowston, *Fabricating Women*, 43; Jones, *Sexing la Mode*, 191; Ribeiro, *Dress in Eighteenth-Century Europe*, 207; Roche, *Culture of Clothing*, 143–45; Waugh and Woodward, *Cut of Women's Clothes*, 73.

2. Chrisman-Campbell, *Fashion Victims*, 77; Lasic, "Ethnicity," 155–57; Redondo, "Polonesa del Siglo XVIII," 4.

3. Boucher, *20,000 Years of Fashion*, 300–303; Chrisman-Campbell, *Fashion Victims*, 242–43; Chrisman-Campbell, "Minister of Fashion," 267–72; Delpierre, *Dress in France in the Eighteenth Century*, 18–19, 67–68; Leloir, *Histoire du costume de l'Antiquité à 1914*, 12:18–24; Pietsch, "Eastern Influences on French Fashion in the Late 18th Century," 210–13; Pietsch, "On Different Types of Women's Dresses," 400–403, 405–6; Ribeiro, *Dress in Eighteenth-Century Europe*, 226–28.

4. Boucher, *20,000 Years of Fashion*, 229; Chrisman-Campbell, *Fashion Victims*, 220–21; Delpierre, *Dress in France in the Eighteenth Century*, 21, 59; Leloir, *Histoire du costume de l'Antiquité à 1914*, 12:32–34; Lister, "La Mantua," 58; Pietsch, "On Different Types of Women's Dresses," 403–4; Ribeiro, *Dress in Eighteenth-Century Europe*, 222.

5. Chrisman-Campbell, *Fashion Victims*, 226–29; Delpierre, *Dress in France in the Eighteenth Century*, 21; Leloir, *Histoire du costume de l'Antiquité à 1914*, 12:30; Pietsch, "On Different Types of Women's Dresses," 406.

6. Ashelford, "'Colonial Livery' and the Chemise a la Reine, 1779–1784," 224; Boucher, *20,000 Years of Fashion*, 303; Chrisman-Campbell, *Fashion Victims*, 174–75; Leloir, *Histoire du costume de l'Antiquité à 1914*, 12:29; Pietsch, "On Different Types of Women's Dresses," 406.

7. Blum, *Eighteenth-Century French Fashion Plates*, vii; Coulomb, "Empire des modes," 67; Crowston, *Fabricating Women*, 43; Delpierre, *Dress in France in the Eighteenth Century*, 21; Pietsch, "On Different Types of Women's Dresses," 408.

8. Leloir, *Histoire du costume de l'Antiquité à 1914*, 12:28; Pietsch, "On Different Types of Women's Dresses," 408–10.

9. Arnold, "Cut and Construction of Women's Clothes," 133; Boucher, *20,000 Years of Fashion*, 303; Panckoucke, *Encyclopédie méthodique*, s.v. "Fourreau," 2:67; Juranek, *Przemiany "robe en chemise*," 13; Pietsch, "On Different Types of Women's Dresses," 405.

10. Crowston, *Fabricating Women*, 47; Leloir, *Histoire du costume de l'Antiquité à 1914*, 12:52.

11. Ribeiro, *Art of Dress*, 64; Ribeiro, *Dress in Eighteenth-Century Europe*, 222. See patterns for mantuas/nightgowns in Arnold, *Patterns of Fashion . . . c. 1660–1860*, 23; Arnold et al., *Patterns of Fashion 6*, 44–45, 68–70, 71–73; Baumgarten, Watson, and Carr, *Costume Close-up*, 13; Waugh and Woodward, *Cut of Women's Clothes*, diagrams XIV, XVI, XVII.

12. Arnold, "Cut and Construction of Women's Clothes," 128; Buck, *Dress in Eighteenth-Century England*, 41–43; Ribeiro, *Dress in Eighteenth-Century Europe*, 138, 222.

13. "Robe à l'anglaise de pékin verd pomme unie" (1778), *GDM*, 13/4.

14. Buck, *Dress in Eighteenth-Century England*, 14–17.

15. Ribeiro, *Art of Dress*, 66.

16. Beaumarchais, *Eugénie*, 3–4.

17. Michel-Barthélémy Ollivier, *La Partie des dames*, ca. 1765, painting; Michel-Barthélémy Ollivier, *Le Thé à l'anglaise servi dans le salon des Quatre-Glaces au palais du Temple, mai 1766*, 1766, painting.

18. *Courrier de la mode ou le Journal du goût, Ouvrage périodique, contenant le détail de toutes les nouveautés du mois* (hereafter *CDLM*), Dec. 1768, 77. The term *fourreau* was sometimes used interchangeably with *robe*.

19. *CDLM*, June 1769, 122–23.

20. Arnold, "Cut and Construction of Women's Clothes," 129; Boucher, *20,000 Years of Fashion*, 299; Delpierre, *Dress in France in the Eighteenth-Century*, 21; Delpierre, "Marie-Antoinette, reine de la mode," 43; Pietsch, "On Different Types of Women's Dresses," 403–5; Ribeiro, *Art of Dress*, 66–67; Ribeiro, *Dress in Eighteenth-Century Europe*, 222; Ribeiro, *Fashion in the French Revolution*, 27–28; Trey, *Mode à la cour de Marie-Antoinette*, 84; Waugh and Woodward, *Cut of Women's Clothes*, 72. See patterns for *robes à l'anglaise* in Arnold, *Patterns of Fashion . . . c. 1660–1860*, 36, 39, 41; Arnold et al., *Patterns of Fashion 6*, 74–75; Baumgarten, Watson, and Carr, *Costume Close-up*, 27; Waugh and Woodward, *Cut of Women's Clothes*, diagram XXII.

21. "Robe à l'anglaise de pékin verd pomme unie" (1778), *GDM*, 13/4.

22. Ribeiro, *Art of Dress*, 67; Ribeiro, *Dress in Eighteenth-Century Europe*, 222.

23. Panckoucke, *Encyclopédie méthodique*, s.v. "Couturiere," 1:224.

24. Arnold, "Cut and Construction of Women's Clothes," 129; Pietsch, "On Different Types of Women's Dresses," 404; Ribeiro, *Art of Dress*, 67; Ribeiro, *Dress in Eighteenth-Century Europe*, 226.

25. In addition to the patterns in this book, see patterns for *robes à la polonaise* in Arnold et al., *Patterns of Fashion 6*, 101–3, 104–7; *Moda en sombras, Museo Nacional del Pueblo Español*, back cover. See patterns for *robes à la circassienne* in Arnold et al., *Patterns of Fashion 6*, 108–9. See additional patterns for *robes à la turque* in Arnold et al., *Patterns of Fashion 6*, 110–12.

26. Van Cleave and Welborn, "'Very Much the Taste and Various Are the Makes,'" 2.

27. Pietsch, "Eastern Influences on French Fashion," 213; Ribeiro, "Elegant Art of Fancy Dress," 157; Schoeser, "Oriental Connections," 176.

28. Boucher, *20,000 Years of Fashion*, 300, 302; Chrisman-Campbell, *Fashion Victims*, 242; Delpierre, *Dress in France in the Eighteenth Century*, 18; Delpierre, "Marie-Antoinette, reine de la mode," 43; Giorgi, "La Moda de la Robe à la Polonaise," 101; Pietsch, "On Different Types of Women's Dresses," 401; Pietsch, "Eastern Influences on French Fashion," 210; Redondo, "Polonesa del Siglo XVIII," 2; Ribeiro, *Dress in Eighteenth-Century Europe*, 226; Trey, *Mode à la cour de Marie-Antoinette*, 82; Van Cleave and Welborn, "'Very Much the Taste and Various Are the Makes,'" 5–8.

29. "Robe à la polonoise d'étoffe unie à coqueluchon" (1778), *GDM*, 7/2; "Jeune dame vêtue à l'austrasienne" (1778), *GDM*, 15/2. The *parfait contentement* (perfect contentment) was the name for the decorative rosette or bow that was frequently placed at the breast center front, on top of the closure (Blum, *Eighteenth Century French Fashion Plates*, xiv; Boucher, *20,000 Years of Fashion*, 302).

30. Boucher, *20,000 Years of Fashion*, 307; Chrisman-Campbell, *Fashion Victims*, 243; Delpierre, *Dress in France in the Eighteenth Century*, 19; Pietsch, "On Different Types of Women's Dresses," 402, 405; Pietsch, "Eastern Influences on French Fashion," 211; Ribeiro, *Fashion in the French Revolution*, 28.

31. Panckoucke, *Encyclopédie méthodique*, s.v. "Couturiere," 1:225.

32. "Demoiselle en caraco de taffetas coiffée d'un demi bonnet" (1778), *GDM*, 12/6.

33. "Cette robe à la circassienne d'un nouveau gout" (1778), *GDM*, 13/1.

34. *Magasin des modes nouvelles, françaises et anglaises, décrites d'une manière claire & précise, & représentées par des planches en taille-douce, enluminées* (hereafter *MDM*), June 30, 1788, 196.

35. Cornu, *Galerie des modes et costumes français*, xiii; Giorgi, "Moda de la Robe à la Polonaise," 102.

36. "Demoiselle élégante coeffée d'un bonnet anglais" (1778), *GDM*, 15/5.

37. Delpierre, *Dress in France in the Eighteenth Century*, 165–66; Pietsch, "On Different Types of Women's Dresses," 401–2, 405; Pietsch, "Eastern Influences on French Fashion," 210–11; Redondo, "Polonesa del Siglo XVIII," 2, 5; Ribeiro, *Dress in Eighteenth-Century Europe*, 226; Van Cleave and Welborn, "'Very Much the Taste and Various Are the Makes,'" 8–10; Waugh and Woodward, *Cut of Women's Clothes*, 73.

38. Some scholars refer to the *compère* stomacher as a "zone," a term that some have taken to refer to the cutaway, triangular shape of the bodice opening itself. This usage of *zone* appears to date to C. Willett Cunnington and Phillis Cunnington's *Handbook of English Costume in the Eighteenth Century*, in which they write of the "ENGLISH GOWN with Fourreau Back, or 'Robe à L'Anglaise,'" "Open without robings and worn with a false waistcoat or zone (from 1770's). The bodice was closed at the pit of the bosom and then sloped away to the sides leaving a triangular gap with the base below. The gap was filled by a 'zone' or false waistcoat sewn to the linings of the inner sides of the bodice, or as described under 'waistcoat with polonese gowns.' The 'zone' varied in design but was always in the form of an inverted stomacher, and was sometimes scalloped or, in the 1780s, vandyked with a falling collar to match, the collar edging the décolletage and joining the zone at the apex of the triangle" (Cunnington and Cunnington, *Handbook of English Costume*, 274). They go on to write of the *polonaise:* "A zone was used where the front gap was small." For sources, they point to an article in the *Ipswich Journal* (1788), which declared, "No stomachers or any decoration whatever in their place, the bodice being entirely plain, not even a zone which was so universal last year." However, all mentions of "zones" that I have found in eighteenth-century sources point to it being a belt, which is the only relevant definition found in the *Oxford English Dictionary*. The Cunningtons further present a line drawing of a "zone," which is now at the Colchester & Ipswich Museum Service. This item does appear to be a stomacher, but it is not cut in the shape necessary to fill in the gap created by a cutaway gown.

39. *MDM*, Jan. 30, 1787, 59. See Boucher, *20,000 Years of Fashion*, 307.

40. *MDM*, June 30, 1788, 196.

41. *Caraco et jupe*, 1780–90, cotton and linen, Palais Galliera, musée de la Mode de la Ville de Paris, GAL1920.1.2370; *Caraco mit halblangen Ärmeln*, France, 1786–90, linen, Bayerisches Nationalmuseum, Munich, 96/178; *Dress*, England, 1770–80, cotton, Royal Ontario Museum, Toronto, 978.101.2; *Dress*, 1780, silk, Worthing Museum & Art Gallery, UK, 1972/59/1; *Dress*, 1781–85, cotton, linen, metal, silk, Museum of London, 65.80/1; *Polonaise dress*, 1775, Killerton, Devon, UK, NT 1362010; *Robe à la Turque, manteau de robe, corsage et jupon ayant appartenu à Anne-Élisabeth Oberkampf*, ca. 1785, cream silk pékin, Musée de la Toile de Jouy, Jouy-en-Josas, France, 000.4.6, 001.1.13.2.a, 001.13.2.b. *Woman's overdress*, France, 1775–99, cotton, Palazzo Mocenigo, Venice, Cl. XXIV no. 0239.

42. *Caraco*, 1770–80, cotton, Palais Galliera, musée de la Mode de la Ville de Paris, GAL1992.177.X; *Caraco à la Polonaise*, France, ca. 1760–70, silk, linen, Bayerisches Nationalmuseum, Munich, 96/143; *Caraco et jupe*, 1770–80, silk, cotton, Palais Galliera, musée de la Mode de la Ville de Paris, GAL1966.33.1; *Casaca*, 1760–70, silk, linen, Centre de Documentació i Museu Tèxtil, Terrassa, Spain, 11732; *Casaca*, Centre de Documentació i Museu Tèxtil, Terrassa, Spain, 11819; *Embroidered jacket and skirt*, Sweden, 1780s, silk, Nordiska Museet, Stockholm, NM.0991090A; *Hüftlanger Caraco mit ovalem Halsausschnitt*, Netherlands?, ca. 1780–1800, silk, linen, Bayerisches Nationalmuseum, Munich, 96/145; *Mädchencaraco*, Italy, ca. 1775–85, silk, linen, Bayerisches Nationalmuseum, Munich, 96/182; *Manteau à la polonaise*, ca. 1770–80, silk, linen, Collection Gilles Labrosse #1, Sept. 22, 2020, lot no. 95, Encheres Sadde SARL, Moulins, France; *Polonaise*, Great Britain, ca. 1780, silk and linen, Victoria & Albert Museum, London, T.20-1945; *Robe à la polonaise*, ca. 1770–90, silk, Gemeentemuseum, The Hauge, 0556545; *Robe à la polonaise*, France, ca. 1772–80, silk, linen, and cotton, National Gallery of Victoria, Melbourne, 2018.321.1-b; *Robe à la polonaise*, Europe, 1775–85 (altered later), silk and linen, Colonial Williamsburg Foundation, Williamsburg, VA, 2006-42; *Robe à la polonaise*, ca. 1778, Palais Galliera, musée de la Mode de la Ville de Paris, 62-108-14; *Robe à la polonaise*, ca. 1780, silk, Coutau-Bégarie & Associés, Linge, dentelles, tissus, Feb. 9, 2012, lot no. 303; *Robe à la polonaise*, ca. 1778, silk, Collections d'etoffes et costumes ancien, June 15, 2012, lot no. 287, Drouot, Paris; *Vestido*, Spain, ca. 1775–80, silk, linen, Museo del Traje, Madrid, CE001005.

43. Similarly shaped stomachers survive with a 1780s *robe à la française* (French, 1778–85, linen and silk, Metropolitan Museum of Art, New York, C.I.65.13.2a-c), as well as a Swedish jacket ensemble that also includes a separate waistcoat (*Klänning*, 1782–1848, Sweden, taffeta, Nordiska Museet, Stockholm, NM.0222648A-E).

44. *Robe à la polonaise*, France, silk, Art islamique et indien, tableaux, mobilier et objets d'art, mode, Oct. 31, 2018, lot no. 269, Drouot, Paris.

45. With sewn-in false front: *Day dress worn by Hon. Mrs Graham*, Scotland, ca. 1790–92, yellow-brown silk, cream silk, trimmed with cream silk ribbon, private collection, in Belsey, *Gainsborough's Beautiful Mrs Graham*, 42; *Woman's Dress (Robe à l'anglaise) with Zone Front*, American, ca. 1785–93, cotton and linen, Philadelphia Museum of Art, 1955-98-9. Without stomacher or underbodice: *Klänning*, Sweden, ca. 1790, silk, Nordiska Museet, Stockholm, NMA.0052362; *Polonesa*, ca. 1775–85, silk, linen, Museo del Traje, Madrid,

CE000592; *Robe à la circassienne,* probably Italian, ca. 1787, silk, Metropolitan Museum of Art, New York, 1983.32.

46. Pietsch, "On Different Types of Women's Dresses," 401; Pietsch, "Eastern Influences on French Fashion," 210; Redondo, "Polonesa del Siglo XVIII," 2; Trey, *Mode à la cour de Marie-Antoinette,* 82; Waugh and Woodward, *Cut of Women's Clothes,* 73.

47. Van Cleave and Welborn, "'Very Much the Taste and Various Are the Makes,'" 5–8.

48. *Manteau à la polonaise,* ca. 1770–80, silk, linen, Collection Gilles Labrosse #1, Sept. 22, 2020, lot no. 95, Encheres Sadde SARL, Moulins, France; *Robe à la polonaise,* France, ca. 1772–80, silk, linen, and cotton, National Gallery of Victoria, Melbourne, 2018.321.1-b. See Arnold et al., *Patterns of Fashion 6,* 101–7.

49. Panckoucke, *Encyclopédie méthodique,* s.v. "Couturiere," 1:224–25.

50. Other examples include: *Caraco,* 1770–80, cotton, Palais Galliera, musée de la Mode de la Ville de Paris, GAL1992.177.X; *Embroidered jacket and skirt,* Nordiska Museet, Stockholm NM.0991090A; *Robe à la Turque, manteau de robe, corsage et jupon ayant appartenu à Anne-Élisabeth Oberkampf,* ca. 1785, cream silk pékin, Musée de la Toile de Jouy, Jouy-en-Josas, France, 000.4.6, 001.1.13.2.a, 001.13.2.b.

51. Other examples include: *Caraco eines zweiteiligen Mädchenkleides,* France, ca. 1785, silk with linen lining, Bayerisches Nationalmuseum, Munich, 96/191.1; *Caraco et jupe,* 1780–90, cotton and linen, Palais Galliera, musée de la Mode de la Ville de Paris, GAL1920.1.2370; *Caraco mit halblangen Ärmeln,* France, 1786–90, linen, Bayerisches Nationalmuseum, Munich, 96/178; *Dress,* England, 1770–80, cotton, Royal Ontario Museum, Toronto, 978.101.2; *Polonaise,* Victoria & Albert Museum, London, T.20–1945; *Dress,* 1781–85, cotton, linen, metal, silk, Museum of London, 65.80/1; *Polonaise dress,* 1775, Killerton, Devon, UK, NT 1362010; *Robe,* Sweden, 1700s, silk taffeta with linen lining, Göteborgs Stadsmuseum, Sweden, GM:7703; *Robe à la polonaise,* France, ca. 1772–80, silk, linen, and cotton, National Gallery of Victoria, 2018.321.1-b; *Robe à la polonaise,* Europe, 1775–85 (altered later), silk and linen, Colonial Williamsburg Foundation, Williamsburg, VA, 2006–42; *Robe à la polonaise,* ca. 1778, Palais Galliera, musée de la Mode de la Ville de Paris, 62-108-14; *Robe à la circassienne,* probably Italian, ca. 1787, silk, Metropolitan Museum of Art, 1983.32; *Woman's overdress,* France, 1775–99, cotton, Palazzo Mocenigo, Venice, Cl. XXIV no. 0239.

52. Dowdell, "The Multiple Lives of Clothes," 130–31. I am grateful to Dr. Dowdell for sharing her research on this piece.

53. "Fraque à la polonoise vu par derriere" (1779), *GDM,* 17/3. See Van Cleave and Welborn, "'Very Much the Taste and Various Are the Makes,'" 18.

54. *Cabinet des modes, ou les Modes nouvelles, décrites d'une manière claire & précise, & représentées par des planches en taille-douce, enluminées* (hereafter *CDM*), Mar. 6, 1786, 59.

55. "Jeune dame en robe à la polonoise" (1780), *GDM,* 30/6.

56. Based on written sources, it seems unlikely that the numerous extant gowns that were cut with separate waist seams but worn *retroussée*—like the *Dress* at the Museum of London, Figs. 58–60—would have been considered *robes à la polonaise* (Pietsch, "Object in Focus"; Pietsch, "On Different Types of Women's Dresses," 404–5).

57. See the pattern for this dress in Arnold, "Cut and Construction of Women's Clothes," 131; and Arnold, *Patterns of Fashion; The Content, Cut, Construction and Context of Englishwomen's Dress,* 98–99. The *Day Dress Worn by Hon. Mrs Graham,* another later example, also separates the skirt from the bodice (Belsey, *Gainsborough's Beautiful Mrs Graham,* 42).

58. "Caraco à la polonoise garni de gaze" (1780), *GDM,* 28/3; "Demoiselle élégante coiffée d'un bonnet anglais" (1778), *GDM,* 15/5.

59. "Caraco à la polonoise garni de gaze" (1780), *GDM,* 28/3; "Femme en déshabillé du matin" (1778), *GDM,* 9/3; "Femme en robe à la polonoise" (1778), *GDM,* 7/1; "Jeune dame tenant son enfant dans ses bras" (1779), *GDM,* 27/4; "Jeune femme vêtue d'un caraco à la polonoise" (1780), *GDM,* 30/3; "Robe de tafetas de couleur changeante" (1779), *GDM,* 27/2.

60. Robert, *L'Entrée du Tapis vert.*

61. Jean-Laurent Mosnier, *Portrait de la reine Marie-Antoinette,* 1775, miniature painting on ivory, Christie's.

62. Elisabeth Louise Vigée Le Brun, *Presumed Portrait of the Duchesse de Chartres,* ca. 1778, oil on canvas, 27 × 21 in., private collection; Jean Laurent Mosnier, *Portrait of the Duchess of Fitz-James, née Thiard de Bissy,* ca. 1871, miniature painting on round box, diam. 6.5 cm, Musée du Louvre.

63. *Robe à la polonaise,* France, ca. 1772–80, silk, linen, and cotton, National Gallery of Victoria, Melbourne, 2018.321.1-b.

64. *Robe à la polonaise,* France, ca. 1772–80.

65. Boucher, *20,000 Years of Fashion,* 300, 302; Buck, *Dress in Eighteenth-Century England,* 28; Cornu, *Galerie des modes et costumes,* xiii; Delpierre, *Dress in France in the Eighteenth Century,* 18; Delpierre, "Marie-Antoinette, reine de la mode," 43; Giorgi, "Moda de la Robe à la Polonaise," 101; Pietsch, "On Different Types of Women's Dresses," 401; Pietsch, "Eastern Influences on French Fashion," 210; Redondo, "Polonesa del Siglo XVIII," 2; Ribeiro, *Art of Dress,* 66; Ribeiro, *Dress in Eighteenth-Century Europe,* 226; Ribeiro, *Fashion in the French Revolution,* 28; Trey, *Mode à la cour de Marie-Antoinette,* 83; Waugh and Woodward, *Cut of Women's Clothes,* 73.

66. Van Cleave and Welborn, "'Very Much the Taste and Various Are the Makes,'" 4–5.

67. "Demoiselle à la promenade du matin" (1778), *GDM*, 9/6; "Femme en robe à la polonaise" (1778), *GDM*, 7/1.

68. *Dictionnaire de l'Académie française,* 4th ed. (1762), s.v. "retrousser," Univ. of Chicago: ARTFL Dictionnaires d'autrefois Project, https://artfl-project.uchicago.edu/content/dictionnaires-dautrefois (hereafter ARTFL).

69. Pietsch, "On Different Types of Women's Dresses," 404; Ribeiro, *Dress in Eighteenth-Century Europe*, 222.

70. "Cette petite fille est vêtue d'un foureau" (1780), in Cornu, *Galerie des modes,* pl. 146; "Elégante en chapeau de paille à l'anglaise," *Collection d'habillements modernes et galants avec les habillements des princes et seigneurs [Gallerie des Modes]* (hereafter *CDH*), D 23; "Habit de bal avec des manches à la Gabrièle" (1779), *GDM*, 18/3; "Habit à l'insurgente" (1779), *GDM*, 28/6; "Jeune dame coëffée à la dauphine" (1778), *GDM*, 13/3; "Jeûne [*sic*] dame vétue d'une robe à l'anglaise," *CDH* (Paris, 1781), B 12eme F; "Jeûne [*sic*] dame vétue d'une robe à l'anglaise," *CDH*, C 17eme F; "Jeune demoiselle vétue d'une robbe à l'anglaise retroussée," *CDH*, no. e 29me F; "Jolie femme, vetue d'une robe à l'anglaise," *CDH*, D 20; "La Nymphe galante dont le port oest majestueux" (1785), *Gallerie des modes et costumes français*, 1778, *Gallerie des modes et costumes français*, 1778, Bibliotheque municipale de Versailles, Bibliothèque municipale de Versailles, Rés I 70_fol 13; "La petite fille vue de face" (1780), in Cornu, *Galerie des modes,* pl. 145; "Robe à l'anglaise le corpsage lace par derriere" (1784), in Cornu, *Galerie des modes,* pl. 186; "Robe à l'anglaise retroussée" (1782), in Cornu, *Galerie des modes,* pl. 168; "Robe à la Versailloise de gros de Naples couleur grise" (1778), 13/2.

71. *Robe à la polonaise,* Colonial Williamsburg Foundation.

72. *Robe à la circassienne,* probably Italian, ca. 1787, silk, Metropolitan Museum of Art, New York, 1983.32. See Arnold, *Patterns of Fashion 6*, 109.

73. Boucher, *20,000 Years of Fashion*, 303; Pietsch, "On Different Types of Women's Dresses," 402; Ribeiro, *Dress in Eighteenth-Century Europe*, 228.

74. "Jeune dame en circassienne garnie de blonde" (1778), *GDM*, 8/2; "Robe à la circassienne" (1780), *GDM*, 28/4.

75. "Jeune dame en circassienne de gaze d'Italie" (1778), *GDM*, 13/5.

76. Chrisman-Campbell, *Fashion Victims,* 243; Delpierre, *Dress in France in the Eighteenth Century,* 19; Pietsch, "On Different Types of Women's Dresses," 405; Pietsch, "Eastern Influences on French Fashion," 211; Ribeiro, *Fashion in the French Revolution,* 28; Trey, *Mode à la cour de Marie-Antoinette,* 83.

77. Boucher, *20,000 Years of Fashion*, 303; Pietsch, "On Different Types of Women's Dresses," 408; Pietsch, "Eastern Influences on French Fashion," 211; Ribeiro, *Dress in Eighteenth-Century Europe*, 226; Van Cleave and Welborn, "'Very Much the Taste and Various Are the Makes,'" 11–12.

78. See patterns for two likely pierrots in Arnold et al., *Patterns of Fashion 6*, 148–54.

79. *Dictionnaire de l'Académie française,* 4th ed. (1762), s.v. "détrousser," ARTFL.

80. "Jeune dame vétue d'une polonoise longue de satin," *Gallerie des modes et costumes français,* 1778, Bibliothèque municipale de Versailles, Rés I 70_fol 67.

81. The other is at the Museum of London (*Dress*, 1781–85, cotton, linen, metal, silk, Museum of London, 65.80/1).

82. "Jeune actrice bourgeoise étudiant son rôle" (1780), *GDM*, 28/5.

83. Panckoucke, *Encyclopédie méthodique,* s.v. "Couturiere," 1:225.

84. "Bourgeoise élégante se promenant à la campagne" (1778), *GDM*, 9/5; "Circassienne de taffetas à bandes de rubans" (1779), *GDM*, 21/6.

85. Louis Carrogis Carmontelle, *Madame Moreau et mademoiselle de Flinville,* 1762 [ca. 1780], watercolor and gouache. This image has the year 1762 written upon it, but based on the clothing and hairstyles, it must date after 1780 (Gruyer, *Chantilly,* 216).

86. See also *Caraco a la polonesa de seda azul celeste*, Spain, 1782–87, silk, Museu del Disseny de Barcelona, MTIB 88009-0; *Dress,* Worthing Museum & Art Gallery, UK, 1972/59/1; *Manteau à la polonaise,* ca. 1770–80, silk, linen, Collection Gilles Labrosse #1, Sept. 22, 2020, lot no. 95, Encheres Sadde SARL, Moulins, France; *Polonaise,* Victoria & Albert Museum, London, T.20-1945; *Polonaise dress,* Scotland, United Kingdom, 1780–81, silk and linen, Kelvingrove Art Gallery and Museum, Glasgow, 1932.51.I; *Robe,* Sweden, 1700s, silk taffeta with linen lining, Göteborgs Stadsmuseum, Sweden, GM:7703; *Robe à la polonaise,* Colonial Williamsburg Foundation, Williamsburg, VA, 2006-42; *Robe à la polonaise,* after 1772, wool, silk, Musée d'Histoire de Marseille, France, A/83/391.

87. Pietsch, "On Different Types of Women's Dresses," 401.

88. Redondo, "Polonesa del Siglo XVIII," 5; Ribeiro, *Dress in Eighteenth-Century Europe*, 226.

89. Boucher, *20,000 Years of Fashion,* 300, 302; Delpierre, *Dress in France in the Eighteenth Century,* 166; Delpierre, "Marie-Antoinette, reine de la mode," 43; Giorgi, "Moda de la Robe à la Polonaise," 102; Redondo, "Polonesa del Siglo XVIII," 5; Trey, *Mode à la cour de Marie-Antoinette,* 83; Van Cleave and Welborn, "'Very Much the Taste and Various Are the Makes,'" 10–11.

90. Boucher, *20,000 Years of Fashion*, 303, 307; Chrisman-Campbell, *Fashion Victims,* 242–43; Delpierre, *Dress in France in the Eighteenth Century,* 19, 166; Lehnert, "Robes à la turque," 198; Pietsch, "On Different Types of Women's Dresses," 403, 405; Pietsch, "Eastern Influences on French Fashion," 211; Ribeiro, *Dress in Eighteenth-Century Europe,* 228; Trey, *Mode à la cour de Marie-Antoinette,* 83.

91. "Jeune dame en circassienne garnie de blonde" (1778), *GDM*, 8/2.

92. Delpierre, *Dress in France in the Eighteenth Century*, 67.

93. "Demoiselle en polonoise unie en buras" (1778), *GDM*, 12/5; "Jeune dame en polonoise avec des manches à la circassiene" (1778), *GDM*, 10/3; "Jeune dame tenant son enfant dans ses bras" (1779), *GDM*, 27/4; "Jeune femme vêtue d'un caraco à la polonaise de toile vermicelle" (1780), *GDM*, 30/3. *Amadis* (or *amadices*) were a tight, wrist-length sleeve (Blum, *Eighteenth-Century French Fashion Plates*, xiii; Chrisman-Campbell, *Fashion Victims*, 200; Delpierre, *Dress in France in the Eighteenth Century*, 166; Jullien, *The Opera before the Revolution*, 213).

94. Chrisman-Campbell, "Minister of Fashion," 268; Giorgi, "Moda de la Robe à la Polonaise," 100; Redondo, "Polonesa del Siglo XVIII," 4; Ribeiro, *Art of Dress*, 239n66; Trey, *Mode à la cour de Marie-Antoinette*, 83. Pietsch joins me in questioning this assumption ("Different Types of Women's Dresses," 401).

95. Boucher, *20,000 Years of Fashion*, 300; emphasis added.

96. Van Cleave and Welborn, "'Very Much the Taste and Various Are the Makes,'" 16.

97. *Gazette du commerce*, Apr. 9, 1763, 16.

98. *Public Advertiser*, Jan. 1, 1768; emphasis added.

99. Rothstein, *Four Hundred Years of Fashion*, 125; Van Cleave and Welborn, "'Very Much the Taste and Various Are the Makes,'" 8.

100. *Public Advertiser*, Jan. 13, 1768.

101. The *Gallerie des modes* declared that the introduction of the jacket version (the *caraco à la polonaise*) does not date before 1772 ("Demoiselle en caracot de taffetas" [1778], *GDM*, 12/6).

102. *CDLM*, Apr. 8, 1768, 6. The *Tronchine* was a short dress without *paniers* suitable for walking outdoors, recommended by physician Théodore Tronchin (1709–81) (Martin, *Dairy Queens*, 130). Thus far, I have found no sources describing the *Hollondaise*.

103. "Comptes de Madame du Barry," Français 8157.

104. Louis Carrogis (called Carmontelle), *Mme du Dreneuc*, 1771, graphite, watercolor, gouache, sanguine on paper; Louis Carrogis (called Carmontelle), *Mme de Saint-Amarante*, ca. 1770, drawing, watercolor; Louis Carrogis (called Carmontelle), *Mmes les comtesses de Fitz-James et du Nolestin*, 1771, graphite, watercolor, gouache, sanguine on paper; Marie Louise Elisabeth Vigée-Le Brun, *Study of a Woman*, n.d., drawing, red chalk (the date of 1772 is suggested by Baillio, *Elisabeth Louise Vigée Le Brun*, 30).

105. Germann, *Picturing Marie Leszczinska*, 184; Marschner, "Ceremonial Dress," 12; Ribeiro, *Art of Dress*, 239n66; Ribeiro, *Dress in Eighteenth-Century Europe*, 226.

106. Turnau, *History of Dress in Central and Eastern Europe*, 80–81, 165. See also Boucher, *20,000 Years of Fashion*, 300; Delpierre, *Dress in France in the Eighteenth Century*, 59, 67.

107. Blum, *Eighteenth-Century French Fashion Plates*, vii; Chrisman-Campbell, *Fashion Victims*, 242; Pietsch, "On Different Types of Women's Dresses," 402; Pietsch, "Eastern Influences on French Fashion," 210; Ribeiro, *Dress in Eighteenth-Century Europe*, 226; Scher, "Relations militaires entre la France et la Pologne," 68–77; Van Cleave and Welborn, "'Very Much the Taste and Various Are the Makes,'" 16–17.

108. Germann, *Picturing Marie Leszczinska*, 184.

109. Interestingly, the only late-eighteenth-century fashion plate that mimics this treatment is a woman's *habit à l'Insurgente/robe à l'anglaise*, referencing the American Revolution ("Habit à l'insurgente: cette robe est une robe à l'angloise" [1779], *GDM*, 28/6).

110. "Jeune dame en circassienne garnie de blonde" (1778), *GDM*, 8/2.

111. Ribeiro, *Art of Dress*, 193–95; Ribeiro, *Dress in Eighteenth-Century Europe*, 276.

112. Solnon, *Turban et la stambouline*, 322–23. See also Van Cleave and Welborn, "'Very Much the Taste and Various Are the Makes,'" 17.

113. Blum, *Eighteenth-Century French Fashion Plates*, vii; Boucher, *20,000 Years of Fashion*, 294; Leloir, *Histoire du costume de l'Antiquité à 1914*, 12:48–49; Pietsch, "On Different Types of Women's Dresses," 400; Pietsch, "Eastern Influences on French Fashion," 211; Redondo, "Polonesa del Siglo XVIII," 5.

114. "Jeune dame en circassienne garnie de blonde" (1778), *GDM*, 8/2; "Papiers Bourbon-Busset," 1776–87, T//265/8; *Affiches de Bordeaux*, July 24, 1777, 140–41.

115. Besleney, *The Circassian Diaspora in Turkey*, 53; Boer and Bal, *Disorienting Vision*, 45; Chrisman-Campbell, *Fashion Victims*, 242.

116. Figal, "The Caucasian Slave Race," 164–66, 169–70; Foster, "Colonialism and Gender in the East," 13; Jirousek, *Ottoman Dress and Design in the West*, 173; M. Martin, "French Harems," 1; Zlatnik, "Myth, Vision, and the Harem in French Painting," 8.

117. Pietsch, "Eastern Influences on French Fashion," 211; Ribeiro, *Dress in Eighteenth-Century Europe*, 270.

118. *Affiches de Bordeaux*, July 24, 1777, 140–41; "Femme en robe à la polonoise" (1778), *GDM*, 7/1.

119. Moheng, "Whalebone Bodies and Panniers," 118–20.

120. Arnold, *Patterns of Fashion 5*, 26; Moheng, "Whalebone Bodies and Panniers," 116–18.

121. Redondo, "Polonesa del Siglo XVIII," 6; Ribeiro, *Art of Dress*, 64; Ribeiro, *Dress in Eighteenth-Century Europe*, 222.

122. Roland de la Platiere, "Bourse, Boursier," in Panckoucke, *Encyclopédie méthodique*, 1:86–87. See Arnold, *Patterns of Fashion 5*, 27; Delpierre, *Dress in France in the Eighteenth Century*, 18; Ribeiro, *Dress in Eighteenth-Century Europe*, 222. According to satirical English prints, rumps were also made of cork; it is quite possible that cork rumps existed in France as well.

123. *Panier*, France, 1750–90, linen, horsehair, paper, KA 1126, Amsterdam Museum; *Underklädsel*, Sweden, 1770–1810, Nordiska Museet, Stockholm, NM.0001008. See Arnold, *Patterns of Fashion 5*, 27.

124. It is possible, however, that the term *bouffante* did not strictly refer to hoops but also included pads, particularly as the *bouffante pour lévite* does not include whalebone or cane.

125. "Robe à la polonoise de satin leger" (1780), *GDM*, 31/1.

126. "Mémoires quittancés et quittances de fournisseurs pour le service de la garde-robe de la comtesse d'Artois et de la comtesse de Provence" (1771), T//265/3, Papiers d'origine privée, vol. 3, Archives Nationales (France).

127. "Memoir des ouvrages je quais fois est fournir poure madame la comtesse Dartois don le couran d'en cartier de janvier est avril par ordre de madame la comtess de Bourbon-busse dame d'atours de madame la comtesse Dartois: Fais est fourni par motte au l'année 1779," Apr. 1779, cotte 19, Papiers Bourbon-Busset, T//265/4-T//265/5.

128. "Jeune dame coeffée d'un bonnet rond" (1778), *GDM*, 8/4.

129. Cradock, *Journal de Mme Cradock*, 58.

130. *CDM*, May 15, 1786, 98. The *aune* was the standard measurement for cloth. In Paris it measured 118 cm or 46 7/16 in. (Vrignaud, *Vêture et parure en France au dix-huitième siècle*, 171).

131. "Robe à la lévite, a deux plis par derriere" (1779), in Cornu, *Galerie des modes et costumes français*, pl. 83.

132. I am grateful to Dr. Serena Dyer for sharing her research on this doll's ensemble.

133. "Nouvelle lévite de taffetas uni" (1780), *GDM*, 31/2.

134. Arnold et al., *Patterns of Fashion 6*, 110.

135. See the pattern for the Philadelphia Museum of Art *turque* in Arnold, "Cut and Construction of Women's Clothes," 131; and Arnold, *Patterns of Fashion . . . c. 1720–1860*, 98–99.

136. Delpierre, *Dress in France in the Eighteenth Century*, 33; Moheng, "Whalebone Bodies and Panniers," 112–13; Waugh and Woodward, *Cut of Women's Clothes*, 77.

137. "Tailleur costumier essayant un cor à la mode" (1778), *GDM*, 15/1.

138. Panckoucke, *Encyclopédie méthodique*, s.v. "Couturiere," 1:225.

139. "Memoire: Des Ouvrages et fournitures fait pour madame la comtesse d'Artois à lordre de madame la comtesse de Bourbon Busset: Par la Sigly couturiere," Apr. 4, 1779, cotte 19, Papiers Bourbon-Busset, T//265/4-T//265/5; "Memoire: Des Ouvrages et fournitures pour le service de madame la comtesse d'Artois fait à lordre de madame la comtesse de Bourbon Busset par la Sigly couturiere," Oct. 25, 1776, cotte 16, Papiers Bourbon-Busset, T//265/4-T//265/5; Chatenet-Calyste, "Pour paraître à la cour," 34.

140. The *chemise à la reine* was also occasionally depicted this way (Bissonnette, Chartrand, and Karbonik, "Dress & Historical Escapism").

141. Adélaïde Labille-Guiard, *Femme au ruban bleu*, 1782, pastel, in Jeffares, "Labille-Guiard, Adélaïde," *Dictionary of Pastellists before 1800*, online edition, updated July 10, 2018, www.pastellists.com/Articles/LabilleGuiard.pdf; Adélaïde Labille-Guiard, *Portrait of a Lady, Half Length, Wearing a Pink Dress*, 1786, oil on canvas; Ludwig Guttenbrun, *Ritratto di Giuseppina di Lorena-Armagnac*, 1784–86, oil on canvas; Louis Rolland Trinquesse, *Portrait of a Lady*, 1780, painting, oil on canvas.

142. Pierre Alexandre Wille, *The Double Reward of the Merit or the Return from the American War of Independence*, 1781, oil on canvas.

4. FASHION AND NATIONAL IDENTITY

1. Chrisman-Campbell suggests that *marchandes de modes* may have been another significant creator of style names (*Fashion Victims*, 155).

2. "Avis divers," *Affiches du Poitou*, July 12, 1781, 112; emphasis added.

3. Barthes, *The Fashion System*, 3, 8.

4. Barthes, *The Fashion System*, 13.

5. Bryant, "Names and Terms Used in the Fashion World," 168.

6. Miller, "Why Some Things Matter," 3.

7. Chrisman-Campbell, *Fashion Victims*, 150; Delpierre, *Dress in France in the Eighteenth Century*, 65. See also Arnold et al., *Patterns of Fashion 6*, 3; Boucher, *20,000 Years of Fashion*, 299; Lehnert, "Robes à la turque," 198; Sheriff, "Dislocations of Jean-Etienne Liotard," 113.

8. König, "Glossy Words," 207.

9. The *Trésor de la Langue Française* links the term *manteau* to *mantel*, an outerwear garment that dates from the tenth century: "[a] garment that hangs from the shoulders to the bottom of the knees and that one wears over all other garments" (*TLF*, s.v. "manteau"). The English term for the gown, *mantua*, connects to the silks made in that Italian city and was in use from the sixteenth century (*Oxford English Dictionary*, s.v. "mantua").

10. In this period, *robe de X* can also refer to a dress made of *X* (generally a textile), but it was occasionally substituted for *robe à la X*.

11. Moline, "A Manner of Doing and a Manner of Being," 174; Raus, "L'Evolution de la locution 'à la turque,'" par. 63.

12. Féraud, *Dictionaire critique de la langue française*, vol. 2, s.v. "françois," ARTFL.

13. Féraud, *Dictionaire critique de la langue française*, vol. 1, s.v. "a," ARTFL.

14. Coignard, *Le Dictionnaire de l'Académie française*, vol. 2, s.v. "vestir," ARTFL.

15. Le Maistre, *Recueil de divers plaidoyers et harangues, prononcez au Parlement*, 121; Mézeray and Chalcondyle, *L'Histoire de la décadence de l'Empire grec*, 2:20. Earlier references to the *française* tend to use the older term *robe de chambre*, although confusingly these are referring to the fashionable gown, not the dressing gown that inspired it (Gorguet-Ballesteros, "Caractériser le costume de cour," 62; Vinha and Örmen, *Dans la garde-robe de Marie-Antoinette*, 45).

16. Beaumont, *Magasin des adolescentes*, 4:202.

17. *Gazette du commerce*, Apr. 9, 1763, 16.

18. Chrisman-Campbell, *Fashion Victims*, 153; emphasis added.

19. Lasic, "Ethnicity," 156. See also Trey, *Mode à la cour de Marie-Antoinette*, 83.

20. Jones, *Sexing la Mode*, 191.

21. *MDM*, Aug. 30, 1788, 228.

22. Ponce, "Révolutions des modes Françaises," 55–56.

23. For the *Gallerie des modes*, this study included all the plates in Paul Cornu's 1912 published compilation, as well as the collections at the Bibliothèque municipale de Versailles, Bunka Gakuen University Library, and Museum of Fine Arts, Boston. Every issue of the other titles was surveyed for the dates listed, using the collections of the Bibliothèque nationale de France and Bunka Gakuen University Library.

24. Roche, *Culture of Clothing*, 121–22.

25. Chrisman-Campbell, *Fashion Victims*, 150, 177.

26. "Robe à la lévite, a deux plis par derriere" (1779), in Cornu, *Galerie des modes*, pl. 83. See Boucher, *20,000 Years of Fashion*, 300; Chrisman-Campbell, *Fashion Victims*, 123; Delpierre, *Dress in France in the Eighteenth Century*, 67; Pietsch, "Eastern Influences on French Fashion," 212; Pietsch, "On Different Types of Women's Dresses," 403; Trey, *Mode à la cour de Marie-Antoinette*, 83. It is also mentioned as a fashionable gown that same year in Marsy, *Le Petit chansonnier françois*, 3:391–92.

27. Bachaumont, *Mémoires secrets*, 17:226.

28. Jirousek, *Ottoman Dress and Design in the West*, 173.

29. Bar, *Recueil de tous les costumes des ordres religieux et militaires*, 2:254ng.

30. Louis-René Boquet, *1 maquette du costume pour Athalie*, 1770, drawing; Louis-René Boquet, *Athalie [maquette du costume]*, 1770, drawing.

31. "Habillement d'Athalie au théatre de la Comédie Françoise" (1779), in Cornu, *Galerie des modes*, pl. 87. The "*pectoral*" is difficult to translate. According to the *Dictionaire critique de la langue française*, it could refer to something worn on the breast, in which case it may be the stomacher or underbodice (1787, s.v. "pectoral," ARTFL). Alternatively, it could refer to a "pectoral Cross, that which the Bishops wear on their breasts, as a mark of their dignity, and in which there are sometimes relics," although there is no jewel pictured on the breast in the fashion plate (*Dictionnaire de l'Académie française*, 4th ed., 1762, s.v. "pectoral," ARTFL). According to an early nineteenth-century dictionary, it could also refer to an "Ornament garnished with precious stones that the high priest of the Jews wore on the chest" (*Dictionnaire de l'Académie française*, 6th ed., 1835, s.v. "pectoral," ARTFL). Anything flared could be called *en pagode* and was a generally Eastern reference (Martin and Koda, *Orientalism*, 17).

32. Charnois, *Costumes et annales des grands theatres de Paris*, 91–93. The *Trésor de la Langue Française* defines an *éphod* as a "liturgical garment of the Levites, of Hebrew priests" (*TLF*, s.v. "éphod"). The *dalmatique* is a "garment of Deacons and Sub-Deacons, when they serve the Priest at the High Mass" (*Dictionaire critique de la langue française* [1787], s.v. "dalmatique," ARTFL). Its name refers to Dalmatia (*TLF*, s.v. "dalmatique"). Now part of Croatia and Montenegro, in the seventeenth century, Dalmatia was part of the Ottoman Empire; in the eighteenth, the Republic of Venice. Landini argues that the full, loose garments worn by those in public service were based on sixteenth-century styles and reminded observers of Islamic clothing ("Dress for the Body," 18).

33. Blum, *Eighteenth-Century French Fashion Plates*, vii; Pietsch, "On Different Types of Women's Dresses": 403; Pietsch, "Eastern Influences on French Fashion," 212; Ribeiro, *Dress in Eighteenth-Century Europe*, 228; Trey, *Mode à la cour de Marie-Antoinette*, 83.

34. Panckoucke, *Encyclopédie méthodique*, s.v. "Couturiere," 1:224.

35. "Robe à la lévite, a deux plis par derriere" (1779), in Cornu, *Galerie des modes*, pl. 83. See Boucher, *20,000 Years of Fashion*, 300.

36. "Autre lévite, la juppe de couleur différente" (1780), *GDM*, 28/2; "Cette femme est vetuë d'un lévite ajusté" (1780), *GDM*, 31/4; "Femme vêtue d'un lévite uni" (1780), *GDM*, 29/1; "Habit en lévite enrichi de glands" (1780), in Cornu, *Galerie des modes*, pl. 118; "Jeune dame répétant une danse" (1782), in Cornu, *Galerie des modes*, pl. 169; "Lévite de taffetas, ajustée" (1780), in Cornu, *Galerie des modes*, pl. 148; "Lévite de taffetas, ajustée" (1782), in Cornu, *Galerie des modes*, pl. 163; "Lévite ornée de brandebourgs" (1779), *GDM*, 27/6.

37. "Jeune dame répétant une danse" (1782), in Cornu, *Galerie des modes*, pl. 169.

38. "Femme vêtue d'un lévite uni" (1780), *GDM*, 29/1; Panckoucke, *Encyclopédie méthodique*, s.v. "Couturiere," 1:224.

39. Panckoucke, *Encyclopédie méthodique*, s.v. "Couturiere," 1:225.

40. "Habit en lévite enrichi de glands" (1780), in Cornu, *Galerie des modes*, pl. 118.

41. Panckoucke, *Encyclopédie méthodique*, s.v. "Couturiere," 1:224.

42. "Autre lévite, la juppe de couleur différente" (1780), *GDM*, 28/2.

43. Delpierre, *Dress in France in the Eighteenth Century*, 19; Pietsch, "On Different Types of Women's Dresses," 403; Pietsch, "Eastern Influences on French Fashion," 212; Trey, *Mode à la cour de Marie-Antoinette*, 83.

44. Boucher, *20,000 Years of Fashion*, 300.

45. Redondo, "Polonesa del Siglo XVIII," 3.

46. Delpierre, *Dress in France in the Eighteenth Century*, 166.

47. "Nouvelle robe dite la Longchamps" (1779), *GDM*, 27/3; "Robe à la turque ou espèce de circassienne" (1779), *GDM*, 21/2. "Longchamps" is a reference to the racecourse in the Bois de Boulogne, Paris.

48. Chrisman-Campbell, *Fashion Victims*, 161.

49. Bachaumont, *Lettres sur les peintures, sculptures et gravures*, 318.

50. Chrisman-Campbell, *Fashion Victims*, 242.

51. Panckoucke, *Encyclopédie méthodique*, s.v. "Couturiere," 1:224–25.

52. Dyer, *Material Lives*, 161–77.

53. Dyer, *Material Lives*, 173.

54. *Closed gown and petticoat*, ca. 1780–90, green silk, Tirelli Costumi, Rome, MCCT-D20.

55. See the pattern for this gown in Arnold et al., *Patterns of Fashion 6*, 124–27.

56. *Open gown (lewitka?) in silk gauze with embroidered robings*, Muzeum Narodowe, Krakow, MNK-XIX-2802. See the pattern in Arnold et al., *Patterns of Fashion 6*, 120–21.

57. Geczy, *Fashion and Orientalism*, 10.

58. *MDM*, Jan. 10, 1787, 42–43.

59. Chrisman-Campbell, *Fashion Victims*, 243, 249.

60. "Jeune dame en Circassienne garnie de blonde" (1778), *GDM*, 8/2.

61. "Robe à la turque ou espèce de circassienne" (1779), *GDM*, 27/3; "Jeune dame en polonoise avec des manches à la circassiene" (1778), *GDM*, 10/3.

62. *Dress*, 1760–80, silk, Centre de Documentació i Museu Tèxtil, Terrassa, Spain, 11679(b)(3); *Dress*, French, 1778–80, silk, Metropolitan Museum of Art, C.I.60.40.3a,b.

63. The Musée d'art et d'histoire de Provence gown survives without waistcoat or stomacher; it has ties sewn to the back interior demonstrating that it was worn *retroussé* (*Robe*, Musée d'art et d'histoire de Provence, Grasse, France, 2012.0.7). The private collection gown has a sewn-in false-front stomacher and no evidence of its skirt being worn up (*Dress*, probably French, ca. 1780s, silk with linen lining, private collection).

64. *Dress*, ca. 1770s, silk, Museum of London, 85.553.

65. Trey, *Mode à la cour de Marie-Antoinette*, 83.

66. Claude-Louis Desrais, *Jeune dame vétue d'une polonoise longue de satin*, 1701–1800, colored engraving, Bibliothèque municipale de Versailles, Res I 70_fol 67.

67. *Lady's Magazine*, Dec. 1780, 621; *Lady's Magazine*, Mar. 1781, 153.

68. "Femme en robe à la polonoise" (1778), *GDM*, 7/1.

69. "Robe à la polonoise d'étoffe unie à coqueluchon" (1778), *GDM*, 7/2.

70. "Femme de qualité en déshabillé" (1778), *GDM*, 7/4. The term *bas* usually refers to the separate trained overskirt worn with formal court gowns, and so here probably means the trained skirt portion of the dress.

71. "Demoiselle à la promenade du matin" (1778), *GDM*, 9/6.

72. "Demoiselle habillée en caracot" (1778), *GDM*, 10/6.

73. "Jeune bourgeoise vêtue d'une polonoise" (1778), *GDM*, 11/5.

74. "Demoiselle en polonoise unie en buras" (1778), *GDM*, 12/5.

75. "Jeune dame vêtue à l'austrasienne" (1778), *GDM*, 15/2.

76. "Demoiselle élégante coeffée d'un bonnet anglais" (1778), *GDM*, 15/5.

77. "Jeune dame coëffée d'un chapeau anglais" (1779), *GDM*, 21/4.

78. "Jeune dame en robe à la polonoise" (1780), *GDM*, 30/6.

79. "Robe à la polonoise de satin leger" (1780), *GDM*, 31/1.

80. "Circassienne de taffetas à bandes de rubans" (1779), *GDM*, 21/6.

81. "Jeune actrice bourgeoise étudiant son rôle" (1780), *GDM*, 28/5.

82. "Nouvelle circassienne en gaze d'Italie doublée" (1780), *GDM*, 29/2.

83. "Circassienne fond du coleur" (1780), *GDM*, 30/4.

84. *MDM*, Nov. 10, 1788, 286.

85. "Robe de cour à la turque" (1787), in Cornu, *Galerie des modes*, pl. 301.

86. *MDM*, Jan. 30, 1787, 59–60.

87. *MDM*, Dec. 11, 1788, 11.

88. Ribeiro, *Dress in Eighteenth-Century Europe*, 228; Van Cleave, "The Lévite Dress."

89. Hamilton, *The Oxford Handbook of European Romanticism*, 808–10.

90. Dobie, *Trading Places*, 117–20.

91. Panckoucke, *Encyclopédie méthodique*, s.v. "Couturiere," 1:225.

92. Panckoucke, *Encyclopédie méthodique*, s.v. "Couturiere," 1:225.

93. Panckoucke, *Encyclopédie méthodique*, s.v. "Fourreau," 2:67. See a pattern for the girl's *fourreau* in Arnold et al., *Patterns of Fashion 6*, 76–78.

94. Boucher, *20,000 Years of Fashion*, 303; Juranek, *Przemiany "robe en chemise,"* 102; Pietsch, "On Different Types of Women's Dresses," 405. See the patterns for roundgowns in Arnold, *Patterns of Fashion . . . c. 1660–1860*, 42; "Kjole i engelsk snit fra 1780'erne," Nationalmuseet, Copenhagen. Examples of *fourreaux* with open-front skirts include *CDM*, Apr. 10, 1787, pl. 1; "Robe en foureau" (1784), in Cornu, *Galerie des modes*, pl. 184; "Robe en foureau à queue simple" (1784), in Cornu, *Galerie des modes*, pl. 187.

95. Gouvernet, *Journal d'une femme de cinquante ans*, 1:92. See Boucher, *20,000 Years of Fashion*, 303; Panckoucke, *Encyclopédie méthodique*, s.v. "Couturiere," 1:224. Back-closing gowns were very rare in the eighteenth century. Other than boned stays with coordinating sleeves, thus far, the only source I have located that qualifies as a back-closing adult woman's garment is a fashion plate in the *Gallerie des modes* featuring a "robe à l'anglaise the bodice laced in back the skirt *retroussé*" (Cornu, *Galerie des modes*, pl. 186).

96. "Jeune dame de qualité en grande robe" (1778), *GDM*, 8/2; "Robe à la levantine garnie en hermine" (1779), *GDM*, 17/1.

97. "Cette figure est vêtue d'un lévite taille à l'anglaise" (1781), *GDM*, 27e suite, II.200(bis); "Lévite de satin rose garni de cordonnets" (1782), *GDM*, 28/1; "Nouvelle lévite de taffetas uni" (1780), *GDM*, 31/2.

98. "Cette femme est vetuë d'un lévite ajusté" (1780), *GDM*, 31/4; "Cette figure est vêtue d'un lévite taille à l'anglaise" (1780), *GDM*, 26e suite, jj.193; "Lévite ajuste a queue trainante comme les robes a l'anglaises" (1779), in Cornu, *Galerie des modes*, pl. 163.

99. The lack of extant examples of the *lévite* may be due to two factors. Given that early versions were cut similarly to dressing gowns, from large, simple shapes, they would have been particularly good candidates to remake into later styles. For example, a circa 1790 jacket at the Germanischen Nationalmuseum has the kind of rounded shawl collar typical of the *lévite* but is cut with the kind of high waistline typical of the late 1790s; could this garment have been remade from an earlier style (*Jacke*, ca. 1790, cotton, linen, Germanischen Nationalmuseum, Nuremberg, T1377)? Secondly, *lévites* may exist in collections but be mistaken for dressing gowns, *robes à l'anglaise*, or redingotes.

100. Chrisman-Campbell, "L'Angleterre et la mode en Europe au XVIIIe siècle," 52.

101. Boucher, *20,000 Years of Fashion*, 311; Roche, *Culture of Clothing*, 131.

102. Delpierre, "Marie-Antoinette, reine de la mode," 38.

103. Cornu, *Galerie des modes*, pl. 138 and 233.

104. Pierre-Thomas Le Clerc (designer), Nicolas Dupin (engraver), Esnauts et Rapilly (publisher), *Gallerie des Modes et Costumes Français. 37e Cahier des Costumes Français, 29e Suite d'Habillemens à la mode en 1781. nn.216* "Lévite pelisse à parement et Colet," 1781, hand-colored engraving on laid paper, 15¼ × 10 in., Museum of Fine Arts, Boston. See Boucher, *20,000 Years of Fashion*, 303.

105. Pietsch, "On Different Types of Women's Dresses," 406.

106. See patterns for redingotes in Arnold et al., *Patterns of Fashion 6*, 128–30; "Woman's Dress (Redingote)," *Undertaking the Making*.

107. It is possible that this transition was first made in England, as between 1785 and 1787 a London "Great-coat" maker advertised "levettes . . . for ladies wear" (*Daily Universal Register*, Jan. 1, 1785; and *Morning Herald*, Sept. 8, 1787). See Ribeiro, *Dress in Eighteenth-Century Europe*, 230.

108. Éloffe, *Modes et usages*, 1:23n5, 88, 92, 136, 168, 297, 442–43, 448.

109. Styles related to the *chemise à la reine* went by many different names: variations on the term *chemise* (*chemise, chemise à la reine, robe en chemise, chemise à la Floricourt*, and *chemise à la Jesus*) were most common, but *gaulle, robe à la créole*, and *robe-peignoir* appear to have referred to similar gowns.

110. Ashelford, "Colonial Livery," 224–25; Gorguet-Ballesteros, "De la Robe chemise à la robe droite," 219–22; Chrisman-Campbell, *Fashion Victims*, 193; Dobie, *Trading Places*, 117–19; Juranek, *Przemiany "robe en chemise,"* 50; Louis, *Hommes en noir, femmes en blanc?*, 12.

111. Arnold, "Cut and Construction of Women's Clothes," 133; Ashelford, "Colonial Livery," 224; Boucher, *20,000 Years of Fashion*, 303; Chrisman-Campbell, *Fashion Victims*, 172–75; Gorguet-Ballesteros, "De la Robe chemise à la robe droite," 219–28. See patterns for the same chemise gown in Goodman, "Devil in a White Dress," 109; and Waugh and Woodward, *Cut of Women's Clothes*, diagram XXV.

112. Bissonnette, Chartrand, and Karbonik, "Dress & Historical Escapism"; Juranek, *Przemiany "robe en chemise,"* 116–17. It is interesting to note that the numerous back pleats of the Musée de la Toile de Jouy *chemise* (*Robe droite*, France, ca. 1785–95, cotton muslin, Musée de la Toile de Jouy, Jouy-en-Josas, France, 000.4.10) resembles those on the Tirelli Costumi *lévite* (*Closed gown and petticoat*, c. 1780–90, green silk, Tirelli Costumi, Rome, MCCT-D20). This technique is explored in Lazaro and Warner, "All-Over Pleated Bodice," 15–24.

113. Panckoucke, *Encyclopédie méthodique*, s.v. "Couturiere," 1:225. Unfortunately, I have been unable to locate any other use of the term *quinzevine*.

114. Boucher, *20,000 Years of Fashion*, 303.

115. Landini and Niccoli, *Moda a Firenze, 1540–1580*, 109–17.

116. This plate was originally published in a 1786 almanac (*Les Fantaisies aimables, ou les Caprices des belles représentés par les costumes les plus nouveaux*) with the caption "*l'abbé Mardrigal.*" The same images were republished in this later series using style names, including "*lévite à trois collets*" (Savigny de Moncorps, *Almanachs illustrés du XVIIIe siècle*, 114–15).

117. Grimm and Diderot, *Correspondance littéraire*, 13:45.

118. Panckoucke, *Encyclopédie méthodique*, s.v. "Couturiere," 1:225.

119. Chrisman-Campbell, "Minister of Fashion," 331.

120. "L'Anacade," in Mercier, *Tableau de Paris*, 9:49.

121. Maillard, "Contributions à l'histoire du costume."

122. *CDM*, Nov. 15, 1785, pl. 1; *Journal de Paris*, Oct. 5, 1790, 2; Feb. 7, 1791, iii; Mar. 23, 1791, iii; Apr. 18, 1791, 4; Oct. 12, 1792, 3; and Mar. 16, 1794, 3.

123. Jules Baudin, *Portrait de femme au livre*, 1789, painting, oil on canvas.

5. *TURQUERIE*, ENLIGHTENMENT THOUGHT, AND THE FRENCH FASHION PRESS

1. Ellison, "Rousseau and the Modern City," 497; Jones, "Repackaging Rousseau," 940; Roche, *Culture of Clothing*, 400; Roche, *People of Paris*, 173; Shovlin, *The Political Economy of Virtue*, 5–6.

2. Chrisman-Campbell, *Fashion Victims*, 177; Crowston, *Fabricating Women*, 63–64; Geczy, *Fashion and Orientalism*, 73; Grélé, "Et si l'habit faisait l'utopie," 35:117; Roche, *Culture of Clothing*, 46.

3. Alyea, "Dress, Childhood and the Modern Body," 55–127; Pellegrin, "L'Uniforme de la santé," 131–32.

4. Israel, *Radical Enlightenment*, 515–17.

5. Grieder, *Anglomania in France*, 8; Israel, *Democratic Enlightenment*, 344.

6. Bolton, *AngloMania*, 12–13; Nordmann, "Anglomanie et anglophobie en France au XVIIIe siècle," 791.

7. Arnold, "Cut and Construction of Women's Clothes," 133; Delpierre, *Dress in France in the Eighteenth Century*, 23; Jones, "Repackaging Rousseau," 945–46; Pellegrin, *Les Vêtements de la liberté*, s.v. "Anglomanie"; Ribeiro, *Art of Dress*, 30, 35; Ribeiro, *Fashion in the French Revolution*, 21, 35, 44; Trey, *Mode à la cour de Marie-Antoinette*, 106–7; Zieseniss, Bourhis, and Metropolitan Museum of Art, *The Age of Napoleon*, x.

8. Grieder, *Anglomania*, 11–12.

9. Chrisman-Campbell, *Fashion Victims*, 216, 220. See also Boucher, *20,000 Years of Fashion*, 296; Chrisman-Campbell, "L'Angleterre et la mode en Europe au XVIIIe siècle," 50–53.

10. Beaumarchais, *Eugénie*, 3–4; "Spectacles: Comédie Italienne," *L'Avantcoureur: feuille hebdomadaire, où sont annoncés les objects particuliers des sciences & des arts, le cours & les nouveautés des spectacles, & les livres nouveaux en tout genre*, Oct. 14, 1765, 643–44.

11. Boucher, *20,000 Years of Fashion*, 296; Chrisman-Campbell, *Fashion Victims*, 221.

12. Grieder, *Anglomania*, 18–19.

13. Maillard, "Contributions a l'histoire du costume."

14. Boucher, *20,000 Years of Fashion*, 296; Jones, *Sexing la Mode*, 183–84; Ribeiro, *Fashion in the French Revolution*, 36–39.

15. *CDM*, April 5, 1768, 18; emphasis added.

16. "Habit de printems, cannelé" (1778), in Cornu, *Galerie des modes*, pl. 45.

17. "Les delices de la maternité," *Seconde suite d'estampes pour servir à l'histoire des moeurs et du costume des français dans le dix-huitième siècle*.

18. Chrisman-Campbell, *Fashion Victims*, 155, 242.

19. Joubin, "Islam and the Arabs through the Eyes of the Encyclopedie," 197–98.

20. Harvey, *French Enlightenment and Its Others*, 73.

21. Delpierre, *Dress in France in the Eighteenth Century*, 18; Jones, "Repackaging Rousseau," 949.

22. Chrisman-Campbell, *Fashion Victims*, 155.

23. Matossian, "Et je ne portai plus d'autre habit," 19–20; Kahf, *Western Representations of the Muslim Woman*, 143–44; Roche, *Culture of Clothing*, 420.

24. Crowe, "Le Manteau arménien," 9.

25. Crowe, "Manteau arménien," 3.

26. Rousseau, *Confessions and Correspondence*, 503.

27. Crowe, "Manteau arménien," 9; Zaretsky and Scott, *The Philosophers' Quarrel*, 105, 114–16.

28. Fordham, "Allan Ramsay's Enlightenment," 508–24; Matossian, *Et je ne portai plus d'autre habit*, 22n22.

29. Coller, "Rousseau's Turban," 72; Matossian, *Et je ne portai plus d'autre habit*, 23. See also Geczy, *Fashion and Orientalism*, 50.

30. Biernat, "Whalebone Stays and Corsets for Children," 129, 138–39; Pellegrin, "Uniforme de la santé," 134–36.

31. Ballexserd, *Dissertation sur l'éducation physique des enfans*, 145.

32. Grivel, *Théorie de l'éducation*, 291.

33. Alphonse Louis Vincent LeRoy, *Recherches sur les habillemens des femmes et des enfans, ou examen de la maniere dont il faut vêtir l'un et l'autre sèxe* (Paris: Le Boucher, 1772), 241–42.

34. Le Fébure, *Le Manuel des femmes enceintes*, 191–94.

35. Venel, *Essai sur la santé et l'éducation médicinale des filles*, 176.

36. Halma, *De l'éducation*, 211.

37. Bretonne, *Les Gynographes, ou Idées de deux honnêtes-femmes*, 68.

38. Bretonne, *Les Contemporaines, ou Avantures des plus jolies femmes*, 543.

39. Bretonne, *L'Andrographe, ou Idées d'un honnête-homme*, 66.

40. Riballier, *De l'Éducation physique et morale des enfants des deux sexes*, 118–19.

41. Chrisman-Campbell, *Fashion Victims*, 77.

42. Jones, "Repackaging Rousseau," 964; Jones, *Sexing la Mode*, 185.

43. Apostolou, "Apparence extérieure de l'Oriental": par 26–27; Avcıoğlu, *"Turquerie" and the Politics of Representation*, 27–28; Geczy, *Fashion and Orientalism*, 48; Moussa, "Peuples primitifs, peuples décadents," 185–97; Stein, "Exoticism as Metaphor," 204.

44. Maréchal, *Costumes civils actuels de tous les peuples connus*, 13; Montesquieu, *Spirit of the Laws*, 225.

45. Jones, "Repackaging Rousseau," 947.

46. L. E. Miller, "An Enigmatic Bourgeois," 52; Stein, "Exoticism as Metaphor," 204.

47. Roche, *People of Paris*, 160–61.

48. Roche, *Culture of Clothing*, 157, 418–19; Shovlin, "The Cultural Politics of Luxury," 577–78; Shovlin, *Political Economy of Virtue*, 133.

49. Jones, *Sexing la Mode*, 180.

50. Roche, *Culture of Clothing*, 401, 418.

51. Ellison, "Rousseau and the Modern City," 513–14; Jones, "Repackaging Rousseau," 944; Roche, *Culture of Clothing*, 417–19; Starobinski, *Jean-Jacques Rousseau*, 5.

52. Rousseau, *Emile*, 1:133.

53. Ellison, "Rousseau and the Modern City," 499.

54. Rousseau, *Emile*, 4:54–55. See Jones, "Repackaging Rousseau," 945.

55. Rousseau, *Emile*, 4:132–33.

56. Rousseau, *Emile*, 1:311.

57. Rousseau, 4:55; Rousseau, 1:311–12.

58. Rousseau, 1:313.

59. Pellegrin, "Uniforme de la santé," 134; Roche, *Culture of Clothing*, 457, 461.

60. *CDM*, May 15, 1786, 98.

61. "Demoiselle en polonoise unie en buras" (1778), *GDM*, 12/5.

62. "Femme vêtue d'un lévite uni" (1780), *GDM*, 29/1.

63. Giorgi, "Moda de la Robe à la Polonaise," 102; Van Cleave and Welborn, "'Very Much the Taste and Various Are the Makes,'" 18–19.

64. "Cette petite fille est vêtue d'un foureau de toile peinte" (1780), in Cornu, *Galerie des modes*, pl. 146.

65. Van Cleave and Welborn, "'Very Much the Taste and Various Are the Makes,'" 18.

66. "Femme de qualité en déshabillé" (1778), *GDM*, 7/4.

67. Chatenet-Calyste, "Consommation aristocratique," 279.

68. The *turque* was also worn with a train, but this feature did not elicit particular commentary in fashion magazines.

69. "Robe à l'angloise, queue trainante" (1779), *GDM*, 23/3.

70. Rousseau, *Oeuvres de M. Rousseau de Genève*, 1:11. See Pellegrin, "Uniforme de la santé," 134.

71. "Nouvelle Circassienne en gaze d'Italie doublée" (1780), *GDM*, 29/2.

72. "Demoiselle en caracot de taffetas" (1778), *GDM*, 12/6; *MDM*, Feb. 10, 1788, 65. See Benoît, *La Provence et le Comtat Venaissin*, 122; Pellegrin, *Vêtements de la liberté*, s.v. "Arlésiennes"; Picard-Cajan, "Typologie d'un costume-garde-robe de femme," 28; Tétart-Vittu, "Incidence de la mode française à Arles," 17. Tétart-Vittu connects the *drolet* with the *polonaise* ("Incidence de la mode française à Arles," 17).

73. "La Petite mère au rendez-vous des Champs Elisées" (1779), *GDM*, 11/3.

74. "Femme en robe à la polonoise, de tafetas rayé" (1778), *GDM*, 7/2; "Robe à la polonoise de toille blanche" (1779), *GDM*, 23/2.

75. Jones, "Repackaging Rousseau," 947.

76. Roche, *Culture of Clothing*, 46.

77. Bevilacqua and Pfeifer, "Turquerie," 30, 104–5.

78. Moronvalle, *"Recueil de cent estampes représentant différentes nations du Levant,"* 18–19. Thus, these styles also had erotic connotations (see chap. 6).

79. "Jeune dame en circassienne garnie de blonde" (1778), *GDM*, 8/2.

80. *CDM*, Jan. 15, 1786, 33–34.

81. "Grande robe à la sultane fermée sur le devant du corsage" (1782), in Cornu, *Galerie des modes*, pl. 167; "Robe de cour à la turque, coeffure orientale," in Cornu, *Galerie des modes*, pl. 301; "Robe de cour au grand orient," in Cornu, *Galerie des modes*, pl. 297; "Grande robe de cour dans le goût asiatique," in Cornu, *Galerie des modes*, pl. 274.

82. Çırakman, *From the "Terror of the World,"* 109; Çırakman, "From Tyranny to Despotism," 59; Geczy, *Fashion and Orientalism*, 48; Kaiser, "Evil Empire," 26; Rubiés, "Oriental Despotism and European Orientalism," 113.

83. Geczy, *Fashion and Orientalism*, 48–49. See also Bevilacqua and Pfeifer, "Turquerie," 30; Egler, Gorguet-Ballesteros, and Maeder, "L'Orient et la mode en Europe," 62.

84. Mercier, *Tableau de Paris*, 7:141; Rousseau, *Emile*, 4:35. See Bevilacqua and Pfeifer, "Turquerie," 111.

85. Crowley, *Invention of Comfort*, 392. See also Odile-Bernez, "Comfort, the Acceptable Face of Luxury," 15. Although not a scholarly source, DeJean demonstrates that the same processes were at work in France (*Age of Comfort*).

86. Lasic, "Ethnicity," 157.

87. Egler, Gorguet-Ballesteros, and Maeder, "L'Orient et la mode en Europe," 63; Giorgi, "Moda de la Robe à la Polonaise," 101; Redondo, "Polonesa del Siglo XVIII," 6.

88. "Femme en déshabillé du matin couchée négligement" (1778), *GDM*, 9/3.

89. "Discourse préliminaire," *Seconde suite d'estampes pour servir à l'histoire des moeurs et du costume des Français*, ii.

90. "Robe à la lévite, a deux plis par derriere" (1779), in Cornu, *Galerie des modes*, pl. 83.

91. Boucher, *20,000 Years of Fashion*, 303; Delpierre, *Dress in France in the Eighteenth Century*, 67–68; Pietsch, "Eastern Influences on French Fashion," 213.

92. "Robe à la Levantine garnie en hermine" (1779), *GDM*, 17/1.

93. Raveux, "Fashion and Consumption," 51.

94. Nougaret, *Sottises et les folies parisiennes*, 64. Nougaret was supposedly quoting "a small writing" printed and circulated in Paris by a fabric merchant.

95. "Femme en robe à la polonoise, de tafetas rayé" (1778), *GDM*, 7/1.

96. "La Petite mère au rendez-vous des Champs Elisées" (1779), *GDM*, 11/3.

97. LeRoy, *Recherches sur les habillemens*, 244.

98. Ballexserd, *Dissertation sur l'éducation physique des enfans*, 145.

99. *CDLM*, Apr. 8, 1768, 6.

100. Redondo, "Polonesa del Siglo XVIII," 2.

101. "Lévite ornée de brandebourgs" (1779), *GDM*, 27/6; "Robe à la turque ou espèce de circassienne" (1779), *GDM*, 21/2.

102. *CDM*, Mar. 6, 1786, 59; "Caraco à la polonoise garni de gaze" (1780), *GDM*, 28/3.

103. Pellegrin, "Uniforme de la santé," 132–33; Roche, *Culture of Clothing*, 417–18.

104. Roche, *Culture of Clothing*, 417.

105. Savary, *Lettres sur l'Égypte*, 161.

106. Delon, "The Ancien Régime of the Body," 89–90; Pellegrin, "Uniforme de la santé," 136–37.

107. *MDM*, Jan. 20, 1788, 50.

108. Brace, "Rousseau, Maternity and the Politics of Emptiness," 364; Jones, "Repackaging Rousseau," 946–47; Lasic, "Ethnicity," 158.

109. "Jeune dame coeffée d'un bonnet rond" (1778), *GDM*, 8/4.

110. "Jeune dame se faisant porter son enfant dans une barcelonette" (1780), in Cornu, *Galerie des modes*, pl. 142. See Darrow, "French Noblewomen and the New Domesticity," 42.

111. Delon, "Ancien Régime of the Body," 91.

112. Rousseau, *Emile*, 1:86.

113. Ballexserd, *Dissertation sur l'éducation physique des enfans*, 145; Le Fébure, *Manuel des femmes enceintes*, 191–94.

114. *CDLM*, Aug. 1769, 141.

115. "Premiere, seconde, etc. figures" (1780), *Gallerie des modes et costumes français*, 32e Cahier; emphasis added.

116. "Bourgeoise se promenant avec sa fille," (1778), in Cornu, *Galerie des modes*, pl. 9; "Cette petite fille est vêtue d'un foureau" (1780), in Cornu, *Galerie des modes*, pl. 146; "Habillemens d'enfans dans le nouveau goût" (1780), in Cornu, *Galerie des modes*, pl. 134; "Jeune fille en petit juste à la paysanne (1780), in Cornu, *Galerie des modes*, pl. 147; "La Petite fille vue de face" (1780), in Cornu, *Galerie des modes*, pl. 145; "Le Plus petit de ces enfans" (1780), in Cornu, *Galerie des modes*, pl. 144.

117. "Le Plus petit de ces enfans" (1780), in Cornu, *Galerie des modes*, pl. 144; "La Petite fille vue de face" (1780), in Cornu, *Galerie des modes*, pl. 145.

6. MARIE-ANTOINETTE À *LA TURQUE*

1. Fraser, *Marie Antoinette*, 135.
2. Gruder, "The Question of Marie-Antoinette," 273–74.
3. Weber, *Queen of Fashion*, 4.
4. Weber, *Queen of Fashion*, 105–10. See also Chrisman-Campbell, *Fashion Victims*, 24–25, 27–28; Hosford, "The Queen's Hair," 196; Thomas, *The Wicked Queen*, 86; Vinha and Örmen, *Dans la garde-robe de Marie-Antoinette*, 52–61; Trey, *Mode à la cour de Marie-Antoinette*, 8.
5. Campan, *Mémoires sur la vie privée de Marie-Antoinette*, 1:96.
6. Geczy, *Fashion and Orientalism*, 74.
7. Chrisman-Campbell, "Minister of Fashion," 18–20; Sapori, *Rose Bertin*, 87–88; Thomas, *Wicked Queen*, 86.
8. Ashelford, "Colonial Livery," 218–19, 236; Chrisman-Campbell, "Minister of Fashion," 23–24, 35–36; Delpierre, *Dress in France in the Eighteenth Century*, 106; Delpierre, "Marie-Antoinette, reine de la mode," 37; Germann, *Picturing Marie Leszczinska*, 209; Larkin, "Marie-Antoinette and Her Portraits," 224–26; Leclerq, "Sur la garde-robe de Marie Leczinska et de Marie Antoinette," 33; Sheriff, "Portrait of the Queen," 52; Weber, *Queen of Fashion*, 134.
9. Crewe, *An English Lady in Paris*, 135. On the *petit-maîtresse*, see Chrisman-Campbell, *Fashion Victims*, 32.
10. Chrisman-Campbell, *Fashion Victims*, 27, 31, 260; James-Sarazin and Régis Lapasin, "Marie-Antoinette, prescriptrice de tendances ou 'Fashion Victim'?," 15–17; Leclerq, "Sur la garde-robe," 30–34; Roche, *Culture of Clothing*, 186–87; Tétart-Vittu, "Toilettes royales," 55–59.
11. Crowston, *Fabricating Women*, 28.
12. Harris, *Queenship and Revolution in Early Modern Europe*, 140; Martin, *Dairy Queens*, 202.
13. Chrisman-Campbell, *Fashion Victims*, 177–78.
14. Ashelford, "Colonial Livery," 228; Chrisman-Campbell, *Fashion Victims*, 177–78, 184–86; Delpierre, *Dress in France in the Eighteenth Century*, 109–10; Jones, "Repackaging Rousseau," 946; Ribeiro, *Art of Dress*, 71.
15. Ashelford, "Colonial Livery," 227; Geczy, *Fashion and Orientalism*, 73–74; Giorgi, "Moda de la Robe à la Polonaise," 101; Larkin, "Marie-Antoinette," 260n58; Sheriff, *The Exceptional Woman*, 171; Tétart-Vittu, "Toilettes Royales," 60; Trey, *Mode à la cour de Marie-Antoinette*, 80.

16. Larkin, "'Je ne suis plus la reine, je suis moi,'" 115; Sapori, *Rose Bertin*, 132–33, 155–57; Sheriff, *Exceptional Woman*, 171; Sheriff, "Portrait of the Queen," 59.

17. James-Sarazin and Lapasin, "Marie-Antoinette," 20–21.

18. Marie-Antoinette to Louise de Hesse-Darmstadt, May or June 1780, in *Lettres de la reine*, 2–3.

19. Panckoucke, *Encyclopédie méthodique*, s.v. "Couturiere," 1:225.

20. Ashelford, "Colonial Livery," 218.

21. Delpierre, "Marie-Antoinette, reine de la mode," 42–43.

22. Chrisman-Campbell, "Minister of Fashion," 108–9; Delpierre, *Dress in France in the Eighteenth Century*, 92–94; Delpierre, "Robes de grande parure du temps de Louis XVI," 2; Ribeiro, *Fashion in the French Revolution*, 27; Trey, *Mode à la cour de Marie-Antoinette*, 10, 42.

23. Gorguet-Ballesteros, "Caractériser le costume de cour," 58–62; Moheng, "Whalebone Bodies and Panniers," 120.

24. Chatenet, "Pour paraître à la cour," par. 35; Chrisman-Campbell, *Fashion Victims*, 112–15; Delpierre, *Dress in France in the Eighteenth Century*, 94; Delpierre, "Marie-Antoinette, reine de la mode," 43–44; Delpierre, "Robes de grande parure," 2–4, 8; Gorguet-Ballesteros, "Caractériser le costume du cour," 62; Gorguet-Ballesteros, "Exchanging Looks," 57, 62–63; Ribeiro, *Fashion in the French Revolution*, 27; Trey, *Mode à la cour de Marie-Antoinette*, 44.

25. Campan, *Mémoires sur la vie privée*, 1:19; Delpierre, "Robes de grande parure," 2; James-Sarazin and Lapasin, "Marie-Antoinette," 12; Mansel, *Dressed to Rule*, 35; Ribeiro, *Fashion in the French Revolution*, 27; Trey, *Mode à la cour de Marie-Antoinette*, 10. The term *parure* can also mean an ensemble, so context is important.

26. Urbain, "'Dans un instant, la toilette aura tout gâté,'" 244–46.

27. Campan, *Mémoires sur la vie privée*, 1:19; Ruano, "The Négligé in Eighteenth-Century French Portraiture," 93–94.

28. "Camisole à la polonaise" (1780), *GDM*, 31/6.

29. Sarah Livingston Jay to Mary White Morris, Nov. 14, 1782, in Jay and Jay, *Selected Letters of John Jay and Sarah Livingston Jay*, 123.

30. "Bourgeoise aisée en robe de satin rayé" (1779), in Cornu, *Galerie des modes*, pl. 70; "Bourgeoise élégante se promenant à la campagne" (1778), *GDM*, 9/5; "Demoiselle à la promenade du matin" (1778), *GDM*, 9/6; "Femme en déshabillé du matin" (1778), *GDM*, 9/3.

31. "Femme de qualité en déshabillé" (1778), *GDM*, 7/4.

32. Jean Démosthène Dugourc, *The Garden Façade of Bagatelle*, 1779, drawing; Louis Nicolas de Lespinasse, called the Chevalier de Lespinasse, *The Château de Versailles Seen from the Gardens*, 1779, drawing; Hubert Robert, *The Terrace at the Château de Marly*, ca. 1780, painting.

33. Jacques-Antoine-Marie Lemoine, *Portrait of Elisabeth-Louise Vigée-Lebrun Reading a Letter Seated in a Garden*, 1783, drawing; Pierre-Alexandre Wille, "Young Woman with Miniature," 1778.

34. Lady Mary Coke, Aug. 30, 1775, quoted in Walpole, *Yale Edition of Horace Walpole's Correspondence*, 7:345n14.

35. Angélique de Mackau Bombelles to Marc Bombelles, Oct. 24, 1778, in Bombelles and Bombelles, *"Que je suis heureuse d'être ta femme,"* 80.

36. Marie-Antoinette to Comte de Mercy-Argenteau, Mar. 2, 1780, in Marie-Antoinette (reine de France), *Lettres de Marie-Antoinette*, 1:209–10. The *"petite robe"* was a ceremonial court gown worn over slightly smaller hoops (Ribeiro, *Fashion in the French Revolution*, 30).

37. *CDM*, May 15, 1786, 97–98.

38. Chrisman-Campbell, "Le Grand habit et la mode en France au XVIIIe siècle," 224–25; Chrisman-Campbell, "Minister of Fashion," 285–86.

39. Vinha and Örmen, *Dans la garde-robe de Marie-Antoinette*, 5–6.

40. Vinha and Örmen, *Dans la garde-robe de Marie-Antoinette*, 103–6.

41. "Etat des grands habits, robes et polonoises necessaire par année pour le service de la garderobe de la reine," Estate de la garderobe de Marie Antoinette et dépense pour cet objet, Comptes de la maison du roi, no. 25, K//506.

42. Ossun, *Gazette des atours de Marie-Antoinette*. Other fashionable styles included are *robes à l'anglaise* and redingotes. No *polonaises* or *circassiennes* are included, although one page of *lévites* originally had the categories *"polonaises"* and *"robe turque,"* which are now crossed out. Percale was a very fine, tightly woven cotton fabric that was bleached white after weaving (Vrignaud, *Vêture et parure en France*, 174). *Basin* was a cotton fiber fabric that could be solid, striped, or cross-barred (171).

43. "Habillements de printemps qui [unintelligible] a la garderobe de la reine, pour server au printemps 1782," Estate de la garderobe de Marie Antoinette et dépense pour cet objet, Comptes de la maison du roi, K//506 no. 25.

44. "Relevé des mémoires de Mlle Bertin, quartier de janvier 1782," Comptes de la maison du roi, K//506 no. 25.

45. "Relevé des mémoires de Mlle Bertin, quartier de janvier 1782," "Memoires de Mlle Bertin, année entière 1783," "Memoire de Mlle Bertin 2e du janvier 1784," Comptes de la maison du roi, K//506 no. 25.

46. Bachaumont, *Mémoires secrets*, (1789), 34:176–77. See Weber, *Queen of Fashion*, 171–72.

47. Éloffe, *Modes et usages*, 1:70, 98, 137. *Mirfas* were a "type of sleeve ruffle that were worn frequently in mourning," according to Reiset. He ascribes the name to either the dressmaker who invented it, a character in a comedy, or "oriental" origin. The Eastern origin seems most likely, as Mirfas is currently an Indian first name. Alternatively, this could be a mistranscription of the word *mirsas*, which appears to be

an alternative spelling for *mirzas*, a historical title of Persian origin frequently mentioned in connection with the Tatars. *Peau de soie* was a heavy silk taffeta with a coarse weave (Vrignaud, *Vêture et parure en France*, 174).

48. Éloffe, *Modes et usages*, 1:92, 168, 347.

49. "Mémoires quittancés et quittances de fournisseurs pour le service de la garde-robe de la comtesse d'Artois et de la comtesse de Provence" (1771), Papiers d'origine privée, T//265/3.

50. Papiers Bourbon-Busset, T//265/8. On the comtesse's ceremonial court wardrobe, see Gorguet-Ballesteros, "Petite étude du grand habit à travers les mémoires quittancés," 197–212.

51. Boucher argues that Germans were the first to copy Ottoman braided trim, and thus this trim was called "Brandenburgs" (*20,000 Years of Fashion*, 247); these *polonnaises* are another connection between Turkish trimmings and Polish dress. In its entry on "Passementier," the *Encyclopédie méthodique* declares, "The *simple circle* is also a *cartisane* ["thread, silk, gold or silver twisted on small pieces of fine cardboard, which is used for lace or embroidery" (Féraud, *Dictionaire critique de la langue française*, s.v. "cartisane")] whose figure is expressed by its particular name, & the rose is only an ornament of the same nature, divided into several branches, forming many rays composed of a single strand folded in two rays which move away from each other at the same time as from the common center, & whose angles are rounded almost like the leaves of a rose. This sort of ornament is used in the composition of *polonoises* for men's suits" (Panckoucke, *Encyclopédie méthodique*, s.v. "Passementier," 1:255).

52. "Garde robe des atours de madame la comtesse d'Artois, etat des fournitures faites par Bertin du grand mogol, d'ordre de madame la comtesse de Bourbon-Busset," Oct. 1776, Papiers Bourbon-Busset, T//265/8.

53. "Fourni pour madame comtesse d'Artois suivant les ordres de madame la comtesse de Bourbon Busset sa dame datours," Jan. 1786, Papiers Bourbon-Busset, T//265/8.

54. *Gazette des atours d'été de Madame Elisabeth*, 1792, AE/I: Armoire de fer; Carton n° 8: Louis XVI, Marie-Antoinette et Mme Elisabeth, Grands documents de l'histoire de France; Armoire de fer, AF-100180, Archives nationales de France.

55. Lady Clermont to Georgiana, Duchess of Devonshire, Nov. 5, 1775, in Cavendish, *Georgiana*, 28–29.

56. Panckoucke, *Encyclopédie méthodique*, s.v. "Couturiere," 1:225; Ribeiro, *Dress in Eighteenth-Century Europe*, 228; Roche, *Culture of Clothing*, 143.

57. Lady Sarah Napier to Lady Susan O'Brien, May 10, 1785, in Lennox, *The Life and Letters of Lady Sarah Lennox*, 374.

58. Ashelford, "Colonial Livery," 227; Tétart-Vittu, "Toilettes Royales," 60; Weber, *Queen of Fashion*, 147–49.

59. Campan, *Mémoires sur la vie privée*, 1:194.

60. Campan, *Mémoires sur la vie privée*, 3:97–98. Taffeta was a silk fabric; "Florentine" was a kind of silk satin, so "Florence" is probably related (Vrignaud, *Vêture et parure en France*, 173).

61. Images of the queen in Ottoman-inspired fashion that are unconnected with the Trianon include, in *polonaise*: Louis-Charles Gauthier d'Agoty, *Portrait de Marie-Antoinette assise dans un canapé*, n.d., painting; François Dumont, *Marie-Antoinette écrivant assise à son bureau*, ca. 1777, miniature on ivory; J. B. Gautier Dagoty, *Marie-Antoinette en buste*, n.d., in Blanc, *Portraits de femmes*, 124; Alexandre Moitte, *Mme Elisabeth et Marie Antoinette s'embrassant*, drawing; *La Reine annonçant à Mme. de Bellegarde, des juges, et la liberté de son mari; en mai 1777* (Fig. 122); Robert, *L'Entrée du Tapis vert*. In *robe à la turque*: Charles Le Clercq, *Marie Antoinette and Her Children*, 1781, painting, in Arizzoli-Clémentel and Salmon, *Marie-Antoinette*, 163. There is also a portrait traditionally identified as the queen and the Princesse de Lamballe in a garden; one wears a *lévite*, the other a long-sleeved gown with cutaway front (French school, *Portrait de jeunes femmes traditionnellement dit de Marie-Antoinette et Mme de Lamballe*, ca. 1770 [ca. 1780], painting).

62. François Dumont, *Marie-Antoinette* (1784), gouache, in Nolhac, "François Dumont," 3:329–33. See also Larkin, "Marie-Antoinette and Her Portraits," 260n58; Perrin V. Stein, "Marie Antoinette in the Park of Versailles," in Fahy, *The Wrightsman Pictures*, 252–54.

63. François Dumont l'Aîné, *Portrait de la reine Marie-Antoinette, de sa fille et de son second fils* (detail), 1790, paint on ivory; Jean-Baptiste-André Gautier-Dagoty, *Marie-Antoinette devant le temple d'Amour*, ca. 1780, painting. The low neckline and shawl collar suggest the *lévite*, although the lack of sash detracts from such an identification. This could be a *lévite* influenced by the redingote as discussed in chapter 4. Alternately, this dress could be a *robe à l'anglaise, fourreau*, or another style.

64. Claude-Louis Châtelet, *Illumination du Belvédère du Petit Trianon*, 1781, painting; Hubert Robert, *Fête de nuit, donnée par la reine au Comte du Nord, à Trianon*, n.d., painting.

65. Niclas Lafrensen d.y., *Hovfest i Trianons Park*, 1784, gouache on paper. See Jallut, *Marie Antoinette and Her Painters*, 42.

66. "Drottning Marie Antoinette Av Frankrike Med Två Av Sina Barn Promenerande i Trianons Park"; Hyde, "Notes on a Scandal," 14; Olausson, *Marie-Antoinette, porträtt av en drottning*, 33; Pietsch, "On Different Types of Women's Dresses," 406; Pietsch, "Eastern Influences on French Fashion," 212; Ribeiro, *Art of Dress*, 75.

67. Ashelford, "Colonial Livery," 217–19; Chrisman-Campbell, *Fashion Victims*, 172; Larkin, "Je ne suis plus la reine,"

111; Sheriff, *Exceptional Woman*, 143; Sheriff, "Portrait of the Queen," 5–46; Weber, *Queen of Fashion*, 161–62.

68. Sheriff, *Exceptional Woman*, 143, 145, 165, 174; Sheriff, "Portrait of the Queen," 45.

69. Sheriff, *Exceptional Woman*, 168, 171, 175; Sheriff, "Portrait of the Queen," 68.

70. Lescure, *Correspondance secrète inédite sur Louis XVI*, 420.

71. Cradock, *Journal*, 58.

72. Bachaumont, *Mémoires secrets* (1786), 30:165; Bouyon, *Minos au sallon*, 25; Gorsas, *Deuxième promenade de critès au sallon*, 15; Hyde, "Marie-Antoinette, Wertmüller, and Scandal of the Garden Variety," 69, 75; Hyde, "Notes on a Scandal," 9–12; Olausson, *Marie-Antoinette*, 33, 37; *Mercure de France*, Oct. 1, 1785, 34; "Observations sur les peintures & sculptures exposées au salon du Louvre," 15.

73. Van Cleave, "Contextualizing Wertmüller's 1785 Portrait of Marie-Antoinette," 56–80.

74. Roche, *Culture of Clothing*, 147, 401; Weber, *Queen of Fashion*, 159, 173.

75. Paresys, "La Cour de France," 237.

76. Soulavie, *Mémoires historiques*, 38–41. While Soulavie clearly disapproved, the factual nature of his memoirs—that Marie-Antoinette mingled with the bourgeoisie at Trianon and Saint-Cloud, and this was associated with her simplified dress—is confirmed by the Comte de Vaublanc's memoirs (Vaublanc, *Souvenirs*, 230–32).

77. Grélé, "Et si l'habit faisait l'utopie," 26; Jones, *Sexing la Mode*, 146–47, 180, 199.

78. Reigny, *Les Lunes de cousin Jaques*, 147–48.

79. Vinha and Örmen, *Dans la garde-robe*, 35–36; Roche, *Culture of Clothing*, 186–87.

80. Bevilacqua and Pfeifer, "Turquerie," 104–5.

81. Chrisman-Campbell, "Minister of Fashion," 326–27; Lasic, "Ethnicity," 158; Weber, *Queen of Fashion*, 156–57.

82. Bachaumont, *Mémoires secrets*, 14:305. Chrisman-Campbell argues there were also concerns about Ottoman-inspired styles not requiring as much fabric as traditionally French gowns (*Fashion Victims*, 246).

83. *Journal politique, ou Gazette des gazettes*, Feb., first fortnight, 1780, 54–55; *Journal politique*, second fortnight, 1780, 51. Gentleman also reportedly gave up the less formal *frac* coat.

84. Soulavie, *Mémoires historiques*, 40–42.

85. Ahmed, "Western Ethnocentrism," 524–25; Bevilacqua and Pfeifer, "Turquerie," 108–9; Boer, *Disorienting Vision*, 47; Çevik, "Boudoirs and Harems," 29–30; Çırakman, *From the "Terror of the World,"* 155, 160; Kahf, *Western Representations of the Muslim Woman*, 113; Landini, "Dress for the Body," 19–20; Nefedova-Gruntova, *Journey into the World of the Ottomans*, 47; Solnon, *Turban et la stambouline*, 323, 327; Wheatcroft, *Infidels*, 266–67; Williams, *Turquerie*, 50–51; Zlatnik, "Myth, Vision, and the Harem in French Painting," 91.

86. Boer, *Disorienting Vision*, 79; Peyraube, *Le Harem des lumières*, 128; Solnon, *Turban et la Stambouline*, 327; Stein, "Amedee Van Loo's Costume Turc," 420.

87. Geczy, *Fashion and Orientalism*, 64; Larkin, "Je ne suis plus la reine," 130; Solnon, *Turban et la stambouline*, 329, 331; Stein, "Amedee Van Loo," 417; Stein, "Exoticism as Metaphor," 188–95; Stein, "Madame de Pompadour and the Harem Imagery at Bellevue," 40. Du Barry was also an early adopter of "natural" fashions, including the *robe en chemise* (Hyde, "Beautés rivales," 2–3; Ribeiro, *Dress in Eighteenth-Century Europe*, 228).

88. Price, "Vies privées et scandaleuses," 176–92; Sheriff, "Portrait of the Queen," 52; Schama, *Citizens: A Chronicle of the French Revolution*, 220. Marie-Antoinette was more frequently called after Valeria Messalina, third wife of Roman Emperor Claudius, who had a reputation for promiscuity and supposedly conspired against her husband (Fraser, *Marie Antoinette*, 200, 258, 266, 442).

89. Chrisman-Campbell, *Fashion Victims*, 242; Raus, "Evolution de la locution 'à la turque,'" par. 54.

90. Lasic, "Ethnicity," 157.

91. *CDM*, Jan. 15, 1786, 33–34.

92. Roche, *People of Paris*, 178–79.

93. Mayeur de Saint-Paul, *Tableau du nouveau Palais-Royal*, 1:185–86.

94. Landini, "Dress for the Body," 18.

95. Crowston, "The Queen and Her 'Minister of Fashion,'" 93–94.

96. Jones, "Coquettes and Grisettes," 26.

CONCLUSION

1. Chrisman-Campbell, *Fashion Victims*, 237. See also Ribeiro, *Fashion in the French Revolution*, 39.

2. *MDM*, Nov. 20, 1786, 2, 5; Nov. 30, 1786, 10; Dec. 10, 1786, 24; Dec. 30, 1786, 39; Jan. 30, 1787, 58–61; Feb. 28, 1787, 86; Apr. 10, 1787, 117; Apr. 20, 1787, 124; Apr. 30, 1787, 132; May 20, 1787, 147–48; June 20, 1787, 169; July 30, 1787, 203; Sept. 10, 1787, 236; Nov. 30, 1787, 13; Jan. 20, 1788, 49; Feb. 10, 1788, 65; Feb. 20, 1788, 73, 75; Mar. 10, 1788, 91; Mar. 20, 1788, 97; May 30, 1788, 154; June 10, 1788, 163; June 20, 1788, 170; June 30, 1788, 198; July 30, 1788, 207; Aug. 20, 1788, 222; Sept. 20, 1788, 246; Nov. 10, 1788, 284–86; Dec. 11, 1788, 11; Jan. 1, 1789, 27; Jan. 11, 1789, 36; Jan. 21, 1789, 43; Mar. 21, 1789, 89; Apr. 11, 1789, 107; Apr. 21, 1789, 115; May 1, 1789, 124; June 11, 1789, 157; June 21, 1789, 165; July 1, 1789, 171; Dec. 11, 1789, 274, 279.

3. Chrisman-Campbell, *Fashion Victims*, 241, 250–55; Martin, "Tipu Sultan's Ambassadors at Saint-Cloud," 49–50.

4. *MDM*, Aug. 30, 1788, 228.

5. Pietsch argues that these "*robes*" should be read as *robes à l'anglaise*, but that discounts the strong influence of the *fourreau* ("Different Types of Women's Dresses," 404).

6. *MDM*, Jan. 1, 1789, 27–28; emphases added.

7. Chrisman-Campbell, *Fashion Victims*, 270; Ribeiro, *Fashion in the French Revolution*, 70.

8. Hunt, "Freedom of Dress in Revolutionary France," 231.

9. Fairchilds, "Fashion and Freedom in the French Revolution," 425; Harris, "The Red Cap of Liberty," 285.

10. Fairchilds, "Fashion and Freedom," 425–26.

11. *Journal de la mode et du goût, ou Amusemens du salon et de la toilette* (hereafter *JDLM*), Mar. 5, 1790, 17.

12. Chrisman-Campbell, *Fashion Victims*, 270; Kleinert, "Révolution et la premier journal," 286–87, 302–3; Ribeiro, *Fashion in the French Revolution*, 53, 58–59, 76; Roche, *Culture of Clothing*, 148.

13. *JDLM*, Feb. 5, 1792, 1; *Album Maciet, Gravures. Mode. XVIIIe Siècle. Révolution.* (1792), 1:55, Musée des Arts Décoratifs, Paris.

14. Kleinert, "Révolution et la premier journal," 308–9; Ribeiro, *Fashion in the French Revolution*, 21; Roche, *Culture of Clothing*, 148.

15. Chrisman-Campbell, *Fashion Victims*, 289–95; Chrisman-Campbell, "French Connections," par. 8; Delpierre, *Dress in France in the Eighteenth Century*, 59; Ribeiro, *Art of Dress*, 30.

16. "Fashionable Parties of Faro for the Present Week," *Times*, Apr. 29, 1793. See Van Cleave and Welborn, "'Very Much the Taste and Various Are the Makes,'" 21.

17. *The Gallery of Fashion*, Apr. 1794, Fig. 3; May 1794, Fig. 7; Nov. 1794, Fig. 16; Dec. 1794, Fig. 35; Jan. 1795, Fig. 37, Fig. 38; Feb. 1795, Fig. 41, Fig. 42; Apr. 1795, Fig. 48; Nov. 1795, Fig. 77; Jan. 1796, Fig. 82, 83; Feb. 1796, Fig. 85; June 1796, Fig. 184; Aug. 1796, Fig. 110; Aug. 1797, Fig. 150; Nov. 1797, Fig. 161.

18. This cut may relate to the style explored by Lazaro and Campbell Warner in "All-Over Pleated Bodice," 5–24. See patterns for related gowns in Arnold, *Patterns of Fashion . . . c. 1660–1860*, 45; Waugh and Woodward, *Cut of Women's Clothes*, diagram XXXIV.

19. Palmer, "Looking at Fashion," 286–87.

20. Cage, "The Sartorial Self," 193–94.

21. Hunt, "Freedom of Dress," 244.

22. Bissonnette and Nash, "The Re-Birth of Venus," 13–15; Lubrich, "The Little White Dress," 275.

23. Bissonnette and Nash, "Re-Birth of Venus," 11; Cage, "Sartorial Self," 208; Lajer-Burcharth, "Fleshing Out the Revolution," 2:par. 13.

24. Lasic, "Ethnicity," 159; Ribeiro, *Art of Dress*, 228.

25. Lubrich, "Little White Dress," 284.

26. Apostolou, *Orientalisme des voyageurs français*, 303; Boulaire, "Rencontre de l'Autre," 123; Denny, "Images of Turks and the European Imagination," 9; Jirousek, "More Than Oriental Splendor," 24; Sheriff, "Dislocations of Jean-Etienne Liotard," 113; Tezcan and Delibaş, *Topkapı Saray Museum*, 26.

27. Denny, "Images of Turks and the European Imagination," 9; Jirousek, "More Than Oriental Splendor," 24; Sheriff, "The Dislocations of Jean-Etienne Liotard," 113; Williams, *Turquerie*, 97.

28. Apostolou, *Orientalisme des voyageurs français*, 305; Jirousek, *Ottoman Dress and Design in the West*, 34–35; Jirousek, "More Than Oriental Splendor," 26.

29. Landweber dates this to 1778, but the Mysore embassy occurred in 1788 ("French Delight in Turkey," 278).

30. "Femme vêtue d'un lévite uni" (1780), *GDM*, 29/1; "Jeune dame en caracot à la flamande" (1787), in Cornu, *Galerie des modes*, pl. 286; *MDM*, May 20, 1787, 148. See Boucher, *20,000 Years of Fashion*, 303.

31. Jirousek, *Ottoman Dress and Design in the West*, 175–76.

32. *MDM*, July 10, 1787, 189. See Chrisman-Campbell, "Minister of Fashion," 8. The term *pouf* is used in fashion magazines from 1778 through 1787, but not after that date. It has become confused after Weber's application of the term to women's high hairstyles of the late 1770s and early 1780s in *Queen of Fashion*, but a review of primary sources proves that the term was applied to the caps worn on top of these hairstyles, not the hairstyle itself.

33. Apostolou, "Apperence extérieure de l'oriental," 6; Apostolou, *Orientalisme des voyageurs français*, 301–2; Baktir, *Representation of the Ottoman Orient*, 177–78; Kahf, *Western Representations of the Muslim Woman*, 6, 111–12.

34. *Journal des dames et des modes*, "Turban à calotte plate" (1797), "Turban en spirale, garni de perles de jais" (year VI), "Turban et spencer à l'algérienne" (year VII), "Turban à la caravane" (year VII).

35. *Journal des dames et des modes*, 15 Vendémiaire year VII, 42.

36. Jirousek, *Ottoman Dress and Design*, 201.

37. Geczy, *Orientalism*, 81.

38. *Journal des dames et des modes*, year X, pl. 369, 391, 393, 407, 413; year XI, pl. 422, 431; year XII, pl. 572; year XIII, pl. 594, 596. See Palmer, "Looking at Fashion," 297n15.

39. *Journal des dames et des modes*, 11 Brumaire year VII, 128.

40. "Modes," *Le Miroir*, July 31, 1797, 5–6. Maurice Herbette makes the identification of Madame Tallien (*Ambassade turque sous le directoire*, 169).

41. "Modes," *Journal de Marseille*, Aug. 16, 1797, 205.

42. *Journal des dames et des modes*, year VI, Fig. 51; year VII, Figs. 67, 71, 87; year VIII, Figs. 205, 222; year IX, Fig. 305; year X, Figs. 360, 369; 1808, Figs. 16, 879; 1810, Fig. 1103.

43. Lubrich, "Little White Dress," 287–99.

44. *Tableau général du goût, des modes et costumes de Paris,* Aug. 1799, 165.

45. *Journal des dames et des modes,* Apr. 7, 1800, 42–43; emphasis added.

46. Lévi-Strauss, *The Cashmere Shawl,* 14–16.

47. Ames, *The Kashmir Shawl and Its Indo-French Influence,* 135; Calvi, "Imperial Fashions," 161–63; Geczy, *Fashion and Orientalism,* 101–3; Lévi-Strauss, *Cashmere Shawl,* 16; Maskiell, "Consuming Kashmir," 30–35, 39.

48. *Journal des dames et des modes,* 15 Vendémiaire year VII, 42; year XI, pl. 429; Mar. 5, 1804, 278.

49. *L'Arlequin: Journal de pièces et de morceaux,* Aug. 12, 1799, 63–64.

50. Hiner, *Accessories to Modernity,* 83–84; Hiner, "Lust for 'Luxe,'" 77; Lévi-Strauss, *Cashmere Shawl,* 16.

51. Geczy, *Fashion and Orientalism,* 104; Lévi-Strauss, *Cashmere Shawl,* 16–19.

52. Geczy, *Fashion and Orientalism,* 100; Hiner, *Accessories to Modernity,* 83–84; Hiner, "Lust for 'Luxe,'" 77.

53. Boucher, *20,000 Years of Fashion,* 303.

54. Martin, *The Ceaseless Century,* 53–54, 61; Simon, *Fashion in Art,* 58, 96–101.

55. Martin, *Ceaseless Century,* 53–54.

56. Breward, *The Culture of Fashion,* 154; Mitchell, "Victorian Faddishness," 3, 7–9; Van Cleave and Welborn, "'Very Much the Taste and Various Are the Makes,'" 21.

57. Baumgarten, Watson, and Carr, *Costume Close-up,* 6–7; Dowdell, "Multiple Lives of Clothes," 1–2, 222–23, 239; Dowdell, "'No Small Share of Ingenuity,'" 119–207; Hayward, "Clothing," 178.

58. Inal, "Women's Fashions in Transition," 243–72; Ipek, "Ottoman Fabrics During the 18th and 19th Centuries"; Scarce, "Turkish Fashion in Transition," 144–67.

59. Koç and Koca, "The Westernization Process in Ottoman Women's Garments," par. 4–8.

60. Scarce, *Women's Costume of the Near and Middle East,* 56, 60.

61. Jirousek, *Ottoman Dress and Design,* 158.

62. Jirousek, 159.

63. Jirousek, 179–82.

64. Thoral, "Sartorial Orientalism," 60–61.

65. Craik, "Exotic Narratives in Fashion," 97–118; Ellington, "Black Hair and Cornrows"; Jansen, *Moroccan Fashion,* 91–112; Kawamura and Jong, *Cultural Appropriation in Fashion and Entertainment,* 118–39; Marcketti and Karpova, *The Dangers of Fashion,* 144–49; Palmer, "Introduction," 1–20; Pozzo, "Fashion Between Inspiration and Appropriation," 1–26; Turaga, "Being Fashionable," 73–96.

66. Thoral, "Sartorial Orientalism," 75–76.

APPENDIX 1

1. "Modes," *Nouveau Mercure de France,* 1775, no. 1, 109.

2. Landini and Niccoli, *Moda a Firenze,* 109–17.

3. *Dictionnaire de l'Academie française,* 4th ed., s.v. "simarre," vol. 2, 1762, ARTFL.

4. Boucher, *20,000 Years of Fashion,* 303; Delpierre, *Dress in France in the Eighteenth Century,* 67–68; Landweber, "Turkish Delight," 205.

5. "Robe à la levantine garnie en hermine" (1779), *GDM,* 17/1.

6. Boucher, *20,000 Years of Fashion,* 303; Pietsch, "On Different Types of Women's Dresses," 406; Ribeiro, *Dress in Eighteenth-Century Europe,* 270.

7. *Journal de Paris,* Sept. 17, 1780, 1059.

8. "Grande robe à la sultane fermée sur le devant" (1782), in Cornu, *Galerie des modes,* pl. 167.

9. Pierre Thomas Le Clerc, Janinet workshop (designer), Wossinik (engraver), Esnauts et Rapilly (publisher), *Gallerie des Modes et Costumes Français. 34e Cahier (bis) des Costumes Français, 31e Suite d'Habillemens à la mode en 1782. rr.240 "Robe à la Sultane,"* 1782, hand-colored engraving on laid paper, 15 × 10 in., Museum of Fine Arts, Boston.

10. Panckoucke, *Encyclopédie méthodique,* s.v. "Couturiere," 1:225.

11. "La belle Zulima vetue d'une robe à la sultane" (ca. 1787), in Cornu, *Galerie des modes,* pl. 317.

12. *MDM,* Jan. 30, 1787, 59.

13. *MDM,* Jan. 11, 1789, 36.

14. *MDM,* Jan. 21, 1789, 43.

15. *MDM,* Mar. 21, 1789, 89. The *marinière* cuff was a menswear-derived style typically worn with riding habits. It was "a small round cuff with slightly scalloped vertical flap edged with three to four buttons" (Ribeiro, *Dress in Eighteenth-Century Europe,* 91).

16. *Journal de Paris,* Mar. 2, 1790, iv.

17. "Beauté du Panthéon, vêtue d'une robe à l'asiatique" (1787), in Cornu, *Galerie des modes,* pl. 246.

18. "Grande robe de cour dans le goût asiatique" (ca. 1786–87), in Cornu, *Galerie des modes,* pl. 274.

19. "Robe de cour au grand orient" (ca. 1787), in Cornu, *Galerie des modes,* pl. 297.

20. "Robe de cour à la turque" (ca. 1787), in Cornu, *Galerie des modes,* pl. 301.

21. *MDM,* Mar. 2, 1788, 97–98.

22. Borderioux, "Presse française," 279; Boucher, *20,000 Years of Fashion,* 329; Korchounova and Tarassova, "La Mode française et le costume de cour dans la Russie du XVIIIe siècle," 209; Mansel, *Dressed to Rule,* 53.

23. *MDM,* Aug. 30, 1788, 228.

24. Chrisman-Campbell, *Fashion Victims,* 241, 250–55; Martin, "Tipu Sultan's Ambassadors at Saint-Cloud," 49–50.

25. *MDM,* Aug. 30, 1788, 230.

26. *MDM,* Feb. 10, 1788, 65.

27. Berry, *Extracts from the Journals and Correspondence of Miss Berry,* 144.

28. Moszyński, *Journal de voyage, I: La France, 1784–1785,* 136.

29. *MDM,* Sept. 20, 1788, 246.

30. *MDM,* Apr. 11, 1789, 107.

31. *Journal de Paris,* Mar. 2, 1790, iii.

32. *Journal de Paris,* Mar. 2, 1790, iv.

33. *Journal de Paris,* Oct. 5, 1790, iv.

34. Grimm, *Correspondance littéraire,* 1:402.

35. *Collection d'habillements modernes et galants avec les habillements des princes et seigneurs [Gallerie Des Modes]* (Paris, 1781), no. 44 G.

36. *Journal de Paris,* Apr. 18, 1791, 3.

APPENDIX 2

1. I am grateful to Carolyn Dowdell for sharing her research about this piece.

2. I am grateful to Carolyn Dowdell for sharing her research about this piece.

3. I am grateful to Johannes Pietsch of the Bayerisches Nationalmuseum for providing additional information about these and other garments in the collection, and for confirming my identifications.

4. Inventory information comes from Arnold et al., *Patterns of Fashion 6,* 120–21.

5. Inventory information comes from Arnold et al., *Patterns of Fashion 6,* 124–27.

6. I am grateful to Ned Lazaro of Historic Deerfield for sharing information about this piece.

BIBLIOGRAPHY

PRIMARY SOURCES

MONOGRAPHS AND SERIES

Bachaumont, Louis Petit de. *Lettres sur les peintures, sculptures et gravures de Mrs. de l'Académie royale, exposés au sallon du Louvre depuis MDCCLXVII jusqu'en MDCCLXXIX*. London: J. Adamson, 1780.

———. *Mémoires secrets pour servir à l'histoire de la république des lettres en France, depuis MDCCLXII jusqu'à nos jours*. Vols. 14–34. London: John Adamson, 1780, 1783.

Ballexserd, Jacques. *Dissertation sur l'éducation physique des enfans, depuis leur naissance jusqu'à l'âge de puberté*. Paris: Vallat-La-Chapelle, 1762.

Bar, Jacques-Charles. *Recueil de tous les costumes des ordres religieux et militaires avec un abrégé historique et chronologique*. Vol. 2. 2 vols. Paris: Chez l'Auteur, 1778.

Beaumarchais, Pierre-Augustin Caron de. *Eugénie: drame en 5 actes en prose: enrichi de figures en taille-douce; avec un Essai sur le drame sérieux*. Paris: Merlin, 1767.

Beaumont, Jeanne-Marie Leprince de. *Magasin des adolescentes, ou Dialogues entre une sage gouvernante & plusieurs de ses élèves de la première distinction*. Vol. 4. London: J. Nourse, 1760.

Bouyon, Louis Bonnefoy de. *Minos au Sallon, ou La Gazette infernale*. Paris: Hardouin & Gattey, 1785.

Bretonne, Nicolas-Edme Rétif de La. *L'Andrographe, ou Idées d'un honnête-homme, sur un projet de reglement: Proposé à toutes les Nations de l'Europe, pour opérer une Réforme générale des mœurs, & par elle, le bonheur du Genre-humain*. The Hague: Gosse & Pinet, 1782.

———. *Les Contemporaines, ou Avantures des plus jolies femmes de l'âge présent*. Vol. 12. Leipzig: Büschel, 1783.

———. *Les Gynographes, ou Idées de deux honnêtes-femmes sur un projet de reglement proposé à toute l'Europe, pour mettre les femmes à leur place, & opérer le bonheur des deux sexes: avec des notes historiques et justificatives, suivies des noms des femmes célèbres*. The Hague: Gosse & Pinet, 1777.

Charnois, Jean Charles Le Vacher de. *Costumes et annales des grands theatres de Paris: Accompagnes de notices interessantes et curieuses avec privilege du roi*. Paris: Bureau général de la Souscription, 1786.

"Éloge de Madame Favart." In *Les Spectacles de Paris, ou calendrier historique & chronologique des théâtres*, 22:20–21. Paris: Duchesne, 1773.

Les Fantaisies aimables, ou les Caprices des belles représentés par les costumes les plus nouveaux. Paris: Jubert, 1786.

Gorsas, Antoine Joseph. *Deuxième promenade de Critès au sallon*. Paris: chez les marchands de nouveautés, 1785.

Grimm, Friedrich Melchior, and Denis Diderot. *Correspondance littéraire, philosophique et critique, adressée a un souverain d'Allemagne depuis 1770 jusqu'en 1782*. Vols. 1 and 13. 1812. Reprint, Paris: Chez Furne et Ladrange, 1830.

Grivel, Guillaume. *Théorie de l'éducation*. Vol. 1. Paris: Moutard, 1775.

Halma, Nicolas B. *De l'éducation*. N.p.: A. Bouillon, 1791.

Le Fébure, Guillaume-René. *Le Manuel des femmes enceintes, de celles qui sont en couches et des mères qui veulent nourrir*. Paris: J.-F. Bastien, 1777.

Le Maistre, Antoine. *Recueil de divers plaidoyers et harangues, prononcez au Parlement*. Paris: Michel Bobin, 1652.

LeRoy, Alphonse Louis Vincent. *Recherches sur les habillemens des femmes et des enfans, ou Examen de la maniere dont il faut vêtir l'un et l'autre Sèxe*. Paris: Le Boucher, 1772.

Lescure, Adolphe de. *Correspondance secrète inédite sur Louis XVI, Marie-Antoinette la cour et la ville de 1777 à 1792.* Vol. 1. 2 vols. Paris: Plon, 1866.

Louis XV. *Ordonnance du Roi, concernant sa cavalerie: Du 1er décembre 1761.* Paris, 1761.

———. *Ordonnance du Roi, concernant sa cavalerie: Du 21 décembre 1762.* Paris, 1763.

Louis XVI. *Règlement arrêté par le Roi, concernant l'habillement et l'équipement de ses troupes. Du 31 mai 1776.* Paris: L'Imprimerie Royale, 1776.

Maréchal, Sylvain. *Costumes Civils actuels de tous les Peuples connus.* 2 vols. Paris: Pavard, 1784.

Marsy, Claude-Sixte Sautreau de. *Le Petit chansonnier françois, ou Choix des meilleures chansons sur des airs connus.* Vol. 3. Geneva: Veuve Duchesne, 1778.

Mayeur de Saint-Paul, François-Marie. *Tableau du nouveau Palais-Royal.* Vol. 1. Paris: Maradan, 1788.

Mercier, Louis-Sébastien. *Tableau de Paris.* Vols. 7–9. Amsterdam: N.p., 1783–88.

Mézeray, François Eudes de, and Laonicus Chalcondyle. *L'Histoire de la décadence de l'Empire grec et establissement de celuy des Turcs.* Vol. 2. Paris: Mathieu Guillemot, 1650.

Montandre-Longchamps, François Edme de, Alexandre de Montandre, and Jacques de Roussel. *Etat militaire de France, pour l'année 1758–[1793].* Paris: chez Guillyn, 1787.

Montesquieu, Baron de. *The Spirit of the Laws.* Translated by Thomas Nugent. London: Haffner Publishing Company, 1966.

Nougaret, Pierre-Jean-Baptiste. *Les Sottises et les folies parisiennes.* Vol. 1. Paris: Veuve Duchesne, 1781.

———. *Tableau mouvant de Paris, ou variétés amusantes,* Vol. 3. London: Thomas Hookham, 1787.

"Observations sur les peintures & sculptures exposées au salon du Louvre." In *L'Année littéraire,* 5:289–304. Paris: Mérigot le jeune, 1785.

Panckoucke, Charles, ed. *Recueil de planches de l'encyclopédie, par ordre de matières.* Vol. 6. Paris: Panckoucke, 1786.

———. "Bourse, Boursier." In *Encyclopédie méthodique ou par ordre de matières: Art, métiers et mécaniques,* Vol. 1, Manufactures, Arts et Métiers, 83–90. Paris: Panckoucke, 1785.

Paris vu tel qu'il est. Paris: N.p., 1781.

Ponce, M. "Révolutions des modes françaises." In *Almanach littéraire, ou Etrennes d'Apollon,* 49–60. Paris: Veuve Duchesne et Defer de Maisonneuve, 1789.

Reigny, L.-A. Beffroy de. *Les Lunes de cousin Jaques.* Paris: Lesclapart, 1785.

Remi, Ch. *Mon oisiveté.* Amsterdam: Gueffier & Moreau, 1779.

Riballier. *De l'Éducation physique et morale des enfants des deux sexes.* Paris: Nyon aîné, 1785.

Rousseau, Jean-Jacques. *The Confessions and Correspondence, Including the Letters to Malesherbes.* Edited by Christopher Kelly, Chretien Guillaume de Lamoignon de Malesherbes, Roger D. Masters, and Peter G. Stillman. Vol. 5. Hanover: Univ. Press of New England for Dartmouth College, 1995.

———. *Emile, ou, De l'éducation.* 4 vols. Amsterdam: J. Néaulme, 1765.

———. *Oeuvres de M. Rousseau de Genève.* Vol. 1. Neuchâtel: Marc Michel Rey, 1764.

Savary, Claude Etienne. *Lettres sur l'Égypte: où l'on offre le parallèle des moeurs anciennes et modernes de ces habitans.* Vol. 1. Paris: Flon, 1786.

Seconde suite d'estampes pour servir à l'histoire des moeurs et du costume des français dans le dix-huitième siècle: Année 1776. Paris: Prault, 1777.

"Theatres, Comedie Francaise." In *Journal helvétique: ou, Annales littéraires et politiques de l'Europe et principalement de la Suisse,* 56–64. Neuchatel: la Société Typographique, 1782.

Venel, Jean-André. *Essai sur la santé et l'éducation médicinale des filles destinées au mariage.* Yverdon: chez la Société littéraire et typographique, 1776.

PERIODICALS

Les Affiches americaines
Affiches de Bordeaux
Affiches du Poitou
Affiches Generales de la Bretagne
Annonces, affiches et avis divers pour la ville du Mans et pour la province
Annonces, affiches, nouvelles et avis divers de la Province du Poitou
Annonces, affiches, nouvelles et avis divers de l'Orléanais
L'Arlequin: Journal de pièces et de morceaux
L'Avantcoureur: Feuille hebdomadaire, où sont annoncés les objects particuliers des sciences & des arts, le cours & les nouveautés des spectacles, & les livres nouveaux en tout genre
Cabinet des modes, ou les Modes nouvelles, décrites d'une manière claire & précise, & représentées par des planches en taille-douce, enluminées
Courrier de la mode ou le Journal du goût, Ouvrage périodique, contenant le détail de toutes les nouveautés du mois
Daily Universal Register
The Gallery of Fashion
Gazette du commerce
Journal de Guienne
Journal de la mode et du goût, ou Amusemens du salon et de la toilette
Journal de l'Orléanais ou Annonces, affiches et avis diver
Journal de Marseille

Journal de Paris

Journal des dames et des modes

Journal politique, ou Gazette des gazettes

The Lady's Magazine

Magasin des modes nouvelles, françaises et anglaises, décrites d'une manière claire & précise, & représentées par des planches en taille-douce, enluminées

Mercure de France

Mercure galant

Le Miroir

Morning Herald

Nouveau Mercure de France

Public Advertiser

Tableau général du goût, des modes et costumes de Paris

The Times (London)

FASHION PLATE COLLECTIONS

Collection d'habillements modernes et galants avec les habillements des princes et seigneurs [Gallerie des modes]. Paris, 1781. Bunka Gakuen Univ. Library, Tokyo. https://digital.bunka.ac.jp/kichosho_e/index.php.

Collection d'habillements modernes et galants: avec les habillements des princes et seigneur [Gallerie des modes]. Paris: André Basset, 1775–81. Muzeum Narodowe, Warsaw.

Collection Maciet. Musée des Arts Décoratifs, Paris.

Cornu, Paul, ed. *Galerie des modes et costumes français, dessinés d'après nature, 1778–1787*. Paris: É. Lévy, 1912.

Gallerie des modes et costumes français. Bibliothèque municipale de Versailles, France. http://www.banqueimages.chateauversailles-recherche.fr/.

Gallerie des modes et costumes français. The Elizabeth Day McCormick Collection. Museum of Fine Arts, Boston. https://collections.mfa.org/.

Gallerie des modes et costumes française dessinés d'après nature graves par les plus célèbres artistes en ce genre. Esnauts & Rapilly, Paris, 1778–88. Muzeum Narodowe, Warsaw.

Gallerie des modes et costumes français: dessinés d'après nature: gravés par les plus célèbres artistes en ce genre. Paris, 1778. Bibliothèque nationale de France, Paris.

Gallerie des modes et costumes français: dessinés d'après nature: gravés par les plus célèbres artistes en ce genre, et colorés avec le plus grand soin par Madame Le Beau: ouvrage commencé en l'année 1778. 2 vols. Paris: Esnauts et Rapilly, 1778. Bunka Gakuen Univ. Library, Tokyo. https://digital.bunka.ac.jp/kichosho_e/index.php.

PUBLISHED ACCOUNTS, CORRESPONDENCE, DIARIES, AND MEMOIRS

Bénet, Armand, ed. "E. 112., Serie E." In *Inventaire sommaire des archives départementales antérieures à 1790: Seine-et-Oise*, 10:18. Versailles: Cerf & Fils, 1873.

———. "H. Suppl. 1814-H. 96, Serie H Supplément—Honfleur." In *Inventaire sommaire des archives départementales antérieures à 1790: Calvados*, 10:311. Caen: Charles Valin, 1900.

Berry, Mary. *Extracts from the Journals and Correspondence of Miss Berry: From the Year 1783 to 1852*. Vol. 1. London: Longmans, Green, 1866.

Bombelles, Marc de. *Journal*. Edited by Jean Grassion and Frans Durif. Genève: Droz, 1977.

Bombelles, Marc de, and Angélique de Mackau Bombelles. *"Que je suis heureuse d'être ta femme": Lettres intimes, 1778–1782*. Edited by Évelyne Lever. Paris: Tallandier, 2009.

Campan, Madame. *Mémoires sur la vie privée de Marie-Antoinette; suivis de souvenirs et anecdotes historiques sur les règnes de Louis XIV, de Louis XV et de Louis XVI*. 3 vols. Paris: Baudouin frères; Mongie aîné, 1823.

Cavendish, Georgiana Spencer. *Georgiana; Extracts from the Correspondence of Georgiana, Duchess of Devonshire*. London: Murray, 1955.

Cradock, Anna Francesca. *Journal de Mme Cradock: Voyage en France (1783–1786)*. Translated by Mme O. Delphin-Balleyguier. Paris: Perrin, 1896.

Crewe, Frances Anne. *An English Lady in Paris: The Diary of Frances Anne Crewe 1786*. Edited by Michael Allen. London: Oxford-Stockley Publications, 2011.

Éloffe, Mme. *Modes et usages au temps du Marie-Antoinette: Livre-Journal de Madame Éloffe: Couturière lingère ordinaire de la Reine*. Edited by Gustave Armand Henri de Reiset. Paris: Mesnil, 1885.

"La Garde-robe d'une champenoise au XVIIIe siècle." In *Revue de Champagne et de Brie*, 17:413–15. Arcis-sur-Aube: Léon Frémont, 1884.

Gouvernet, Henriette Lucie Dillon, marquise de La Tour du Pin. *Journal d'une femme de cinquante ans, 1778–1815*. Vol. 1. Paris: M. Imhaus & R. Chapelot, 1914.

Jay, John, and Sarah Livingston Jay. *Selected Letters of John Jay and Sarah Livingston Jay: Correspondence by or to the First Chief Justice of the United States and His Wife*. Jefferson, NC: McFarland, 2010.

Le Gouil-Bauzin, Delphine, ed. "Inventaire de François Guillaume Claude Trousseau, ancien avocat au Parlement 19 Décembre 1775—MC/ET/LXXIII/968." https://identitesvestimentaires.wordpress.com/dans-les-actes-notaries-de-paris/annee-1775/inventaire-de-francois-guillaume-claude-trousseau-ancien-avocat-au-parlement-19-decembre-1775-mcetlxxiii968/.

Lennox, Sarah. *The Life and Letters of Lady Sarah Lennox, 1745–1826 Daughter of Charles, 2nd Duke of Richmond, and Successively the Wife of Sir Thomas Charles Bunbury, Bart., and of the Hon. George Napier; Also a Short Political Sketch* of the Years 1760 to 1763 by Henry Fox, 1st Lord Holland.* Edited by Giles Stephen Holland Fox-Strangways 6th Earl of Ilchester, and Mary Eleanor Anne Countess of Dawson. London: J. Murray, 1901.

Marie-Antoinette, Queen consort of Louis XVI King of France, and Landgrave Louise Caroline Henriette de Hesse. *Lettres de la reine Marie-Antoinette à la landgrave Louise de Hesse-Darmstadt.* Paris: Henri Plon, 1865.

Marie-Antoinette (reine de France). *Lettres de Marie-Antoinette: recueil des lettres authentiques de la reine.* Edited by Maxime de La Rocheterie and le Marquis de Beaucourt. Vol. 1. Paris: A. Picard et fils, 1895.

Monnard, Marie-Victoire. *Les Souvenirs d'une femme du peuple.* Edited by Olivier Boutanquoi. Senlis, France: Impr. réunies de Senlis, 1928.

Moszyński, August Fryderyk. *Journal de voyage, I: La France, 1784–1785.* Edited by Guillaume Calafat. Paris: CNRS A. Baudry, 2010.

Ossun, Geneviève de Gramont. *Gazette des atours de Marie-Antoinette: garde-robe des atours de la reine: gazette pour l'année 1782.* Paris: Réunion des musées nationaux, Archives nationales, 2006.

Péage, P. Denis du. "Inventaire après décès de Madame de Podenas—Persée." *Revue du Nord* 87 (1936): 175–86.

Soulavie, Jean-Louis. *Memoires historiques et politiques du regne de Louis XVI: depuis son mariage jusqu'a sa mort.* Vol. 6. Paris: Treuttel et Würtz, 1801.

Vaublanc, Vincent Marie Viennot comte de. *Souvenirs.* Paris: G. A. Dentu, 1841.

Walpole, Horace. *Yale Edition of Horace Walpole's Correspondence.* https://libsvcs-1.its.yale.edu/hwcorrespondence/.

REFERENCE SOURCES

"Dictionnaires d'autrefois, the ARTFL Project." Chicago: Univ. of Chicago. https://artfl-project.uchicago.edu/content/dictionnaires-dautrefois.

Furetière, Antoine. *Dictionnaire universel, contenant generalement tous les mots françois tant vieux que modernes, et les termes de toutes les sciences & des arts.* Rotterdam: Chez A. et R. Leers, 1690.

Panckoucke, Charles, ed. *Encyclopédie méthodique ou par ordre de matières: Manufactures, arts et métiers.* Vol. 1. Paris: Panckoucke, 1785.

———. *Encyclopédie méthodique ou par ordre de matières: Manufactures et arts.* Vol. 2. Paris: Panckoucke, 1784.

———. *Encyclopédie méthodique ou par ordre de matières: Arts et métiers mécaniques.* Vol. 6. Paris: Panckoucke, 1789.

EXTANT GARMENTS

See Appendix 2: Extant Garments. Other garments cited:

Jacke. ca. 1790. Cotton, linen. T1377. Germanischen Nationalmuseum, Nuremberg.

Kjole i engelsk snit fra 1780'erne. Printed cotton. W.18. Nationalmuseet, Copenhagen. https://natmus.dk/historisk-viden/temaer/modens-historie/1700–1790/engelsk-kjole/.

Panier. France. 1750–90. Linen, horsehair, paper. KA 1126. Amsterdam Museum.

Robe droite. France. ca. 1785–95. Cotton muslin. 000.4.10. Musée de la Toile de Jouy, Jouy-en-Josas, France.

Underklädsel. Sweden. 1770–1810. NM.0001008. Nordiska Museet, Stockholm.

"Woman's Dress (Redingote)." *Undertaking the Making: LACMA Costume and Textiles Pattern Project.* Los Angeles County Museum of Art. https://www.lacma.org/patternproject.

ARTWORKS

Agoty, Louis-Charles Gauthier d.' *Portrait de Marie-Antoinette assise dans un canapé.* n.d. Painting, oil on canvas, 16¼ × 13 in. Comte et Comtesse Niel. Une passion partagée, Apr. 16, 2012, lot no. 108. Christie's, Paris.

Baudin, Jules. *Portrait de femme au livre.* 1789. Painting, oil on canvas. Tableaux anciens & modernes mobilier & objets d'art chasse, Nov. 23, 2011, lot no. 118. Coutau-Bégarie & Associés, Paris.

Bonnet, Louis-Marin after Jean-Baptiste Hüet. *Les Échasses, jeux des enfants.* ca. 1790. Color stipple engraving on laid paper, 6⅝ × 7⅝ in. National Gallery of Art, Washington, DC.

Boquet, Louis-René. *1 maquette de costume pour Athalie.* 1770. Drawing, metallic gall ink, 285 × 230 mm. Bibliothèque nationale de France, département Bibliothèque-musée de l'opéra, Paris.

———. *Athalie [maquette de Costume].* 1770. Drawing, metallic gall ink, 253 × 159 mm. Bibliothèque nationale de France, département Bibliothèque-musée de l'opéra, Paris.

———. *Josabeth // Mlle Dubois [maquette du costume].* 1770. Drawing, 262 × 178 mm. Bibliothèque nationale de France, Paris.

———. *Mme Favart dans "Les Trois Sultanes."* 1760. Ink and watercolor on paper. Bibliothèque nationale de France, Bibliothèque-Musée de l'Opéra, Paris.

———. *Polonoise, polonois (maquette de costume).* Eighteenth century. Drawing, iron gall ink, 255 × 325 mm. Bibliothèque nationale de France, Paris.

Boissieu, Jean-Jacques de. *La Danse des enfants.* Painting, oil on canvas, 30 × 38.5 cm. Petit Palais, Musée des Beaux-arts de la Ville de Paris.

Carmontelle, Louis Carrogis. *Madame Millin du Perreux and Her Son, with a Painted Portrait of Monsieur Jérôme-*

Robert Millin du Perreux. ca. 1760. Drawing, red chalk, black chalk, and watercolor, heightened with white chalk or paint? on cream laid paper, 12⅜ × 7¹⁵⁄₁₆ in. Cleveland Museum of Art.

———. *Madame Moreau et mademoiselle de Flinville.* 1762 [ca. 1780]. Watercolor and gouache, 0.325 × 0.2 m. Musée Condé, Chantilly, France.

Carrogis, called Carmontelle, Louis. *Mme de Saint-Amarante.* ca. 1770. Drawing, watercolor, 0.325 × 0.2 m. Musée Condé, Chantilly, France.

———. *Mme du Dreneuc,* 1771. Graphite, watercolor, gouache, sanguine on paper, 30 × 18 cm, Musée Condé, Chantilly, France.

———. *Mmes les comtesses de Fitz-James et du Nolestin,* 1771. Graphite, watercolor, gouache, sanguine on paper, 34 × 20.5 cm, Musée Condé, Chantilly, France.

———. *Monsieur N., fermier général, avec sa fille.* n.d. Watercolor and gouache, 0.205 × 0.31 m. Musée Condé, Chantilly, France.

Châtelet, Claude-Louis. *Illumination du Belvédère du Petit Trianon.* 1781. Painting, oil on canvas, 58.3 × 80.4 cm. Palace of Versailles, France.

Dagoty, J. B. Gautier. *Marie-Antoinette en buste.* n.d. In Olivier Blanc, *Portraits de femmes: artistes et modèles à l'époque de Marie-Antoinette.* Paris: Ed. Didier Carpentier, 2006.

Desfossés, Charles Henri (designer), Antoine Jean Duclos (engraver), Basan et Poignant (publisher). *Marie Antoinette: The Queen of Fashion: Marie Antoinette Visiting Mme Bellegarde / La Reine annonçant à Mme de Bellegarde, des juges, et la liberté de son mari; en mai 1777.* 1779. Etching and engraving, 375 × 485 mm. Rijksmuseum, Amsterdam.

Desrais, Claude Louis. *Filles publiques chassées par ordonnance de police. Elles sont conduits, en charrette, tondues, jusqu'à la "Maison de santé."* n.d. Drawing, pen and black ink, brown wash over black pencil lines and red lines, 25.5 × 38.5 cm. Old Master Drawings, Nov. 27, 2013. Tajan, Paris.

———. *Petits métiers, cris de Paris.* Eighteenth century. Drawing, 34 × 22.5 cm. Bibliothèque nationale de France, Paris.

Drouais, François-Hubert. *Le Comte de Nogent, enfant.* 1765. Painting, oil on canvas, 0.710 × 0.600 cm. Musée du Louvre, Paris.

Ducreux, Joseph. *Ritratto di Maria Antonietta d'Asburgo.* 1780–92. Painting, pastel on paper, 72 × 61 cm. Musei Reali, Palazzo Reale, Turin, Italy.

Dugourc, Jean Démosthène. *The Garden Façade of Bagatelle.* 1779. Drawing, pen and black ink, watercolor over traces of black chalk, 11⅛ × 15¹³⁄₁₆ in. Metropolitan Museum of Art, New York.

Dumont, François. *Marie-Antoinette.* 1784. Gouache, model of a color engraving. Private collection. In Pierre de Nolhac, "François Dumont," *Gazette des Beaux Arts* 3, no. 6e period (1930): 328–34.

———. *Marie-Antoinette écrivant assise à son bureau.* ca. 1777. Miniature on ivory, 09 × 90mm. May 16, 1995. Christie's, Geneva.

Dumont l'Aîné, François. *Portrait de la reine Marie-Antoinette, de sa fille et de son second fils.* 1790. Paint on ivory, 0.195 × 0.143 m. Musée du Louvre, Paris.

Duplessis, Joseph. *Portrait of Louise Marie Adélaïde de Bourbon (1753–1821), duchesse de Chartres.* 1777–78. Painting, oil on canvas, 38.1 × 51.1 in. Musée Condé, Château de Chantilly.

French school. *Portrait de jeunes femmes traditionnellement dit de Marie-Antoinette et Mme de Lamballe.* ca. 1770 [ca. 1780]. Painting, oil on canvas. Tableaux, Sculptures et Dessins Anciens et du XIXe siècle, June 16, 2016, lot 48. Sotheby's, Paris.

Gautier-Dagoty, Jean-Baptiste-André. *Marie-Antoinette devant le temple d'Amour.* ca. 1780. Painting, oil on canvas, 41 × 33.3 cm. Palace of Versailles, France.

Guttenberg, Carl Gottlieb (printer), after Jean Michel Moreau. *Le Rendez-vous pour Marly, Le Monument du costume.* 1776–77. Etching, 410 × 318 mm. Rijksmuseum, Amsterdam.

Guttenbrun, Ludwig. *Ritratto di Giuseppina di Lorena-Armagnac.* 1784–86. Oil on canvas, 89.5 × 69 cm. Castello Reale, Turin, Italy.

Labille-Guiard, Adélaïde. *Femme au ruban bleu.* 1782. Pastel, 72 × 58 cm. In Neil Jeffares, ed., "Labille-Guiard, Adélaïde," *Dictionary of Pastelists before 1800,* online edition, 2018, www.pastellists.com/Articles/LabilleGuiard.pdf.

———. *Portrait of a Lady, Half Length, Wearing a Pink Dress.* 1786. Oil on canvas, 31¼ × 25 in. Old Master Paintings, Jan. 31, 2013, lot 184. Sotheby's, New York.

Lafrensen d.y., Niclas. *Hovfest i Trianons Park.* 1784. Gouache on paper, 37 × 29 cm. Östergötlands Museum, Sweden.

Le Clercq, Charles. *Marie Antoinette and Her Children.* 1781. Painting, oil. Château de Sassenage, France. In Pierre Arizzoli-Clémentel and Xavier Salmon, *Marie-Antoinette: Galeries nationales du Grand Palais, Paris, 15 mars–30 juin 2008* (Paris: Réunion des musées nationaux, 2008).

Lemoine, Jaques-Antoine-Marie. *Portrait of Elisabeth-Louise Vigée-Lebrun Reading a Letter Seated in a Garden.* 1783. Drawing, black chalk, stumped, 19⅝ × 16⅜ in. Christie's, New York.

Lemoine, Marie-Victoire. *Portrait de Marie-Thérèse-Louise de Savoie-Carignan, princesse de Lamballe.* 1779. Oil on canvas, 61 × 49.5 cm. Private collection.

———. *Portrait of a Young Boy Feeding Two Birds.* Before 1820. Painting, oil on canvas, 21.6 × 17.9 in. Old Master Paintings, Jan. 31, 2013, lot no. 269. Sotheby's, New York.

Lespinasse, Louis Nicolas de, called the Chevalier de Lespinasse. *The Château de Versailles Seen from the Gardens*. 1779. Drawing, pen and black ink, watercolor, heightened with white, over traces of graphite, 8 1/16 × 11 15/16 in. Metropolitan Museum of Art, New York.

Moitte, Alexandre. *Mme Elisabeth et Marie Antoinette s'embrassant*. n.d. Drawing, black pencil, 0.36 × 0.32 m. Palais des Beaux-Arts, Lille, France.

Naudet (publisher). *Fille de joie se battant avec le coiffeur qui l'a tondue*. 1778. Engraving. Bibliothèque nationale de France, Paris.

Ollivier, Michel-Barthélémy. *La Partie des Dames*. c 1765. Painting, 43.5 × 35.5 cm. Musée Cognacq-Jay, Paris.

———. *Le Thé à l'anglaise servi dans le salon des Quatre-Glaces au palais du Temple, mai 1766*. 1766. Painting, oil on canvas, 54 × 69.6 cm. Palace of Versailles, France.

Raspal, Antoine. *The Couturier's Workshop*. ca. 1785. Painting, oil on canvas. Musée Reattu, Arles, France.

———. *Intérieur de Cuisine*. ca. 1780. Oil on canvas, 36 × 46 cm. Musée Réattu, Arles, France.

———. *Portrait de Femme*. ca. 1780. Painting, oil on canvas. Collection Fragonard Parfumeur, Grasse, France. http://www.museereattu.arles.fr/eng/antoine-raspal-pinxit-eng.html.

———. *Portrait de Madame de Privat et Ses Enfants*. 1780–81. Painting, oil on canvas, 93 × 72.5 cm. Museon Arlaten, Arles, France.

Robert, Hubert. *L'Entrée du Tapis vert*. 1777. Painting, oil on canvas, 124 × 191 cm. Palace of Versailles, France.

———. *Fête de nuit, donnée par la reine au Comte du Nord, à Trianon*. n.d. Painting, oil on wood, 60 × 75 cm. Musée des beaux-arts de Quimper, France.

———. *The Terrace at the Château de Marly*. ca. 1780. Painting, oil on canvas, 35 1/4 × 52 1/4 in. Nelson-Atkins Museum of Art, Kansas City.

Roslin, Alexander. *Marie Jeanne Puissant (1745–1828)*. 1781. Painting, oil on canvas, 74 × 59 cm. Rijksmuseum Twenthe, Enschede, Netherlands.

Trinquesse, Louis-Rolland (attr.). *Portrait d'un enfant tenant des fruits*. 1782. Painting, oil on canvas, 25 1/2 × 21 3/8 in. Le Haras d'Estimauville; Oeuvres et Objects d'Art provenant des Collections Rothschild, Oct. 26–27, 2010, lot no. 310. Christie's, Paris.

———. *Portrait of a Lady*. 1780. Painting, oil on canvas, 36 × 27.7 in. National Museum, Warsaw (now missing).

Vallayer-Coster, Anne. *Portrait of an Elderly Lady with Her Daughter*. Painting, oil on canvas. Bowes Museum, Barnard Castle, County Durham, UK.

Vestier, Antoine. *Portrait présumé de la famille de Bergeret de Grancourt*. ca. 1785. Painting, oil on canvas, 1.92 × 1.45 m. Musée des Beaux-Arts, Brest, France.

Vigée Le Brun, Elisabeth Louise. *Marie Antoinette in a Park*. ca. 1780–81. Black, stumped, and white chalk on blue paper, 23 3/16 × 15 7/8 in. Metropolitan Museum of Art, New York.

———. *Study of a Woman*. n.d. Drawing, red chalk, 9 1/2 × 5 7/8 in. Museum of Fine Arts, Boston.

Vigée Le Brun, Élisabeth-Louise (after). *Marie-Antoinette*. After 1783. Oil on canvas, 36 1/2 × 28 3/4 in. National Gallery, Washington, DC.

Watteau, François Louis Joseph (called Watteau de Lille). *Gathering in a Park*. n.d. Painting, oil on canvas, 65 × 82 cm. Musée Cognacq-Jay, Paris.

———. *Père de famille donnant la Saint Nicolas à ses enfants*. 1788. Painting, oil on wood, 34.5 × 27 cm. Musée des Beaux-Arts, Lille, France.

Watteau, Louis Joseph. *La 14ème expérience aérostatique de M. Blanchard*. 1785. Painting, oil on canvas, 99 × 189 cm. Musée de L'Hospice Comtesse, Lille, France.

Wertmüller, Adolf Ulrik. *Portrait de Mme Claudine Rousse, née Morin*. 1780. Collection of Mme Ingrid Frykman, Sweden. In Gunnar W. Lundberg, *Le Peintre suédois, Adolf Ulrik Wertmüller à Lyon, 1779-1781* (Lyon: Impr. Audin, 1972).

———. *Queen Marie Antoinette of France and Two of Her Children Walking in the Park of Trianon*. 1785. Painting, oil on canvas, 108.6 × 76.3 in. Nationalmuseum, Stockholm.

Wille, Pierre Alexandre. *The Double Reward of the Merit or the Return from the American War of Independence*. 1781. Painting, oil on canvas, 162 × 129 cm. Musée National de la Cooperation Franco-Americaine, France.

———. *La Famille malheureuse*. 1777. Painting, oil on canvas, 0.735 × 0.99 m. Musée des Beaux-Arts, Angers, France.

———. *Portrait d'un amateur et de sa famille*. 1786. Painting, 112 × 131 cm. Faïences et céramiques, tableaux, argenterie, mobilier et objets d'art, Nov. 17, 2004, lot no. 79. Collin du Bocage, Paris.

———. *Young Woman with Miniature*. 1778. Deaccessioned from the Seattle Art Museum. http://www1.seattleartmuseum.org/deaccessions.

MANUSCRIPT COLLECTIONS

"Bernier d'Archet [famille]." 1755–85. Papiers de famille d'Ancien Régime. FR/FR-AD078/E 112. Archives départementales des Yvelines.

"Comptes de la maison du roi, Monuments Historiques." 1784–92 and 1730–91. K//505 and K//506. Archives nationales, Paris.

"Comptes de Madame du Barry." Eighteenth century. Français 8157. Bibliothèque nationale de France. Département des manuscrits. http://archivesetmanuscrits.bnf.fr/ark:/12148/cc567849/ca19918925, 5r.

"Dufort de Lorge (duchesse de)." Eighteenth century. Papiers de famille. E/SUP 523. Archives départementales des Yvelines, France.

"Gazette des atours d'été de Madame Elisabeth." Paris, 1792. AE/I/6/3: Armoire de fer; Carton n° 8: Louis XVI, Marie-Antoinette et Mme Elisabeth, Grands documents de l'histoire de France; Armoire de fer. Archives nationales, France.

Larrivée, Henry. 1777–86. Bibliothèque nationale de France, département Bibliothèque-musée de l'opéra, NLAS-256.

"Papiers Bourbon-Busset." Archives des particuliers émigrés ou condamnés pendant la Révolution, Première partie. 1776–87. T//265/4–8. Archives nationales, France.

"Papiers d'origine privée." 1776–87. T//265/3. Archives nationales, France.

SECONDARY SOURCES

Abler, Thomas S. *Hinterland Warriors and Military Dress: European Empires and Exotic Uniforms.* Oxford: Berg, 1999.

Ahmed, Leila. "Western Ethnocentrism and Perceptions of the Harem." *Feminist Studies* 8 (Oct. 15, 1982): 521–34.

Aldis, Janet. *Madame Geoffrin: Her Salon and Her Times, 1750–1777.* London: Methuen & Company, 1906.

Alyea, Caroline Dinsmore. "Dress, Childhood and the Modern Body: The Body Politics of Children's Dress Reform in Eighteenth-Century Europe." PhD diss., Harvard Univ., 1997.

Ames, Frank. *The Kashmir Shawl and Its Indo-French Influence.* Woodbridge, UK: Antique Collectors' Club, 1997.

Andersen, Ellen. *Moden i 1700-årene: Danske dragter.* København: Nationalmuseet, 1977.

Apostolou, Irini. "L'Apparence extérieure de l'Oriental et son rôle dans la formation de l'image de l'autre par les voyageurs français au xviiie siècle." *Cahiers de la Méditerranée,* no. 66 (June 15, 2003): 181–200.

———. *L'Orientalisme des voyageurs français au XVIIIe siècle: Une Iconographie de l'Orient Méditerranéen.* Paris: Presses de l'Université Paris-Sorbonne, 2009.

Appadurai, Arjun. "Introduction: Commodities and the Politics of Value." In *The Social Life of Things: Commodities in Cultural Perspective,* edited by Arjun Appadurai, 3–63. Cambridge: Cambridge Univ. Press, 1986.

Aravamudan, Srinivas. *Enlightenment Orientalism: Resisting the Rise of the Novel.* Chicago: Univ. of Chicago Press, 2012.

Arizzoli-Clémentel, Pierre, and Xavier Salmon. *Marie-Antoinette: Galeries nationales du Grand Palais, Paris, 15 mars–30 juin 2008.* Paris: Réunion des musées nationaux, 2008.

Arnold, Janet. "The Cut and Construction of Women's Clothes in the Eighteenth Century." In *Revolution in Fashion: European Clothing, 1715–1815,* edited by Jean Starobinski, 126–34. New York: Abbeville Press, 1989.

———. "A Mantua c. 1708–9 Clive House Museum, College Hill, Shrewsbury." *Costume* 4, no. 1 (June 1, 1970): 26–31.

———. *Patterns of Fashion: Englishwomen's Dresses & Their Construction, c. 1660–1860.* New York: Drama Book Specialists, 1964.

———. *Patterns of Fashion: The Content, Cut, Construction and Context of Englishwomen's Dress c. 1720–1860.* 2nd ed. New York: School of Historical Dress, 2021.

———. *Patterns of Fashion 5: The Content, Cut, Construction and Context of Bodies, Stays, Hoops and Rumps c. 1595–1795.* London: School of Historical Dress, 2018.

Arnold, Janet, Sébastien Passot, Claire Thornton, and Jenny Tiramani. *Patterns of Fashion 6: The Content, Cut, Construction and Context of European Women's Dress c. 1695–1795.* London: School of Historical Dress, 2021.

Aschengreen, Cristina Piacenti, Syed Mohamad Albukhary, and Roberta Orsi Landini, eds. "The Costumes of the Islamic Peoples: Simple Shapes and Splendid Materials." In *Dress for the Body, Body for the Dress: When Islamic and Western Styles Meet,* 82–99. Kuala Lumpur: Islamic Arts Museum Malaysia, 2000.

———, eds. "Men's Dress, the Invention of the Tailored Shape." In *Dress for the Body, Body for the Dress: When Islamic and Western Styles Meet,* 62–71. Kuala Lumpur: Islamic Arts Museum Malaysia, 2000.

———, eds. "The Woman's Cuirass: From Outer to Under Wear." In *Dress for the Body, Body for the Dress: When Islamic and Western Styles Meet,* 72–81. Kuala Lumpur: Islamic Arts Museum Malaysia, 2000.

Ashelford, Jane. "'Colonial Livery' and the Chemise à la Reine, 1779–1784." *Costume* 52, no. 2 (2018): 217–39.

Avcıoğlu, Nebahat. *"Turquerie" and the Politics of Representation, 1728–1876.* Burlington, VT: Ashgate, 2011.

Baillio, Joseph. *Elisabeth Louise Vigée Le Brun, 1755–1842.* Fort Worth, TX: Kimbell Art Museum, 1982.

Baird, Ileana Popa. "Introduction: Peregrine Things: Rethinking the Global in Eighteenth-Century Studies." In *Eighteenth-Century Thing Theory in a Global Context: From Consumerism to Celebrity Culture,* edited by Christina Ionescu and Ileana Popa Baird, 1–16. Burlington, VT: Ashgate, 2013.

Baktir, Hasan. *The Representation of the Ottoman Orient in Eighteenth Century English Literature: Ottoman Society and Culture in Pseudo-Oriental Letters, Oriental Tales and Travel Literature.* New York: Columbia Univ. Press, 2010.

Barthes, Roland. *The Fashion System.* New York: Hill and Wang, 1983.

Baumgarten, Linda, John Watson, and Florine Carr. *Costume Close-up: Clothing Construction and Pattern, 1750–1790.* Williamsburg, VA: Colonial Williamsburg Foundation, in association with Quite Specific Media Group, 1999.

Beer, Esmond S. de. "King Charles II's Own Fashion: An Episode in Anglo-French Relations 1666–1670." *Journal of the Warburg Institute* 2, no. 2 (Oct. 1938): 105–15.

Belsey, Hugh. *Gainsborough's Beautiful Mrs Graham.* Edinburgh: National Gallery of Scotland, 2003.

Bendall, Sarah A. *Shaping Femininity: Foundation Garments, the Body and Women in Early Modern England.* New York: Bloomsbury Visual Arts, 2022.

Benhamou, Reed. "Fashion in the Mercure: From Human Foible to Female Failing." *Eighteenth-Century Studies* 31 (Fall 1997): 27–43.

Benoît, Fernand. *La Provence et le Comtat Venaissin: Arts et traditions populaires.* Avignon: Aubanel, 1975.

Berlanstein, Lenard R. *Daughters of Eve: A Cultural History of French Theater Women from the Old Regime to the Fin de Siècle.* Cambridge, MA: Harvard Univ. Press, 2001.

Bertrand, Colette. "'Le Monument du costume' de Rétif de La Bretonne." *Dix-Huitième Siècle. Aliments et Cuisine,* no. 15 (1983): 389–406.

Besleney, Zeynel Abidin. *The Circassian Diaspora in Turkey: A Political History.* New York: Routledge, 2014.

Bevilacqua, Alexander, and Helen Pfeifer. "Turquerie: Culture in Motion, 1650–1750." *Past & Present* 221, no. 1 (Nov. 2013): 75–118.

Biedrońska-Słota, Beata, and Maria Molenda. "The Emergence of a Polish National Dress and Its Perception." In *Dress and Cultural Difference in Early Modern Europe,* edited by Cornelia Aust, Denise Klein, and Thomas Weller, 113–36. European History Yearbook 20. Berlin: De Gruyter Oldenbourg, 2019.

Biernat, Anaïs. "Whalebone Stays and Corsets for Children from the Seventeenth to the Nineteenth Centuries." In *Fashioning the Body: An Intimate History of the Silhouette,* edited by Denis Bruna, 129–41. Published for Bard Graduate Center, Decorative Arts, Design History, Material Culture. New Haven, CT: Yale Univ. Press, 2015.

Bissonnette, Anne, Josée Chartrand, and Katelin Karbonik. "Dress & Historical Escapism: The Dress Research Exhibition Series, Part 1 of 3: Dress Artifacts & Curatorial Practices, A Virtual (and Evolving) Exhibition: The Chemise Dress." https://ales-cms.ales.ualberta.ca/clothingtextiles/dhe_chemise-dress/.

Bissonnette, Anne, and Sarah Nash. "The Re-Birth of Venus." *Dress* 41, no. 1 (May 2015): 1–20.

Blanc, Olivier. *Portraits de femmes: Artistes et modèles à l'époque de Marie-Antoinette.* Paris: Ed. Didier Carpentier, 2006.

Blum, Stella, ed. *Eighteenth-Century French Fashion Plates in Full Color: 64 Engravings from the "Galerie Des Modes," 1778–1787.* New York: Dover Publications, 1982.

Boer, Inge E., and Mieke Bal. *Disorienting Vision: Rereading Stereotypes in French Orientalist Texts and Images.* New York: Rodopi, 2004.

Bohanan, Donna. *Fashion beyond Versailles: Consumption and Design in Seventeenth-Century France.* Baton Rouge: Louisiana State Univ. Press, 2012.

Bolton, Andrew. *AngloMania: Tradition and Transgression in British Fashion.* New York: Metropolitan Museum of Art, 2006.

Bonnaud, M. Louis. "La Mode féminine à Limoges il y a deux cents ans." *Bulletin de la Société archéologique et historique du Limousan* 118 (1990): 202–7.

Borchard, George E. "Reflections on the Polish Nobleman's Attire in the Sarmatian Tradition." *Costume* 4, no. 1 (June 1, 1970): 13–22.

Borderioux, Xénia. "La Presse française, miroir des 'modes russes' à Paris." *Revue des études slaves* 86, no. 3 (Nov. 30, 2015): 267–90.

Boucher, François. *20,000 Years of Fashion: The History of Costume and Personal Adornment.* Translated by Yvonne Deslandres. New York: Harry N. Abrams, 1967.

Boulaire, Vanessa. "La Rencontre de l'Autre dans le théâtre français de la Saint-Barthélémy à la Révolution française: Enjeux politiques et philosophique (XVIIème–XVIIIème siècles)." Musique, musicologie et arts de la scène, Université de la Sorbonne nouvelle—Paris III, 2013.

Brace, Laura. "Rousseau, Maternity and the Politics of Emptiness." *Polity* 39, no. 3 (2007): 361–83.

Breskin, Isabel. "'On the Periphery of a Greater World': John Singleton Copley's Turquerie Portraits." *Winterthur Portfolio* 36, no. 2/3 (2001): 97–123.

Breward, Christopher. *The Culture of Fashion: A New History of Fashionable Dress.* Studies in Design and Material Culture. Manchester: Manchester Univ. Press, 1995.

Bruna, Denis. "Puffed out Chests and Paunched Bellies: The Broadening of Men's Bodies from the Fourteenth to the Sixteenth Century." In *Fashioning the Body: An Intimate History of the Silhouette,* edited by Denis Bruna, 39–45. Published for Bard Graduate Center, Decorative Arts, Design History, Material Culture. New Haven, CT: Yale Univ. Press, 2015.

Bryant, Margaret M. "Names and Terms Used in the Fashion World." *American Speech* 45, no. 3/4 (1970): 168–94.

Buck, Anne. *Dress in Eighteenth-Century England.* New York: Holmes & Meier, 1979.

Bull, Duncan. "The Artist." In *Jean-Baptiste Vanmour: An Eyewitness of the Tulip Era,* 25–40. Istanbul: Kocbank, 2003.

Cage, E. Claire. "The Sartorial Self: Neoclassical Fashion and Gender Identity in France, 1797–1804." *Eighteenth-Century Studies* 42, no. 2 (2009): 193–215.

Calefato, Patrizia. *The Clothed Body.* Oxford: Berg, 2004.

Calvi, Giulia. "Imperial Fashions: Cashmere Shawls between Istanbul, Paris, and Milan (Eighteenth and Nineteenth Centuries)." In *Dress and Cultural Difference in Early Modern Europe,* edited by Cornelia Aust, Denise Klein, and Thomas Weller, 159–74. Berlin: De Gruyter Oldenbourg, 2019.

Carlson, Marvin. "The Eighteenth-Century Pioneers in French Costume Reform." *Theatre Survey* 28, no. 1 (1987): 37–47.

Carrière, Charles, and Marcel Courdurié. "Un Sophisme économique. Marseille s'enrichit en achetant plus qu'elle ne vend. (Réflexions sur les mécanismes commerciaux levantins au XVIIIème siècle)." *Histoire, économie & société* 3, no. 1 (1984): 7–51.

Carson, Susannah. "L'Economique de la Mode: Costume, Conformity, and Consumerism in 'Le Mercure Galant.'" *Seventeenth-Century French Studies* 27 (Aug. 2005): 133–46.

Cavallaro, Dani, and Alexandra Warwick. *Fashioning the Frame: Boundaries, Dress and Body*. Oxford: Berg, 1998.

Çevik, Gülen. "Boudoirs and Harems: The Seductive Power of Sophas." *Journal of Interior Design* 43, no. 3 (2018): 25–41.

Chatenet-Calyste, Aurélie. "Pour paraître à la cour: les Habits de Marie-Fortunée d'Este, princesse de Conti (1731–1803)." *Apparence(s)*, no. 4 (Feb. 7, 2012). http://journals.openedition.org/apparences/1184.

———. "Une Consommation aristocratique et féminine à la fin du XVIIIe siècle: Marie-Fortunée d'Este, princesse de Conti (1731–1803)." Theses, Univ. de Limoges, 2010.

Chazin-Bennahum, Judith. *The Lure of Perfection: Fashion and Ballet, 1780–1830*. New York: Routledge, 2005.

Chrisman-Campbell, Kimberly. "L'Angleterre et la mode en Europe au XVIIIe siècle." In *Modes en miroir: la France et la Hollande au temps des Lumières: Musée Galliera, 28 avril–21 août 2005*, edited by Pascale Gorguet Ballesteros, 50–53. Paris: Paris musées, 2005.

———. *Fashion Victims: Dress at the Court of Louis XVI and Marie-Antoinette*. New Haven, CT: Yale Univ. Press, 2015.

———. "French Connections: Georgiana, Duchess of Devonshire, and the Anglo-French Fashion Exchange." *Dress* 31 (Jan. 2004): 3–14.

———. "Le Grand habit et la mode en France au XVIIIe siècle." In *Fastes de cour et cérémonies royales: le Costume de cour en Europe, 1650–1800*, edited by Pierre Arizzoli-Clémentel and Pascale Gorguet-Ballesteros, 222–25. Paris: Établissement public du musée et du domaine national de Versailles; Réunion des musées nationaux, 2009.

———. "Minister of Fashion: Marie-Jeanne 'Rose' Bertin, 1757–1813." PhD diss., Univ. of Aberdeen, 2002.

Çırakman, Aslı. *From the "Terror of the World" to the "Sick Man of Europe": European Images of Ottoman Empire and Society from the Sixteenth Century to the Nineteenth*. New York: P. Lang, 2002.

———. "From Tyranny to Despotism: The Enlightenment's Unenlightened Image of the Turks." *International Journal of Middle East Studies* 33, no. 1 (2001): 49–68.

Clay, Lauren R. *Stagestruck: The Business of Theater in Eighteenth-Century France and Its Colonies*. Ithaca, NY: Cornell Univ. Press, 2013.

Coller, Ian. "Rousseau's Turban: Entangled Encounters of Europe and Islam in the Age of Enlightenment." *Historical Reflections* 40, no. 2 (Summer 2014): 56–77.

Collins, Mary, and Joanna Jarvis. "The Great Leap from Earth to Heaven: The Evolution of Ballet and Costume in England and France in the Eighteenth Century." *Costume* 50, no. 2 (2016): 168–93.

Coquery, Natacha. "The Language of Success: Marketing and Distributing Semi-Luxury Goods in Eighteenth-Century Paris." *Journal of Design History* 17, no. 1 (2004): 71–89.

Coulomb, Clarisse. "L'Empire des modes: du grand habit à la cocarde: Livre-journal de Madame Eloffe 1787–1793." PhD diss., Univ. Paris 1, 1993.

Craik, Jennifer. "Exotic Narratives in Fashion: The Impact of Motifs of Exotica on Fashion Design and Fashionable Identities." In *Modern Fashion Traditions: Negotiating Tradition and Modernity through Fashion*, edited by M. Angela Jansen and Jennifer Craik, 97–118. London: Bloomsbury Academic, 2018.

Crane, Diana. *Fashion and Its Social Agendas: Class, Gender, and Identity in Clothing*. Chicago: Univ. of Chicago Press, 2000.

Crowe, Yolande. "Le Manteau arménien de Jean-Jacques Rousseau." In *Festschrift en honneur de Dickran Kouymjian*. Fresno, CA: Rousseau Studies, 2007. http://rousseaustudies.free.fr/articlemanteauarmenien.html.

Crowley, John E. *The Invention of Comfort: Sensibilities & Design in Early Modern Britain & Early America*. Baltimore: Johns Hopkins Univ. Press, 2001.

Crowston, Clare. "The Queen and Her 'Minister of Fashion': Gender, Credit and Politics in Pre-Revolutionary France." *Gender & History* 14, no. 1 (2002): 92–116.

Crowston, Clare Haru. *Fabricating Women: The Seamstresses of Old Regime France, 1675–1791*. Durham, NC: Duke Univ. Press, 2001.

Culcasi, Karen. "Constructing and Naturalizing the Middle East." *Geographical Review* 100, no. 4 (2010): 583–97.

Cunnington, C. Willett, and Phillis Cunnington. *Handbook of English Costume in the Eighteenth Century*. Boston: Plays, 1972.

Cunningham, Patricia A. "Eighteenth Century Nightgowns: The Gentleman's Robe in Art and Fashion." *Dress* 10, no. 1 (1984): 2–11.

Dal-Prà, Patricia. "Rapport d'intervention de restauration sur la robe à la turque appartenant au musée de la Toile de Jouy." Jouy-en-Josas, France: Musée de la Toile de Jouy, 2015.

Dandois, Nadège. "Les Journaux de mode en France (1785–1792)." Mémoire de Master 1 "Sciences humaines et sociales." Grenoble, France: Univ. Pierre Mendès-France, 2014.

Darrow, Margaret H. "French Noblewomen and the New Domesticity, 1750–1850." *Feminist Studies* 5, no. 1 (Spring 1979): 41–65.

Davis, Fred. *Fashion, Culture, and Identity*. Chicago: Univ. of Chicago Press, 1992.

DeJean, Joan E. *The Age of Comfort: When Paris Discovered*

Casual—and the Modern Home Began. New York: Bloomsbury, 2009.

Delaney, Carol. "Untangling the Meanings of Hair in Turkish Society." *Anthropological Quarterly* 67, no. 4 (Oct. 1994): 159–72.

Delon, Michel. "The Ancien Régime of the Body." In *Fashioning the Body: An Intimate History of the Silhouette,* edited by Denis Bruna, 89–93. Published for Bard Graduate Center, Decorative Arts, Design History, Material Culture by Yale Univ. Press, 2015.

Delpierre, Madeleine. *Dress in France in the Eighteenth Century.* Translated by Caroline Beamish. New Haven, CT: Yale Univ. Press, 1997.

———. "Marie-Antoinette, reine de la mode." *Versailles: Revue des Société Suisse des Amis de Versailles,* no. 59 (1975): 37–46.

———. "Robes de grande parure du temps de Louis XVI." *Bulletin du Musée Carnavalet,* no. 1 (June 1966): 2–19.

Delpierre, Madeleine, and Arnauld Pontier, eds. *Modes et révolutions 1780–1804.* Paris: Paris-Musées, 1989.

Denny, Walter B. "Images of Turks and the European Imagination." In *Court and Conquest: Ottoman Origins and the Design for Handel's Tamerlano at the Glimmerglass Opera,* edited by Judy Levin, 3–18. Kent, OH: Kent State Univ. Museum, 1998.

Dobie, Madeleine. *Trading Places: Colonization and Slavery in Eighteenth-Century French Culture.* Ithaca, NY: Cornell Univ. Press, 2010.

Dotlačilová, Petra. "Costume in the Time of Reforms: Louis-René Boquet Designing Eighteenth-Century Ballet and Opera." PhD diss., Stockholm Univ., 2020.

Dowdell, Carolyn Anne. "The Multiple Lives of Clothes: Alteration and Reuse of Women's Eighteenth-Century Apparel in England." PhD diss., Queen's Univ., 2015.

———. "'No Small Share of Ingenuity': An Object-Oriented Analysis of Eighteenth-Century English Dressmaking." *Costume* 55, no. 2 (2021): 186–211.

"Drottning Marie Antoinette av Frankrike med två av sina barn promenerande i Trianons park." Nationalmuseum, Stockholm. https://digitaltmuseum.se/021046508049/drottning-marie-antoinette-av-frankrike-med-tva-av-sina-barn-promenerande.

Dyer, Serena. *Material Lives: Women Makers and Consumer Culture in the 18th Century.* London: Bloomsbury Publishing, 2021.

Egler, Zelda, Pascale Gorguet Ballesteros, and Edward Maeder. "L'Orient et la mode en Europe au temps des Lumières." In *Modes en miroir: la France et la Hollande au temps des Lumières: Musée Galliera, 28 avril–21 août 2005,* edited by Pascale Gorguet Ballesteros, 62–64. Paris: Paris musées, 2005.

Eicher, Joanne B., and Mary E. Higgins Roach. "Definition and Classification of Dress: Implications for Analysis of Gender Roles." In *Dress and Gender: Making and Meaning,* edited by Ruth Barnes and Joanne B. Eicher, 8–28. New York: Berg Publishers, Inc., 1992.

Eicher, Joanne Bubolz, and Barbara Sumberg. "World Fashion, Ethnic, and National Dress." In *Dress and Ethnicity: Change across Space and Time,* 295–306. Berg Ethnic Identities Series. Oxford: Berg, 1995.

Ellington, Tameka N. "Black Hair and Cornrows." In *Berg Encyclopedia of World Dress and Fashion: Global Perspectives,* 1. Oxford: Berg, 2010.

Ellison, Charles Edward. "Rousseau and the Modern City: The Politics of Speech and Dress." *Political Theory* 13, no. 4 (1988): 497–533.

Elmarsafy, Ziad. "Submission, Seduction, and State Propaganda in Favart's Soliman II, Ou Les Trois Sultanes." *French Forum* 26, no. 3 (Sept. 1, 2001): 13–26.

Eysturlid, Lee W. "'Where Everything Is Weighed in the Scales of Material Interest': Anglo-Turkish Trade, Piracy, and Diplomacy in the Mediterranean During the Jacobean Period." *Journal of European Economic History* 22, no. 3 (Winter 1993): 613–25.

Fairchilds, Cissie. "Fashion and Freedom in the French Revolution." *Continuity & Change* 15, no. 3 (Dec. 2000): 419–33.

———. "The Production and Marketing of Populuxe Goods in Eighteenth-Century Paris." In *Consumption and the World of Goods,* edited by John Brewer and Roy Porter, 228–48. London: Routledge, 1993.

Faroqhi, Suraiya. "Women, Wealth and Textiles in 1730s Bursa." In *Living the Good Life: Consumption in the Qing and Ottoman Empires of the Eighteenth Century,* edited by Elif Akçetin and Suraiya Faroqhi, 213–35. Boston: Brill, 2017.

Fennetaux, Ariane. "Du Boudoir au salon: l'Intimité et la mode en Europe au XVIIIe siècle." In *Modes en miroir: la France et la Hollande au temps des Lumières: Musée Galliera, 28 avril–21 août 2005,* edited by Pascale Gorguet Ballesteros, 72–74. Paris: Paris musées, 2005.

———. "'J'étais pittoresque et beau': de quelques paradoxes de la robe de chambre." In *À la mode: l'art de paraître au 18e siècle,* 267–70. Gand: Snoek, 2021.

Figal, Sara. "The Caucasian Slave Race: Beautiful Circassians and the Hybrid Origin of European Identity." In *Reproduction, Race, and Gender in Philosophy and the Early Life Sciences,* edited by Susanne Lettow, 163–86. Albany: State Univ. of New York Press, 2014.

Figeac, Michel. *La Douceur des Lumières: Noblesse et art de vivre en Guyenne au XVIIIe siècle.* Bordeaux: Mollat, 2001.

Font, Auguste. *Favart: l'Opéra comique et la comédie-vaudeville aux XVIIe et XVIIIe siècles.* Paris: Fischbacher, 1894.

Fordham, Douglas. "Allan Ramsay's Enlightenment: Or, Hume and the Patronizing Portrait." *Art Bulletin* 88, no. 3 (Sept. 2006): 508–24.

Foster, Shirley. "Colonialism and Gender in the East: Representations of the Harem in the Writings of Women Travellers." *The Yearbook of English Studies* 34 (2004): 6–17.

Foster, Susan Leigh. *Choreography & Narrative: Ballet's Staging of Story and Desire*. Bloomington: Indiana Univ. Press, 1996.

Fraser, Antonia. *Marie Antoinette: The Journey*. New York: Anchor Books, 2002.

Fraser, Elisabeth. "The Color of the Orient: On Ottoman Costume Albums, European Print Culture, and Cross-Cultural Exchange." In *Visual Typologies from the Early Modern to the Contemporary: Local Contexts and Global Practices*, edited by Tara Zanardi and Lynda Klich, 45–59. New York: Routledge, 2019.

Gaudriault, Raymond. *Répertoire de la gravure de mode française des origines à 1815*. Paris: Promodis-Editions du Cercle de la librairie, 1988.

Gauffin, Axel. "A Propos de l'exposition de l'art Suedois à Paris." *La Revue d'Art* 56 (1929): 49–70.

Geczy, Adam. *Fashion and Orientalism: Dress, Textiles and Culture from the 17th to the 21st Century*. New York: Bloomsbury Academic, 2013.

Germann, Jennifer G. *Picturing Marie Leszczinska (1703–1768): Representing Queenship in Eighteenth-Century France*. Farnham, UK: Routledge, 2017.

Giorgi, Arianna. "La Moda de la robe à la polonaise. Memoria de una historia artística." *Imafronte*, no. 19–20 (2008): 95–103.

Göçek, Fatma Müge. *East Encounters West: France and the Ottoman Empire in the Eighteenth Century*. New York: Oxford Univ. Press, 1987.

Goodman, Dena. *The Republic of Letters: A Cultural History of the French Enlightenment*. Ithaca, NY: Cornell Univ. Press, 1996.

Goodman, Sarah. "Devil in a White Dress: Marie-Antoinette and the Fashioning of a Scandal." MA thesis, San Jose State Univ., 2017.

Gorguet-Ballesteros, Pascale. "Caractériser le costume de cour: propositions." In *Fastes de cour et cérémonies royales: le costume de cour en Europe, 1650–1800*, edited by Pierre Arizzoli-Clémentel and Pascale Gorguet-Ballesteros, 54–69. Paris: Établissement public du musée et du domaine national de Versailles; Réunion des musées nationaux, 2009.

———. "De la Robe chemise à la robe droite: Variations picturales autour du blanc." In *À la mode: l'art de paraître au 18e siècle*, 219–28. Gand: Snoek, 2021.

———. "La Double vie de la robe volante, 1700–1735." In *À la mode: l'art de paraître au 18e siècle*, 193–99. Gand: Snoek, 2021.

———. "Exchanging Looks: Codes of Dress at Versailles." In *Visitors to Versailles: From Louis XIV to the French Revolution*, edited by Daniëlle Kisluk-Grosheide and Bertrand Rondot, 56–67. New York: Metropolitan Museum of Art, 2018.

———. "Petite étude du grand habit à travers les mémoires quittancés de la comtesse d'Artois (1773–1780)." In *Se vêtir à la Cour en Europe (1400–1815)*, edited by Isabelle Paresys and Natacha Coquery, 197–212. Villeneuve d'Ascq: Univ. Lille 3–Charles-de-Gaulle, 2011.

Grehan, James. *Everyday Life and Consumer Culture in Eighteenth-Century Damascus*. Seattle: Univ. of Washington Press, 2007.

Grélé, Denis D. "Et si l'habit faisait l'utopie: Concevior un vêtement idéal au XVIIIe siècle." In *Proceedings of the Western Society for French History*, 35:107–26. Ann Arbor: MI: Scholarly Publishing Office, Univ. of Michigan Library, 2007.

Grieder, Josephine. *Anglomania in France, 1740–1789: Fact, Fiction, and Political Discourse*. Genève: Librairie Droz, 1985.

Gruder, Vivan R. "The Question of Marie-Antoinette: The Queen and Public Opinion Before the Revolution." *French History* 16, no. 3 (2002): 269–98.

Grüßhaber, Gerhard. *The German Spirit in the Ottoman and Turkish Army, 1908-1938: A History of Military Knowledge Transfer*. Boston: Walter de Gruyter GmbH, 2018.

Gruyer, François-Anatole. *Chantilly: les Portraits de Carmontelle*. Paris: Plon-Nourrit et cie, 1902.

Hamilton, Paul. *The Oxford Handbook of European Romanticism*. Oxford: Oxford Univ. Press, 2016.

Hammerbeck, David. "Les Trois Sultanes: French Enlightenment Comedy and the Veil." *Journal of Dramatic Theory and Criticism* 18, no. 2 (Spring 2004): 55–78.

Harris, Carolyn. *Queenship and Revolution in Early Modern Europe: Henrietta Maria and Marie Antoinette*. Basingstoke, UK: Springer, 2016.

Harris, Jennifer. "The Red Cap of Liberty: A Study of Dress Worn by French Revolutionary Partisans, 1789–94." *Eighteenth-Century Studies* 14, no. 3 (Winter 1981): 283–312.

Hart, Avril. "The Mantua: Its Evolution and Fashionable Significance in the Seventeenth and Eighteenth Centuries." In *Defining Dress: Dress as Object, Meaning, and Identity*, edited by Amy De La Haye and Elizabeth Wilson, 93–103. Manchester: Manchester Univ. Press, 1999.

Hart, Avril, Leonie Davis, Susan North, and Richard Davis. *Historical Fashion in Detail: The 17th and 18th Centuries*. London: V&A Publications, 2007.

Harvey, David Allen. *The French Enlightenment and Its Others: The Mandarin, the Savage, and the Invention of the Human Sciences*. New York: Palgrave Macmillan, 2012.

Hayward, Maria. "Clothing." In *The Routledge Handbook of Material Culture in Early Modern Europe*, edited by Tara Hamling, Catherine Richardson, and David Gaimster, 172–84. London: Routledge, 2017.

Heller-Greenman, Bernadine. "Moreau le Jeune and the Monument du Costume." *Athanor* 20 (2002): 67–75.

Herbette, Maurice. *Une Ambassade turque sous le directoire.* Paris: Perrin et cie, 1902.

Hill, June. "The Influences of Ottoman Culture." In *Encyclopedia of World Dress and Fashion,* edited by Joanne Bubolz Eicher, 5:66–68. Oxford: Oxford Univ. Press, 2010.

Hiner, Susan. *Accessories to Modernity: Fashion and the Feminine in Nineteenth-Century France.* Philadelphia: Univ. of Pennsylvania Press, Project MUSE, 2010.

———. "Lust for 'Luxe': 'Cashmere Fever' in Nineteenth-Century France." *Journal for Early Modern Cultural Studies* 5, no. 1 (2005): 76–98.

Hollander, Anne. *Seeing through Clothes.* New York: Viking Press, 1978.

Hollander, Martha. "Vermeer's Robe: Costume, Commerce, and Fantasy in the Early Modern Netherlands." *Dutch Crossing: A Journal of Low Countries Studies* 35, no. 2 (July 1, 2011): 177–95.

Hosford, Desmond. "The Queen's Hair: Marie-Antoinette, Politics, and DNA." *Eighteenth-Century Studies* 38, no. 1 (Fall 2004): 183–200.

Hughes, Brittany Lynne. "Fashioning the Other: Sartorial Turquerie in Ancien Régime France." MA thesis, Univ. of Colorado, 2020.

Hunt, Lynn. "Freedom of Dress in Revolutionary France." In *From the Royal to the Republican Body: Incorporating the Political in Seventeenth- and Eighteenth-Century France,* edited by Sara E. Melzer and Kathryn Norberg, 224–49. Berkeley: Univ. of California Press, 1998.

Hyde, Melissa. "Notes on a Scandal: The Critical Fortunes and Misfortunes of Adolf Ulrik Wertmüller." Presented at the Theorizing Early Modern Studies Collaborative, Univ. of Minnesota, Apr. 12, 2012. http://tems.umn.edu/2011-2012.php.

Hyde, Melissa Lee. "Beautés rivales: les portraits de Mme Du Barry et de la Reine Marie-Antoinette." In *Cultures de cour, Cultures du corps,* edited by Catherine Lanoe and Mathieu Da Vinha, 185–205. Paris: Presses de l'Université Paris-Sorbonne & Centre de recherche du Chateau de Versailles, 2011.

———. "Marie-Antoinette, Wertmüller, and Scandal of the Garden Variety: Portraying the Queen at Petit Trianon." In *Disciples of Flora: Gardens in History and Culture,* edited by Victoria Emma Pagan, Judith W. Page, and Brigitte Weltman-Aron, 68–91. Newcastle upon Tyne: Cambridge Scholars Publishing, 2015.

Inal, Onur. "Women's Fashions in Transition: Ottoman Borderlands and the Anglo-Ottoman Exchange of Costumes." *Journal of World History* 22, no. 2 (June 2011): 243–72.

Ipek, Selin. "Ottoman Fabrics During the 18th and 19th Centuries." *Textile Society of America Symposium Proceedings,* 2012. http://digitalcommons.unl.edu/tsaconf/697.

Israel, Jonathan I. *Democratic Enlightenment: Philosophy, Revolution, and Human Rights 1750–1790.* New York: Oxford Univ. Press, 2011.

———. *Radical Enlightenment: Philosophy and the Making of Modernity 1650–1750.* Oxford: Oxford Univ. Press, 2003.

Jallut, Marguerite. *Marie Antoinette and Her Painters.* Paris: A Noyer, 1955.

James-Sarazin, Ariane, and Régis Lapasin. "Marie-Antoinette, prescriptrice de tendances ou 'fashion victim'?" In *Gazette des atours de Marie-Antoinette: Garde-robe des atours de la reine: Gazette pour l'année 1782,* 5–32. Paris: Réunion des musées nationaux: Archives nationales, 2006.

Jansen, M. Angela. *Moroccan Fashion: Design, Tradition and Modernity.* London: Bloomsbury Academic, 2015.

Jasienski, Adam. "A Savage Magnificence: Ottomanizing Fashion and the Politics of Display in Early Modern East-Central Europe." *Muqarnas: An Annual on the Visual Cultures of the Islamic World* 31 (2014): 173–205.

Jirousek, Charlotte. "The Kaftan and Its Origins." In *Encyclopedia of World Dress and Fashion,* edited by Joanne Bubolz Eicher, 5:134–38. Oxford: Oxford Univ. Press, 2010.

———. "More Than Oriental Splendor: European and Ottoman Headgear, 1380–1580." *Dress* 22, no. 1 (1995): 22–33.

———. *Ottoman Dress and Design in the West: A Visual History of Cultural Exchange.* Bloomington: Indiana Univ. Press, 2019.

———. "Ottoman Influences in Western Dress." In *Ottoman Costumes: From Textile to Identity,* edited by Suraiya Faroqhi and Christoph K Neumann, 231–51. İstanbul: Eren, 2004.

Jones, Jennifer M. "Coquettes and Grisettes: Women Buying and Selling in Ancien Régime Paris." In *The Sex of Things: Gender and Consumption in Historical Perspective,* edited by Ellen Furlough and Victoria De Grazia, 25–53. Berkeley: Univ. of California Press, 1996.

———. "Repackaging Rousseau: Femininity and Fashion in Old Regime France." *French Historical Studies* 18 (Fall 1994): 939–67.

———. *Sexing la Mode: Gender, Fashion and Commercial Culture in Old Regime France.* New York: Berg, 2004.

Joubin, Rebecca. "Islam and the Arabs through the Eyes of the Encyclopedie: The 'Other' as a Case of French Cultural Self-Criticism." *International Journal of Middle East Studies* 32, no. 2 (May 2000): 197.

Jullien, Adolphe. *The Opera before the Revolution.* London: Boussard, Valadon & Co., 1888.

Juranek, Gabriela. *Przemiany "robe en chemise" i "fourreau" we Francji w latach 1785–1794.* Łódź: ArchaeGraph Wydawnictwo Naukowe, 2018.

Kahf, Mohja. *Western Representations of the Muslim Woman from Termagant to Odalisque.* Austin: Univ. of Texas Press, 1999.

Kaiser, Susan B. *Fashion and Cultural Studies.* New York: Berg, 2012.

Kaiser, Thomas. "The Evil Empire? The Debate on Turkish Despotism in Eighteenth-Century French Political Culture." *Journal of Modern History* 72, no. 1 (Mar. 2000): 6.

Kallander, Amy Aisen. *Women, Gender, and the Palace Households in Ottoman Tunisia.* Austin: Univ. of Texas Press, 2013.

Kawamura, Yuniya, and Jung-Whan Marc de Jong, eds. *Cultural Appropriation in Fashion and Entertainment.* London: Bloomsbury, 2022.

Kidwell, Claudia Brush. "Are Those Clothes Real? Transforming the Way Eighteenth-Century Portraits Are Studied." *Dress (Costume Society of America)* 24 (Nov. 1997): 3–15.

Kirillova, Ekaterina. "Tailleurs d'habits et couturières à Reims en 1716. Une étude de cas pour l'histoire sociale." *Histoire, Economie et Société*, no. 1 (Mar. 2021): 86–99.

Kirkness, W. John. *Le Français du Théâtre italien d'après le Recueil de Gherardi, 1681-1697. Contribution à l'étude du vocabulaire français à la fin du 17e siècle.* Genève: Droz, 1971.

Kleinert, Annemarie. "La Révolution et le premier journal illustré paru en France (1785–1793)." *Dix-huitième siècle: Montesquieu et la révolution*, no. 21 (1989): 285–309.

Knauer, Elfriede R. "Toward a History of the Sleeved Coat: A Study of the Impact of an Ancient Eastern Garment on the West." *Expedition* 21, no. 1 (Oct. 15, 1978): 18–36.

Koç, Fatma, and Emine Koca. "The Westernzation Process in Ottoman Women's Garments: 18th Century–20th Century." *Asian Journal of Women's Studies* 13, no. 4 (2007): 57–84, 92.

König, Anna. "Glossy Words: An Analysis of Fashion Writing in British Vogue." *Fashion Theory* 10, no. 1–2 (2006): 205–24.

Konuk, Kader. "Ethnomasquerade in Ottoman-European Encounters: Reenacting Lady Mary Wortley Montagu." *Criticism* 46, no. 3 (Summer 2004): 393–414.

Korshunova, Tamara. *The Art of Costume in Russia: 18th to Early 20th Century.* Leningrad: Aurora Art Publishers, 1983.

Korchounova, Tamara, and Nina Tarassova. "La Mode française et le costume de cour dans la Russie du XVIIIe siècle." In *Fastes de cour et cérémonies royales: le costume de cour en Europe, 1650–1800*, edited by Pascale Gorguet-Ballesteros and Pierre Arizzoli-Clémentel, 202–11. Paris: Réunion des musées nationaux, 2009.

Kuchta, David. *The Three-Piece Suit and Modern Masculinity: England, 1550–1850.* Berkeley: Univ. of California Press, 2002.

Kugler, Emily M. N. *Sway of the Ottoman Empire on English Identity in the Long Eighteenth Century.* Leiden: Brill, 2012.

Kurz, Otto. "Pictorial Records of Favart's Comedy 'Les Trois Sultanes.'" In *Etudes d'art français offertes à Charles Sterling,* edited by Albert Châtelet and Nicole Reynaud, 311–17. Paris: Presse Universitaires de France, 1975.

Lajer-Burcharth, Ewa. "Fleshing out the Revolution." In *Classic and Modern Writings on Fashion.* Oxford: Berg, 2009. http://dx.doi.org.jpllnet.sfsu.edu/10.5040/9781847887153.v2-0052.

Landini, Roberta Orsi. "Dress for the Body, Body for the Dress." In *Dress for the Body, Body for the Dress: When Islamic and Western Styles Meet,* edited by Cristina Piacenti Aschengreen, Syed Mohamad Albukhary, and Roberta Orsi Landini, 16–28. Kuala Lumpur: Islamic Arts Museum Malaysia, 2000.

Landini, Roberta Orsi, and Bruna Niccoli. *Moda a Firenze, 1540–1580: lo stile di Eleonora di Toledo e la sua influenza.* Florence: Pagliai Polistampa, 2005.

Landweber, Julia. "Celebrating Identity: Charting the History of Turkish Masquerade in Early Modern France." *Romance Studies* 23, no. 3 (Nov. 2005): 175–89.

———. "How Can One Be Turkish? French Responses to Two Ottoman Embassies." In *Europa und die Türkei im 18. Jahrhundert = Europe and Turkey in the 18th Century,* edited by Barbara Schmidt-Haberkamp, 403–16. Bonn: Bonn Univ. Press, 2011.

———. "'This Marvelous Bean': Adopting Coffee into Old Regime French Culture and Diet." *French Historical Studies* 38, no. 2 (2015): 193–223.

———. "Turkish Delight: The Eighteenth-Century Market in 'Turqueries' and the Commercialization of Identity in France." *Proceedings of the Western Society for French History* 30 (Jan. 2002): 202–11.

Larkin, T. Lawrence. "Je ne suis plus la reine, je suis moi': Marie-Antoinette at the Salon of 1783." *Aurora, The Journal of the History of Art* 4 (Jan. 1, 2003): 109–34.

Larkin, Todd Lawrence. "Marie-Antoinette and Her Portraits: The Politics of Queenly Self-Imaging in Late Eighteenth-Century France." PhD diss., Univ. of California–Santa Barbara, 2000.

Lasic, Barbara. "Ethnicity." In *A Cultural History of Dress and Fashion in the Age of Enlightenment,* edited by Peter McNeil, 139–60. London: Bloomsbury Academic, 2017.

Lazaro, David E., and Patricia Campbell Warner. "All-Over Pleated Bodice: Dressmaking in Transition, 1780–1805." *Dress* 31 (Jan. 2004): 15–24.

Leclant, Jean. "Le Café et les cafés à Paris (1644–1693)." *Annales. Histoire, Sciences Sociales* 6, no. 1 (Mar. 1951): 1–14.

Leclerq, Jean-Paul. "Sur la garde-robe de Marie Leczinska et de Marie Antoinette." *L'Oeil: Magazine International d'art,* no. Jan.-Feb. (1996): 30–39.

Leeds-Hurwitz, Wendy. *Semiotics and Communication: Signs, Codes, Cultures.* New York: Routledge, 1993.

Lehnert, Gertrud. "Des 'Robes à la turque' et autres orientalismes à la mode." In *Les Mondes coloniaux à Paris au*

XVIIIe siècle. Circulation et enchevêtrement des savoirs, 183–210. Paris: Karthala Editions, 2010.

Leloir, Maurice. *Histoire du costume de l'Antiquité à 1914*. Vol. 11, *Epoque Louis XV, 1725 à 1774*. Paris: H. Ernst, 1938.

———. *Histoire du costume de l'Antiquité à 1914*. Vol. 12, *Epoque Louis XVI et révolution, 1775-1795*. Paris: Henri, 1949.

Lemire, Beverly. "Fashioning Global Trade: Indian Textiles, Gender Meanings and European Consumers, 1500–1800." In *How India Clothed the World: The World of South Asian Textiles, 1500–1850*, edited by Giorgio Riello and Tirthankar Roy, 365–89. Boston: Brill, 2009.

Lemire, Beverly, and Giorgio Riello. "East & West: Textiles and Fashion in Early Modern Europe." *Journal of Social History* 41, no. 4 (Summer 2008): 887–916.

Lenotre, G. *Mémoires et souvenirs sur la Révolution et l'Empire: Le Tribunal Révolutionnaire (1793-1795)*. Paris: Perrin et cie, 1910.

Lévi-Strauss, Monique. *The Cashmere Shawl*. New York: Harry N. Abrams, 1988.

Lewis, Reina. *Rethinking Orientalism: Women, Travel, and the Ottoman Harem*. New Brunswick, NJ: Rutgers Univ. Press, 2004.

Lilti, Antoine. *The World of the Salons: Sociability and Worldliness in Eighteenth-Century Paris*. Oxford: Oxford Univ. Press, 2015.

Lister, Jenny. "La Mantua." In *Modes en miroir: la France et la Hollande au temps des Lumières: Musée Galliera, 28 avril–21 août 2005*, edited by Pascale Gorguet Ballesteros, 58–59. Paris: Paris musées, 2005.

Louis, Abel A. *Hommes en noir, femmes en blanc?: La culture des apparences à l'épreuve du système esclavagiste en Martinique—(1765-1848)*. Paris: L'Harmattan, 2020.

Lubar, Stephen, and David W. Kingery. "Introduction." In *History from Things: Essays on Material Culture*, edited by Stephen Lubar and David W. Kingery, viii-xvii. Washington, DC: Smithsonian Institution, 2013.

Lubrich, Naomi. "The Little White Dress: Politics and Polyvalence in Revolutionary France." *Fashion Theory: The Journal of Dress, Body & Culture* 20, no. 3 (June 2016): 273–96.

Luebbers, Leslie. "Documenting the Invisible: European Images of Ottoman Women, 1577–1867." *Print Collector's Newsletter* 24 (Apr. 3, 1993): 1–7.

Lundberg, Gunnar W. *Le Peintre suédois, Adolf Ulrik Wertmüller à Lyon, 1779-1781*. Lyon: Impr. Audin, 1972.

Mackinney-Valentin, Maria. *Fashioning Identity: Status Ambivalence in Contemporary Fashion*. London: Bloomsbury Academic, 2017.

Maillard, Pascale. "Contributions à l'histoire du costume dans la noblesse parisienne à la fin du XVIIIe siècle." Maîtrise, Université Paris 1, 1979.

Mansel, Philip. *Dressed to Rule: Royal and Court Costume from Louis XIV to Elizabeth II*. New Haven, CT: Yale Univ. Press, 2005.

Maquet, Jacques. "Objects as Instruments, Objects as Signs." In *History from Things: Essays on Material Culture*, edited by Stephen Lubar and David W. Kingery, 30–40. Washington, DC: Smithsonian Institution, 2013.

Marcketti, Sara B., and Elena E. Karpova. *The Dangers of Fashion: Towards Ethical and Sustainable Solutions*. London: Bloomsbury Publishing, 2020.

Marly, Diana de. "King Charles II's Own Fashion: The Theatrical Origins of the English Vest." *Journal of the Warburg and Courtauld Institutes* 37 (1974): 378–82.

Marschner, Joanna. "Ceremonial Dress: Great Britain Meets Poland." In *Crossroads of Costume and Textiles in Poland: Papers from the International Conference of the ICOM Costume Committee at the National Museum in Cracow, September 28-October 4, 2003*, edited by Beata Biedrońska-Słotowa, 11–14. Cracow: NM, 2005.

Martin, Meredith. *Dairy Queens: The Politics of Pastoral Architecture from Catherine de' Medici to Marie-Antoinette*. Cambridge, MA: Harvard Univ. Press, 2011.

———. "Tipu Sultan's Ambassadors at Saint-Cloud: Indomania and Anglophobia in Pre-Revolutionary Paris." *West 86th: A Journal of Decorative Arts, Design History, and Material Culture* 21, no. 1 (2014): 37–68.

Martin, Morag. "French Harems: Images of the Orient in Cosmetic Advertisements, 1750–1815." *Proceedings of the Western Society for French History* 31 (Jan. 2003): 125–37.

Martin, Richard Harrison. *The Ceaseless Century: 300 Years of Eighteenth-Century Costume*. New York: Metropolitan Museum of Art, 1998.

Martin, Richard, and Harold Koda. *Orientalism: Visions of the East in Western Dress*. New York: Metropolitan Museum of Art, 1994.

Maskiell, Michelle. "Consuming Kashmir: Shawls and Empires, 1500–2000." *Journal of World History* 13, no. 1 (2002): 27–65.

Matossian, Chaké. *"Et je ne portai plus d'autre habit": Rousseau l'Arménien*. Geneva: Droz, 2014.

Mayer, Tara. "Cultural Cross-Dressing: Posing and Performance in Orientalist Portraits." *Journal of the Royal Asiatic Society* 22, no. 2 (Apr. 2012): 281–98.

McCabe, Ina Baghdiantz. *Orientalism in Early Modern France: Eurasian Trade, Exoticism, and the Ancien Régime*. Oxford: Berg, 2008.

McNeil, Peter. "Introduction." In *A Cultural History of Dress and Fashion in the Age of Enlightenment*, edited by Peter McNeil, 1–21. London: Bloomsbury Publishing, 2018.

Mele, Flora. *Le Théâtre de Charles-Simon Favart: Histoire et inventaire des manuscrits*. Paris: Champion, 2010.

Melman, Billie. *Women's Orients—English Women and the Middle East, 1718-1918: Sexuality, Religion, and Work.* Ann Arbor: Univ. of Michigan Press, 1992.

Micklewright, Nancy. "Ottoman Dress." In *Encyclopedia of World Dress and Fashion,* edited by Joanne Bubolz Eicher, 5:126–33. Oxford: Oxford Univ. Press, 2010.

Miller, Daniel. "Why Some Things Matter." In *Material Cultures: Why Some Things Matter,* edited by Daniel Miller, 3–21. London: Taylor & Francis Group, 1997.

Miller, Lesley Ellis. "An Enigmatic Bourgeois: Jean Revel Dons a Nightgown for His Portrait." *Costume: Journal of the Costume Society,* no. 44 (June 2010): 46–55.

Mitchell, Rebecca N. "Victorian Faddishness: The Dolly Varden from Dickens to Patience." *Journal of Victorian Culture* 26, no. 2 (2021): 1–19.

Moda en sombras, Museo Nacional del Pueblo Español. Madrid: Ministerio de Cultura, 1991.

La Mode et l'enfant, 1780-2000. Paris: Paris musées, 2001.

Moheng, Anne-Cécile. "Whalebone Bodies and Panniers: The Mechanics of Good Carriage in the Eighteenth Century." In *Fashioning the Body: An Intimate History of the Silhouette,* edited by Denis Bruna, 109–27. Published for Bard Graduate Center, Decorative Arts, Design History, Material Culture. New Haven, CT: Yale Univ. Press, 2015.

Moindrot, Isabelle. "The 'Turk' and the 'Parisienne': From Favart's Soliman Second, ou Les trois sultanes (1761) to Les trois sultanes (Pathé, 1912)." In *Ottoman Empire and European Theatre. I, The Age of Mozart and Sekim III (1756-1808),* edited by Michael Hüttler and Hans Ernst Weidinger, 427–66. Vienna: Hollitzer, 2013.

Moline, Estelle. "A Manner of Doing and a Manner of Being: A la mode de (SN) vs à la mode." *Revue Romane* 48, no. 1 (2013): 163–82.

Moronvalle, Jeff. "Le Recueil de cent estampes représentant différentes nations du Levant: une Image de l'Orient à la française." In *Modes ottomanes: la Gravure de l'Orient au siècle des Lumières,* 15–44. Amiens: Bibliothèques d'Amiens métropole, 2012.

———. "Le Recueil Ferriol (1714) et la mode des turqueries." *Dix-huitieme siecle* n° 44, no. 1 (Sept. 12, 2012): 425–46.

Moulinier, Axel, and Sophie Vesin. "Women's Undergarments and the Submission of the Body in the Sixteenth Century." In *Fashioning the Body: An Intimate History of the Silhouette,* edited by Denis Bruna, 57–64. Published for Bard Graduate Center, Decorative Arts, Design History, Material Culture. New Haven, CT: Yale Univ. Press, 2015.

Moussa, Sarga. "Peuples primitifs, peuples décadents: l'Imaginaire anthropologique de quelques artistes-voyageurs en Orient." In *Visualisation,* edited by Roland Mortier, 185–97. Berlin: Verlag; Arno Spitz GmbH, 1999.

Nefedova-Gruntova, Olga. *A Journey into the World of the Ottomans: The Art of Jean-Baptiste Vanmour, 1671-1737.* Milan: Skira, 2009.

Neumann, Iver B. *Uses of the Other: "The East" in European Identity Formation.* Minneapolis: Univ. of Minnesota Press, 1999.

Nevinson, J. L. *Origin and Early History of the Fashion Plate.* Philadelphia: D. N. Goodchild, 2014.

Newton, Charles. *Images of the Ottoman Empire.* New York: V&A Publications, 2007.

Nolhac, Pierre de. "François Dumont." *Gazette des Beaux Arts* 3, 6e period (1930): 328–34.

Nordmann, Claude. "Anglomanie et anglophobie en France au XVIIIe siècle." *Revue du Nord* 66, no. 261–62 (1984): 787–803.

Odile-Bernez, Marie. "Comfort, the Acceptable Face of Luxury: An Eighteenth-Century Cultural Etymology." *Journal for Early Modern Cultural Studies* 14, no. 2 (2014): 3–21.

Olausson, Magnus. *Marie-Antoinette, porträtt av en drottning.* Stockholm: Nationalmuseum, 1989.

Palmer, Alexandra. "Introduction." In *A Cultural History of Dress and Fashion in the Modern Age,* edited by Alexandra Palmer, 1–20. London: Bloomsbury Academic, 2017.

———. "Looking at Fashion: The Material Object as Subject." In *The Handbook of Fashion Studies,* edited by Sandy Black, Amy de la Haye, Joanne Entwistle, Regina Root, Agnès Rocamora, and Helen Thomas, 268–300. London: Bloomsbury, 2014.

Paresys, Isabelle. "La Cour de France, fabrique de normes vestimentaires à l'époque moderne." In *La Fabrique de la norme: Lieux et modes de production des normes au Moyen Âge et à l'époque moderne,* edited by Véronique Beaulande-Barraud, Julie Claustre, and Elsa Marmursztejn, 223–38. Rennes: Presses univ. de Rennes, 2019.

Peck, Amelia. "Trade Textiles at the Metropolitan Museum: A History." In *Interwoven Globe: The Worldwide Textile Trade, 1500-1800,* edited by Amelia Peck, 2–11. New York: Metropolitan Museum of Art, 2013.

Pellegrin, Nicole. "L'Uniforme de la santé: Les Médecins et la réforme du costume." *Dix-Huitième Siècle* 23 (1991): 129–40.

———. "Les Vertus de 'l'ouvrage': Recherches sur la feminisation des travaux d'aiguille (XVIe–XVIIIe siecles)." *Revue d'Histoire Moderne & Contemporaine* 46, no. 4 (Oct. 1999): 747–69.

———. *Les Vêtements de la liberté: Abécédaire des pratiques vestimentaires en France de 1780 à 1800.* Aix-en-Provence: Alinea, 1989.

Peyraube, Emmanuelle. *Le Harem des Lumières: l'Image de la femme dans la peinture orientaliste du XVIIIe siècle.* Paris: Éditions du patrimoine, Centre des monuments nationaux, 2008.

Pfiefer, Emily Catherine. "Undressed: Undergarments as Cultural Limina in Eighteenth-Century France." PhD diss., Univ. of California–Riverside, 2014.

Picard-Cajan, Pascale. "Typologie d'un costume-garde-robe de femme." In *Façon Arlésienne: étoffes et costumes au XVIIIe siècle*, 23–56. Arles: Museon Arlaten, 1998.

Pierre, Aurore. "From the Doublet to the Justaucorps: A Man's Silhouette in the Seventeenth and Eighteenth Centuries." In *Fashioning the Body: An Intimate History of the Silhouette*, edited by Denis Bruna, 95–107. Published for Bard Graduate Center, Decorative Arts, Design History, Material Culture. New Haven, CT: Yale Univ. Press, 2015.

Pietsch, Johannes. "Eastern Influences on French Fashion in the Late 18th Century." In *In Between: Culture of Dress Between the East and the West: ICOM's Costume Committee: Proceedings of the 64th Annual Conference, September 25–30, 2011*, edited by Mirjana Menković, 209–17. Belgrade: Ethnographic Museum, 2012.

———. "Object in Focus: Naming a Woman's Gown Dating to about 1775—85." Fashioning the Early Modern. http://www.fashioningtheearlymodern.ac.uk/object-in-focus/naming-a-womans-gown/.

———. "On Different Types of Women's Dresses in France in the Louis XVI Period." *Fashion Theory: The Journal of Dress, Body & Culture* 17, no. 4 (Sept. 2013): 397–416.

Pointon, Marcia R. *Hanging the Head: Portraiture and Social Formation in Eighteenth-Century England*. Published for the Paul Mellon Centre for Studies in British Art. New Haven, CT: Yale Univ. Press, 1993.

Pozzo, Barbara. "Fashion Between Inspiration and Appropriation." *Laws* 9, no. 1 (Mar. 2020): 1–26.

Price, Leah. "Vies Privées et Scandaleuses: Marie-Antoinette and the Public Eye." *The Eighteenth Century* 33, no. 2 (1992): 176–92.

Raus, Rachele. "L'Evolution de la locution 'à la turque.'" *Langage et société* 105, no. 3 (Sept. 1, 2003): 39–68.

Raveux, Olivier. "Fashion and Consumption of Painted and Printed Calicoes in the Mediterranean during the Later Seventeenth Century: The Case of Chintz Quilts and Banyans in Marseilles." *Textile History* 45, no. 1 (2014): 49–67.

———. "Spaces and Technologies in the Cotton Industry in the Seventeenth and Eighteenth Centuries: The Example of Printed Calicoes in Marseilles." *Textile History* 36, no. 2 (Nov. 2005): 131–45.

Redondo, María. "Polonesa del Siglo XVIII." *Modelo del Mes*, 2007. http://www.culturaydeporte.gob.es/mtraje/dam/jcr:7cda2f17-20fd-4d53-bbc9-2b5fcc073079/06-2007.pdf.

Ribeiro, Aileen. *The Art of Dress: Fashion in England and France 1750 to 1820*. New Haven, CT: Yale Univ. Press, 1995.

———. *Dress in Eighteenth-Century Europe, 1715–1789*. New Haven, CT: Yale Univ. Press, 2002.

———. *The Dress Worn at Masquerades in England, 1730 to 1790, and Its Relation to Fancy Dress in Portraiture*. New York: Garland, 1984.

———. "The Elegant Art of Fancy Dress." In *An Elegant Art: Fashion and Fantasy in the Eighteenth Century from the Los Angeles County Museum of Art Collection of Costumes and Textiles*, edited by Edward Maeder, 139–65. Los Angeles: Los Angeles County Museum of Art, 1983.

———. *Fashion in the French Revolution*. New York: Holmes & Meier, 1988.

Rimbault, Caroline. "La Presse féminine de langue française au XVIIIème siècle: Place de la femme et système de la mode." Thèse 3ème cycle Hist. des cult., des savoirs et de l'éduc., EHESS, 1981.

Roche, Daniel. *The Culture of Clothing: Dress and Fashion in the "Ancien Régime."* Translated by Jean Birrell. Cambridge: Cambridge Univ. Press, 1994.

———. *The People of Paris: An Essay in Popular Culture in the 18th Century*. Berkeley: Univ. of California Press, 1987.

Rodenbeck, John. "Dressing Native." In *Unfolding the Orient: Travellers in Egypt and the Near East*, edited by Paul Starkey and Janet Starkey, 65–100. Ithaca: Reading, 2001.

Rothstein, Natalie, ed. *Four Hundred Years of Fashion*. London: Victoria & Albert Museum in association with W. Collins, 1984.

Ruano, Elise Urbain. "The Négligé in Eighteenth-Century French Portraiture." *The Journal of Dress History* 1, no. 1 (Spring 2017): 92–99.

Rubiés, Joan-Pau. "Oriental Despotism and European Orientalism: Botero to Montesquieu." *Journal of Early Modern History* 9, no. 1 (2005): 109–80.

Said, Edward W. *Orientalism*. New York: Vintage Books, 1979.

Saint-Beuve, Charles Augustin. "L'Abbé Prévost." *Revue de Paris* 29 (1831): 203–25.

Sanciaud-Azanza, Anne. "L'Evolution du costume enfantin au XVIIIe siècle: Un Enjeu politique et social." *Revue d'Histoire Moderne & Contemporaine* 46, no. 4 (1999): 770–83.

Sapori, Michelle. *Rose Bertin: ministre des modes de Marie-Antoinette*. Paris: Regard: Institut français de la mode, 2003.

Savigny de Moncorps, Vte de. *Almanachs illustrés du XVIIIe siècle*. Paris: Librarie Henri Leclerc, 1909.

Scarce, Jennifer M. "Turkish Fashion in Transition." *Costume* 14, no. 1 (Jan. 1, 1980): 144–67.

———. *Women's Costume of the Near and Middle East*. London: Unwin Hyman, 1987.

Schama, Simon. *Citizens: A Chronicle of the French Revolution*. London: Penguin, 1989.

Scher, Lydia. "Relations militaires entre la France et la Pologne aux XVII° et XVIII° Siècles." *Revue historique des armées*, no. 162 (1986): 68–77.

Schmidt, Benjamin. *Inventing Exoticism: Geography, Globalism, and Europe's Early Modern World.* Philadelphia: Univ. of Pennsylvania Press, 2015.

Schoeser, Mary. "Oriental Connections: Merchant Adventurers and the Transmission of Cultural Concepts." In *Fashion Prints in the Age of Louis XIV: Interpreting the Art of Elegance,* edited by Kathryn Norberg, Sandra Rosenbaum, and Françoise Tétart-Vittu, 167–84. Lubbock: Texas Tech Univ. Press, 2014.

Scholz, Susanne. "English Women in Oriental Dress: Playing the Turk in Lady Mary Wortley Montagu's Turkish Embassy." In *Early Modern Encounters with the Islamic East: Performing Cultures,* edited by Ralf Hertel, Sabine Lucia Müller, and Sabine Schülting, 85–98. New York: Routledge, 2016.

Sheriff, Mary D. "The Dislocations of Jean-Etienne Liotard, Called the Turkish Painter." In *Cultural Contact and the Making of European Art since the Age of Exploration,* edited by Mary D. Sheriff, 97–121. Chapel Hill: Univ. of North Carolina Press, 2010.

———. *The Exceptional Woman: Elisabeth Vigée-Lebrun and the Cultural Politics of Art.* Chicago: Univ. of Chicago Press, 1996.

———. "The Portrait of the Queen." In *Marie-Antoinette: Writings on the Body of a Queen,* edited by Dena Goodman, 45–72. New York: Routledge, 2003.

Shovlin, John. "The Cultural Politics of Luxury in Eighteenth-Century France." *French Historical Studies* 23, no. 4 (Oct. 1, 2000): 577–606.

———. *The Political Economy of Virtue: Luxury, Patriotism, and the Origins of the French Revolution.* Ithaca: Cornell Univ. Press, 2006.

Simon, Marie. *Fashion in Art: The Second Empire and Impressionism.* Paris: Editions Hazan, 1995.

Smentek, Kristel. "Jean-Etienne Liotard, the Turkish Painter." *Ars Orientalis* 39 (2010): 84–112.

Solnon, Jean-François. *Le Turban et la stambouline: l'Empire ottoman et l'Europe, XIVe–XXe siècle, affrontement et fascination réciproques.* Paris: Perrin, 2009.

Starobinski, Jean. *Jean-Jacques Rousseau, Transparency and Obstruction.* Chicago: Univ. of Chicago Press, 1988.

Steele, Valerie. *Fashion and Eroticism: Ideals of Feminine Beauty from the Victorian Era to the Jazz Age.* New York: Oxford Univ. Press, 1985.

Stein, Perrin. "Amedee Van Loo's Costume Turc: The French Sultana." *Art Bulletin* 78, no. 3 (Sept. 1996): 417–38.

———. "Exoticism as Metaphor: 'Turquerie' in Eighteenth-Century French Art." New York: New York Univ., 1997.

———. "Madame de Pompadour and the Harem Imagery at Bellevue." *Gazette Des Beaux-Arts* 123 (1994): 29–44.

———. "Marie Antoinette in the Park of Versailles." In *The Wrightsman Pictures,* edited by Everett Fahy, 252–54. New York: Metropolitan Museum of Art, 2005.

Stobart, Jon. "Introduction: Comfort, the Home and Home Comforts." In *The Comforts of Home in Western Europe, 1700–1900,* 1–16. London: Bloomsbury Publishing, 2020.

Straszewska, Anna. "Poland: Urban Dress up to 1900." In *Encyclopedia of World Dress and Fashion,* edited by Joanne Bubolz Eicher, 9:222–29. Oxford: Oxford Univ. Press, 2010.

Swain, Margaret H. "Nightgown into Dressing Gown: A Study of Mens' [*sic*] Nightgowns Eighteenth Century." *Costume* 6, no. 1 (June 1, 1972): 10–21.

Takeda, J. T. "French Mercantilism and the Early Modern Mediterranean: A Case Study of Marseille's Silk Industry." *French History* 29, no. 1 (2015): 12–17.

Tarrant, Naomi E. A. *The Development of Costume.* Edinburgh: National Museums of Scotland in conjunction with Routledge, 1994.

———. "Lord Sheffield's Banyan." *Costume* 11, no. 1 (Jan. 1, 1977): 92–97.

Taszycka, Maria. "Symbols of Nationhood: History of the Polish Sash." *Hali* 17 (1996): 72–77.

Tekin, Beyza Ç. *Representations and Othering in Discourse: The Construction of Turkey in the EU Context.* Philadelphia: John Benjamins Pub. Co., 2010.

Tétart-Vittu, Françoise. "Dessinateurs et diffusion de la mode par la gravure et la presse." In *À la mode: l'Art de paraître au 18e siècle,* 145–50. Gand: Snoek, 2021.

———."La Gallerie des modes et costumes français." *Nouvelles de l'estampe* 91 (Mar. 1987): 16–21.

———. "Incidence de la mode française à Arles." In *Façon Arlésienne: Étoffes et Costumes au XVIIIe Siècle,* 15–22. Arles: Museon Arlaten, 1998.

———. "Toilettes royales: La Reine et ses fournisseurs." In *Marie-Antoinette: Femme réelle, femme mythique,* edited by Élisabeth Maisonnier and Catriona Seth, 53–61. Paris: Magellan, 2008.

Tezcan, Hülya, and Selma Delibaş. *The Topkapı Saray Museum: Costumes, Embroideries and Other Textiles.* Translated by J. M. Rogers. London: Thames and Hudson, 1986.

Thepaut-Cabasset, Corinne. "Fashion Encounters: The 'Siamoise,' or the Impact of the Great Embassy on Textile Design in Paris in 1687." In *Global Textile Encounters,* edited by Marie-Louise Nosch, Feng Zhao, and Lotika Varadarajan, 165–70. Philadelphia: Oxbow Books, 2014.

Thoisy-Dallem, Anne de. "La Robe de chambre d'Oberkampf: Un Témoignage rare du vêtement d'intérieur à la fin du XVIII siècle." *La Revue du Louvre et des musées de France,* no. 3 (2008): 82–85.

———. "La Vieille robe de chambre de Diderot et les vêtements d'intérieur masculins au Siècle des Lumières."

Thomas, Chantal. *The Wicked Queen: The Origins of the Myth of Marie-Antoinette*. New York: Zone Books, 1999.

Thoral, Marie-Cecile. "Sartorial Orientalism: Cross-Cultural Dressing in Colonial Algeria and Metropolitan France in the Nineteenth Century." *European History Quarterly* 45, no. 1 (2015): 57–82.

Thunder, Moira. "New Object in Focus: Man's Banyan." *Fashioningtheearlymodern* (blog). http://fashioningtheearlymodern.wordpress.com/2012/02/17/new-object-in-focus-mans-banyan/.

Tiramani, Jenny. *Seventeenth-Century Women's Dress Patterns: Book 2*. New York: Abrams, 2012.

Tiramani, Jenny, Richard Davis, Paul Robins, and Susan North. *Seventeenth-Century Women's Dress Patterns*. London: V&A Publications, 2011.

Trey, Juliette. *La Mode à la cour de Marie-Antoinette*. Paris: Gallimard, 2014.

Turaga, Janaki. "Being Fashionable in the Globalization Era in India: Holy Writing on Garments." In *Modern Fashion Traditions: Negotiating Tradition and Modernity through Fashion*, edited by M. Angela Jansen and Jennifer Craik, 73–96. London: Bloomsbury Academic, 2018.

Turnau, Irena. "The Dress of the Polish Jews in the 17th and 18th Centuries." *World Congress of Jewish Studies*, Div. D, vol. ii (Jerusalem, 1990): 101–8.

———. *History of Dress in Central and Eastern Europe from the Sixteenth to the Eighteenth Century*. Warszawa: Institute of the History of Material Culture, Polish Academy of Sciences, 1991.

———. "The Main Centres of National Fashion in Eastern Europe from the Sixteenth to the Eighteenth Centuries." *Textile History* 22, no. 1 (Spring 1991): 47–65.

———. "Pour une histoire du costume: A Varsovie au XVIIIe siècle: les Costumes bourgeois." *Annales. Histoire, Sciences Sociales* 15, no. 6 (Nov. 1, 1960): 1127–37.

Turner, Terence S. "The Social Skin." In *Not Work Alone: A Cross-Cultural View of Activities Superfluous to Survival*, edited by Jeremy Cherfas and Roger Lewin, 112–40. London: Temple Smith, 1980.

Urbain, Élise. "'Dans un instant, la toilette aura tout gâté': Négligences et légèreté dans la peinture et la mode en France au dix-huitième siècle." In *Le Siècle de la légèreté: Émergences d'un paradigme du dix-huitième siècle français*, edited by Marine Ganofsky and Jean-Alexandre Perras, 237–54. Liverpool: Liverpool Univ. Press on behalf of Voltaire Foundation, Univ. of Oxford, 2019.

Van Cleave, Kendra. "Contextualizing Wertmüller's 1785 Portrait of Marie-Antoinette through Dress." *Costume* 54, no. 1 (2020): 56–80.

———. "The Lévite Dress: Untangling the Cultural Influences of Eighteenth-Century French Fashion." *The Social Fabric: Deep Local to Pan Global; Proceedings of the Textile Society of America 16th Biennial Symposium*, Jan. 1, 2018. https://digitalcommons.unl.edu/tsaconf/1119.

Van Cleave, Kendra, and Brooke Welborn. "'Very Much the Taste and Various Are the Makes': Reconsidering the Late-Eighteenth-Century Robe à La Polonaise." *Dress* 39, no. 1 (May 1, 2013): 1–24.

Van Dyk, Garritt. "The Embassy of Soliman Aga to Louis XIV: Diplomacy, Dress, and Diamonds." *Emaj*, 2017. http://emajartjournal.com/cosmopolitan-moments/.

Vickery, Amanda. "Mutton Dressed as Lamb? Fashioning Age in Georgian England." *Journal of British Studies* 52, no. 4 (Oct. 2013): 858–86.

Vinha, Mathieu da, and Catherine Örmen. *Dans la garde-robe de Marie-Antoinette*. Paris: Réunion des musées nationaux, Grand Palais Versailles Château de Versailles, 2018.

Vittu, Françoise. "Presse et diffusion des modes françaises." In *Modes et révolutions: 1780–1804*, 129–36. Paris: Musée Galliera, 1989.

Vogelsang, Willem. "History of Dress and Fashion." In *Encyclopedia of World Dress and Fashion*, edited by Joanne Bubolz Eicher and Oxford Univ. Press, 5:14–23. Oxford: Oxford Univ. Press, 2010.

Vogelsang-Eastwood, Gillian. "Introduction to Dress and Fashion in Central and Southwest Asia." In *Encyclopedia of World Dress and Fashion*, edited by Joanne Bubolz Eicher, 5:3–8. Oxford: Oxford Univ. Press, 2010.

Vrignaud, Gilberte. *Vêture et parure en France au dix-huitième siècle*. Paris: Editions Messene, 1995.

Waugh, Norah. *Corsets and Crinolines*. New York: Routledge/Theatre Arts Books, 2000.

Waugh, Norah, and Margaret Woodward. *The Cut of Women's Clothes, 1600–1930*. New York: Theatre Arts Books, 1968.

Weber, Caroline. *Queen of Fashion: What Marie Antoinette Wore to the Revolution*. New York: H. Holt, 2006.

Wheatcroft, Andrew. *Infidels: A History of the Conflict between Christendom and Islam*. New York: Random House, 2004.

Williams, Haydn. *Turquerie: An Eighteenth-Century European Fantasy*. London: Thames and Hudson, 2014.

Wolff, Larry. *Inventing Eastern Europe: The Map of Civilization on the Mind of the Enlightenment*. Redwood City, CA: Stanford Univ. Press, 1994.

———. *The Singing Turk: Ottoman Power and Operatic Emotions on the European Stage from the Siege of Vienna to the Age of Napoleon*. Redwood City, CA: Stanford Univ. Press, 2017.

Yermolenko, Galina I. *Roxolana in European Literature, History and Culture*. Burlington, VT: Ashgate, 2010.

Zaretsky, Robert, and John T. Scott. *The Philosophers' Quarrel: Rousseau, Hume, and the Limits of Human Understanding.* New Haven, CT: Yale Univ. Press, 2009.

Zieseniss, Charles-Otto, Katell Le Bourhis, and Metropolitan Museum of Art. *The Age of Napoleon: Costume from Revolution to Empire, 1789–1815.* New York: Metropolitan Museum of Art, 1989.

Zlatnik, Gail Parson. "Myth, Vision, and the Harem in French Painting: From Fontainbleau through the Nineteenth Century." PhD diss., Univ. of Iowa, 1998.

REFERENCE SOURCES

Jeffares, Neil, ed. *Dictionary of Pastellists before 1800.* Online edition, 2018. www.pastellists.com.

Oxford English Dictionary. https://www.oed.com.

Sgard, Jean, ed. *Édition électronique revue, corrigée et augmentée du dictionnaire des journaux (1600–1789).* Voltaire Foundation. http://dictionnaire-journaux.gazettes18e.fr/

Trésor de la Langue Française informatisé. Centre national de la recherche scientifique and Université de Lorraine. http://atilf.atilf.fr/.

INDEX

Page numbers in italics refer to illustrations.

Aga, ou Gentilhomme (Scotin after Vanmour), *17*
ailes (wings), 86–87
à la Créole, 135–36
à la française, defined, 112–13. See also *robes à la française*
à la paysanne (peasant), 147
Album Maciet, gravures, *137*
Alembert, Jean Le Rond d', *34*
Alexandre, Mademoiselle, 162
Algeria, cultural cross-dressing, 179
amadis (sleeves), 98
anglaise. See *robes à l'anglaise*
anteris (caftans), 37, 85
Aravamudan, Srinivas, 12
Arlequin, and Ottoman inspiration (1785–1810), 9, *172*, 177
"Armenian" clothing, and Rousseau, 142
Arnoult, Nicolas, *42*
art, Ottoman dress in, 16–19, *17, 18*. See also *individual names of artworks*
Artois, Comte d' (Charles Philippe), 162
Artois, Comtesse d' (Marie-Thérèse of Savoy), 29, 110, 161, 162
Athalie (Racine), 116–19, *119*
Augustus III (King of Poland), *40*
Avcıoğlu, Nebahat, 5, 12
Avion, Mademoiselle d', 99

Bachaumont, Louis Petit de, 122, 125
Bal des ifs (Cochin the Younger), 20
Balexert, Jacques, 143, 151, 152
Ballet des Créoles, 135–36
Barnaby Rudge (Dickens), 178
Baron, Bernard, *117*
Barthes, Roland, 112
Basan et Poignant, *105*

Baudin, Jules, 138
Beaumarchais, Pierre-Augustin Caron de, 56
bed design, clothing influenced by, *100*, 101
Bendall, Sarah A., 35, 43
Bertin, Rose, 138, 156, 161, 162, 168
Bevilacqua, Alexander, 4
Blouin, Marie-Madeleine, 117–19
Bodin, A., *177*
Boissieu, Jean-Jacques de, 27, *27*
Bombelles, Marquise de, 160
bonnet rouge, 170
bonnets, *174*
Boquet, Louis-René, *21, 22, 23*, 100
Bosse, Abraham, *42*
Boucher, François, 19, *20*, 99, *141*
bouffantes (puffings), 103–6, *104*
Bretonne, Restif de la, 143
Broglie, Madame de, 11, 23
Bruyn, Abraham de, *39*
Bryant, Margaret M., 112
Buisson, François, 10, *96*, *132*, 160
busks, 41, *108*, 152

Cabinet des modes: and clothing perspectives, East and West, 24; Enlightenment thought and *turquerie*, 145–46, 148; and *fourreau à la Lévite*, *138*; French print culture expansion (eighteenth century), 9, 10; and Marie-Antoinette's fashion influence, 160; on naming trends for fashion, 114; Ottoman fashionability and appeal to demographic groups, 24; and *pierrot*, *96*; on *robe à l'anglaise*, 76; and *robe à la turque*, 63, 106
caftans: *anteris*, 37, 85; defined, 36; as dressing gowns, 42–43; *kontusz*, *39, 40*, 41, 100; *kürdiyye*, 38, 115, 116; *lévite* modeled after, 119–20, *120*; *robe à la Levantine*, 150, *150*; robe (Turkish caftan, ca. 1720), *15*, 15–

16; Western and Eastern approaches to dress, 33, *35*, 36–39, *37*, 41–44, 47; *zupan*, 41. See also *lévites*
Cage, E. Claire, 173
Calefato, Patrizia, 4
camisoles à la polonaise, 158
Campan, Madame, 156, 163
The Capoudgi Bachi, Grandmaster of the Seragli (Vanmour), *63*
caraco à la Arlaise (Duhamel after Defraine), *147*
caracos (jackets): à la *lévite*, 135–36; *caraco à la circassienne*, 130; *caraco à la polonaise* and Enlightenment thought, 147, *149*; *caraco à la polonaise* and Ottoman influence (1760–90), 63, 75, 85–86, *87*–90, 95–97, *96*, 98; *caraco à l'Arlaise*, 147, *147*; *caraco à la turque*, 130; *caraco à l'Indienne*, 169
Caravanne du Sultan à la Mecque (Vien), 20, *20*
Caribbean influence. See *chemise à la reine*
Carmontelle, Louis de, 100, *101*
Catherine the Great (Empress of Russia), 16
Cavallaro, Dani, 4
Chartres, Duchesse de, 85, 122, *122*–26
Châtelet, Albert, 163
Chatenet-Calyste, Aurélie, 31
chemise à la reine: defined, 118; inventories, 26; *lévite* and Caribbean influence, 111, 131, *135*–37, 135–38; Marie-Antoinette's wearing of, *157*, 158, 163, *164, 165*; Ottoman fashionability and appeal to demographic groups, 24–26, 29
Chéreau, Jacques, *48*
children and children's dress: *Circassienne à l'enfant*, 130; Enlightenment and effect on, 140, *141*, 143, 145, 151–53, *152, 153*; *fourreau*, 132; Ottoman fashionability and appeal to demographic groups, 24, 28–29

243

Choadar, Servant of the Ambassador (Vanmour), 37
Chrisman-Campbell, Kimberly: on Anglomania and fashion, 141; on consumption patterns (eighteenth century), 8; on French Revolution and clothing, 170; on Marie-Antoinette's clothing, 157, 158, 167; on naming fashions, 113; on Ottoman inspiration (1785–1810), 169
Circassian Style Dress (Desrais), *95*
circassienne. See *robes à la circassienne*
class. See demographics and class
Classicism and Enlightenment philosophy, 144
Clermont, Lady, 163
clothing perspectives, East and West, 11–31; Franco-Ottoman alliance (renewal in late seventeenth century), 11; popularity and demographics of Turkish-inspired dress, 24–31, *27–30*; *turquerie* and French dress, 11–24, *14*, *16–21*, *23*
Cochin the Younger, 20
Coiffure à l'Egyptienne, 176
Coke, Lady Mary, 160
Colbert, Jean-Baptiste, 7
Coller, Ian, 143
Comédie Italienne (theatrical production), 23
comfort of dress: and Enlightenment philosophy, 148–51, *149*, *150*; and *robe de chambre* as formal dress, 51–52; Western and Eastern approaches to dress, 33. See also Ottoman influence, defining (1760–90); underpinnings
compère (false front), 67
Confessions (Rousseau), 142
contentement (decorative rosette), 61, 63
Conti, Princesse de, 25, 31, 110, 146
corsage, 67, 71, 162
corsets: *corps de baleine*, 35, 41, *107*, 152; names for, 67; stays, *107–9*, 107–10; Western and Eastern approaches to dress, 35, 36, 43
costume, defined, 3
costume à la Jeanne d'Arc, 61
Costumes de différents pays (De Saint-Saveur), *102*
côtes (sides), 86–87
cotton, growth in popularity, 150–51, 167
Couple Wearing the Latest French Fashion (De Saint-Igny), *35*
Courrier de la mode ou le Journal du goût: and Enlightenment thought and *turquerie*, 141, 151, 153; French print culture expansion (eighteenth century), 9; and origins of *robes*, 99–100; on *robe à l'anglaise*, 56
court dresses, 98, 107, 112, 114, 130, 148, *148*, *157*, 158, 160
The Couturier's Workshop (Raspal), 28, *29*
Craddock, Anna, 166
Crane, Diana, 4
cross-cultural studies. See geographic terminology; national identity and French fashion; Ottoman Empire
Crowley, John E., 149
Crowston, Clare Haru, 8, 46–47, 167–68
culs (rumps), 103–6, *104*
cutaway fronts, 61–72. See also Ottoman influence, defining (1760–90)

Dame met fontange, open waaier in de hand (etching on paper), *47*
Dames en Manteaux (engraving with etching on laid paper), *48*
Dauvel, Etienne, 35
David, Jules, 177
Davis, Fred, 4–5
"deep surface," dress as, 4
Defraine (designer), *147*, 160
Delafosse, Jean Charles, 101
demi-polonaise, 97, 114, 130, 146, 158–59
demographics and class: fashion and identity, 7–8; French interest in "oriental" culture (seventeenth to eighteenth centuries), 1–3; and French Revolution, 169–71, 173; and Marie-Antoinette's fashion influence, 156, *157*, 158–61, *164*, 165; and popularity of Turkish-inspired dress (eighteenth century), 24–31, *27–30*; social class and corsets, 43; theatrical representations of Ottoman dress, *21*, 21–24, *23*. See also *individual names of royals*
Desfossés, Charles Henri, 105
deshabillé (informal ensemble), 2, 26, 56, 158–59, 162
Desrais, Claude-Louis, 10, *95*, *96*, *104*, *134*
Dickens, Charles, 178
Dictionaire critique de la langue française, 112–13
Dictionnaire de l'Académie français, 113
Diderot, Denis, *34*, 140
Doll, in a white linen dress with trimmings of muslin, silk ribbon and color-printed cotton (Powell family), *124*, 125
Doll's mantua (silk damask lined with silk taffeta), *46*
"Dolly Varden" gown, *177*, 178
dolman, 37, 143
The Dreamer (Watteau), 18, *18*
dress, defined, 3, 4
drolet jacket, 29, *147*
Du Barry, Comtesse (Jeanne Bécu), 100, 167
The duchesse de Chartres in the presence of the vessel the Saint-Esprit (Duplessis), *122*, 122–25
Duclos, Antoine Jean, 105
Duhamel, A. B., *96*, *132*, *134*, *147*, 160
Dumont, François, 163
Dupin, Nicolas, *56*, *120*, *135*, 148, *153*
Duplessis, Joseph, *122*, 122–25

East, as geographic term, 5–8, *6*
Eastern Europe: countries defined as, 13–14; dress (sixteenth to eighteenth century), 38–41, *39*, *40*; as geographic term, 5–8, *6*
Efendi, Mehmed Said, 14
Eicher, Joanne, 4
Elisabeth, Madame, 161, 162–63
Ellison, Charles, 145
Éloffe, Madame, 134–35, 161
Émile, ou De l'éducation (Rousseau), 140
Encyclopédie (Diderot), 140
Encyclopédie méthodique: on French fashion elements in *robes*, 58, 62, 97, 103, 106, 109; on *lévite* and variations, 119–21, 125, *131*, 131–33, 135, 138, 158, 163

engageantes (sleeve style), 98
England: English dress and Enlightenment philosophy, 140–41, 143, 146–47, 151; English press on Ottoman inspiration (1785–1810), 171–72, *172*; and naming conventions/trends for fashion, 113, 116; and origins of *robes*, 99; Ottoman dress in masquerades, 20; Ottoman inspiration (1785–1810), 169. See also *robes à l'anglaise*
English Levant Company, 15
Enlightenment philosophy, 139–53; and Classicism, 144; and comfort of dress, 148–51, *149*, *150*; dress (sixteenth to eighteenth centuries), 39; dress and construction of social identity, 8; and English dress, 140–41, 143, 146–47, 151; health/morality and effect on fashion, 151–53, *152–53*; intellectual exploration of, 139–40; Marie-Antoinette's interest in, 155, 157, 163, 166; and naturalism, 139–42, 144–48, *146–48*; and Ottoman dress, *142*, 142–43; and *turquerie* in French fashion press, overview, 144
erotic images of fashion, 123, 149, 167–68, 177
Esnault, Jacques, 10
Esnauts & Rapilly: *camisole à la polonaise*, *96*; *caraco à la polonaise*, 86; *chemise à la reine*, 135; *circassienne*, *104*; lack of waist seam, 72; *lévite*, 120, 133, *136*, *137*, 152, *153*; *polonaise* worn *retroussée*, *91*; *pouf* (headdress), *174*; *robe à la levantine*, *150*; *robe à l'anglaise*, 56; *robe à la turque*, 106, 148
Essai sur la santé et sur l'éducation médicinale des filles destinées au mariage (Venel), 143
Eugenie (Beaumarchais), 56
Evening Party Given by the Queen Marie-Antoinette (Robert), 163
Extraordinaire du mercure galant, 33

fabric industry: cotton and growth in popularity, 150–51, 167; French silk industry, 150–51, 166–67; loom invention (thirteenth and fourteenth centuries), 35
fabrics. See Western and Eastern approaches to dress
fashion: changing cycle concept, 4; defined, 3; dress and construction of social identity, 8; wardrobe inventories, 25–27, 114, 141, 161–68. See also clothing perspectives, East and West; Enlightenment philosophy; fashion press; Marie-Antoinette (Queen of France); national identity and French fashion; Ottoman influence, defining (1760–90); Ottoman inspiration (1785–1810); *turquerie*; Western and Eastern approaches to dress
fashion press: and Classicism, 144; and comfort of clothing, 148–51, *149*, *151*; consistent publication of (beginning in 1778), 25; Enlightenment philosophy and *turquerie* in, overview, 139–40, 144; expansion in eighteenth century, 8–10; and health/morality and effect on clothing, 151–53, *152*, *153*; national identity and influence of, 111; and naturalism, 139–42, 144–48, *146–48*. See also *Gallerie des modes et costumes français* (fashion plates); *and individual names of magazines*

244   INDEX

Favart, Charles Simon, 22, 23
Favart, Marie-Justine, 22, *23*
Favray, Antoine de, 19
Femme de qualité en Sultane (Saint-Jean), *47*
Femme en déshabillé rosé et caraco olive allongée sur un sofa (Galerie des modes), *149*
"Femme Turque, qui repose sur le Sopha sortant du bain" (Le Hay and Scotin after Vanmour), *123*
Fille de joie se battant avec le coiffeur qui l'a tondue (Naudet, publisher), *28*
"Fille Turque, prenant le Caffé sur le Sopha" (Haussard after Vanmour), *17*
Fitz-James, Duchesse de, 85
Flinville, Mademoiselle de, 97
Fonds d'estampes du XVIIIème siècle (Galerie des modes), *134*, *149*
Fourment, Helene, 101
fourreau (gowns), 54, 56; defined, 118; and Enlightenment thought, 145, 153; fashion and national identity, 131–32, *132*, *133*, 138; Ottoman fashionability and appeal to demographic groups, 25, 28, *29*
frac coat, 141
française. See *robes à la française*
France: colonialism by, 178–79; fashion press and influence on, 9–10; Franco-Ottoman alliance (renewal in late seventeenth century), 11, 12–13; French dress, defined, 43; and French fashion world dominance, 1–3; French Revolution, 9, 169–71, 173; *polonaise* timing in, 99–100; silk industry, 150–51, 167. *See also* fashion press; Marie-Antoinette (Queen of France); national identity and French fashion
François I (King of France), 12
Franse edelvrouw gekleed volgens de Franse mode van ca. 1630 (engraving on paper), *42*
Freudenberge, Sigmund, *102*
Frith, William Powell, 178

Gallerie des modes et costumes français (fashion plates): Enlightenment thought and *turquerie*, 139, 141, 146, *146*, 149, 150, 151, *152*, 153; *Femme en déshabillé rosé et caraco olive allongée sur un sofa*, *149*; on French fashion elements in *robes*, 56, 61–63, *72*, *73*, *85*, *86*, *88*, *91*, *91*, *95*, *96*, 96–98, 101–6, *106*, *109*; and *lévite*, 116, 119, 120, *120*, 121, 126, 130, 132–38, *133*, *136*, *137*; and Marie-Antoinette's fashion influence, 158, 160–61; on naming trends for fashion, 114, 116; Ottoman fashionability and appeal to demographic groups, 24–28, 30–31; and Ottoman inspiration (1785–1810), 174, *174*; publication type and production of, 9, 10; on theatrical costumes, 23
Gardes français et hussard trinquant (print), *19*
garment construction. *See* Western and Eastern approaches to dress
Gaussian, Madame, 11
Gazette des atours (register of fabric swatches), 161, 162–63
Gazette du commerce, and origins of *robes*, 99
Geczy, Adam, 4, 149, 177

Geoffrin, Marie Thérèse Rodet, 16, 100
geographic terminology: Levant, 150; and naming conventions for fashion, 112–14; and naming trends for fashion, 114–16, *115*; "oriental" references, 2; for Ottoman Empire territories, 5–8, *6*
Gigot, Mademoiselle, 99
gömlek (shirt), 36–37
Gorguet-Ballesteros, Pascale, 42
Goubaud et Fil, 177
grande robe à la française, 158
grand habits, 42, 158, 160–62
Grandval, Madame, 11
Greek clothing: Enlightenment thought on, 143; Ottoman influence on (1760–90), *60*; and Ottoman inspiration (1785–1810), 172, 176–77; *robe à la grecque*, 99, 113
Grieder, Josephine, 140–41
Guer, Jean-Antoine, 19, 20
Gustav III (King of Sweden), 163
Guttenberg, Carl Gottlieb, *86*

Halma, Nicolas, 143
Haussard, Jean-Baptiste, *17*
headwear (Ottoman-inspired fashions, 1785–1810), 169–70, *170*, 173–76, *174*, *175*, 178
health, Enlightenment thought on, 151–53, *152–53*
Hickel, Joseph, 156, *156*
Hilaire, Jean-Baptiste, 159, *159*
Hiner, Susan, 177
hirka, 37
hoops. *See paniers* (hoops)
horizontal pleat technique, 72, *73*. *See also* pleats
Hungary: Eastern Europe, defined, 13–14; Hussar uniforms, 19, *19*
Hunt, Lynn, 170

Illumination of the Belvédère of the Petit Trianon (Châtelet), 163
India: house gowns, 44; Indian-inspired fashion in France, 169, 174; saris, 36; *turquerie*, French dress, and ambassadorial visits from Mysore, 15
inventories, wardrobe, 25–27, 114, 141, 161–68

James-Sarazin, Ariane, 158
Japanese kimonos and yukatas, 36, 44
Jasienski, Adam, 39
Jeaurat, Etienne, *47*
Jewish gowns. *See lévites*
Jirousek, Charlotte, 21, 50–51, 116, 175, 178
Jones, Jennifer, 8, 113, 144, 168
Joseph II (Emperor of Austria), 165
Joséphine (Empress of France), 177
Journal de la mode et du goût: French print culture expansion (eighteenth century), 9, 10; *lévite*, *134*; on naming trends for fashion, 114; and Ottoman inspiration (1785–1810), 170, *171*, 174; on redingote, *134*
Journal de Marseille, and Ottoman inspiration (1785–1810), 176
Journal des dames et des demoiselles, and Ottoman inspiration (1785–1810), *177*
Journal des dames et des modes: inception of, 9, 172; and naming trends, 115; on naming trends for fashion, 114; and Ottoman inspiration (1785–1810), 172, 174, *175*, 176, *177*
Journal helvétique, Ottoman fashionability and appeal to demographic groups, 31
"Juif" (Le Hay and Baron after Vanmour), *117*
jupons (petticoats), 46
justaucorps (men's coat), 141

Kaiser, Susan B., 4
Klänning (dress), 71, *80*, 95
Kleinert, Annemarie, 9
Koç, Fatma, 178
Koca, Emine, 178
Koda, Harold, 36
König, Anna, 112
kontusz (caftan), *39*, *40*, 41, 100
kürdiyye (caftan), 38, 115, 116
kuşak/kemer (belt/sash), 38

La Danse des enfants (Boissieu), 27, *27*
Lafrensen, Niclas, 163
La Grenadiere (*circassienne* variation), 130
Landweber, Julia, 5, 174
Langlois, François, 42
La Partie de dames (Ollivier), 56
Lapasin, Régis, 158
L'Arlequin, and Ottoman inspiration (1785–1810), 9, 172, 177
Lasic, Barbara, 113
L'Audiance Magnifique donnée par le Roy Louis XV à Mehemet Effendi (print), *14*
layering effect, 21, 36, 39, 43, 47, 54, 60, 62, 98, 110. *See also* Ottoman influence, defining (1760–90)
Le Beau, Madame, 9, *91*, *133*, *135*
Le Beau, Pierre Adrien, 42, *120*, *157*
Le Brun, Jean-Antoine, 10
Lebrun-Tossa, Jean-Antoine, 134
Le Clerc, Pierre Thomas: *caraco à la polonaise*, *86*; *chemise à la reine*, *135*, 153; *Gallerie* work of, 10; *lévite*, *120*, *133*, 153; *pierrot*, *96*; polonaise with *cul*, *104*; *polonaise* worn *retroussée*, *91*; *robe à l'anglaise*, 56
Le Fébure, Guillaume-René, 143, 152
Le Grand, Louis, 42
Le Hay, Jacques, *117*, *123*
Le lever (Romanet after Freudenberge), *102*
Le Miroir, and Ottoman inspiration (1785–1810), *175*
Lemoine, Marie-Victoire, *109*, 160
Le Rendez-vous pour Marly (Guttenberg after Moreau), *86*
LeRoy, Alphonse, 140, 143, 151
Les Trois sultanes (theatrical production), 22, *23*
Le Thé à l'anglaise servi dans le salon des Quatre-Glaces au palais du Temple (Ollivier), 56
Levant, defined, 7
lévites: and Caribbean influence, 131, 135–37, 135–38; collars of, 121–26, *124*; defined, 24; depiction of, in artwork, *109*, 110; and English influence, 131–34, 131–35; Enlightenment thought and effect on, 143, 144, 146,

INDEX 245

lévites (cont.)
149, 150, *152*, 152–53, *153;* extant examples of, 178; fashion popularity (late eighteenth century), 3; *fourreau à la Lévite,* *138;* French fashion press and influence on, 111; and Marie-Antoinette's fashion influence, 155, *158,* 160–63, 165, 167; naming conventions, 112–14; naming trends, 114–16, *115;* Ottoman fashionability and appeal to demographic groups, 24–28, 30–31; and Ottoman inspiration (1760–90), 53, 60; and Ottoman inspiration (1785–1810), 172, *173,* 176; popularity, 116–25, *117, 119, 120, 122–24;* redesigned, combined, reinvented styles, 126–31, *127–29;* silhouette, 61, 106–7
lining techniques: *polonaises,* 73, 78; *turques,* 80
Liotard, Jean Étienne, 18, *18*
lits à la polonaise (bed design), *100,* 101
looped-up skirts, 61. *See also* Ottoman influence, defining (1760–90)
Louis XIV (King of France), 1, 7, 42
Louis XV (King of France), *14,* 40, 156
Louis XVI (King of France), 117, 156, 162
Lubrich, Naomi, 173
Lying-in Room of a Distinguished Turkish Woman (Vanmour), *38*

Magasin des modes: on cultural influence on French fashion, 1; on French fashion elements in *robes,* 63, 67, *84, 108, 109, 126, 130, 132, 134;* on naming conventions for fashion, 113; on naming trends for fashion, 114; Ottoman inspiration (1785–1810), 169–70, 174
Maillard, Pascale, 25–26, 138
mantua and manteau, 33, 45, *46–48,* 46–51, 55, *55,* 112
marchandes de modes (female merchants), 8
Maréchal, Sylvain, 144
mari (trimming), 135
Marie Anne légitimée de France, fille de Louis le Grand (engraving, watercolor), *42*
Marie-Antoinette (Queen of France), 155–68; and *Athalie* (Racine), 117; biographical information and characterization of, 155–58; dress categories separated by occasion during reign of, 158–61, *159, 160; Marie Antoinette, 1755–1793, Archduchess of Austria, Queen of France* (Hickel), 156, *156; Marie Antoinette: The Queen of Fashion* (etching and engraving), *105,* 105–6, *135; Marie Antoinette* (after Le Brun), 138, *165; Marie Antoinette archide d'Autriche* (Le Beau), 42, *157; Marie Antoinette in a Park* (Le Brun), *157, 158; Mémoires secrets,* 30–31; Petit Trianon of, *157,* 158, 163, *164,* 165; redingote-style *lévite* of, 134–35; silhouette of dresses, 85; turban worn by, 174; Turkish-inspired dress in wardrobe of, 3, 161–68; wardrobe inventories of, 26, 161–68; Wertmüller portrait of, 163–65, *164*
Marie Antoinette in a Park (Vigée Le Brun), *157,* 163
Marie Joséphine of Savoy. *See* Artois, Comtesse d' (Marie-Thérèse of Savoy)

Marie Leszczyńska (Queen of France), 40, 156
Mariette, Denis, *47*
Martin, J.-B., 10, *148*
Martin, Richard, 36
masquerade: fashion and identity, 3–5; Ottoman dress in (eighteenth century), 20, *20*
Matossian, Chakè, 143
Melchior, Friedrich, 16
Mémoires & Quîttances d'ouvriers pour differns ouvrages, 155
Mémoires secrets: on *lévite,* 116; on Marie-Antoinette's wardrobe, 30–31, 161–62
men's fashion: Enlightenment philosophy and effect on, 141; men's coats, *34;* Ottoman dress, 36–37, *37;* and Ottoman inspiration (1785–1810), 170, 171, 173, 175; *polonaises* and seaming influenced by, 73–76; riding habit and redingote influenced by, 54; eighteenth century and documentation, 2; shirts and tunic origins, 34
Mercier, Louis-Sébastian, 149
Mésangère, Pierre de la, *175,* 176
Michel, Jean-Baptiste, *142*
Middle East, as geographic term, 5–8, *6*
Miller, Daniel, 112
Mitan (designer), *132*
Moeurs et usages des Turcs (Guer after Boucher), 19, *20*
Monnard, Marie-Victoire, 27
Mon oisiveté (Remi), 111
Montagu, Mary Wortley, *15,* 15–16
Montesquieu, Baron de, 144
Monument du costume: and Enlightenment thought and *turquerie,* 141, 146, 150; French print culture expansion (eighteenth century), 9, 85, *86*
morality, Enlightenment thought on, 151–53, *152–53*
Moreau, Jean Michel, *86*
Mosnier, Jean-Laurent, 85

naming of fashions: conventions, 112–14; fashion magazines on named styles, 126; trends, 114–16, *115*
national identity and French fashion, 111–38; and Caribbean influence, 131, *135–37,* 135–38; definitions, 118; fashion press and influence on, 111; *lévite* and English influence, *131–34,* 131–35; *lévite* popularity, 116–25, *117, 119, 120, 122–24;* naming conventions, 112–14; naming trends, 114–16, *115;* and redesigned, combined, reinvented styles, 126–31, *127–29*
Nattier, Jean-Marc, 11, 23
naturalism and Enlightenment philosophy, 139–42, 144–48, *146–48*
Naudet (publisher), 28
négligés, 2, 63, 66, 85, 130, 158–59, 162
neoclassical modes and Ottoman inspiration (1785–1810), 172, 173, 175, 176
nervures (back seam trim), 151
Nougaret, Jean-Baptiste, 150–51
nursing of children, Enlightenment thought on, 141, 142, *142*

Oberkampf, Anne-Élisabeth, *65,* 68, *97*

Ollivier, Michel-Barthélémy, 56
oriental, defined, 13
Orientalism (Said), 5
Orientalism and otherness, 5–8, 12
otherness: Enlightenment thought and Ottoman dress, 142; Orientalism as, 5–8, 12; *turquerie* and French dress (eighteenth century), 15–16. *See also* geographic terminology
Ottoman Empire: Circassia, 101; formation of, 12; Franco-Ottoman alliance (renewal in late seventeenth century), 11; French image of, 166; geographic terminology for, 5–8, *6;* military uniforms of, *19,* 19–20; Ottoman references and otherness, 5–8, 12, 15–16, 142; Ottoman/Turkey/Turkish, as interchangeable terms, 7
Ottoman Empire and influence on French fashion, 1–10; fashion and identity, 3–5; fashion of, as erotic, *123,* 149, 167–68, 177; French fashion press on, 8–10; French interest in "oriental" culture (seventeenth to eighteen centuries), 1–3; geographic terminology, 5–8, *6. See also* Enlightenment philosophy
Ottoman influence, defining (1760–90), 53–110; cutaway front, 61–72, *62–71;* popularity and demographics, 24; *robe à l'anglaise* features, 54–58, *55–57; robes à la polonaise, circassienne,* and *turque* commonality and definitions, 58–60; *robes à la polonaise, circassienne,* and *turque* layering effects, 60, *61; robes à la polonaise, circassienne,* and *turque* looped-up skirts, 61; *robes à la polonaise, circassienne,* and *turque* origins, 99–102, *100, 101; robes à la polonaise, circassienne,* and *turque* sashes, 61; *robes à la polonaise, circassienne,* and *turque* skirts, 86–97, *91–97; robes à la polonaise, circassienne,* and *turque* sleeves, 98, *98; robes à la polonaise, circassienne,* and *turque* soft silhouettes, 61, 85–86, *86–90; robes à la polonaise, turque,* and *circassienne* vs. *lévite* uniqueness, 53; stays, *107–9,* 107–10; and thematic groups of fashion, 54; tunic cut, 72–84, *72–84;* underpinnings, 103–7, *104–6*
Ottoman inspiration (1785–1810), 169–79; *doliman,* 176, *176;* and English-inspired styles, 169; English press on, 171–72, *172;* fashion press suspended (1794–1797), 171–72; and French Revolution, 169–71, 173; headwear, 169–70, *170,* 173–76, *174, 175,* 178; and neoclassical modes, 172, 173, 175, 176; *robe à la turque* and iterations, 169–74, *173, 176,* 178–79; shawls, 172, *177*

paniers (hoops), 103–7, *104–6,* 119
parure (*robes parées*), 158–62, *160,* 166
pas kontuszowy (sash), 41
Patas, Charles Emmanuel, *86, 104, 152*
peasant (*à la paysanne*), 147
Pelicier, J., *133*
Pelissier, Jean Joseph, *95, 96*
Petit Trianon, *157,* 158, 163, *164,* 165

petticoats: *The duchesse de Chartres in the presence of the vessel the Saint-Esprit* (Duplessis), 125; *jupons*, 46; and Ottoman influence on *robes*, overview (1760–90), 53; for *robe à l'anglaise*, 55, 56, *57;* for *robe à la polonaise*, 65, 68, 69, 76, 79, 86, 89, 90, 96–98, *97,* 106–7, 109
Pfeifer, Helen, 4
Philosophe, éloquent, sensible / Il nous a peint l'humanité (Michel), 142
Picart, Jean, *35*
pièce d'estomac, 46. See also stomacher (underbodice)
pierrot jackets: in *Cabinet des modes, 96;* in Marie-Antoinette's wardrobe, 161; Ottoman fashionability and appeal to demographic groups, 25, 30. See also *caracos* (jackets)
pleats: horizontal pleat technique, 72, *73;* of *lévite*, 120, *120,* 121, *124,* 125–27, *127,* 128, 131–32; vertical (silhouette) (*see* Ottoman influence, defining [1760–90])
Podenas, Vicomtesse de, 25
Poland: dress (sixteenth to eighteenth century), 38–41, *39, 40;* Eastern Europe, defined, 13–14; Lancer uniforms, 19, *19;* and naming conventions for fashion, 113; partition of, and origins of *robes*, 99–102; Polish costume and *turquerie* in art, *18*. See also *robes à la polonaise*
polonaise: à la Jean-Jacques, 146, *146;* à la liberté, 146; naming conventions, 113. See also *robes à la polonaise*
Polonoise, polonois (maquette de costume) (Boquet), *21*
Pompadour, Marquise de, 167, 178
Portrait de femme au livre (Baudin), 138
Portrait de Marie-Thérèse-Louise de Savoie-Carignan, princesse de Lamballe (Lemoine), *109*
Portrait of an Elderly Lady with Her Daughter (Vallayer-Coster), 30, *30*
Portrait of Augustus III of Saxony (De Silvestre), *40*
pouf (headdress), 169, 174, *174*
Powell family, *124*
Promenade dans un parc (Hilaire), 159, *159*
Provence, Comtesse de, 26, 161, 162
Province du Poitou, on *polonaise*, 53

Queen of Fashion (Weber), 156
queue (train), 86–87
quinzevine, 135, 138

Racine, Jean, 116–19, *119*
Ramsay, Allan, 142
Rapilly, Michel, 10
Raspal, Antoine, 28, *29*
Ravenet, Simon Francis, *18*, 18–19
Recherches sur les habillemens des femmes et des enfans (LeRoy), 143
Recueil de cent estampes representant différentes nations du Levant, 16–17, *17,* 20, *117, 123*
Recueil de diverses figures étrangères (Ravenet), *18*, 18–19

Recueil de planches (Diderot and Alembert, eds.), *34*
redingotes: and *circassienne*, 130; defined, 118; Enlightenment philosophy and effect on, 141; and *lévite*, 121, 131, *134,* 134–35; and Marie-Antoinette's fashion influence, 157, 162; Ottoman fashionability and appeal to demographic groups, 25, 26, 29, 30; and Ottoman influence (1760–90), 54; and Ottoman inspiration (1785–1810), 169
Reigny, Beffroy de, 166
Remi, Ch, 111
retroussée (skirt style), 87–96, *91, 95*
Ribeiro, Aileen, 7, 20, 100
riding habit, 25, 54
Rimbault, Caroline, 9
Riocourt, Madame la Comtesse de, 25
robe à la Tippoo-Saïb, 113, 169
robe à l'austrasienne, 61
robe de cour, 42, 112, *148*
Robe d'intérieur de femme (silk and cloth of gold), *35*
Robe jaune d'or et redingote gris-bleu, grand chapeau blanc à rayures dorées (Desrais), *134*
Robert, Hubert, 85, 163
robes: defined, 36, 54, 112; naming conventions, 112–14; naming trends, 114–16, *115;* short definitions (charts), 45, 59, 118; styles (1660–1770s), definitions, 35. *See also individual types of robes*
robes à la chinoise (Chinese), 88
robes à la circassienne: Circassienne à l'enfant, 130; cutaway front of, 61–72, *62, 71;* defined, 53, 58, 59; Enlightenment thought and effect on, 143, 146–49; extant examples of, *178;* fashion popularity (late eighteenth century), 3; jacket versions of, 96; and *lévite*, 120, 121, 126, 127; and Marie-Antoinette's fashion influence, 160–63, 167; naming conventions, 113; origin of, 99–102; Ottoman fashionability and appeal to demographic groups, 24–27, 29, 30; Ottoman influence (1760–90), overview, 53–54, 61–62; and Ottoman inspiration (1785–1810), *170,* 171, 172, *178; polonaise* and *turque* commonality, 53, 58; silhouette of, 61, 85–86; skirts of, 91, *95,* 96, *97;* sleeves of, 98; stays of, 107–10; tunic cut of, 72–84; underpinnings of, 103–7, *104;* variations of, 130; Western and Eastern approaches to dress, 50
robes à la française: à la française, defined, 112–13; clothing perspectives, East and West, *30;* cutaway front of, 61; defined, *30,* 45; and Enlightenment thought, 141, 146, *147,* 149–51; *grande robe à la française,* 158; and *lévite*, 120; naming conventions, 112–13; and *robe à l'anglaise, 128;* skirts, 102; sleeves, 98; Western and Eastern approaches to dress, 43, 45, 50–52, *50–52*
robes à la grecque, 99, 113
robes à la Levantine, 150, *150*
robes à la lévite. See *lévites*
robes à l'anglaise: Cabinet des modes on, Ottoman influence (1760–90), 76; defined, 59; Enlightenment philosophy and effect on, 141, 143, 146–47, 151; features of, 62, 63, 67, 72, 76–77, *84,* 88, 96, 98, 102; *lévite* and English influence, 111, *131–34,* 131–35; and Marie-Antoinette's fashion influence, 157, 161, 163; Ottoman fashionability and appeal to demographic groups, 24–26, 29, 31; and Ottoman influence (1760–90), 54–58, *55–57;* and Ottoman inspiration (1785–1810), 169; *and robes à la française, 128;* Western and Eastern approaches to dress, 50, 51
robes à la polonaise: caracos à la polonaise, 63, 75, 85–86, 87–90, 95–97, *96,* 98; *circassienne* and *turque* commonality, 53, 58; cutaway front of, 61–72, *62, 64–71;* defined, 59; *demi-polonaise*, 146; fashion popularity (late eighteenth century), 3; and *lévite*, 120, 121, 126–27, *127,* 128, 132; and Marie-Antoinette's fashion influence, 155, *157,* 158–63, *159,* 167; naming conventions, 113; origin of, 99–102, *101;* Ottoman fashionability and appeal to demographic groups, 24, 25, 27, *27*–31, *29;* Ottoman influence (1760–90), overview, 53–54, 61–62; polonaise à la Jean-Jacques, 146, *146;* polonaise à la liberté, 146; polonaise longue (trained version), 65, 67, 68, 69, 96, *96, 97;* silhouette of, 85–86; skirts of, 86–97, *91–97;* sleeves of, 98, *98;* soft silhouettes, 61, 85–86, *86–90;* stays of, 107–10; subvariants, naming conventions, 114; tunic cut of, 72–80, *72–84;* underpinnings of, 103–7, *104, 105;* variations of, 130; Western and Eastern approaches to dress, 50
robes à la turque: circassienne and polonaise commonality, 53, 58; cutaway front of, 61–72, *63, 69–71;* defined, 59; Enlightenment thought and effect on, 143, 145–49, *147, 148,* 152; extant examples of, 178; fashion popularity (late eighteenth century), 3; jacket versions of, 96; and *lévite*, 120–22, 126, *127;* and Marie-Antoinette's fashion influence, 155, 160–67, *164;* naming conventions, 113; origin of, 99, 101, 102; Ottoman fashionability and appeal to demographic groups, 24–31; Ottoman influence (1760–90), overview, 53–54, 61–62; Ottoman inspiration (1785–1810), 169–74, *173,* 176, 178–79; skirts of, 91, 94, *95, 97;* sleeves of, 91, 94, *95, 97;* soft silhouette, 61, 85–86; stays of, 107–10; tunic cut of, 72–84, *80–84;* underpinnings of, 103–7, *106;* variations of, 130, 132; Western and Eastern approaches to dress, 50
robes de chambre: defined, 45; and first wave *turquerie* (1670s–1705os), 43–47, *44;* as formal dress, 51–52; *lévite* modeled after, 119–20, *120;* and *robe volante*, 49–50
robes parées (parure), 158–62, *160,* 166
robes volante, 43, 45, *49,* 49–50, 98
Roche, Daniel, 3, 26–29, 148
Romanet, Antoine Louis, *102*
roundgown, 132

Rousseau, Jean-Jacques: Enlightenment thought and effect on clothing, 139, 140, 142–47, 149, 151–53; and Marie-Antoinette's clothing, 157; in *Philosophe, éloquent, sensible / Il nous a peint l'humanité* (Michel), *142*
Rubens, Peter Paul, 101
Russia: Catherine the Great, 16; Eastern Europe, defined, 13–14

sabots (cuffs), *15*, *62*, *72*, *86*, *91*, *98*, *98*, *104*, *146*, *149*, *159*, *161*
Said, Edward, 5, 12
Saint-Aubin, Augustin de, *10*, *148*
Sainte-Beuve, Charles Augustin, 13
Saint-Igny, Jean de, *35*
Saint-Jean, Jean Dieu de, *47*
Saint-Saveur, Jacques Grasset de, *102*
şalvar (trousers), 23, 36–37
Sarmatism, 40–41
sashes: defined, 61; Enlightenment thought and *turquerie*, 151; *kuşak/kemer* (belt/sash), 38; of *lévite*, 121–26, *124*; *pas kontuszowy*, 41. See also Ottoman influence, defining (1760–90)
Savary, Claude Etienne, 151
schall (shawls), 177
Scholz, Suzanne, 43
Schomberg, Baronne de (Cecile), 26, 28–29
Scotin, Gérard Jean Baptiste, I, 17, *17*, *123*
seams: cutaway front, *65*; tunic cut, 72, 73, *75*, *76*; Western and Eastern approaches, 34, 45, 52
Selim I (Sultan of Ottoman Empire), 12
Sellèque (publisher), *175*, *176*
sexuality (erotic images) of fashion, *123*, 149, 167–68, 177
Siam, ambassadorial visits to France (1684), 14, *15*
silhouette. See Ottoman influence, defining (1760–90); underpinnings
Silvestre, Louis de, *40*
simarre (loose overgown), 136
skirts: and Enlightenment thought, 146; and Ottoman influence (1760–90), 61, 86–97. See also *ailes* (wings); *bouffantes* (puffings), *côtes* (sides); *queue* (train); train; *and individual names of* robes
"social skin," 4
Soliman second ou les trois sultanes (theatrical production), 22
Solnon, Jean-François, 101
sopravveste femminile (woman's overdress), 75–77
soubreveste, 67, 98
Soulavie, Jean-Louis Girard, 166, *167*
spiral turban, *175*
Stanislaw August (King of Poland), 16
Stanisław Leszczyński (King of Poland), 40
Steele, Valerie, 43
stomacher (underbodice): and definitions of robes, 45, 59; in manteau, 46; in *robes à la polonaise, circassienne,* and *turque*, 58, 64, 66, 67–68, 71, 79, 85–86, 96, 98, 109; in *robe volante*, 49
Suite du recueil de planches sur les sciences, *52*
Suleiman I (Sultan of the Turks), 12, 22
sultane gowns, 47, *47*, 148
sultanes, 67. See also corsets

Tableau de Paris, on chemise, 138
Tableau général du goût, and Ottoman inspiration (1785–1810), 176
Tableau mouvant de Paris, Ottoman fashionability and appeal to demographic groups, 24–25
"Tailleur d'Habits, Pieces d'étaillées d'un Habit" (*Recueil de planches*, Diderot and Alembert, eds.), *34*
Tallien, Madame (Thérésa Cabarrus), 176
Tapis Vert (Robert), *85*
Tarrant, Naomi, 33–34
tente Tartare, 101, *101*
Tessin, Comte de, 11
thing theory, 5
Thoral, Marie-Cecile, 179
Tinville, Antoine Quentin Fouquier de, 26–27
Tour, Maurice Quentin de la, 142
Tour du Pin, Marquise de la, 132
train: and Enlightenment thought, 146–47; of *polonaise longue*, 65, 67, 68, 69, 96, *96*, *97*; *queue*, 86–87
Trousseau, Madame, 25
tülbent (turban), 37
tunics: shirts and tunic origins, 34; tunic cut (1760–90), 72–84, *72–84*; tunic cut, Western and Eastern approaches, 33–36, *35*
turbans: and Marie-Antoinette, 174; spiral, *175*; *tülbent*, 37
Turkey: geographic terminology, 7; and naming conventions for fashion, 113. See also Ottoman Empire
Turnau, Irena, 38, 100
Turner, Terence, 4
turque. See *robes à la turque*
turquerie: ambassadorial visits and influence on French society, 14, *15*; defined, 3; Enlightenment philosophy and French fashion press, overview, 144; and French fashion (1670s–1750s), 43–52, *44*, *46–52*; Ottoman dress in art, 16–19, *17*, *18*; Ottoman dress in masquerades, 20, *20*; Ottoman dress in theater, *21*, 21–24, *23*; Ottoman dress in travel writings, 15–16, *16*; Ottoman military uniforms, *19*, 19–20; study of, 178–79; *Turquerie: An Eighteenth-Century European Fantasy* (Williams), 11; *turquerie*, defined, 3, 11, 13–14. See also Enlightenment philosophy; Western and Eastern approaches to dress
Twaalf Polen en Hongaren, gekleed volgens de mode van ca. 1580 (engraving on paper), *39*

underpinnings: busks, 41, *108*, 152; *corps de baleine*, 35, 41, *107*, 152; corsets, 35, 36, 43, 67, *107*–9, *107–10*; *culs* (rumps), 103–6, *104*; Enlightenment thought on health/morality and, 151–53, *152*, *153*; hoops, 35, 36, 41, 48–49, 103–7, *104–6*; and Marie-Antoinette's fashion influence, 158; Ottoman influence, overview (1760–90), 103. See also corsets; petticoats

Vallayer-Coster, Anne, 30, *30*
Vanmour, Jean Baptiste, 17, *17*, 20, *37*, *38*, *63*, *117*, *123*
veils, 38
Venel, Jean-Andre, 143
Versailles Palace, Petit Trianon of, *157*, 158, 163, *164*, *165*. See also Marie-Antoinette (Queen of France)
veste (waistcoat), 67
Vien, Joseph-Marie, 20, *20*
Vigée Le Brun, Élisabeth, 19, *85*, 138, *157*, 163, 164
Villars, Duchesse de, 161
Voltaire, 140
Von Grimm, Baron, 16
Voysard, Etienne Claude, *104*

waistcoats, 58, 59, 61, 68, 71, 85, 98, *108*, 109, 118, 120, 122, 123, 130, 132, 152, 161, 162, 166
wardrobe inventories, 25–27, 114, 141, 161–68
Warwick, Alexandra, 4
Watteau, Jean Antoine, 18, *18*
Watteau de Lille (Joseph Watteau), 10
Weber, Caroline, 156
Wertmüller, Adolf Ulrik, 163–65, *164*
Western and Eastern approaches to dress, 33–52; clothing for "comfort," 33, 41, 43, 46, 52; definitions of robe styles (1660–1770s), 45; Eastern European dress (sixteenth to eighteenth century), 38–41, *39*, *40*; French female dress (seventeenth century), 41–42, *42*; manteau, 33, 45, *46*–48, 46–51; and medieval-era technology, 33, *34*, *35*; Ottoman dress (eighteenth century), 36–38, *37*, *38*; popularity and demographics, 24; *robe à la française*, 43, 45, 50–52, *50–52*; *robe de chambre*, 43–47, *44*, 49–52; *robe volante*, 43, 45, 49, *49–50*; tunic cut, 33–36, *35*; *turquerie* and French fashion (1670s–1750s), 43
Wille, Pierre-Alexandre, 160
Williams, Haydn, 11
Woman in Turkish Dress, Seated on a Sofa (Liotard), 18, *18*

yaşmak (veils), 38
yelek, 37
"Young Woman with Miniature" (Wille), *160*

zupan (caftan), 41